TWENTY YEARS
OF RATIONAL
THERAPY

TWENTY YEARS OF RATIONAL THERAPY

PROCEEDINGS OF THE FIRST NATIONAL CONFERENCE ON RATIONAL PSYCHOTHERAPY

Editors

JANET L. WOLFE, Ph.D. and EILEEN BRAND

Institute for Rational Living, New York

Library of Congress Catalog No. 76-57312

ISBN No. 0-917476-08-5

Publisher:

Institute for Rational Living, Inc.
45 East 65th Street
New York, New York 10021

Printed in the United States of America

First National Conference on Rational Psychotherapy

PROGRAM COMMITTEE

Herdie Baisden
Dana Lehman-Olson
Janet L. Wolfe

CONFERENCE CENTER COORDINATORS

Dorothy Arfer
Betty Barry
Virginia Anne Church

LOCAL ARRANGEMENTS

Kathy Thome, Coordinator
Kenneth Peiser
Sanford Silverstein
LaVaughn Silverstein
Martin Steigman

PUBLICITY

Betty Barry

AUDIOVISUAL ARRANGEMENTS

Raymond J. Christianson

REGISTRAR

William Dunn

Preface

Rational-emotive therapy (RET) is a common-sense, action-oriented approach which emphasizes people's ability to solve their problems by uprooting irrational attitudes about themselves, other people, and the surrounding world.

Originator of the rational-emotive approach to psychotherapy is the free-thinking, icon-smashing, innovative psychologist, Albert Ellis, Ph.D., whose outspoken views sparked the sexual revolution, defied Freud, upset the American psychiatric establishment, and so outraged Governor Orval Faubus back in the early 1960's that he banned Dr. Ellis from the state of Arkansas.

Hailed by some and damned by others when Dr. Ellis first presented his theories in 1955, rational psychotherapy has moved ahead to become the seminal influence on the new action-oriented therapies featured in nearly every contemporary psychology text. Currently, rational-emotive therapy is being used extensively in the fields of psychology, law, social work, medicine, psychiatry, and education, with applications to virtually every problem known to man, woman, and child.

The First National Conference on Rational Psychotherapy held in Glen Ellyn, Illinois, June 6-8, 1975, served many purposes. It celebrated twenty years of rational psychotherapy. It brought the proponents of the burgeoning movement together in a national conclave where they could share philosophies, professional and personal interests, and come to know each other better. It provided workshops, lectures, and panels, conducted by leading specialists from across the country in order to aid participants in developing greater skills and flexibility in applying rational therapy to a broad spectrum of therapeutic and educational activities — in school, home, business, therapy, and personal growth. It focused on expanding the rational-therapy network and fostering regional centers to transmit new ideas and techniques.

Conference participants heard a lively array of speakers, and the papers included in this volume represent a generous sampling of conference presentations. Though excessively busy schedules prevented a few of the participants from providing their presentations for inclusion in this book, it encompasses the sweep of topics that animated the conference and the unique talents and expertise that have helped rational psychotherapy emerge as the leader of the new psychotherapies.

Predictably, the movement's emphasis on individual development toward effective and enjoyable living has attracted a richly diverse and individualistic lot of proponents. These proceedings reflect that treasured individuality in scholarly plain-speaking, scientific plumbing of the efficacy of RET, the personal reminiscences of the titans in the field, and enlightened dedication to helping people learn to live rationally in an irrational world.

For the pioneering work of Albert Ellis, for the efforts of all the RET therapists and the thousands of individuals who have enjoyed the benefits of rational-emotive therapy, for the good sense of all the professionals and lay people in nearly every field who have applied RET principles to their lives and work, for the skill and zeal of those who organized the conference and the enthusiasm of all who attended it, and especially for the contributions of the conference participants to this volume, we are grateful.

The Editors

Contents

If thou art pained by any external thing,
it is not this thing that disturbs thee,
but thy own judgment about it. And it is
in thy power to wipe out this judgment now.

— Marcus Aurelius

Irrational Ideas

The idea that you must — yes, *must* — have sincere love and approval almost all the time from all the people you find significant.

The idea that you must prove yourself thoroughly competent, adequate, and achieving; or that you must at least have real competence or talent at something important.

The idea that people who harm you or commit misdeeds rate as generally bad, wicked, or villainous individuals and that you should severely blame, damn, and publish them for their sins.

The idea that life proves awful, terrible, horrible, or catastrophic when things do not go the way you would like them to go.

The idea that emotional misery comes from external pressures and that you have little ability to control your feelings or rid yourself of depression and hostility.

The idea that if something seems dangerous or fearsome, you must become terribly occupied with and upset about it.

The idea that you will find it easier to avoid facing many of life's difficulties and self-responsibilities than to undertake some rewarding forms of self-discipline.

The idea that your past remains all-important and that, because something once strongly influenced your life, it has to keep determining your feelings and behavior today.

The idea that people and things should turn out better than they do; and that you have to view it as awful and horrible if you do not quickly find good solutions to life's hassles.

The idea that you can achieve happiness by inertia and inaction or by passively and uncommittedly "enjoying yourself."

The idea that you must have a high degree of order or certainty to feel comfortable; or that you need some supernatural power on which to rely.

The idea that you can give yourself a global rating as a human and that your general worth and self-acceptance depend upon the goodness of your performances and the degree that people approve of you.

— Albert Ellis

Abbreviations

AA	Alcoholics Anonymous
AII	Adult Irrational Ideas
AIII	Adult Irrational Ideas Inventory
AP	attention-placebo
ART	Association for Rational Thinking
CBT	cognitive-behavior therapy
CC	client-centered
CES	conditioned emotional stimulus
CPI	California Psychological Inventory
EPI	Eysenck Personality Inventory
GSC	galvanic skin conductance
GSR	galvanic skin response
IBT	Irrational Beliefs Test
MMPI	Minnesota Multiphasic Personality Inventory
NT	no treatment
NTL	National Training Laboratories
PBI	Personal Beliefs Inventory
PIRL	programmed instruction in rational living
PSA	public-speaking anxiety
RBT	rational behavior therapy or rational behavior training
REB	rational-emotive behavior
REBT	rational-emotive behavior therapy
REI	rational-emotive imagery
REM	rational-emotive meditation
RET	rational-emotive therapy
RSA	rational self-analysis
RSC	rational self-counseling
RSDH	rational stage directed hypnotherapy
RSDI	rational stage directed imagery
RSDT	rational stage directed therapy
SD	systematic desensitization
S.H.A.R.P.	Self Help Alcoholism Research Project
SIT	self-instructional training
16 PF	Sixteen Personality Factor Questionnaire
SRSR	Self-Rating Scale for Rationality
STAI	State Trait-Anxiety Inventory
TA	transactional analysis
TM	transcendental meditation
TMA	Taylor Manifest Anxiety Scale
VA	Veterans Administration
VR	vocational rehabilitation

Introduction to the Conference

JANET L. WOLFE, Ph.D.

Associate Director, Institute for Advanced Study in Rational Psychotherapy

What an incredibly beautiful sight — this impressive group of people . . . seven hundred strong . . . psychologists, counselors, psychiatrists, educators, physicians, lawyers, social workers, and rational thinkers from forty states (and Canada)! You may never have been in Glen Ellyn before this weekend, but if you felt as I did last night when people came from all over the country to register and gather together at the welcoming reception, you must share my sense that, at last, we're home.

I'd like to take you on a tour of the course of events that has culminated in our being here today. Over the years, as some of us have traveled around the country, meeting each other perhaps by chance, we have talked of the many exciting things going on among teachers, researchers, and practitioners of rational therapy. And we have lamented that we so rarely got an opportunity to meet each other and exchange ideas. In a way, many of us have known each other for a long time. I've been at the Institute for Rational Living in New York for ten years but until yesterday I had never met, face to face, a good number of people with whom I've corresponded over the years — people whose ideas I know well from reading their books and papers. It's time to get together, some of us thought. So . . . out of a series of convivial evenings that took place in one Greek restaurant, two Japanese restaurants, and our local friendly Madison Avenue French restaurant, Dana Lehman-Olson and Herdie Baisden and I appointed ourselves the fomenters of the First National Conference on Rational Therapy.

It appears that the time was auspicious indeed. This year — 1975 — marks the twentieth anniversary of the first presentation of the theory of rational-emotive therapy by its founder, Albert

Ellis. It marks a time, too, when RET — far from being viewed as the heretical underground approach that it once was — is now featured in ever-increasing numbers of contemporary counseling and personality tests; is incorporated in dozens of school systems throughout the country; is being applied widely in marital and sexual counseling, guidance, rehabilitation services, and business; is effective in work with prisoners, addicts, alcoholics; and is a valuable tool for self-growth and learning to maximize our pleasure in a basically irrational world. In putting together the conference program, we realized most dramatically just how many areas RET has influenced.

I'd like now to acknowledge the contributions of some of the many hard-working people who brought our dream of a coming-together to its fruition.

First, I'd like to thank Dana Lehman-Olson and Herdie Baisden who, in addition to several trips to New York and I've lost track of how many hours of long-distance calls from Minneapolis, helped put together our spectacular program. Dana has also been working nonstop since early this week to help coordinate the enormous amount of preparatory work here at the conference site.

Thanks go to our vivacious dynamo, Dorothy Arfer, the Administrative Director of the New York Institute for Rational Living, who has been working on arrangements for weeks in New York and in Glen Ellyn; and to the third member of our advance guard, one of the world's nicest and most efficient human beings, Betty Barry of the Madison Association for Rational Thinking.

While we have been staggering through program arrangements and registration in New York, back here at Glen Ellyn has been the miraculous Anne Church, who has calmly helped us work out kinks while running through her modest 120-hours-a-week job of running one of the most exciting law programs in the country. A really special ovation, I think, goes to Scott Church, who for several weeks almost single-handedly organized dormitory and meal ticket arrangements and helped to stretch meeting rooms to accommodate double their normal capacity. We are grateful, too, to Dean Church's office staff, who have fielded the hundreds of phone calls that have poured in and who have amazingly managed to tranquilly work away at their normal jobs while the conference staff commandeered most of their office space.

Ray Christianson, Lewis University Law School's ace audiovisual director, I'd like to steal and take back to New York with us . . . he's responsible for making the arrangements to tape, for posterity, the several hundred hours of presentations that will be taking place over the next three days, and he has arranged for the variety of audio and visual equipment that our creative presenters have requested.

Kathy Thome and Ken Peiser, as far as I can tell, haven't been to sleep all week . . . since just about every time I've seen them, they've been going around making signs to help us thread our way through this extraordinary place. They were responsible for coordinating the large and dedicated staff of Chicago volunteers who have been running the registration desk and working with us all week wherever needed.

Although they're not all here, I want to thank the staff of the Institute for Rational Living in New York for effectively handling the barrage of registration correspondence, and especially Bill Dunn, who flew out here to offer a bit of much-needed stability as preparations grew more and more frantic.

Betty Barry and John Gullo have helped greatly with press relations and publicity, and our ever cheerful and always helpful Sylvia Gullo will be running the placement bulletin board.

I'm hoping that we will continue, in this very special community of special people, to meet and share with each other in what will clearly be only the first of many more exciting get-togethers in years to come. Our work has its rewards. More and more research into the efficacy of the cognitive behavior therapies — of which rational-emotive therapy is among the most highly developed — indicates that we have indeed been on the right track toward developing a system with enormous promise for alleviating some of the misery of the world.

RET as a Personality Theory, Therapy Approach, and Philosophy of Life

ALBERT ELLIS, Ph.D.

Executive Director, Institute for Advanced Study in Rational Psychotherapy, New York City

Though Albert Ellis was once the heretic of the professional psychological community, in recent years professional groups have recognized his creative contributions to psychotherapy. His awards include a special citation in 1973 from the American Psychological Association for Distinguished Contributions to Psychotherapy, and the 1972 Humanist of the Year Award from the American Humanist Association. A Fellow of many professional societies, Dr. Ellis served as President of the Division of Consulting Psychology of the American Psychological Association, as President of the Society for the Scientific Study of Sex, as Vice President of the American Academy of Psychotherapists, and as a member of the Executive Boards of the American Association of Marriage and Family Counselors and of the New York Society of Clinical Psychologists.

Dr. Ellis has served as Associate Editor of many professional journals, including the Journal of Contemporary Psychotherapy, *the* Journal of Individual Psychology, *the* Journal of Marriage Counseling, *the* Journal of Sex Research, *and* Rational Living. *He has published over four hundred and fifty papers in psychological, psychiatric, and sociological journals and anthologies; and has authored or edited thirty-nine books and monographs.*

The topic that I have chosen for this talk sounds great — except that I may have one hell of a time saying anything new about it. I have outlined the RET theory of personality in several books and papers (Ellis, 1962, 1972c, 1973b), especially in a chapter in Arthur Burton's *Operational Theories of Personality* (Ellis, 1974d). As for RET as a therapy approach, I have written and talked about that almost ad nauseam — as I shall probably keep doing for the next ninety-nine years or so. So what shall I say that will sound novel and significant in this twentieth-anniversary presentation? Probably not very much!

Which leaves me with a final and not-too-desperate ploy — to talk to you tonight on the RET philosophy of life. I have strongly suggested in previous writings that rational-emotive therapy does endorse a distinct philosophy, or value system, to live by (Ellis, 1971b, 1972b, 1973c, 1975; Ellis and Harper, 1975). Various other writers, such as Paul Hauck (1974, 1975), William Knaus (1974), John Lembo (1974), Maxie C. Maultsby, Jr. (1976), Kenneth Morris and Mike Kanitz (1975), and Donald Tosi (1974) have also emphasized some of the main philosophic premises of RET and how they can help people lead more satisfactory lives. So what new things can I say tonight on this score?

A few, at least, and some highly personal ones at that. For although I have written autobiographical articles relating my RET philosophy to some significant events of my past life (Ellis, 1972d, 1974a), I don't recall doing one which reviews my present personal philosophy of life and which relates it to RET theory and therapy. Let me try to summarize some of the main tenets of RET and to show how I actualize them — or at least do my damnedest to try to actualize them — in my current existence.

Rational and Irrational Values and Behaviors

RET, as I say in the paper on theory in Burton's book (Ellis, 1974d), holds that virtually all people start with a basic set of value assumptions: They believe that survival and happiness have goodness and that death and misery have less value. More specifically, humans seek happiness in their relationships with themselves, in their social contacts, in their intimate or love relations, in their work, and in their esthetic and recreational pursuits. They consequently define life- and happiness-abetting activities as good or rational and death- and misery-aiding activities as bad or irrational. Following suit, RET views rationality as a method or technique of effectively gaining certain values or life enjoyments and not as anything that exists in any intrinsic or absolutistic sense (Ellis, 1974d; Goodman and Maultsby, 1974; Maultsby, 1976).

Do I follow this view in my own life? For the most part — but not perfectly — I think I do. I definitely value living, and its major subheading, good health, quite strongly. Having had more than my share of physical illnesses during childhood, and having acquired diabetes at the age of forty, I follow fairly strict health rules. These include keeping regular hours, taking my insulin every day, maintaining a very strict diet, rigorously refraining from stimulants and drugs, and almost compulsively performing my goddamned physical fitness exercises 365 days each year. Does this strict regimen give me a royal pain in the ass on many occasions? Indeed it does! But I rationally keep to it because it helps prolong my days and keep me physically healthy. I won't find it, when I finally go, awful or terrible to die. But who the hell wants to piss away some of the relatively few years of aliveness available to us (probably) in all eternity? Certainly not I! So I rationally stick to the health rules and never — well, hardly ever! — overeat or overimbibe anything. Not that I miss the alcohol too much; I never guzzled great quantities even in my prediabetic days. But O those lost and never-to-get-forgotten malteds! *Tough shit, baby!* But not horrible and awful!

What about the rational value of living happily with myself? How do I keep up with that one? Fairly nicely, thank you. In response to Paul Krassner's question about whether I felt happy, in his famous 1960 interview with me which he published in *The Realist*, I replied that I honestly thought myself "one of the relatively few people in the United States, and perhaps in the entire world, who has not had a seriously unhappy day for the last twenty-five years" (Ellis, Krassner, and Wilson, 1960). Now, fifteen years later, if by "seriously unhappy" I mean depressed, anxious, guilty, or angry, I can easily make that a total of forty. And the rest of my answer to Krassner I can restate today in spades: "I find it almost impossible to feel intensely unhappy, hostile, or upset for more than literally a few minutes at a time. I really would have to start working myself up to feel unhappy: I'd have to work hard at it, to practice again, disturbing myself. . . . And because I have so little time and energy to expend at making myself miserable, I derive considerable pleasure, enjoyment, and sometimes sheer bliss out of my life. What more can one ask?"

Which leads me to restate what I have emphasized to many audiences recently — since many crooked thinkers in the field of psychology still foolishly think that *rational* means unemotional, completely calm, or uninvolved: Rationality, when correctly defined, means working your ass off not only to rid yourself of dire misery — especially anxiety, despair, depression, guilt, shame, and feelings of worthlessness — but of actively using your head to help your heart beat more strongly, impassionedly, and joyously.

Do I seek happiness — and try to minimize irrational interferences with unhappiness — in my social contacts, my intimate relations, my work, and my esthetic and recreational pursuits? By all means — but not equally! In my work, I do fine and nobly, and probably feel more involved and get considerably more downright pleasure than 99 percent of the population. Consequently, I see more clients, give more talks and workshops, correspond more, and do more writing than practically anyone else — which, fortunately, gives me variety as well as task-orientation. But time, alas, still amounts to a measly twenty-four hours a day, and something has to give — especially my socializing and my recreational activities. Years ago I took full advantage of the entertaining and entertainment life of New York — still the greatest city in the world for that sort of thing. But not any more. I have so many professional activities to which I keep committed that I feel lucky to have time to screw! And the last full day of leisure I managed to spend with the woman I dearly love, I hardly remember. Fortunately, my professional life provides me with many interesting friends and acquaintances; and my work life has its own entertainments. But I have to admit that my days all seem too short, and life itself much too brief, for half the enjoyable things I would like to do but lack time to fit into my busy schedule. Years back, I would listen to music as much as forty hours a week. Today, I often barely get in five. About which I rationally manage to convince myself: "Too damned bad! As long as I decidedly enjoy what I do manage to do, why must I also make time for everything else?" Answer: I obviously don't have to.

The A-B-C Theory of Personality

The now fairly famous A-B-C theory of RET states that when you have either an appropriate or an inappropriate emotional reaction, at point C (your emotional Consequence), after some Activating Event or Activating Experience (especially of an obnoxious nature) has occurred at point A, A definitely does *not* cause C. Instead, B, your Belief System *about A*, directly causes you to react emotionally at C. And therefore, if you want to change inappropriate or dysfunctional consequences, at C, you can do so fairly quickly by vigorously and incisively Disputing them, with logico-empirical challenges, at D.

Do I use these A-B-C-D's to help myself in my own life? Indeed, I do! A very recent example: Having a very fallible memory, I forgot that this present paper had several perceptive and bright discussants, and expected to give it, along with my other main presentation at this conference, off the cuff, with the preparation of only a brief outline to work from. This, I admit, doesn't always make for the very best talks; but when I have a half thousand other things to do before the conference takes place, and when I have a faculty for making extemporaneous talks alive and absorbing (if not necessarily profound), I normally feel that such three-quarter-ass preparation will suffice.

Not this time, alas! A few weeks before the conference, some of the discussants politely but firmly informed me that they had no intention of voicing their views on a practically nonexistent, and certainly a nonwritten, paper. Would I please, they courteously asked, get them a written one *before* the blasted conference arrived? Not that they stated, or even irrationally implied, that I would rate as a shit if I didn't. But I could suspect what some of them might possibly be thinking.

I could have easily felt, at point C, both angry and self-downing when asked, at point A, that I get the blasted paper to these goddamned rational discussants pronto — in fact, reasonably immediately. But before I could get myself to say even a moderately strong, "Fuck 'em!" (which, as sophisticated RETers among you may note, constitutes a rather irrational Belief, at B), I heard my inner voice determinedly muttering, "Shit! What a drag! What idi — er, person who sometimes acts idiotically — on the Program Committee saddled me with those dratted consultants anyway? How sad, regrettable, and unfortunate! Not to mention, what a pain in the *tuchas!* But it won't — I think — kill me. Though admittedly difficult, I *can* find the time to write the unholy paper in the next week or so. So I will hardly have a chance even to masturbate for a while. No catastrophe! At least I'll still prepare to give the other conference paper off the top of my head and wow them with my impromptu brilliance. It could turn out worse — nearly!"

In other words, as soon as I felt the pangs of anger (at the program committee's scheduling) and self-immolation (at my own forgetfulness) coming on at C, I immediately sensed that I profoundly believed some asinine ideas at B, and went to work to change them to rational beliefs. And I soon succeeded. I must admit that I don't always use the A-B-C's of RET in this rapid-fire and effective manner. But I usually do; and thus, as noted above,

I rarely make myself miserable about any crummy thing that occurs in my life. I think that I did something similar for many years before I created and started using RET with others, but I did it vaguely and somewhat squelchingly. In the old days, I would tell myself, when difficult things occurred, something like, "I don't have to make myself miserable. Anyone who lets himself or herself feel violently unhappy acts in a stupid or ignorant manner." And, believing this, I simply refused to feel depressed, angry, or similarly upset for any length of time.

Probably I did so mainly by convincing myself that things really didn't transpire badly, when they actually did. I just didn't face the fact that situations and events *can* go quite crummily and that intense sorrow and displeasure *do* occur as legitimate feelings. Now I think I fully realize that they do. And I really did let myself feel quite badly — meaning sad and disappointed — when I remembered that I had agreed to have discussants for my paper and therefore would better prepare a written version of it before the conference. But I only got myself to feel sorry about that — and not self-damning and angry. In other words, this time, as most of the time, I almost automatically used the A-B-C's of RET on myself, after noting I had once again made an error; and I wound up feeling 98 percent regretful and only about 2 percent mad at myself and others for making that error. RET successfully rides again!

Confronting and Attacking Irrational Beliefs and Values

RET rather uniquely confronts and attacks a disturbed person's irrational beliefs and self-defeating values; and it does so systematically and vigorously, not merely for practical reasons but because its theory states that humans strongly and dogmatically hold irrational (as well as rational) ideas, and that in many instances they will not likely surrender them, if they or therapists take a namby-pamby approach to uprooting such beliefs. Many cognitive therapists, such as Paul Dubois (1907), Alfred Adler (1929), Jerome Frank (1973), George Kelly (1955), E. Lakin Phillips (1957), Donald Meichenbaum (1974), and Victor Raimy (1975), have clearly indicated that clients' self-defeating and self-disturbing beliefs had better get clearly revealed and uprooted in order for them to receive intensive and elegant help with their emotional problems. Even Sigmund Freud, in his first book with Josef Breuer, originally published in 1895 (Breuer and Freud, 1957), used the term "ideogenic" to describe "a great number of hysterical phenomena, probably more than we suspect today." But none of these theorists seemed to stress (as does RET) the remarkable power with which disturbed individuals almost automatically hold on to their self-sabotaging beliefs, and the desirability of their energetically and incisively attacking and surrendering these cognitions.

Do I use force and vigor in combating my own irrational notions and thereby uprooting my inappropriate feelings? I definitely do! Particularly in regard to feelings of anger, which I plague myself with far more often than I inflict other dysfunctional emotions on myself. As most of you know, I continually go out on the road to give talks, seminars, workshops, and marathons; and, naturally, I run into almost incredible stupidities and inefficiencies on the part of airlines, local arrangement committees, motels, audio-visual technicians, and so on. I also get asked innumerable stupid, baiting, and pejorative questions by members of my audiences who idiotically expect me to endorse various kinds of treatment methods which they personally favor but which I obviously don't endorse, since I consistently do practice RET and *not* these somewhat conflicting techniques. Thus, they apparently assume that I will wax enthusiastic about psychoanalytic dream interpretations, Gestalt therapy's anti-intellectualism, transactional analysis's misleading belief that you mainly get your childish scripts from your Parent, and primal therapy's encouraging you to whine and scream about how your mother severely hurt you twenty years ago and how you have to feel terribly hurt today because she left you alone in the dark a few times when you were four years old.

Naturally, I clearly and forcefully reply that I do not go along with this kind of bullshit — that, in fact, I think it quite iatrogenic (meaning the causing or exacerbating of an ailment by the poor treatment of a physician or a therapist). Naturally, the barbs and recriminations of my questioners then really fly! In the old days, I would violently retort to their nasty aspersions against my intelligence and my manhood, and occasionally I still do. But almost always I now manage to vigorously convince myself, only a few seconds after (and sometimes significantly *before*) my hackles start to rise: "These hostile questioners *should* act exactly as they foolishly do — because they *do* think crookedly and feel inappropriately, and in *these* conditions they *will* react precisely as they now keep reacting. They clearly *have* a right to their mistaken and bigoted beliefs; and I'd better grant them that right, else I shall act just as mistakenly and bigotedly as they do. Too bad that they do not really listen to me and at least consider the possible validity of my viewpoints. But it *only* remains too bad — and not in the least horrible or terrible!"

With this kind of intensive, powerful interrupting of my innate and acquired tendency to totally damn people who partially act contemptibly, I almost always make myself displeased rather than hostile — and sometimes I greatly enjoy confuting their benighted views, and do not even feel very displeased about their having them. Not that I don't at times fail myself in this regard — I do! But for every hundred displays of overt and covert hostility toward me and my views, I think that I make myself angry only a few times these days. Which seems pretty good for someone like me, who used to continually seethe about the stupidities and inefficiencies of many other humans.

Homework Assignments

Rational-emotive therapy, probably more than any other leading therapeutic school, emphasizes behavioristic, *in vivo* homework assignments. To a lesser degree, so do some other schools, such as reality therapy (Glasser, 1965), integrity therapy (Mowrer, 1973), active psychotherapy (Herzberg, 1945), decision therapy (Greenwald, 1975), and behavior therapy (Salter, 1949; Wolpe, 1958).

Actually, I independently created homework assignments long before I contemplated entering the field of psychotherapy, far back in 1932, when I had just reached the age of nineteen. I knew that I behaved too shyly in several important respects, and realized (from reading psychology and philosophy books) that I felt too much afraid of what other people thought of me, and greatly feared failing in their presence. So, while convincing myself that nothing terrible *would* happen if they saw me acting idiotically and thought me pretty worthless, I forced myself to do a graduated series of risk-taking exercises, such as speaking in front of sizable public groups, which I previously had scared myself shitless about. So, in essence, I gave birth to RET — and saw that the damned thing worked beautifully. I not only completely got over my fear of public speaking, but found to my great surprise that I started to enjoy it. Now, just try to stop me from giving a speech!

I still use the homework assignment approach on myself, and combine it with some degree of operant conditioning at times. In writing the present paper, for example, I knew that I had better polish it off on the one Sunday I would have in New York just before the conference. And I knew that I had a good many other interesting and pleasurable things to do that day. So I arranged to let myself read the *New York Times* and go out to dinner with the woman I live with (to celebrate the tenth anniversary of our living successfully in "sin") only *after* I had completed the paper. It worked! — or, rather, *I* worked it. Similarly, I often set myself graduated homework assignments, such as exercising or writing a book, and set myself certain reinforcements as I accomplish them and penalties as I goof on them. I have done this sort of thing for so many years now that I often do not have to use the reinforcements and the penalties to get myself to carry out my self-given assignments. But to some extent, still having a great deal of human fallibility, I expect to keep using the homework and the operant conditioning for the rest of my life.

The Theory of Human Worth

The most up-to-date RET theory of human worth, as outlined in my essay, "Psychotherapy and the Value of a Human Being" (Ellis, 1972c), and other recent writings (Ellis, 1974d, 1975, 1976; Ellis and Harper, 1975) states that human beings really don't have intrinsic value or worth, except by somewhat arbitrary definition; and that if they want to think clearly and act wisely, they'd better not rate themselves, their essences, or their totality either positively or negatively. Instead, they'd better accept their aliveness and their capacity to enjoy life and determinedly work at staying alive and enjoying. Robert Hartman (1967), Abe Maslow (1954), Paul Tillich (1953), and Alan Watts (1959) have stated somewhat similar views, but they don't seem to write as clearheadedly or include the practical applications of this theory of worth as do RET theorists and practitioners.

Do I really accept myself unconditionally these days, and virtually never rate myself, my totality, at all? No, not entirely. I still slip a little in this respect, at times. I sometimes feel a little *too* good about my accomplishments or the pleasurable things that happen to me — and I then suspect myself of some grandiosity or ego-aggrandizement. And I occasionally, for a few seconds, feel ashamed or guilty — and know that I then engage in self-downing or devil-ification. But not for long! I quickly realize that *it* feels good, that this thing I consider pleasurable has happened, and not that *I* rate as a good person because it has occurred or because I have contributed to making it happen. And

I also realize, when I temporarily feel ashamed, that I may well have done the wrong or stupid thing, but that I hardly turn into a bad or rotten person (in RET language, an R.P.) for doing that wrong or stupid thing. So I may at first rate and denigrate myself for acting badly, but I quickly — almost immediately — stop that nonsense.

"Oh, you can do that fairly easily," people object, *"because* you have accomplished so much in life, have made yourself the originator and leader of a popular school of psychotherapy. No wonder you can accept yourself!"

"Quite the contrary," I reply. "I have in all probability done well and helped a popular school of therapy get going *because* I pigheadedly refused to rate myself as I kept creating and promulgating it." I have received enormous amounts of opposition almost every step of the way in beating the drum for RET; and I still do. If I had rated myself (or, better, accepted myself) *because* I succeeded with RET, I would most probably never have succeeded! My unconditional acceptance of my aliveness and my potential for enjoyment have served as perhaps my most important assets in persisting, against so much opposition, with RET. If I now liked myself because of my good traits and because of my successes with therapy, public presentations, and writing, I would serve as a very lousy example of the use of RET and my actions would tend to sabotage some of my basic therapeutic views. But I think that lots of evidence from my past and present life proves otherwise.

Hereditary and Environmental Influences

RET, along with many modern psychological authorities, stresses the strong hereditary as well as the environmental influences on human personality and emotional disturbance (Bender, 1963; Chess, Thomas, and Birch, 1965; Jellinek, 1973; Rimland, 1964; Rosenthal, 1970; Slater and Cowie, 1971). It hypothesizes that we innately have strong tendencies toward "healthy" functioning — toward surviving, seeking for happiness or self-actualization, living cooperatively with others, and intimately relating to or loving a few significant others during our lifetime — and that we also have strong biological tendencies toward "unhealthy" or self-defeating functioning — toward acting oversuggestibly, overcautiously, grandiosely, wishful-thinkingly, and defensively. In addition, we tend to feel intolerant of frustration, and prone to overgeneralization and magical thinking (Ellis, 1962, 1971b, 1973b, 1975).

Do I fit into these categories myself? I certainly seem to! On the one hand, I have strong "natural" tendencies toward irritability, exaggerated devotion to my own hypotheses, and damning others who have the temerity to fail to agree with my obviously superior point of view. On the other hand, I seem to have powerful tendencies to hate inefficiency, to view conventions skeptically, to have a high level of energy, and to delight in fighting against intellectual and emotional opposition. I also tend realistically to accept the fact that no magic exists in the universe and that practically the only way to change yourself involves working and practicing, and then working and practicing some more, to change your innate and acquired tendencies to foolishly "do in" yourself and others.

So I think that my biological predispositions have much to do with my creating RET, with my persistently propagating its tenets and practices, and with my using its theories and methodologies to better my own existence. Of course, this remains a difficult proposition to prove with empirical data. But one of these days, when I have more time, I shall try to present what seems to me some of the confirmatory evidence.

Anti-absolutizing

RET, almost uniquely among therapeutic systems, reveals and vigorously combats the enormous tendency of humans to absolutize, to demand, and to practice arrant *must*urbation. It holds that antiempirical views or misconceptions lead to much of what we call human disturbance; but it also sees as even more important, and to a high degree causative of these antiempirical misconceptions, the natural, and almost certainly biologically predisposed, tendency of people to absolutize and invent magic. Thus, individuals wrongly assume a good chance exists that the airplane in which they might take a trip will fall and plummet them to their death because they devoutly and absolutistically believe that they *must* not die in such a crash and that they *have to* avoid the mistake of riding in a plane that has any chance whatever of falling. Their absolutistic *musts* get them to mistakenly perceive flying as exceptionally dangerous, when all the empirical data that we have about it shows that it remains unusually safe.

I must — oh, well, I'd *better* — admit that I still sometimes find myself lapsing back into some dogmatic *shoulds, oughts,* and *musts* in my private and public life. At times I strongly feel — which means, of course, *believe* — that RET *must* triumph over innumerable amazingly ineffective and harmful types of therapies that still have great popular appeal; that I *must* live long enough to see this great day arrive; and that truth, in general, *has to* prevail over falsehood. But I also firmly realize, most of the time, that this represents arrant bullshit. It would prove nice if knowledge and fact prevailed over superstition and fiction, but I acknowledge full well that they often won't.

Indeed, I take a somewhat pessimistic —or, I think, realistic— view that within the remainder of this century, RET and related sensible and hard-headed therapies will likely retain a minority position while all sorts of magical- and mystical-oriented therapies (especially some forms of transcendental hogwash) will probably prove increasingly popular. For man and woman have great difficulty keeping to the straight paths of science and horse sense, and they easily deflect themselves to profound gibberish. Therefore, although today's psychotherapy turns increasingly into cognitive-behavioral channels, and RET has taken its place as one of the most influential forms of scientifically oriented cognitive-behavior therapy, most people who have severe disturbances still turn to one or another unscientific or antiscientific methodologies, and they probably will continue doing so for quite a number of years to come.

True to my RET position, I pigheadedly refuse to upset myself about this unfortunate human tendency. I still believe, though perhaps wrongly, that truth *eventually* will out and that sanity will *ultimately* prevail over human insanity. Maybe the human race won't keep itself alive that long — will irrationally resort to its own destruction. I don't think so, but I recognize that real possibility. If so, too damned bad! If I live long enough, I intend to go down fighting that insane tendency — at the same time, primarily, still propagating and using on myself the basic principles of RET!

Semantic Therapy

Rational-emotive therapists practice one of the few truly semantic therapies that now exist. They persistently interrupt their clients' inaccurate overgeneralizations and teach them to give up the use of "I *need* love," "I *must* do well," "You *have to* treat me properly," "*That* makes me anxious," "I see myself as a *rotten person,"* "I *can't* stop worrying," "I *always* act badly at public functions," "I find it *awful* to get rejected," and many similar totalitarian statements. I used to make the same kind of mistakes myself and even included some of them in the early editions of my books on RET!

Now I watch my language much more carefully, and rarely make these errors — in print, at least. I stick fairly closely to the principles of general semantics, as originally laid down by the brilliant Alfred Korzybski; and I seem to have emerged as the only leading therapist who writes in E-prime, a form of syntax invented by Korzybski's follower, D. David Bourland, Jr. E-prime means all the words in the English language, minus all forms of the verb *to be.* And my recently published books, *How to Live with a "Neurotic"* and *A New Guide to Rational Living,* exist as the first books ever issued in E-prime. Thanks to my enthusiastic and able helper, Bob Moore, you'll find them bereft of every vestige of *is, was, being, am, have been,* and other forms of *to be.*

I can now say, after writing these two new books in E-prime, that Sigmund Freud very stupidly held that emotional disturbance stems from the *id* rather than from the *is.* Such disturbance (as Korzybski and Bourland have shown) largely stems from the human tendency to overgeneralize and to use the *is* of identity and the *is* of prediction. This *isness makes* your id urges sacred and almost forces you to foolishly upset yourself about them.

Thus, if you strongly feel, "I would like to copulate with my mother, but I'd better not in this anti-incestuous culture," or if you feel, "I would prefer to masturbate in Macy's window but the gendarmerie will take a dim view of this, so I'd better not!" you will hardly get into any trouble. But if you overgeneralize these beliefs and feelings to: "I *must* copulate with my mother and find it terrible that I cannot!" or "I *have to* stop even thinking about incest and I rate as a horrible person when I do think about it!" you make it almost impossible for you to live comfortably with your innate and acquired sexual urges, or your so-called "id."

Freud, in other words, overemphasized masturbation while we in rational-emotive therapy heavily stress *mast*urbation. As I have said around the country for the last six months,

> *Masturbation proves good and delicious,*
> *While musturbation seems bad and pernicious!*

Or *Lusturbate, don't musturbate!* — and your silly id will take care of itself!

Following my lead, a group of RETers in the state of Connecticut have coined the phrase and issued a button declaiming: *"Musturbation is self-abuse!"* Right on! — almost. For the *is* in their slogan seems contradictory. *Mus*turbation may, in *some* conditions and *some* of the time, equal self-abuse. But we cannot legitimately say that it *always*, in *every* condition, leads to self-defeating behavior. At least, we cannot say that without, by that very form of overgeneralization, resorting to *mus*turbation! So let me revise this slogan, using Bourland's form of syntax, and let me say in Anglo-Saxon E-prime:

MUSTurbation means self-abuse!

I wish dear old Siggie could have lived long enough to ruminate on this slogan.

Summary

At this point, I could say, enough rationality is enough. But since that flouts the rules of E-prime, let me just say: enough! In case my charming discussants find little RET personality or therapy theory in this paper to get their teeth into, let me summarize some highly important aspects of rational-emotive theory and practice for them to consider. As a result of my twenty years of formally practicing RET with literally thousands of clients, as well as my more than forty years of using some aspects of it on myself, I can vigorously state the following important hypotheses about many individuals and their emotional disturbances:

1. Practically all people have some very strong innate and acquired tendencies to act irrationally (as well as to act rationally) and to needlessly defeat themselves.

2. They largely create their emotional problems themselves, with significant help from their environment, and they do so cognitively, emotively, and behaviorally.

3. They also have the capacity to understand their irrational thinking, their inappropriate emoting, and their self-sabotaging behavior and to change or eliminate much of it.

4. The most important, elegant, and long-lasting ways they can employ to help undisturb themselves largely consist of cognitive awareness and philosophic restructuring.

5. While people seem to change mainly by emotive and behavioral procedures, underlying cognitive reorganization really motivates and to a large extent directly causes these changes.

6. When they significantly change their dysfunctional thinking, emoting, and behaving, they frequently return, at least temporarily, to their former dysfunctional patterns.

7. Since people powerfully and rigidly hold on to some of their emotional disturbances, they'd better solidly interrupt them with strong counterbeliefs, dramatic emotive moves, and determined behavioral changes.

8. Humans easily get habituated to self-defeating feelings, thoughts, and behaviors and therefore had better persistently and habitually work and practice against such dysfunctional patterns. Repetition often creates as well as ameliorates emotional problems!

9. Along with their profound tendencies toward habituation, people also incessantly change. So do the environmental conditions under which they live. Therefore, they'd better expect no perfect or Utopian solutions to their problems!

10. If our major human values include surviving as long as feasible and remaining reasonably happy and free from needless pain as long as we survive, we can observe that we largely disturb ourselves by thinking and acting in absolutistic, rigid, dogmatic, demanding, damning, intolerant, bigoted, and grandiose ways. *Must*urbation comprises the root of most emotional evil.

11. Effective psychotherapy largely involves a hard-headed, realistic, logico-empirical attitude leading to tolerance, anti-awfulizing, and unconditional acceptance of oneself and of other people.

12. To achieve maximum joy and self-actualization, people had better try to forego rating or assessing their intrinsic worth, their essences, or their totalities. They would better try, instead, to rate their traits, deeds, and performances, so that they may abet their values of living and enjoying.

13. People's identity or uniqueness largely consists of what they, as individual members of the human race, truly desire and enjoy — and what they do not desire and find distasteful. Identity does not consist of what the members of any peer group or other group think that a person *should* or *must* do. To attain maximum happiness, therefore, people had better experiment and try to discover, as distinct individuals, what they really want to do in the course of the one and only life they will ever likely have. For who the hell else can ever tell them *that?*

OK, discussants. Let's see what you think and feel about these RET hypotheses!

Comments by Gerhard Neubeck, Ph.D.

I would like to make a number of comments not necessarily connected with each other. I appreciate having been asked to respond, and it was pointed out to me that I was invited exactly because I am not a RET true believer. I feel a bit like I am in the lion's den here but, practicing RET on myself, I know how to deal with it.

Is there a danger for RET to become institutionalized too soon? *Must*urbation is a danger present even for you. To be doctrinaire stands in the way of your own principles. How are you going to resolve that dilemma?

I think in this paper affective states have been overlooked, and while I could elaborate on that, I want to simply refer here to a study on pornography where respondents evaluated the material on the basis of "how it made them feel," rather than on a cognitive or emotional set of criteria. The affective aspects of behavior, of course, have much to do with our biological selves, and I think that Al is not paying enough attention to that.

I, with Al, think people want to live happily, and that must mean that they want to feel good, which is not only, let us say, the absence of a headache. Also, what people describe subjectively as feeling good may not be what an outsider defines as good. A recent occurrence in my marriage counseling practice will serve as an illustration. I helped a couple in respect to problem-solving, communication, and so on, and their marriage seemed to be going better — only for them to come back a month later to say that they couldn't go on. It seemed their feelings for each other had not been recaptured; and that, they said, made them unable to continue as a couple. I wonder, therefore, if therapy must not be directed toward feeling states.

In respect to RET, I would like to be personal for a moment. We all know that Al has been a diabetic for many years, and so he must have practiced RET on himself in respect to his illness — a physical event — for a long time. I became a diabetic — the mild, old-age one — about a year and a half ago. It came all of a sudden when I experienced symptoms which were then diagnosed as diabetes. This caused some temporary depression, but primarily because my expectations were fanned by my physician and dietician, warning me of eventual loss of circulatory sensitivities, eyesight, and impotence. My dietary habits had to be changed. I would have to eat less, but I managed to overcome these considerations by thinking that nobody could be blamed for this state of affairs and that certainly I would not read this as personal punishment or a consequence of some other personal shortcoming. But with all of that, there was an *activating event* and my dilemma was not solely because I read the event irrationally. The final answer in dealing with my short-term depression was something like this — there is a wonderful bag of goodies out there in this world, but I don't need to have everything. It's not going to kill me — as a matter of fact, to have these goodies is going to kill me!

In respect to RET and interpersonal events, I feel there are some difficulties. RET addresses itself to the work that an individual can do for herself or himself, while relationships exist as a result of contractual responsibilities. In other words, I can work on myself and be less awfulizing and catastrophizing about events, but in a relationship I contracted for certain satisfactions. While I can tell myself I did not need all of these goodies, or didn't need them as often, and I am not a rotten person if I don't get them, etc., etc., etc., I still entered the relationship with a certain set of goals in mind, and indeed I entered the relationship because I didn't want to go it alone.

So no matter what, unless the relationship delivers satisfactions, I must get out of it. That is the direction of change, and not one in myself.

There is a plethora of emotional loadings to which RET addresses itself, but seemingly without consideration as to their qualitative differences — can examination anxieties, a cleanliness phobia, or jealousy all be dealt with in the same way? Perhaps there is a hierarchy of difficulty. I believe there is, and I would put jealousy on the top of that list. And I have had in this conference a good deal of affirmation that jealousy has so far been the most difficult problem to deal with. I look forward to the time when RET can deliver in this area.

Last but not least, I don't think we have studied the therapist, her/him, enough. I cannot believe that a system can work independently of its practitioners; and while Albert has spawned many good RET therapists, he ought to study them as persons and how their effectiveness may differ according to their personalities. As I said before, I have known Al since the late 1940's. I have always respected him — and I have disagreed with him. I have not been a close friend of his, and neither have I been a follower, but I know that Al as a person will remain in my unconscious.

RET's Place and Influence in Contemporary Psychotherapy

ROBERT A. HARPER, Ph.D.

Washington, D.C.

Because I have so long and so intimately been involved with RET and in a fully seemly friendly and collaborative way with its maker, Albert Ellis, I became downright surprised as I undertook the evaluation of the psychotherapeutic scene in preparation for this paper to note that RET's place in contemporary psychotherapy is near, if not at, the top, and its influence is tremendous.

As some of you know, I did not just begin evaluating psychotherapies at the time this meeting topic was assigned to me. Some seventeen years ago I commenced to take a scholarly stance in regard to the plethora of therapies. In addition to this hobby's growing into a noble substitute for seducing the youth of the nation and as a supplement to my avidly racing through the woods with my dog and compulsively replacing clay with compost in my gardens in the Capital Garden Spot where I reside, this same avocation has somewhat amazingly exuded two semischolarly works: *Psychoanalysis and Psychotherapy: 36 Systems* and *The New Psychotherapies*. Those who would like documentation of some of the things I say today about other psychotherapies may consult these works.

I do not intend to line up the eighty or so therapies which have been described in my two books and show how superior rational-emotive therapy is to them all. Nor am I going to compare RET in principle and practice point by point with any other particular therapy. I am going to try to hit significant high spots of content and procedure and results in RET and in what I hope are appropriately selected other therapies.

One other caveat is that what I present here today is the way it all seems to me personally and may not be taken as the official view either of RET or necessarily Albert Ellis's view of the other therapies mentioned. In order to keep the whole thing in clear, crisp declarative sentences I shall speak as if my over-all impressions were facts, but I do not view myself as the voice of official authority.

To understand what has happened and still is happening in the whole area of psychotherapy, we need to make a very sharp distinction between *theories* of man and therapy (which I shall refer to from time to time as the religions of psychotherapy) and *techniques* of therapy (methods designed to help troubled people).

The main religion of psychotherapy when RET came on the scene in 1955 was psychoanalysis. Like Christianity, its more churchly counterpart, the religion of psychoanalysis had had various major schisms and denominational splits. There were clusters of psychoanalytic schools who took as their prophets such persons as Wilhelm Stekel, Carl G. Jung, Otto Rank, Sandor Ferenczi, Karen Horney, Erich Fromm, Harry Stack Sullivan, and Wilhelm Reich. But, as in the Christian analogy with Catholicism, Freudianism stood out as the one true and original faith.

The second major religion of psychotherapy twenty years ago was client-centered therapy. I think it can be viewed somewhat analogously to Mormonism in relation to Christianity: Carl Rogers emerged from psychoanalysis in much the same way Joseph Smith emerged from Christianity, but they both pretty soon got to talking about man and faith so differently that they and their followers turned out to be quite discrete religious phenomena. Although both the Joseph Smith-Brigham Young and Carl Rogers Churches of the Latter Day Saints have become eminently respectable today, they both went through periods of being treated as real pariahs. Rogerianism never made any real headway in the world of the Establishment (psychoanalysis and psychiatry), but found its own Salt Lake City in the desert mecca of academic psychology. When our own brave prophet, Albert the Ellis, stalked upon the stage breathing fire, circa 1955, client-centered therapy appeared to be a firmly established majority religion for psychologist-psychotherapists, and psychoanalysis (and mainly true-church Freudianism) was the established faith for a majority of psychiatrists and a minority of psychologists.

We'll now drop the religious theme for a moment — reminding ourselves that the therapeutic systems we have referred to up to now are the *theories* of man and therapy — and take a quick look at the pre-RET *techniques* of psychotherapy. For those of you who hate to let go of the religious theme, let me assure you that things get very theological soon again as we come to take a look at the multitude of therapeutic faiths that have developed in the last twenty years.

Although psychotherapeutic techniques are often interwoven with psychotherapeutic theories, an understanding of what is going on in psychotherapy cannot be approached without pulling the two apart. From the standpoint of techniques, it is interesting to observe that psychoanalysis and client-centered therapy are really very similar. What is free association but a form of nondirectiveness, and what is reflection of the client's feelings except a kind of interpretation? And free association with an occasional interpretation is allegedly the heart of psychoanalysis just as nondirectiveness with occasional reflection of the client's feelings is supposed to be the methodological center of client-centered therapy.

I say "allegedly" and "supposed" because not only psychoanalytic deviants but purportedly true-blue Freudians have departed flagrantly from what are purportedly proper psychoanalytic techniques. Even twenty years ago, you had to look hard to find a technically classical (as distinguished from a theoretically classical) analyst. Today if you find one, let me know: He is a collector's item worth his weight in Freudian dreams. As for the techniques of client-centered therapy, Carl Rogers himself, by my direct observations of him in workshop situations, did not stick to them with any great fidelity. His followers, however, applied them with assiduity that reached the heights of parody, but what has now happened to the busy client-centered hmm-hmmers of the fifties and early sixties? So far as I can determine, they have gone over the hill to existentialism, experientialism, gestalt therapy, or even in a few academic settings — horror of horrors — behavior therapy.

Just so you won't get lost, what I am still trying to do is set the psychotherapeutic scene, theoretically and technically, for the Grand Entrance of Guru Ellis in 1955. Technically, as we have already observed, many psychoanalysts — certainly at times including Sigmund Freud himself — departed from classical psychoanalytic procedures. Several founders of deviant schools of psychoanalysis made a point of emphasizing the values of more directive methods. These included Stekel, Adler, and (at times) Ferenczi, and later Sullivan, Horney, and Fromm. Theoretically, by 1955, psychoanalysis had had many face-lifting jobs. Freud himself did a lot of modifying and supplementing; he added on a lot of theories in the course of his lifetime, but almost never outrightly scrapped anything. But the main components of Freudian theory that were still knocking around twenty years ago (and even to a considerable extent today) consisted of conscious, preconscious, unconscious; sexual and aggressive drives as basic instincts of human behavior; and id, ego, and superego in cakes and cookies of religiosity of various shapes and sizes and in various stages of consistency — unmixed, baked, and half-baked.

But religious theory had not really seen anything yet until Jung hit the scene, and the Jungians were still exerting some theoretical influence in psychotherapy in the mid-fifties. Today Jungians have not become as rare as the Infernal Snow Man or the classical psychoanalyst, but damned near. Jung made Freud's preconscious his Personal Unconscious, eliminated the dynamic unconscious and substituted the Collective Unconscious, invented a system of opposites and compensations and gave them spiritual names, and generally rendered the already magical Freudian material much more mystical and esoteric.

The Adlerians were also on the scene in 1955, but much less formidably than they are today. Both Al Ellis and I have pointed out the overwhelming parallelisms between individual psychology and RET, along with some few and relatively unimportant differences. Only a few American Adlerians were functioning actively and noticeably twenty years ago, but their functioning from both the theoretical and technical standpoints was all in the direction of an active, directive, rational, purposive teaching approach to behavior problems. How Alfred Adler could have been a pupil of Freud's and could have emerged so unmarred by either the theories or the procedures of psychoanalysis is one of the chief puzzles in this whole mysterious field of psychotherapy. Anyhow, in the United States (and chiefly through the work of our old friend Rudolf Dreikurs and his many followers at the practical level and of Heinz and Rowena Ansbacher and others at the theoretical level), individual psychology has had a strong and steady development in the past twenty years parallel to RET. I will point out later why I think the Adlerian future may be less bright than RET, but right now they are shining along pretty well together (with the Adlerian emphasis, as a result of Dreikurs' influence, being most notable in the family-child-school counseling area). Twenty years ago, though, individual psychology was no great beacon of light in either the theoretical or technical therapeutic seas.

There were a few other therapeutic characters around in both fact and fantasy in 1955 America. Otto Rank had developed some followers and some influence among those who never became followers: The Philadelphia (or "functional") school of social casework was his most outstanding group of American followers, and both the dynamic culturalists (such as Fromm) and the Rogerians were and are in Rank's debt theoretically and technically. With Rank's pitch about the birth trauma as the biggest of behavioral deals, I suppose he can be considered the precursor of primal therapy, which may be considered a kind of watered-down version of the birth scream.

The dynamic culturalists were surely here in 1955, and theoretically they made interesting and occasionally fascinating and sometimes even realistic revisions of the largely biology-based Freudian hypotheses, but they usually went ahead with the therapeutic methodology of the more orthodox psychoanalysts. More accurately stated, both the revisionists and the orthodox proceeded with their unsystematic adaptations of the classical psychoanalytic techniques that had long ago proved considerably unworkable. These haphazard technical alterations of the Freudian techniques did not seem to work much better — mainly, I would say, because even the forthright directivists such as Franz Alexander remained pretty hamstrung with psychoanalytic theory (however revised, still basically Freudian religion).

There were plenty of other so-called schools of psychotherapy hanging around the edges of clinical reality in 1955. Their peripheral influence was not enough to change the basic texture, color, form, or odor of the theoretical and technical therapeutic scene onto which Albert Ellis sprang full-grown from the head of the Statue of Liberty. There was a form of behavior therapy (not yet called that) introduced by Salter (conditioned reflex therapy) and Joseph Wolpe's psychotherapy by reciprocal inhibition was just around the corner. Psychobiologic therapy (Adolf Meyer), directive therapy (Fred Thorne), general semantics (Alfred Korzybski and Wendell Johnson), assertion-structured therapy (Lakin Phillips), and a number of learning theory therapies may be considered (along with the individual psychology of Adler) precursors of RET. As I hope to show soon, however, Ellis put the whole direct teaching of a rational and realistic approach to behavior together much more neatly, simply, and effectively than did these predecessors. He also struck with a much mightier propagandistic sledge-hammer when the therapeutic iron was much hotter than in the years of his forerunners.

Whatever effect these pre-RET pioneers were having on the stage of the early fifties, they were being more than offset by other magical and religious therapeutic influences than those of psychoanalysis and client-centered therapy. I refer to psychodrama (Jake Moreno and followers with its acting-out magic), gestalt therapy (with Fritz Perls' clever combining of the magics of psychoanalysis, psychodrama, and the body-energy hypotheses of Wilhelm Reich with some garbage-pail religiosity of his own), and experiential therapy (with John Warkentin, Carl Whitaker, Thomas Malone, and others of the Atlanta school going back to the deep feeling-tone magic of the Freudian id, the area abandoned by the ego-therapy developments of psychoanalysis).

Why do I put such awful (not to say "terrible" and "catastrophic") terms as "magic" and "religiosity" on such fine people and their therapies? Many of these persons, along with other leaders of therapeutic faiths developed since 1955, were or are my friends, but I assert that what they think about human behavior and its causes (or say they think about human behavior and its causes) and the treatments they undertake to change human behavior (or the treatments they say they undertake) fall into the magical and religious categories for the following reasons:

1. They all posit some mysterious and largely unknowable force (usually called the unconscious, basic and generalized instincts, or the id, but which could just as easily be called God or Beelzebub) that controls human behavior. That is the religion.

2. The magic is the process used — be it psychoanalysis, psychodrama, or nondirective and loving and authentic encountering of the patient by the therapist — somehow vaguely to exorcise evilly designed forces (Beelzebub) in the individual and to replace them by benignly designed forces (God).

Is this oversimplification and misrepresentation of those therapies that held front and center stage in 1955 (psychoanalysis, primarily, and, in the academic theater, client-centered therapy) and those nonrational therapies (experiential, gestalt, and psychodramatic) that hung around the edges? I think not. I am in no way denying that there are a lot of complicated details in all these therapies. Many of these details, incidentally, fall within the categories of ritualism, tautological and definitional thinking, deification and hero worship, intolerance of opposition, mysticism, and unrealism and antiempiricism that we properly associate with religion and magic. But most of the details of theory boil down to mysterious forces, and most of the details of technique reduce themselves to the magic process of exorcism. Let's look a little closer in these two respects at both psychoanalysis and client-centered therapy.

In psychoanalysis we have the unconscious, which is almost exclusively running each human machine. Freud first likened the mind to an optical instrument, later developed a topographic theory, and finally produced a structural hypothesis (id, ego, superego). First there was one force which ran the whole shebang via the unconscious — the libido or sex drive. Then the libido got more desexualized (curiously in harmony with Jung's notion, about which Freud fairly frothed at the mouth when he first encountered it) into a life force (Eros) and was joined by an aggressive drive or death instinct (Thanatos). By 1923, Freud had the unconscious (and these two forces of the unconscious) raging through id, ego, and superego, but, despite valiant efforts of ego and superego at the conscious level, it was very clear that the unconscious (powered by Eros and Thanatos) was somehow accounting for most of the individual's behavior. What do you do about the unconscious, according to Freud? Well, you just let it rip, because you are powerless to do anything else. But if, as it rips, the psychoanalyst tunes in on the verbal manifestations of the ripping (via the patient's free associations and, especially, his free associations about reported dreams), and makes careful interpretations (dogmatically and ritualistically defined) as he holds his own neuroses in abeyance (which is possible only if he has gone through this magical process of free associating for a long time — unless, of course, he is Freud himself), then somehow *magically* (and I would be glad to entertain another appropriate word than "magically" that really fits the process) the nasty old unconscious (Beelzebub) transforms into a mature, fully analyzed, genitally fixated unconscious where Eros and Thanatos are functioning in apple-pie shape (God).

As Freud often made clear in his later writings, he had no overwhelming faith in psychoanalysis as a curative process. He and many of his followers made the chief case for psychoanalysis as a research tool in the study of human behavior — behavior that would go on being pretty sick, but presumably increasingly explainable. But since the explanations about human behavior derived from psychoanalysis are all couched in its own religious dogma, it has yet to be shown that they get anybody anywhere.

Carl Rogers reacted negatively to the religion of psychoanalysis, but then proceeded to set up his own religion and magic. The client-centered religion rests on the proposition that the good forces (called potentialities for growth and development instead of God) in the individual will emerge provided that the person is given a permissive atmosphere to explore himself, to acquire deeper understanding of himself, and gradually to reorganize his perceptions of himself and the world about him. The permissive atmosphere is the Rogerian magic: In this atmosphere the therapist effectively communicates to the client unconditional positive regard and empathic understanding. It's magic because there is no satisfactory cause-and-effect explanation: One takes on faith that the good forces are in the person and that unconditional positive regard and empathic understanding will somehow vaguely release them. And if you don't believe that, you must have somehow been messing around with too many of Fred Skinner's pigeons and got yourself Beelzebubbed up at a point beyond freedom and dignity.

It was into this world, then, that RET was born twenty years ago. What did Ellis bring? Perhaps some other kind of religion and magic? Quite the contrary. He was pilloried by his colleagues for offering such an earthly and earthy model of human behavior, of how that behavior becomes disturbed, and of how the therapist and patient by working hard together rather than by magic can change that behavior. I remember one distinguished colleague at one of the early workshops of the American Academy of Psychotherapists (after listening to a brief exposition of RET by Ellis) having said that this was the oversimplified notion of human behavior that he had believed as a child but had given up by the time he reached high school.

First, Ellis got rid of both Beelzebub and Jehovah. There is no mystical unconscious, no id. There are no specifically patterned forces — good or evil — which grab hold of the individual and run his life for him. The emotions, which psychoanalysis and client-centered therapy and many other therapeutic systems tended to enshrine and treat as autonomous powers toward which one must genuflect in one way or another, were chiefly just the product of what the individual himself thinks, Ellis said. And what the individual thinks, usually prejudiced and distorted and overlaid with nonsense uncritically absorbed from infancy onward, can be changed — not by such magic as unconditional positive regard or free association, but by the hard work of changing the internalized sentences with which he largely created the feelings in the first place.

Secondly, then, Ellis, after getting rid of God and devil, took away the status of high priesthood from the psychotherapist. These therapeutic boys and girls who had been basking in the soft, sweet light of guruhood were told by Cousin Al that the therapist's main job is to teach (and in 1955 therapeutic circles "teach" was almost as horrible a word as another known to occasionally pass the lips of our hero: namely, "bullshit") — that the therapist's main job is to teach his patients to understand exactly how they create their own emotional reactions by telling themselves certain things and how they can create different emotional reactions by telling themselves other things. What hideous perfidy! indicated the colleagues of Albert Ellis. Here is one of our own dear boys who is not only leaving the tabernacle himself, but dares to suggest it would be desirable that the rest of us get our asses out and teach ourselves and others not to be so damned unhappy and disturbed. Let's lynch the son of a bitch!

There are other reasons Albert Ellis has not always met with either lusty cheers or polite applause during the past two decades. He went further with the antireligion and antimagic of his therapeutic theories and techniques. He not only gave an unreligious explanation of disturbed emotions and an unmagical procedure for reducing the individual's disturbance, he went on to specify many of the illogical internalized statements that are almost universal among people in our society. These are the sentences for which the therapist had best look and on which he'd better be prepared to hammer away when a patient enters his sanctuary. Imagine this fellow Ellis having the heresy and gall of not only advocating rational teaching, but also of specifically listing many of the nutty ideas a disturbed person in our society is almost certain to have (in his own unique mix, of course). Besides, where did this guy think he derived the right to say that it is irrational to think one direly needs to be loved and that one makes oneself disturbed by thinking it is terrible, awful, and catastrophic not to get what one wants?

A fourth way that RET offered a nonreligious and nonmagical therapeutic route was by Ellis's showing that his unvague conceptions of human behavior and forthright methods of tackling disturbed behavior were really more depth-centered and intensive and effective than the vague and complicated theories and rituals of psychoanalysis. Causes attributed to unconscious forces by psychoanalysis could be picked (by hard introspective work) right in the here-and-now of the patient's consciousness. Ellis showed patients (and fellow therapists) that their problems, especially their negative feelings (such as anger, depression, anxiety, and guilt), arise not from past events or external situations but from their present irrational attitudes toward these events and situations.

A fifth most important antireligious and antimagical contribution of RET was not yet precisely formulated in 1955, but nevertheless underlay much of the early work in Ellisian theory and practice. This was antiperfectionism, antiegoism, antirating, and related phenomena. If I were asked to pick the one major cause of human unhappiness and emotional disturbance, I would choose perfectionism. This is especially true among the most intelligent and creative individuals I have known, certainly including many psychotherapists. Many of these 1955 and post-1955 therapists had enshrined perfectionism for themselves and their patients, and Ellis came charging into their temples to pitch them out on their less-than-perfect asses. The general religious theme of the times (which unfortunately still widely persists today) was that to be fully worthy I must not only achieve excellently all of the time, but everybody (or at least everybody who matters) must recognize me and approve of me and love me as a constantly excellent achiever. And if I don't and if they don't, then I am a miserable shit who deserves to be shot. That was the religion of the day with which the magic of the day was supposed to deal: A truly fully analyzed person would presumably become so perfect that he would be thus recognized by himself and others and then rise to Heaven to sit at Freud's right hand. How that obviously imperfect Freud ever got to heaven himself was not something that anyone other than maybe Ernest Jones had to struggle with.

This matter of learning not to be a perfectionist and learning not to rate oneself and learning not to get hung up in one's ego on the line with achievements and opinions of others constitutes, in my opinion, by far the toughest and most important one with which RET has had to wrestle. The therapist does not know what hard work really is until he has gone to the mat with a patient on the whole self-worth deal, and a lot of his other work is going to be largely in vain until he can get the patient to come to think one of two things about himself: "(1) I accept as an unprovable axiom that I have dignity and worth regardless of what I do or don't do and regardless of what my associates think of me, and I shall henceforth live in accordance with this axiom"; or (and preferably), "(2) I hereby dispense with and reject as magical nonsense the whole idea of self-worth, and I shall henceforth focus on how I can make my life more interesting and effective and enjoyable rather than on whether I am worthy."

Many more things could be said about the contributions of Albert Ellis and RET to therapeutic theories and techniques, but those are what I consider major ones. What impact have they had and how do I distinguish them from other relatively realistic and direct and rational therapies? In the course of trying to answer that question, I will discuss not only the therapies that existed in 1955, but many of the direct and relatively realistic therapies that have come into existence after that date.

The more directive psychoanalytic deviants (at least those that founded subschools of psychoanalysis) can, I think, be quickly dismissed as realistic competitors of RET in attacking the heart of (or should I say the Head?) of emotional disturbance. The reason for this is that modified psychoanalysis, no matter how direct and forthright its techniques (and they often aren't all that direct and forthright), is still hung up on a lot of mumbo-jumbo theory. I don't mean to belittle this mumbo-jumbo theory because it is really very fascinating stuff — often not at all inferior to a well-written spy or mystery thriller. But that's just the point: Even the most basically rational and realistic therapist and the most intelligent and cooperative patient are bound to be distracted from the major therapeutic tasks at hand by their devoted pursuit of what they are addicted to calling the vicissitudes of psychoanalytic theory.

The exception to all this is, as I have already said, Adlerian therapy, but any relationship between Adlerian theory and practice and Freudian theory and practice is purely coincidental. I am not prepared to argue that RET is essentially more rational and realistic than Adlerian therapy in either theory or practice. There are only two advantages that I see of RET over Adlerian therapy: (1) The rational-emotional therapist is probably less apt to get off the track of tackling the central thinking problems of the patient that are producing his self-defeating emotions and behavior. (The Adlerian therapist can get off on a lot of sidetracks, useful but nevertheless not central to major disturbances. I refer to the therapist helping the patient to develop more social and community interests, change his life style, become more loving, etc. All these things will be of little practical use to the patient in developing a happier life if his screwed-up, disturbance-producing ideas are neglected.) (2) As both Albert Ellis and Maxie Maultsby have demonstrated with their various programmed therapeutic procedures and homework assignments, RET is much more attuned to — and, in fact, is a part of — behavior therapy than is the Adlerian approach. This gives RET a superior flexibility to Adlerian therapy because it is also as well adapted to the conventional face-to-face teaching approach. RET can thus offer a more thoroughgoing multifaceted approach to the patient than Adlerian or any other therapy.

The other therapies which, as of 1955, offered direct techniques and realistic theories are psychobiologic therapy, conditioned reflex therapy, psychotherapy by reciprocal inhibition, directive therapy, general semantics, learning theory therapy, and assertion-structured therapy. Adolf Meyer's psychobiologic therapy consists of really a kind of syncretism and no unifying theory. He suggested, in effect, that the therapist sit down and listen and keep offering suggestions until by some sort of hit-and-miss process he and the patient would arrive at an outlook that would suit them both. Now that's OK, and that's how I sometimes work with very difficult patients who are wholly unresponsive to an RET approach (and some definitely are). But it lacks any neat cutting edge for getting through to emotional disturbance and quickly and efficiently achieving significant behavioral change, as is often possible with RET.

General semantics and the various learning theory therapies are fine as far as they go, but, with one exception, they tend to be rather segmented in theory and sometimes in technique. The exception is the late George Kelly's psychology of personal constructs, which is certainly complete in its theoretical manifestations, but when you get through Kelly's two-volume work (and believe me, you have to be gutsy to make it, for George, who, incidentally, was PO'd with me for calling him a learning theory therapist in my *36 Systems*, wrote long-windedly and atrociously, but was a nice guy). But, anyhow, when you got through Kelly's two-volume work, you knew Freud, with all his magic and religion, was a great writer. George's stuff just had little to do with helping patients, at least as I see it.

As for conditioned-reflex therapy, psychotherapy by reciprocal inhibition, and assertion-structured therapy, they were all forerunners of behavior therapy, and they all, like more recent developments of behavior therapy, miss the general theoretical and technical boat so far as dealing with the broad range of neurotic disorders in an efficient and relatively precise way like RET. These and other behavioral approaches have considerable success in dealing with specific disorders, such as the phobias, but they do not offer a broad and flexible framework within which the therapist can operate in relation to whatever problems or disturbances are brought to him by the patient. RET does provide this.

Of the psychotherapies that have come into being since 1955, reality therapy is the one most often compared to RET. Reality therapy has taken long strides away from the religion and magic of psychoanalysis, but it has not, in my opinion, gone quite far enough. Reality therapists still seem to get themselves and their patients caught up in the magic of the need to be loved and the need to feel worthwhile (the latter to be gained by what they refer to as moral achievements). And William Glasser and his followers do not seem to work directly and concentratedly on self-sentences as the source of disturbed emotions and self-defeating behavior.

Transactional analysis is also often compared to RET. Eric Berne apparently had some kind of block about RET and/or Albert Ellis because most TA people today admit great similarities in the system, but Eric Berne, so far as I know, refused to look at RET. The main deficiency that I can see in TA is that patients and therapists get distracted from the main task of helping people to change their beliefs (and, hence, their self-defeating emotions and behavior) by substituting a whole new mythology for the psychoanalytic magic and religion. While the new mythology of Parent and Adult and Child and recognition and structure hunger and "strokes" and games and scripts is much more realistic and infinitely simpler than the Freudian or Jungian mythology, it still becomes a fascinating distraction from the real business at hand for both therapist and patient. Just as it may be good, clean fun to analyze my Oedipal urges, so it can be a peachy-keen sport to chase my Child through all its manifestations and contaminations. But the real problem of how to get me to enjoy life more by giving up a lot of my damned-foolish thoughts and feelings and actions is not helped by a merry mythological romp through either the Freudian or Berne-ian bogs and marshes. Clearly it is the plain old Ellisian fields that not only appeal to me, but make the best, simplest, and yet most comprehensive therapeutic sense. That, for those of you who have not yet caught on, is my bias.

Although my friend Harold Greenwald probably will not appreciate being dismissed with just a line or two, I don't think direct decision therapy is a new system of psychotherapy. Harold makes commendable emphasis on the importance of decision-making (including the decision of not making a decision) in everyone's life and then proceeds to practice a not-very-modified form of RET.

Then there's the confrontation problem-solving therapy of a Chicago psychiatrist, Harry H. Garner. I don't think Garner has developed a wholly different system, but is valuable in prodding patients to develop problem-solving attitudes and to become involved in observing and more accurately interpreting reality.

What therapies remain? Well, there exists psychosynthesis, invented by Roberto Assagioli, but it gets back to religion and magic with a zest comparable to a Holy Roller's. Psychosynthesis allegedly awakens, releases, and utilizes superconscious spiritual energies which transform and regenerate the personality.

Joseph Shorr, a California psychologist, has come up with psycho-imagination therapy and uses imagination to tap the patient's phenomenological world in a manner that he says reveals the nature of major conflicts and points the way toward effective resolution of these conflicts. This seems all fine as another fascinating game for the therapist and his patients to play. There are self-and-other questions, the most-or-least method, the finish-the-sentence technique, and the gambit of what image is aroused in the patient when the therapist says certain key words. I suspect that Shorr and his patients have some really challenging and thrilling hours together galloping through their respective imaginations, but there is still the grubby, uninspiring business at hand: How are these guys and gals going to live more interesting and effective and enjoyable lives when not playing games with their therapist?

I said at the outset of this paper that I was not going to try to cover all the therapies, but I think I am getting pretty close to it. There are, of course, the body psychotherapies: Reichian, Alexander Lowen's bio-energetic modifications of Reich, primal therapy, autogenic therapy, and some aspects of gestalt therapy. Within these, the religion and magic vary from teaching the brain how involuntarily to do its health-enhancing job (in autogenics) to letting health function again by getting all the strictures and fixations opened up in a few screams (in primal therapy). And that, except for the application of some special techniques to group and family situations, just about constitutes a complete review of the psychotherapies of 1955 and 1975 and the years in between.

What does this tell us about RET's place and influence in contemporary psychotherapy? If we view psychotherapy as the means of helping people to reduce or remove the behavior patterns which are causing them distress, disorganization, frustration, and confusion, I know of no therapeutic system that can realistically declare itself superior to RET. RET's direct, simple, and unmagical attack on the beliefs that produce unhappy feelings and self-defeating behavior proves effective in a high percentage of cases, and this technique is based on an equally direct and simple and realistic (that is, nonreligious) view of human beings and how they function.

As for RET's influence in the field of psychotherapy, I think it has been tremendous. Even many psychotherapists who most strongly criticize the simplicity of the techniques and theories of RET and the supremely objectionable personality of A. Ellis show in their writings and their talks some tightening up of the nuts and bolts of their brands of magic and religion. The more realistic here-and-now emphasis of ego psychology had already begun to pervade psychoanalysis in 1955, and this predisposed some psychoanalysts to be subject to the influence of RET to take them further in the reality-oriented direction. Some client-centered therapists, experientialists, and existentialists have been similarly influenced by RET to cut down considerably on their crap in both a theoretical and technical vein by their encounters with RET. Adlerian therapy and some of the other more rational and realistic approaches to helping people to cope with their problems have been strengthened by their association with RET forces.

A quite large segment of psychotherapy, however, still remains mainly uninfluenced by RET or any of the other more rational and realistic approaches. In 1975, we still have religion and magic in psychotherapy, but I think the proportion of the field thus controlled by the lunatic group is smaller than in 1955, and I think this can be considerably attributed to the influence of RET. A few years ago, it looked as if the feel-deal magic of the encounter movement was going to dominate psychotherapy even more completely than had psychoanalytic magic of an earlier era. But that has waned, and at least as this is being written no new religion or magic is here to replace it. A certain small percentage of any type of magic and religion goes on after its heyday, so we still have a sizable but certainly not overwhelming segment of psychotherapy under the control of one or another brand.

I think there are two main reasons why magic and religion persist in psychotherapy. One reason, and the most obvious one, is that nutty people get attracted to the field in the hope of thus getting over their nuttiness. Instead, some of them settle in, nuttiness and all, and produce and practice these forms of magic and religion which we have been discussing. Some get over their nuttiness, though, and some are really quite sane to begin with when they become psychotherapists, and this leads us to the second reason why magic and religion stick with us in psychotherapy. I think this reason is that therapists, being human and thus imperfect, get bored. And they get tired of working at the tedious process of keeping sane and helping their patients to achieve and maintain sanity. So they lapse into old games — some they picked up in their graduate training or internship — and they invent new ones. They remember it feels good to be loved and now from their patients they can not only be loved, but worshiped. They pontificate, and they like what they think they hear when they pontificate. They become a lot of little spiders who are spinning little webs of magic, and they like that religious glow that comes over them and their patients when everybody gets covered with magical cobwebs.

RET means hard work, and it means hard work for the therapist as well as the patient. It does not seem surprising to me that the price of persistent, lifelong hard work in order to achieve a life of great satisfaction seems too high a price for many human beings, whether patients or therapists. There must be an easier way, a magic way, a way that will get a person a nice fix with the

Almighty and that whole other-world bunch. The surprise is that as many therapists and patients as we have today are willing to hack away at the rational way. So the influence, I contend, of RET has been tremendous. The place of RET might be summed up this way: If man makes it, in the long run, I think RET will make it. And for the human beings who decide they want to try to make it in life, nonmagically, RET will help. Whatever the future of mankind, RET can help make the process between now and then more interesting and enjoyable, but — don't look now — a hell of a lot of hard work.

Comments by Albert Ellis, Ph.D.

Thank you, Bob, and I certainly mean *thank you!* I enjoyed your survey of RET's place and influence in contemporary psychotherapy and your inimitable style of presenting it.

I like your phrase, religions of psychotherapy. In some respects the religions have begun to ebb away, as you suggested in your paper, because things are a little more direct, active, and rational today than they were in 1955. But as the old religions fade, new apostles appear. I'm going to present my thesis of the biological bases of irrationality at the American Psychological Association meetings in the Fall, and I could spend a lot of time showing how psychotherapy itself confirms my thesis. I could devote practically all my scheduled one-hour talk to show how nutty psychotherapists are — including the main theoreticians in the field.

You've given a lot of evidence of that today in your survey, Bob. Just to add to your discussion . . . we don't have some of the old nonsense that we had in 1955. The Freudians lost their magic and had begun to die — in practice if not in theory. Unfortunately, just as we were about to bury them, along came even worse post-Freudian horseshit, called primal therapy. This has revived with a vengeance a great many nutty notions — notably, that you are disturbed today because you whined about your mother and her leaving you alone in the dark years ago. But, of course, you didn't whine nearly enough, so you'd better whine and whine and whine today. That is the new implementation, you might say, of Freudian theory. The old Freudian theory said exactly the same thing — that your problems came from your mother's depriving or neglecting you or something like that. The

Freudians didn't really tell you what to do about it — you were just supposed to understand it and that would magically change you. Now we have the current version in which you not only have to understand it, you have to actively wail your goddamned lungs out! And then that will change you. *Fat chance!*

And, of course, we have in the field of psychotherapy today a sort of new vector, which I'm sure you will go into in your book, *The New Psychotherapies*, Bob. That is the transpersonal psychotherapy which goes all the way back to 1848 (at least in the United States) as advocated by Henry David Thoreau and Bronson Alcott and the transcendentalists. It starts with a good supposition — the Zen Buddhist theme that you can get rid of ego to a large degree; and the idea that nothing is crucially important and you don't have to have insured success to make your life worthwhile. But then, quite typically of those who seek magic, like many of our friends in the Association for Humanistic Psychology, a great many "psychologists" today go further and follow transpersonal psychotherapy. They define "transpersonal" wrongly, as meaning something beyond what you normally do in personality theory and in psychotherapy. But really, more accurately, it means beyond the human or into the realm of the superhuman. And there are hosts of individuals today who call themselves psychotherapists — M.D.'s, Ph.D.'s, M.S.W.'s, etc. — who devoutly believe in transpersonal (beyond human) psychotherapy. So we still have screwballs in the field! Or, more accurately, therapists who often act screwballishly!

I would like to give a good deal of credit, because they certainly influenced me, to a couple of individuals whom you didn't mention prominently. They were two unusual psychoanalysts, both of whom coincidentally happened to be in Chicago at the time their book came out — Franz Alexander and Thomas French. They wrote a very practical book called *Psychoanalytic Therapy*, which I read in 1948. At that time I had already started being skeptical of some of the Freudian concepts, and Alexander and French presented a very direct technique and they helped me. Unfortunately, they did what analysts frequently do: They used the same old Freudian terminology and they never really gave up the id, the ego, and the superego. But what they did as therapists, and what their book advised, was a quite active form of psychotherapy — unrelated . . . in fact quite opposite . . . to what Freudians previously had been doing. They didn't have the guts to throw out the whole psychoanalytic language — the whole kit and kaboodle — and start a truly rational form of psychotherapy, but they were very influential in their day and they helped me.

On the idea of disturbed people getting more plentiful, lest anyone misunderstand, I don't mean that there are more nutty people in the world today or more nutty psychotherapists than there used to be. But I do take a skeptical — and I think realistic — view that human disturbance is very intense, often severe, as it has biological as well as psychological roots. Because of the way we think — and the evidence shows that even therapists and scientists easily think very crookedly! — once we get rid of a lot of nonsense, a lot more often shows up. As one kind of superstition (such as belief in lucky horseshoes) fades, something equally obnoxious and equally magical (such as belief in astrology) seems to rise to take its place. I think we can epitomize the process of social change as a whole with the famous statement: "Truth will out." Things in the field of therapy tend to get better over the years, with more observed fact and less romantic fancy than we once knew. But it's two steps forward and one step back. To extirpate the crap is really a rough go, and we'd better keep working at it!

Finally, let me comment on the unmagical process of working with clients in therapy, which can be a tedious process. Fortunately, I have found that the very tedium of psychotherapy offers some advantage. It has moved me to keep forging ahead to find new theories or add to the old, to change them around and find new techniques or adapt other people's techniques of working in therapy. We in RET have applied a good many of the concepts of operant conditioning of B. F. Skinner, who is hardly known as a great psychotherapist, but who has made significant contributions to the field. And we have adapted some of the best techniques of the encounter movement, though I agree with what Bob said about some of their fundamental hypotheses being faulty and even destructive to certain people who go through encounter-group experiences.

One of the reasons I've been able to originate and adapt new therapeutic methods — why I've pushed myself to do this — is that psychotherapy is so hard and wearing. It is often tedious to try to get individuals to see exactly what they say (and do) to themselves. It is tedious to get them to realize how they block themselves. It is tedious pushing them to stop doing so and to get them to do their goddamned homework assignments; and it is not easy to ferret out what they tell themselves to prevent themselves from doing homework assignments. It may also be a pain in the ass reassigning homework to clients, and helping them to do it by using the principles of operant conditioning.

But I find that, if I take the outlook that I do while seeing many kinds of clients (including a lot of D.C.'s, or difficult customers),

I can turn the tedium to good advantage. If I look at my theories as well as my practice, noting whether certain things work and why they work and how they can be made to work better, that sort of thing relieves a great deal of therapeutic tedium. It prevents the monotony that might ensue if I concerned myself *only* with the one individual before me and with helping him or her to change his or her thinking, emoting, and behavior.

In other words, I find it valuable to put the client in the total context of psychotherapy, and deal not only with this person but with the human condition — with how human beings individually (and in the final run even collectively) can change. As a therapist, I want to help the client change; but as a theorist and something of a revolutionist, I want to discover how *all* people can change and achieve greater enjoyment. By doing therapy in this theoretical as well as practical way, I find it makes the whole process a hell of a lot less tedious and a hell of a lot more interesting and enjoyable.

I certainly am thankful for the quality of the people in RET. There have been a good many high-level people associated in helping me develop RET from the beginning. But the one who has stood by in his own inimitable manner and who has been most effective, in spite of his "eclecticism," in spreading the gospel according to Saint Albert, not to mention the gospel according to Saint Robert, has certainly been Bob Harper! It has been one of my greatest pleasures, for well over thirty years, to know you, work with you, and love you. Let us hope that we somehow manage to struggle on together, you and I, spreading rationality among the heathens of psychotherapy for at least another thirty years!

Basic Principles of Intensive Rational Behavior Therapy: Theory, Goals, Technique, and Advantages

MAXIE C. MAULTSBY, JR., M.D.

Department of Psychiatry, University of Kentucky Medical Center
© Maxie C. Maultsby, Jr., M.D.

Introduction

Intensive RBT is a two-week attempt to give emotionally distressed people the psychotherapeutic benefits they would normally expect to get in three to four months of regular psychotherapy. At first that psychotherapeutic goal may sound overly ambitious. But when you compare the facts about regular psychotherapy to the facts about intensive RBT, you'll see that the goal of intensive RBT is quite reasonable.

Normally the most cooperative patient in regular psychotherapy spends a maximum of five hours in psychotherapeutic activities. Those activities will be one or some combination of (1) individual psychotherapy, (2) group psychotherapy, and (3) some type of self-help activity. That's a maximum of sixty hours of psychotherapeutic activities in three months.

The Intensive Rational Behavior Therapy Program at the University of Kentucky Medical Center gives patients a ten-hour daily combination of individual psychotherapy, group psychotherapy, and rational self-help exercises. Diligent patients are given the opportunity of spending up to fourteen hours per day in some type of therapeutic activity. In two weeks, therefore, intensive RBT patients experience more than twice the amount of therapeutic activity they would normally experience in three months of regular psychotherapy. If patients receiving intensive RBT are as motivated as patients receiving regular therapy, it is logical to expect intensive RBT patients to have more psycho-therapeutic progress at the end of two weeks of intensive RBT than would the same patients at the end of three months of routine psychotherapy. We routinely achieve that expectation because failure to progress in regular psychotherapy is the main reason therapists refer patients to our intensive RBT program.

Theory of Intensive RBT

Intensive RBT is based on the same learning theories of human behavior as regular RBT. Those theories have been described in detail in the psychotherapy literature and will not be discussed here. Instead, I shall describe the six therapeutic assumptions that form the basis of the intensive RBT experience.

Therapeutic Assumption No. 1 — Permanent emotional change is the result of emotional reeducation.

Therapeutic Assumption No. 2 — The five stages in emotional reeducation are the same and follow the same general principles of learning as the five stages in any type of reeducation.

Therapeutic Assumption No. 3 — In the process of rational emotional reeducation, therapists have the sole responsibility for providing patients with an adequate opportunity for efficient emotional analysis, extinction, and auto-conditioning. Patients have the sole responsibility of using that opportunity to put themselves through the five stages of emotional reeducation.

Therapeutic Assumption No. 4 — The time required for patients to pass through the five stages of emotional reeducation depends primarily on patients' ability to learn and willingness to learn new emotional habits.

Therapeutic Assumption No. 5 — Because intensive RBT is based on learning theories, most effective teaching and learning aids can be used to facilitate the emotional reeducational process.

The four teaching and learning aids used most commonly in intensive RBT are (1) frequent individual and small group learning experiences, (2) rational bibliotherapy (Goodman and Maultsby, 1974; Maultsby, 1971c, 1975a, 1975b; Maultsby and Hendricks, 1974a), (3) written and practical therapeutic homework, and (4) analytic study of therapeutic audio and video tapes.

Therapeutic Assumption No. 6 — The events and process of education and reeducation are:

1. Goal-directed repetition of specific perceptions and thoughts produces relatively permanent cognitive habits called attitudes and beliefs. These elicit specific habits of emotional feelings and physical actions.

2. Goal-directed repetition of new perceptions and thoughts about old situations produces new cognitive habits (i.e., new attitudes and beliefs) that elicit new habits of emotional feelings and physical actions which compete with the older habits of emotional and physical actions.

3. At the same time that new cognitive, emotional, and physical habits are being formed, the older, competing habits are simultaneously being extinguished.

The five stages of therapeutic emotional reeducation are (1) intellectual insight, (2) converting practice, (3) cognitive dissonance, (4) emotional insight, and (5) personality trait formation (Maultsby, 1975a). Giving patients rapid, useful understanding of those five stages is essential to efficient therapeutic progress. For that reason, I shall briefly explain each stage now.

Intellectual insight means learning what you will have to practice to obtain the reeducation you hope to achieve. Converting practice means converting your old involuntary emotional habits back to their original voluntary state. That's the only way the newly developing emotional habits can overcome the involuntary competition from the older emotional habits. To do converting practice, you must think, using your intellectual insights, and physically act them out. That activity puts you in the third stage of reeducation, cognitive dissonance. As used in rational behavior therapy, cognitive dissonance means having new thoughts that are illogical for your old, not-yet-extinguished emotional feelings. Emotional insight means having learned to have new emotional feelings that are logical for your new way of thinking. Personality trait formation means you have converted your emotional insight into a relatively permanent involuntary emotional habit.

The first and last two stages of education, or initial learning, are the same as the first and last two stages of reeducation, or new learning with which to replace old learning. For that reason most people are thoroughly familiar with those four stages. That's why they rarely have problems related to them.

Cognitive dissonance, however, is unique to the reeducational process. Most people don't know about it. Therapists must adequately prepare patients for this strange and confusing experience of thinking Yes but having a strong gut impulse that means NO; otherwise many patients will become so frustrated that they give up emotional reeducation and revert to their painful but familiar irrational thoughts with their logical but irrational emotional feelings.

The Two Goals in Intensive RBT

The first goal in Intensive RBT is to give emotionally distressed people a running therapeutic start in the emotional reeducation process. Running therapeutic start means getting people on the emotional insight side of cognitive dissonance. At that point in emotional reeducation, patients are most capable of benefiting maximally for regular psychotherapy and rational self-help activities.

The second goal in intensive RBT is to give patients as rapidly as possible these five kinds of therapeutic insights and skills: (1) recognition of their core emotional conflicts and their main irrational attitudes and beliefs that maintain them; (2) thorough knowledge of the process of rational self-understanding; (3) skill in using the rational emotional self-help techniques; (4) thorough knowledge of the stages in emotional reeducation; and (5) a rational, yet practical, plan for handling the daily events in their various life experiences at home.

From the first day of our intensive RBT program, we repeatedly remind patients that the university setting is both an artificial and unique experience in their lives. We tell them that intensive RBT will help them only to the degree it teaches them self-help skills they can easily carry back and use in their home environment.

The Two Essentials for Intensive RBT

First, you must have a well-trained, enthusiastic staff. Second, you must have appropriate patients. Since the first essential is self-explanatory, I will concentrate on the five types of patients we have found most appropriate for intensive RBT, the way we do it.

First are patients in therapeutic plateau. These patients have stopped showing therapeutic progress for a month or more; but by continuing to come for psychotherapy, they seem to show a sincere desire for further therapeutic change and their therapist can detect unused potential for that change. The second type includes patients needing more intensive, short-term outpatient therapeutic attention than is available in their community, and hospitalization is either undesirable or unneeded. Third are involuntarily resistant patients. These patients have both sincere desire and apparent ability for therapeutic change but their thoroughly learned irrational cognitive styles (explained in the next subsection) involuntarily creates too much resistance to change to be handled efficiently in the regular psychotherapeutic experience. The fourth type of appropriate patients includes patients who want to get in rational control of their problems as quickly as possible. The fifth type of patients could benefit adequately from psychotherapy available in their local community but for personal reasons refuse to get psychotherapy in their hometown.

In the order of their approximate frequency, the most common emotional and behavioral problems we treat in our intensive program are (1) severe neurosis, (2) chronic depression without suicidal ideations, (3) irrational fears, (4) alcohol dependency in people who are meeting their job and family responsibilities but with increasing difficulties, (5) severe problems in effective parenting, and (6) crisis in romantic and marital relationships. In spite of those frequencies, each potential patient is considered for admission on the basis of individual need and our program capabilities, rather than on the basis of diagnostic category. However, unless accompanied by one or both parents, no one under sixteen is accepted in the program.

The most common inappropriate patients for intensive RBT programs are: (1) noncoping psychotics, (2) patients needing significant medical supervision, and (3) involuntary patients.

The Technique of Intensive Rational Behavior Therapy

Intensive RBT begins with each patient being assigned a primary therapist. The primary therapist does an intake evaluation designed to produce three results: (1) an accurate DSM diagnostic label, (2) definition of the patient's three most significant problems, (3) discovery of the patient's major irrational cognitive styles.

As we use the concept, most significant problems have three characteristics. First, they are problems that can be dealt with effectively in the intensive RBT experience. (For example, people with severe money problems will not be able to solve them in our intensive RBT program; but those people will be able to learn more rational emotional reactions to their money problems as well as skill in rationally avoiding such problems in the future.)

Second, they are problems the patients are willing to work on in the intensive RBT program. Third, the elimination of these problems will probably result in significant improvements in the patient's daily life. We restrict ourselves to defining three most significant problems because that's usually the maximum number we can handle in a relatively complete manner in two weeks.

In our experiences irrational cognitive styles often form mental smoke screens that prevent patients from clearly defining their problems. Since precise problem definition is essential for intensive RBT, we emphasize rapid, accurate discovery of irrational cognitive styles.

The six most common irrational cognitive styles that we see at the University of Kentucky Medical Center are:

1. Abuses of generalities; for example, the inaccurate use of always and never.

2. The frequent use of irrational "can't"; for example, saying "I can't" when what is really meant is: "I'm afraid to or I don't want to."

3. Frequent use of irrational "what if's"; for example, refusing to apply for a job because of these thoughts: "What if I do everything wrong?" "What if I really hate everybody who works there?" etc.

4. Frequent use of "yes, but" type thinking to justify ignoring advice that would solve their problems but would also require them to change their behavior; for example, in response to "You could let your teen-agers clean their own room." They say: "Yes, but I just can't stand the thought of a junkyard in my house."

5. Listening to other people but hearing only themselves listening. These are the people who can hear you say, "But you don't have to be suicidally depressed just because your marriage is breaking up." And then respond, "But I do have feelings." They have heard you saying, "You don't have to be suicidally depressed." But they have listened only to themselves saying: "Only people who don't have any feelings wouldn't be upset if their marriage broke up. He thinks I don't have any feelings." Then they respond to themselves and to you with: "But I do have feelings."

6. Irrational emotive imagery; for example, a new waiter mentally picturing himself spilling soup and coffee on customers, rather than mentally picturing correctly serving the soup and coffee; then getting so afraid of making those mistakes he quits the job.

Probably the three most important therapeutic aspects of the intensive RBT experience are structure, structure, and structure.

Intensive RBT patients have numerous complaints. The main therapeutic aim is to find the common irrational logic and irrational attitudinal threads that can tie groups of those numerous complaints together into interrelated parts of one problem. Then patients can see more clearly the general structure of their two or three most significant problems. That relieves most of any initial sense of being overwhelmed by their multitude of complaints. Patients are then better able to work with the therapist in setting appropriate therapeutic priorities. But it isn't necessary for the therapist and patient to have defined three problems before therapy starts. The moment the therapist and the patient agree on one most significant problem, therapy can begin.

From the second day to the end of the intensive treatment period, each day starts with a morning staff conference. Here our professional staff discusses in detail the current therapeutic needs of each patient. The primary therapists use these discussions to make an individualized therapy plan for their patient. That therapy plan determines the content and amount of each patient's individual, group, and self-therapeutic activity for that day. Patients can spend two or more hours per day in any one of these therapeutic activities.

The main self-therapeutic activities are monitored rational self-analysis and rational-emotive imagery sessions and discussions of practical therapeutic homework, to be done outside of the Medical Center. Two other important self-therapeutic activities are listening to and analyzing video and audio taped self-help lectures and taped demonstrations of other patients with similar diagnoses successfully reeducating themselves.

The second week of intensive RBT is essentially a repeat of the first week, but the staff places greater emphasis on how patients can go back to their home environment and use the therapeutic insights and skills gained in the intensive RBT program. In the last two days, patients work with their primary therapist on discharge plans. Those plans always include return to the follow-up care of the referring professionals, who get a full summary of the RBT experience of their patients.

The Three Main Advantages of Intensive RBT

There are three main advantages of intensive RBT: (1) economy of cost, (2) economy of time, and (3) effectiveness in handling patients who are temporarily inappropriate for the regular psychotherapy.

The "E-Priming" of Bob Moore

ROBERT H. MOORE, M.Ed.

Institute for Rational Living, Florida Branch

The year 1975, rational-emotive therapy's twentieth anniversary, saw the revision of three perennial powerful-sellers: Albert Ellis and Robert A. Harper's A Guide to Rational Living *and Albert Ellis's* How to Live with a Neurotic *and* Sex and the Single Man. *Each got taken apart, retitled (*A New Guide to Rational Living, How to Live with a "Neurotic": At Home and at Work, Sex and the Liberated Man), *and put back together with a number of significant additions, but* without, *among other things, even a trace of the verb* to be (am, is, are, was, were, be, been, being).

Revision strategist Bob Moore here reports his seduction by and conversion to the "non-Aristotelian" semantic style of the revised editions.

What ever prompts me routinely to shun the most frequently used words in the English language? Where did I acquire such a habit?

I first picked it up as an undergraduate, actually, from an English instructor at Lehigh. I wrote very colorfully at the time, he told me. Purple! So, it started out as an exercise — leaving the verb *to be* out of everything — to improve my writing. And it probably did, since the style does severely limit one's use of the passive voice and several other fairly noxious constructions.

I took it with me into teaching, a few years later, and socked it to some of my English classes. You'd have thought I cut off their thumbs!

Back then, when a sixteen-year-old just plain didn't know how to cope effectively with somebody, that somebody went down as "weird." And, of course, that almost invariably came out as a straightforward, Aristotelian, identity statement. "He *is* weird!" "Oh yes, he *is*. He's weird! weird! weird!"

And there I stood, my prose down to reddish-brown, still waiting for rational psychology to break into my life.

But we had a ball with it. For one thing, it gave us a chance to go around about objectivity and subjectivity quite a bit. And I think a hell of a lot of learning took place in some of those discussions (maybe even in some of those kids), even if it only beat them back to, "In *my* opinion, he *is* weird!"

Anyway, I got into counseling quickly enough to avoid a second year in the classroom, moved into a clinical setting, then came across the rational model and fell in love. Still, I didn't notice the correspondence between RET and my old writing craze right away.

I guess that remained true until, in about 1969, I caught a *Time* magazine report on David Bourland. That guy, it said, had disciplined himself to *speak* in "E-Prime." (Aha! it had a name!) Back then, I still paid a 50 percent time penalty just to write that way, so I clipped the article and wrote him a fan letter (in E-Prime, of course).

He later put me in touch with Dan Schwartz, a University of California space physicist, responsible for the only doctoral dissertation written in non-Aristotelian language, at the time ("The Spatial Distribution of the Diffuse Component of Cosmic X-Rays").

But no one at that point, I learned, ever had written a whole book in E-Prime.

Then came my better acquaintance with the General Semantics movement. At that point, finally, as I began to explore Korzybski (1933) and non-Aristotelian logic, I made the connection (with RET) — and fell in love again!

I practiced a little harder after that. Earlier, I had written a couple of articles in the style (not in psychology) and had used it during graduate school pretty regularly, but now I began to write most of my letters in E-Prime.

And, of course, nobody ever noticed. (Which Dan also had reported regarding his dissertation.) Even when I made a point of it, hardly anybody got very excited about it. Some insisted that I would sooner or later find at least one tremendously compelling thought that simply would refuse to submit to non-Aristotelian expression. Then, they said, I'd probably blow a fuse — poor Bob!

But so far, so good.

I worked it into my therapy, of course, though I did learn to bring up some of the system's fine philosophic points rather sparingly, both in therapy and out. Apart from a few colleagues, I just didn't find that many people turning on to the discipline

("Aw, that's just semantics!").

Then, about two years ago, just after we opened the Clearwater branch of the Institute, I bit on George Garwood's low-keyed "whip alcoholism philosophically" ad in the "U-U World" (a Unitarian Church "house organ"). And damned if *he* didn't send me a fistful of stuff out of General Semantics, including an old paper on "Semantitherapy" I had never seen before.

In General Semantics, it seems, they teach a non-Aristotelian, cognitive reorientation technique, out of Korzybski, that clearly complements clinical practice. And its compatibility with RET practically knocked me over!

So, at that point, I *re*introduced Albert Ellis to the whole business (go ahead — try to find an idea you can *introduce* him to), stressing E-Prime and feeling as though I'd just discovered intelligent life in outer space.

Well, he bought it, and before long I found myself E-Priming the revised *How to Live With a "Neurotic"* manuscript. We did the old *Guide* over into the *New Guide,* after that. Then we translated *Sex and the Single Man* and finished off Al's and Bill Knaus's newest one, *Overcoming Procrastination.*

Translations, we decided, don't always turn out as smooth, syntactically, as original E-Prime. So, future revisions will get either more substantially rearranged, or completely rewritten. Of course, Al's most recent prose, now thoroughly in keeping with the non-Aristotelian tradition, seems just as terse as ever. (But what a gas it "seemed" to see him "exist as" enthusiastic, as he "kept" getting it together!)

Though I never thought much of a stir would result from the E-Priming aspect of the revisions, I did hope the General Semantics people would take it as a friendly gesture. And they did. Moreover, they gestured back, by publishing the "Introduction to the Revised Edition of HTLWN" in the March 1975 edition of *Etc.,* the journal of the International Society for General Semantics. Then, in the June 1975 issue, they published E. Scott Baudhuin's article, "RET and General Semantitherapy: A Review and Comparison."

Happiness!

I picked up some even more personal rewards, in this connection. I got to draft the Maultsbian definition of rational behavior into Chapter Six of the *New Guide.* And, of course, I also got to salute the General Semantics movement publicly, by introducing E-Prime here at our first national conference. Though I can't imagine who might have cared to hear about it, if we hadn't just gotten those first two revisions into print.

But I must say, it tickles the hell out of me to do the introducing. I hold the conviction that rational psychology and General Semantics have a great deal to share with each other. Not simply because we both recognize the inefficacy of verbal equation-making. But because we both so highly regard and determinedly employ the cognitive processes as mediators of our experience, in the pursuit of emotional health.

In my view, as a committed rational therapist, neither group can afford to overlook the work of the other.

This sort of cross-pollination of ideas, in fact, seems to me one of the key and most rewarding aspects of the national conference. We not only get to share with each other, in this respect, but we have met and touched, briefly, the people we will know even more personally as we grow into and along with our profession.

E-Prime in Principle and Practice

The verb *to be* includes the following parts: *am, is, are, was, were, be, been,* and *being.* Leave them all out.

For good measure, leave out also: *become* and *maybe.* You don't need them either.

"To be" generally appears in only three common grammatical constructions:

1. The predicate nominative
   Example — "He *is* an idiot."

2. The predicate adjective
   Example — "He *is* repulsive."

3. The progressive verb conjugations
   Example — "He *is* puking in my hat."

Infinitives, imperatives, compound verb constructions, the other tenses and persons all fit, somehow, into these three patterns. It doesn't really get any more complicated than this. It only seems as if it does.

How, then, will you replace them? Some examples:

1. "He is an idiot."
   a. "He looks like an idiot."
   b. "He behaves like an idiot."

2. "He *is* repulsive."
   a. "He seems repulsive."
   b. "He behaves repulsively."

3. "He *is* puking in my hat."
   a. "He pukes in my hat."
   b. "I see him puking in my hat."

You may notice that example three, the progressive verb conjugation, does not typically represent the kind of *identity statement* we most wish to delete from our repertoire. True. But having worked up a fairly potent prejudice against all forms of the verb (guilt by association), we generally leave our text scrupulously "*be*-less."

And although you may never have written a line of E-Prime, you very likely practice your profession in the non-Aristotelian tradition — at least to some extent. Examples:

Client: "That's just the way I *am*!"
Therapist: "No, that's just what you generally *do*!"

Client: "This *is* a bad situation!"
Therapist: "You mean, it *looks* pretty bad *to you*!"

Client: "She certainly *is* a nag these days!"
Therapist: "More precisely, she *nags* you a lot these days."

Assertiveness Training

DANA LEHMAN-OLSON, Ph.D.

Director of Family Consultation Center, Burnsville, Minnesota

Assertiveness training procedures have particular relevance for RET practitioners. While largely developed by behavior therapists, assertiveness behaviors and techniques provide guidelines for translating rational beliefs into rational behaviors. Assertiveness training procedures can be enriched by an understanding and analysis of cognitive correlates to assertive and nonassertive behaviors. Thus, several trainers (Lehman-Olson, 1974, 1976; Jakubowski-Spector, 1973; Lange and Jakubowski, 1976; Wolfe and Fodor, 1975) have developed methods which include both cognitive and behavioral techniques.

Assertiveness behavior is generally contrasted with two other types of behavior — passiveness and aggressiveness. Passiveness can be defined as the inability to express one's thoughts, feelings, and desires. It is also nonexpressiveness that is detrimental or inappropriate to the relationship goals. In general, passiveness is an attempt to keep the self hidden and is often correlated with fears of criticism, fears of failure, fears of hurting another, and fears of eliciting the other's anger. More specifically, nonverbal characteristics include avoiding another's eyes, withdrawn body posture, excessive hand movements, affected smiles, "blank" or nonexpressive facial expressions, mumbled words, meek voice tone, and general incongruence between the importance of a message and the nonverbal expression of the message. Verbally, some of the characteristics marking passive expression are overapologies for oneself, takeaways ("I really don't agree with you but I guess I don't have the right to say"), indirect expressions ("Don't you think . . . ?" or "Other people say this is the way it should be done"), overconcern with other persons' reactions ("I know this is really going to offend you and I don't want you to be mad at me, but . . .") and overqualifications ("I know this can be viewed from more than one side and

I'm not really sure and I may see it differently next week," etc., etc.). There are several other characteristics of passive behavior that include avoiding situations such as meetings, parties, or certain people because of not knowing what to do or say; allowing oneself to be easily interrupted and giving up; quietly acquiescing to unreasonable demands; and allowing oneself to become easily distracted by another's nonverbal cues of busyness or disinterest.

Aggressive behavior can be defined as behavior that expresses one's thoughts, feelings, and desires in a hostile, demanding, sarcastic, or put-down manner and with such self-expression usually achieved at another's expense. It is also expressiveness that is detrimental or undermining to the relationship goals. Aggressive behavior in general is an attempt to control another or get the other to acquiesce to one's demands or desires. When acting aggressively, one is out to "win" no matter what. Nonverbal expressions of aggressiveness include glaring or staring eye contact, tense and rigid body posture with the body often leaning toward the other in an exaggerated manner, clenched fists, pointing finger, clenched jaw, inappropriately loud voice, sarcastic tone of voice, and in general a tone and manner that exaggerate the importance of the message. Verbally, some characteristics of aggressive expressions include gross exaggerations ("For the last fifteen years you have never . . . "), absolutisms (*always, never, can't*), righteous language ("This is the way it is," "This is right," "You are wrong," "This is good"), blame ("If it weren't for you," "It's your fault"), demands ("You are inconsiderate if you don't . . . "), name-calling ("You're a slob," "You bastard . . . "), and other attempts to make a person feel self-conscious or put down ("Everybody knows it." "How come you don't seem to follow what's going on?"). Other characteristics include interrupting people or not letting them speak for themselves, controlling a conversation so the other can't get a word in, and unconcern for the other person's feelings or desires.

Assertive behavior can be defined as behavior expressive of one's thoughts, feelings, and desires which is appropriate to the relationship context. Assertive behavior is generally correlated with positive self feelings and general feelings of self-acceptance. Assertive behavior expresses a concern for self and also a concern for others. Nonverbal characteristics of assertive behavior include an ability to maintain direct eye contact, an erect body posture with a slight leaning toward the other, facial expressions congruent with what is being expressed, a clear, easily heard voice tone, a range of inflections to match the importance of the message expressed, and a general nonverbal congruence between the importance or meaning being expressed and body language. Verbal characteristics of assertive behavior include use of personal pronouns to identify one's thoughts, feelings, and desires; clear and direct statements of one's opinions and desires; asking for explanations from others; not allowing others to speak for oneself; and aiming positive and negative responses to the behavior and not to the person. Concern for others is expressed by attempting to facilitate assertive expression from another ("This is what I think. What do you think?"). Other characteristics include not allowing oneself to be easily interrupted or distracted, attempting to elicit clear, direct statements from others, and not giving into others' demands for immediate responses but taking the time necessary to be clear within oneself and to give a clear expression.

Assertiveness and Relationships

In order for assertiveness behaviors and skills to be appropriate, it is important to consider the nature of the relationship between people. What may be appropriate assertive behavior in one relationship may be inappropriate in another or at the very least self-defeating. To illustrate, consider three types of relationships: impersonal, business, and intimate.

Impersonal relationships might include those with store clerks, garage mechanics, doctors' receptionists, and other service-oriented relationships. The goal of these brief relationships is to achieve some desired result, such as returning merchandise or having a bill corrected. Therefore, assertiveness skills center on expressing desires or opinions, making direct requests, persistence, and holding to the result desired. It is not appropriate to be concerned about the other's inconvenience or unenthusiasm to carry out the request.

Business or work relationships, on the other hand, exist over time and are important for carrying out the goals of the organization. Relationships are important but have as their main goal to develop cooperation in carrying out tasks. Assertiveness skills center on expressing opinions, giving positive or negative feedback to plans or strategies, and facilitating expression on the part of others. Voicing opinions about unreasonable requests and striving for mutually agreeable solutions are also important skills. In work relationships it is not necessary to like each person one works with but it is important to be able to work cooperatively.

Intimate relationships are important for developing feelings of closeness and warmth with another. One looks to intimate relationships to satisfy desires for mutual understanding and caring. Assertiveness skills center on expression of feelings as well as desires. It is also important to facilitate expression of feelings from the other person, and to identify uncomfortable patterns that are interfering with the relationship. Working out mutually agreeable solutions to problems as well as agreeable decisions is an important assertiveness skill in close relationships.

Developing Assertiveness Skills

It is important to develop assertiveness skills in at least four areas: How You Think, How You Sound, How You Look, and What You Say. We will consider each of these areas briefly, with examples of practice techniques.

How You Think. This area of practice is to help identify some of the irrational beliefs that affect a person's nonassertiveness. Briefly, passive behavior is often associated with needs for approval, fear of criticism, fear of rejection, fear of appearing foolish, or fear of expressing negative feelings. Aggressive behavior is often correlated with demanding and blaming thoughts, self-righteous anger, and low frustration tolerance. One of many methods that can be used for this purpose is to have each person identify from the past week one example of an aggressive response, a passive response, and an assertive response. Then have each person identify the thoughts she or he was having prior to the response she or he made. With the passive and aggressive responses, have each person identify what an assertive response could have been and what thoughts could have led to the assertive response. Homework assignments can be given to analyze passive and aggressive behaviors for the purpose of identifying the thoughts or beliefs associated with these behaviors.

How You Sound. This area centers on increasing awareness and effectiveness in using voice tone to communicate assertively. One exercise that can be used for this purpose is as follows: In dyads, assign one partner to be passive and the other aggressive. Give the partners time to get in touch with an image of themselves either being passive or aggressive. Then instruct them to use only the words Yes and No and express the various ways they sound when sounding either passive or aggressive.

After a minute or two have the partners switch roles and repeat. Next, have both partners express themselves assertively. Then have the partners discuss how they sounded or other ways they sound when passive, aggressive, and assertive.

Another area of voice tone practice is learning to match the tone of voice and other voice characteristics with the level of meaning or importance of a message. In dyads, have each partner express assertively using only the words "This is what I think" conveying low importance, then moderate importance, and finally high importance. Discussion then centers on various tonal characteristics that can be used to convey levels of importance.

How You Look. This area of practice is to identify body behaviors that communicate passiveness, aggressiveness, and assertiveness. Use exercises in the above section but eliminate the sound by having the person mouth the words. Center discussion and feedback on using body gestures and facial expressions to more accurately express oneself assertively.

What You Say. This area of practice identifies some language skills to express assertiveness. Simple assertive language includes the use of personal pronouns in identifying one's thoughts and feelings and desires, learning to make requests, and making simple direct statements. Exercises center on giving people practice in these expressions. In small groups, people are asked to express a thought about another to describe a feeling about that person, or to make a request of one person. Feedback is given both on language and nonverbal communication.

In addition to simple assertiveness statements, there are at least four other areas that many people identify as difficult assertiveness situations. They are expressing negative and positive feelings, receiving criticism, refusing requests, and dealing with conflict. Here are some suggested assertive skills in each of these areas:

Expressing positive and negative feelings includes a personal statement about what the other did or didn't do that you liked or didn't like, the effect it had on you, and (if appropriate) what is wanted from the other. For example, "When you come home late, I feel upset, and I'd like you to call if you're going to be late." "I really appreciate your thoughtfulness in giving me a call. That really makes me feel good." In small groups, have each person practice giving a positive and negative statement to each person.

Receiving criticism appears almost universally difficult for people. The tendency for most people is to react defensively and either passively withdraw or aggressively counterattack. Assertive alternatives include either Agreeing with What's Agreeable in the criticism or Asking For More Specific Criticism. Agreeing with What's Agreeable is particularly appropriate when the criticism is specific. For example, "You make entirely too many mistakes when typing letters." Usually a person can agree that something *could* have been different or that one would have *wanted* not to have done what was done. For example, "Yes, I feel I can improve and make fewer mistakes" or "I wish that I had checked my work more carefully." What a person never agrees with is that something *should* have been different and one is *terrible* for making mistakes.

Asking For More Criticism is more appropriate when the criticism is vague or generalized such as, "You're a lousy secretary." Asking for more criticism would include such questions as, "What am I doing that you find disagreeable?" or "Is there something specific that I've done?" or "Is there something else that you don't like?" The attempt is to try to lead the criticizer to talk about *specific acts* rather than the *person*. Each person then has an opportunity to practice receiving criticism from others with feedback on both verbal and nonverbal skills.

Refusing a request or learning to say No to things that are not agreeable seems to be particularly difficult for women. Many find themselves doing numerous things they don't want to do, with ensuing feelings of resentment. The verbal skill is learning to use the No-Yes technique. Briefly, the No-Yes technique involves saying No to the request but Yes to the person. A Yes to a person can be expressed as an understanding of the other's frustration or disappointment in being turned down or as an offer of an alternative. As an example:

Mary Lou calls her sister: "Can you babysit for me tomorrow night? I can't find anybody and I'm desperate."

Sister: "Gee, I know it's really tough to find somebody at the last minute. I do have plans and can't help you out. That's probably disappointing to you [empathy response] but I will call a couple of my friends and see if they are available [offer of an alternative]."

There is usually a Yes that can be found appropriate for every No. People are then asked to practice saying No in a simple but tactful manner to various request situations while being prompted at the same time to find a sincere and appropriate Yes.

Dealing with conflict or differences often brings out a power struggle between people to prove one is right and the other wrong. Often one person ends up passively capitulating to the other, and feelings of resentment and anger frequently follow. Assertively dealing with conflict involves the following steps:

1. Verbally state the differences ("You see it one way and I see it another").

2. Offer an alternative or solution that involves a part of what each person wants.

3. Continue the process until both people agree to a solution, or have reached mutual understanding of each other.

4. If a resolution can't be reached at the time, agree to discuss it further at a later time.

5. If a solution or understanding is developed but later doesn't seem workable, then bring it up again and try to arrive at a better resolution.

Techniques of Practice

There are several techniques of practice that can aid the learner in developing understanding and mastery of assertiveness. Role playing will give a person practice in learning the skills. Rehearsing an upcoming situation with a partner can provide knowledge and experience for handling the situation. People can get additional practice from imagery. By rehearsing in their minds, they can begin to develop images of themselves responding to situations assertively. Analyzing situations that have occurred can help teach people to use their mistakes and to think how they could have handled the event differently. Practicing in a group situation using the relationships between people to generate immediate experiences has the advantage of "real life" practice in a supportive environment. Homework assignments that give people practice in areas where they want improvement can begin to bridge the gap between talked-about assertiveness and putting it into practice where it really counts.

Cautions

Assertiveness skills, while sounding simple, are often very difficult for people to master. People who have particularly strong negative feelings and very low self-esteem may require additional counseling before being more successful. It is also easy for people just learning the skills to be overly critical of themselves when they fail to act assertively. It is important to caution people that assertiveness is helping them to act out their rights as human beings and that it doesn't mean they will always get what they want from others. Too easily some people give up trying to increase their skills when they find "it" didn't work, meaning someone didn't go along with them. The emphasis would better be placed on what assertiveness can do for building confidence and self-acceptance in the person rather than on assertiveness as surefire techniques to get somebody else to do something.

Assertiveness training, while not a panacea, has its place in helping people to develop better intrapersonal as well as interpersonal skills. The concepts are easy for people to understand and therefore provide a means by which they can learn self-help techniques for themselves. For the RET practitioner, these cognitive-behavioral skills appear to be meaningful additions to other cognitive techniques.

Working on the E in RET

EDWARD J. GARCIA, C.S.W.

Former Co-Director of Clinical Training, Institute for Advanced Study in Rational Psychotherapy, New York City

If you and I, as clinicians who use rational-emotive therapy as a model, want our clients to live self-benefiting lives, then it would be wise to explore just where the "E" belongs in RET and question what the emotive aspects of the therapy mean to both therapist and client. Too often, perhaps because of the high level of education that we enjoy as a group, we are beguiled by the "R" in RET — that is, the rational and logical aspects — to the partial exclusion of the emotive character of what we are doing.

We are working with people — we are not working only with theory. In applying a rational and logical model, we are working with and trying to help fallible and vulnerable people whose problems and pain have brought them to our offices. In order to become more effective clinicians, I suggest that we would be well advised to delve more fully into the "E" of RET and explore the therapeutic aspects of Empathy, Emotion, and Experience.

Since people appear to be more psychological than logical — at least when it comes to important aspects of their personal lives — the clinician might best consider those factors which most strongly influence people not simply toward intellectual change, but toward behavioral change integrated with emotional freedom. The *integration* of ideational, emotional, and behavioral change is how I view therapeutic growth. It is this kind of therapeutic growth that we are after and not just a superficial change in ideas, or, as is sometimes the case, a mechanical change in behavior.

Unfortunately, when emphasis is placed only on the "R," it is because we sometimes have the mistaken notion that by simply becoming aware of irrational ideas clients will, indeed, change their behavior and feelings. It takes much more than just logical exposition on the part of the therapist to motivate true therapeutic growth.

Along the same line, we sometimes forget that RET is one of the most humanistic of therapies. It accepts people as people, neither intrinsically "good" nor "bad," but rather as fallible and vulnerable, which is what we are. It is a nonjudgmental therapeutic orientation designed not to praise or condemn, but rather to help build emotional self-support systems.

I emphasize the importance of developing emotional self-support systems because without them the rational therapy we teach becomes meaningless didactic jargon. It really takes courage to *become* rational. Unless the fears which are created by our irrational ideas can be *tolerated*, the client will not take *action* to move toward leading a rational life.

There seem to be two main factors involved with translating this theoretical orientation into clinical practice. The first factor is providing insight. The second factor deals with getting people to incorporate this insight into their patterns of daily living. My concern is that many therapists who mainly have a logical/behavioral approach to RET believe that all they have to do is to teach people logical ideas and clients will change their self-defeating behavior.

This may be true, but what therapists tend to forget is that people do things for the *wrong* reasons as well as for the right reasons. Let's not settle for "blind" change, even though it appears "rational." Rather, let's aim for comprehensive therapeutic growth.

On the other hand, there are therapists who overstress the interpersonal relationship as the main motivating factor for therapeutic growth and end up with more dependent clients. It is my belief that the "E" in RET lies between these two poles of logical didactics and interpersonal dependency. In order to stimulate change in the lives of others, we had better use both a logical *and* an empathic approach.

Let's expand the "E" in RET into the following formula: Empathy plus Experience develops Emotional Muscle for more Efficient Therapeutic Growth. What we are concerned with here is making the therapeutic sessions as helpful and as efficient as possible. So let's examine several factors that translate the humanism and logic of RET into efficient clinical techniques.

Certainly EMPATHY is an important factor. The therapist's concern, and the way in which it is expressed toward a client, goes a long way in the process of influencing change.

Unfortunately, people have mistakenly tended to associate certain values with certain words. For example, "need" has become a "good" word and it is often confused with love. The word "independent" seems to imply that people have to do things alone. Words such as "intellectual," "logical," and "rational" tend to imply, to some people, a kind of emotional detachment or aloofness.

It is my conviction that logical and rational ideas can coexist, and indeed have a harmonious relationship, with sensitivity and empathy. RET can be practiced more effectively by emphasizing the sensitivity and empathy which are inherent in its humanistic philosophy. To be rational does not mean to react unemotionally. Empathy, together with acceptance and logic, can be applied in the clinical situation to the furtherance of efficiency by utilizing its influential value.

Empathy is transmitting, verbally or nonverbally, to your client the understanding and acceptance you have of that person's emotions and the value he or she places on the presenting problem. It may be actualized by allowing clients to talk out their problems in the context of their own vocabulary and experience, before you interrupt to point out the "shoulds" and "musts." The expression of empathy within the clinical encounter will go a long way toward translating the humanism of RET into a visible and credible working model which usually tends to increase the client's receptivity to the process.

Expressing empathy may also take the form of altering your rational response to a person's irrational ideas, in short-term deference to their immediate emotional pain. Persons in great emotional pain may not accept your logical statements as to the irrational ideas they have about a problem if you do not express a willingness to accept and understand their pain to begin with. It may be technically correct to transmit certain rational information to them, but keep in mind that it is just as important *how* you say something, at that stage.

Of course, being an empathic therapist is a very personal thing and it would be presumptuous to tell you what to do specifically in any given situation. Perhaps it would be more fruitful to state that it is not only what you say, but also your attitude that conveys that you give a damn about helping the client become more rational. Empathic involvement is important and it is a therapeutic style that requires both courage and restraint.

For one thing, it shows that you are concerned with what is happening to your clients, thereby allowing them to experience the support of your involvement and encouragement as they work on their problems.

Involvement requires courage because you as the therapist, an emotional being in your own right, may find it very difficult to tolerate your own emotional discomfort about the clinical encounter. Let's face it, being a rational therapist is not the same thing as being a therapist who is rational.

Involvement also requires restraint because, while we want to express empathy, we also want our clients to do things for themselves. There is a difference between empathy and, as Paul Hauck states, entering into a "neurotic agreement" with your client. Support is the goal, not dependency. A therapist who is not afraid to combine logic with sensitivity will certainly increase the opportunities to make the sessions more productive and efficient.

Chér Malinski, a very creative and talented person, wrote a lovely poem which was read earlier here at Glen Ellyn. Perhaps it best summarizes the distinction between support and dependency. It is entitled: "I — Am Growing."

When you think that I do not love you
it is because at that moment I do not love myself.

When you see me behave jealously or angrily
it is because I am wrestling with fear and hurt.

And when you hear me blaming
it is because I am feeling guilt.

But I — am growing
and with much pain
I watch you growing too.

But perhaps what is most painful to me
is watching you grow in pain
And not comforting you.

Because when I comfort you or soothe your wounds
I do not let you experience growth
but rather protect you from it.

Or perhaps I do not trust in you
that you can grow.

I am trying
to see and listen with my heart . . .

and toes and skin and nose and mouth
as well as my ears and eyes

. . . to the silences

you are yellow,
I am red.
separate — alone — always

always

I cannot make you grow, you cannot make me
but
always
we can be by each other's side
not to comfort
but to be there and strengthen
until
yellow and red make orange
in the middle.

In addition to empathy, the "R" in RET stands for EMOTION. I divide emotion into two areas — the expression of emotion, and the concept which I call *getting* better versus *feeling* better.

Our efforts as therapists are to influence clients to develop an aspiring rather than a requiring philosophy, since need is the one ideational common denominator that creates so much emotional pain and self-defeating behavior. A famous art critic once said, "We must learn to take things tragically . . . but nothing seriously." In the context of RET, I choose to translate this as meaning that it would be best for us to recognize and accept the appropriateness of experiencing intense emotional feelings associated with not getting important things in our lives, as opposed to making the irrational demands that create our extreme emotional pain, which in turn tends to direct us into self-defeating forms of behavior. Let's allow ourselves to experience the tragic events in our lives as sensitive human beings, without catastrophizing about them.

Emotional expression reflects values that do not always include needfulness. Therefore, it seems to me that when people don't express emotions, they either don't care at all, which is their right, or they may care too much [need] and therefore anesthetize themselves because it is "too painful" to experience. Those who lack appropriate affects may have more serious problems than those who emote more readily.

The expression of "negative" emotions need not be an *automatic* sign of irrationality to the therapist. It could be an appropriate response to a rational value.

Let us learn to distinguish between rational values and needfulness and then make clinical determinations about the expressed behavior. Indeed, if we want to facilitate therapeutic growth, it is important to accept the expression of emotion from both our clients and ourselves.

The second area concerning emotion deals with the concept of *getting* better rather than that of *feeling* better. Most people, it seems, would rather feel better than get better. They strive to attain some level of emotional comfort as their *goal,* and what they cannot see is that comfort, peace, and happiness are the *result* of rational living. When they focus on feeling better, they inevitably fail in their quest. They fail because they cannot *try* to feel anything, they can only *allow* themselves to feel in different ways. It is this constant obsession with feeling comfortable that prevents most clients from acting upon the wisdom they learn.

If we, as clinicians, believe it is important to have individuals translate knowing about something into believing and internalizing it as a way of life, then it would seem logical that we use EXPERIENCE as the major method of bridging that gap between a person's imagination about situations and the reality of what he or she actually experiences.

My purpose in therapy is not to help make the client's life comfortable. I want to teach my clients to *tolerate* discomfort. I want them to develop the "emotional muscle" that is necessary if one is to deal rationally with unpleasant situations and feelings of frustration. People *imagine* that terrible things will happen, and our imaginations are far greater deterrents to rational living than anything else I can think of.

Perhaps another of Malinski's poems would be appropriate on this point. It goes as follows:

Man's best and worst affliction is his
    Imagination.

Are those with infinitely and vividly
    developed capacities
  Blessed or cursed?

The only reply is
    yes.

Our imaginations are like a double-edged sword. It is the imagination of humankind that has inspired us to strive toward the fulfillment of our dreams no matter how far-fetched they may have appeared and it is this same imagination that creates the fears, distortions, and nightmares that psychologically cripple us. It is both our heaven and our hell.

To cut through those ideas that hamper growth, we give clients practical homework assignments and exercises. Since RET contends that our feelings come from the way we think, then it seems to me that it is not enough just to learn about a new idea that is likely to change a person's pattern of living, unless that idea is incorporated into one's belief system. To change an idea into a belief system, it is important to go through the emotional experience of the situation.

To know *about* doing something and to know how to actually do it are two different things. Just having an entire library about how to drive a car will not teach you to operate it. You have to actually drive. Along the same line, being a good therapist is much more than just knowing about clinical theories.

Experience not only helps clients to absorb and internalize the new idea into a belief system, it also teaches them to believe that they can tolerate the emotional discomfort that may be associated with the experience.

These three factors — EMPATHY, EMOTION, and EXPERIENCE — appropriately blended with the theoretical framework of RET, comprise the main focus of this model as an approach for clinicians to practice RET in a comprehensive, creative, and efficient manner.

It is my contention that from a *clinical* point of view there are four main universal irrational concepts which probably constitute nearly all, if not all, of the core problems causing emotional disturbances due to faulty and irrational thinking, as opposed to emotional disturbances caused by organic, biochemical, or hormonal dysfunction.

The first of these is the *need for approval.* Otherwise stated: *I am* what other people think of me. This all-too-familiar concept implies that the totality of a person can be evaluated by the reactions and opinions of other people.

The second universal irrational concept, usually related to the need for approval, is the *need to succeed.* Otherwise stated: *I am* what I do. This implies that a valid rating system based upon what you define as success — such as the kind of car you drive, the amount of money you earn, the grades you get in school — can also be used to define and measure your worth.

The third one deals with low frustration and anxiety tolerance, which I call *the need for comfort.* This is the belief that we need to be anxiety- and frustration-free, that everything must be convenient and not require effort, that everything should be pleasant and enjoyable. To be otherwise would be unbearable and catastrophic.

This third concept sometimes appears to be confusing because the people who adhere to it tend to lead and stick to unbelievably unpleasant, emotionally painful, and self-defeating life styles. In their obsessive quest for immediate comfort, they create many more difficulties for themselves. It's like the old story about the student who spends three hours worrying about how to get out of doing one hour's homework.

The last universal irrational concept is *the belief that things and people external to us cause and control our feelings, and that we can, in turn, also magically control things and people's feelings.*

We must constantly remind our clients that, since people feel the way they think, only they themselves can create — and therefore must be responsible for — their *own feelings*. No one can control anything that is external to him or her. We can sometimes influence things and sometimes things can influence us, but *control* is an attribute of the gods, not of us mere mortals.

Clients can be shown that other people do not control them but rather that they "give" their power away to other people. We may not have the power to control things happening to us, but we do have the power over how we will accept their happening. If clients could be persuaded to spend more time changing their irrational ideas about needing approval, success, and comfort, rather than trying to change the world around them, they would be a great deal healthier and happier.

What is essential in all this is getting the therapist to recognize that no matter how the client expresses himself, no matter what the example, symptom, or problem he presents, the ideation is always related to one, or more, of these four main universal irrational concepts. If the therapist keeps this in mind, he can begin to recognize those concepts even through the verbal smoke screen most clients throw up to protect their feelings. Unless we, as therapists, can get our clients to adopt and internalize a more rational belief system, we have only treated the external manifestations of the real problem. Be problem-solvers, not example-solvers.

Now let's discuss some of the many pitfalls that the rational therapist can fall into, as well as how these "E's," and recognizing the four main universal irrational concepts, can help avoid them.

Too often clinicians become so involved with the theoretical aspects of RET that they do not take the time to translate it into a practical or clinical model which would allow them to understand their clients "conceptually." They get so engrossed in the *example* of the problem, as it is presented to them, that they miss the problem itself. Many examples of irrational behavior may be symptomatic of just one main universal irrational concept. We sometimes become so concerned with the logic of what we are saying about the example presented that we either fail to use techniques and strategies that would *influence* the client to accept our logic, or we deal with the problem in such a narrow fashion that we fail to see the underlying universal irrational concepts that are creating the problem.

An example would be the therapist who is so concerned with catching the client using "can't," "should," "ought," or "must" that the client does not even get the chance to express the problem freely, much less understand it. It is important to listen for the *meaning*, rather than simply the words. It would be wiser to listen to clients, at least at first, in the context of the individual's own mode of expression, so we can then translate what they say into what they really mean. You can't have answers if you don't know the questions or understand the issues.

For instance, if a client says, "Why is this thing happening to me?" it could mean he is asking a genuine question, or (what is most likely) he or she is really saying, "This *should not* be happening to me!" If it is the latter, we can then understand the demand inherent in the "question" and proceed to offer some help in getting the client to understand that people cannot control what others say and do.

A helpful idea that I would like to share with you is learning to recognize that most people who come to us speak in what I call half sentences. For example: "Bill shouldn't be doing that!" is only half a sentence even though it is grammatically correct. When a client makes a statement like that, he is merely describing the behavior of the person about whom he is speaking. The other half of the sentence, which is usually unspoken, is "Bill shouldn't be doing that (*because* I don't like it, I believe it's wrong, and he's a bastard for doing it)!" The second half of the sentence reflects the client's *values* regarding what Bill is doing. Therapists should be looking for those unspoken values in order to get to the main universal irrational concepts more efficiently.

Another pitfall is that therapists too often focus on the client's behavior as the problem rather than seeing it as a mechanism that is used to *protect* his irrational ideas and feelings. The behavior most often is not the problem. If we see the client "conceptually," we see that the main irrational concepts are the real problems and that feelings and behaviors are the painful results and the protective mechanisms we use to cope with life situations.

For example: Joe believes that he *must* get into the school he has applied for, or he will never again be happy. His feelings are anxiety. His behavioral symptom is to drink. If we focus on Joe's presenting problem we might think that it is the drinking. But if we truly understand him conceptually, we begin to understand that he drinks to relieve the anxiety caused by the irrational idea about never being happy academically, which to Joe would be catastrophic. Such an idea is so emotionally painful that Joe uses alcohol as his pacifier.

Now we can better understand the intensity of his irrational ideas — how rigidly Joe holds onto them — and begin to treat the base problem. For if we don't, he may stop drinking only to adopt another form of defensive behavior to relieve his anxiety. It is this comprehensive conceptual overview that can help us determine the best possible approach to the specific client. The presenting problem reflects his irrational ideas, his feelings reflect their intensity, and his behavior reflects how he defends himself.

Another technique I use to understand irrational ideas is what I call the "language" of emotions. If a person believes he "needs" to be loved, he will usually "feel" fear of rejection. Notice the relationship between *need* and *fear*. Need is the idea. Fear is the feeling. The *idea* creates the *feeling*. Thus, if a person can articulate his feelings, you can tell what irrational ideas are causing the feeling and usually the self-defeating behavior used to "protect" those feelings.

Anxiety in my opinion *always* has at least these two ideas: (1) That something, or some person, or some event, is bad, dangerous, or threatening. (2) If it were to happen (or not happen) it would be catastrophic.

Realistically, some things or events may in fact be bad or dangerous, but that doesn't create anxiety. It is the second idea, or the catastrophic value, that one gives to the first idea that creates the anxiety. Thus, when a client tells me he is experiencing anxiety, I already "know" that he is perceiving the situation as "bad," "dangerous," "threatening," *and also* "catastrophic."

It doesn't matter what the situation is about; if he feels anxiety, you can bet the cost of the session that those are his ideas. The same kind of ideational analysis can be applied to anger, guilt, and depression. See if you can figure them out. It's an interesting challenge and you can come up with some very gratifying results.

Begin to understand and view clients as a triangle. They think, feel, and act. In working with clients, look for the interrelationship between thought, feeling, and behavior. It is this interrelationship that expresses the notion of understanding the client "conceptually."

Another pitfall to avoid is the notion that "all people are created equal." That may be fine in the area of democratic freedoms, but in terms of therapy it creates a generalization that is very deceiving. People, psychologically, are not created equal. Some have greater tendencies to be neurotic than others, all other things being equal. Thus, we would better be consciously aware of the biological factors in human disturbance. People learn at different rates. What works for one person may not work for another. And for some there will be very limited therapeutic growth no matter how much logic you provide.

Another major problem area that therapists encounter is the quest that clients have for "happiness." This is related to the client's irrational belief that happiness is being able to *attain* or *achieve* certain things (such as love, approval, success, comfort). This relates to the fourth universal irrational concept that external things or people can give one's life meaning.

I believe that happiness is not simply getting what you want, but rather not being afraid of *either* having it *or* doing without it. When we can *accept* either having something or doing without it, we live without fear and anxiety because we have removed the *need* for things to be a certain way.

When people attain what they *prefer*, they tend to enjoy life more. But when people need, rather than want, they tend to have fear even when they get it. If you need to have someone love you, then you maintain the fear that they may not really love you *and* the fear that they may not continue to love you. Desires can be fulfilled, but needs can never be satisfied.

There are certain things in this world that we cannot do. For example, we cannot force ourselves to love another person and we cannot force ourselves to be happy. These are things we can only *allow* ourselves to experience. The only way to allow ourselves to love and to experience joy is to get rid of our "need" to always experience them.

In sex, for example, you cannot force yourself to be excited or have an orgasm. You can allow yourself to become involved in the process of making love by removing the demands about performance and reaching orgasm. By eliminating our ideas about "needs," we enormously increase our opportunities to do the things we want . . . and enjoy ourselves in the process.

Incidentally, it is quite often the fear of emotional discomfort, or low frustration tolerance, that stops us from doing even simple things. This relates to the universal irrational concept people have about the *need for comfort*. However, as you may well be aware, understanding simple things does not always provide us with the frustration tolerance that is required to accomplish unpleasant tasks.

I constantly stress the differences between "simple" acts and "easy" acts. For example, if a person does not want to gain weight, the procedure is very *simple*. He or she does not have to overeat. One doesn't have to be very intelligent to understand that simple fact. But if he or she continues to overeat, it is usually because of lack of *emotional* tolerance to face the *discomfort* of going through the process of dieting. What we mean is that it is not *easy* to diet. Difficulty and ease relate to our ability to tolerate emotional discomfort. Complexity and simplicity relate to the intellectual process of understanding something.

We often confuse these two notions and fall prey to a common misconception which implies that intelligence should immunize a person against emotional problems and self-defeating behavior. In reality, bright people often have the greatest struggle with simple things that are not easy, because they fail to make that distinction. Whether a person is intelligent or not, our job is not only to help him or her understand rational ideas, but also to help develop the emotional muscle to tolerate discomfort. It is through the development of this emotional muscle that we can go on to experience what we imagine will be intolerably stressful situations, only to find that they are usually less stressful than we had imagined.

It is important to remember that vulnerable people, who have little or no practice tolerating difficult situations, need a graduated program of experiential exercises to develop their emotional muscles. In much the same way that we would not expect a person who leads a completely sedentary life to run a four-minute mile as his first homework assignment in building up his body we cannot expect emotionally flabby persons to successfully deal with difficult assignments at first, in building up their tolerances for discomfort.

Therapists sometimes become angry because they are demanding that their clients do something that is obviously simple, but which they are probably incapable of doing, because it is difficult. An empathic therapist, who has the requisite professional patience to accept different rates of therapeutic growth, probably has a deep awareness of what it is like to be on the other side of that desk. One way for therapists to achieve that level of awareness is to practice RET in their own lives.

After all, it is important that the therapist have a good working knowledge of RET, from both a theoretical and an experiential level, if she or he is to translate that knowledge in a credible manner.

And so we come closer to the crux of our problem as therapists: bridging the gap between getting clients to understand the theory of RET, and getting them to practice what they have learned. The therapist had better have a vast array of strategies, techniques, resources, and clinical insight, if therapeutic growth is to be accomplished efficiently. The following are just a few examples of some of the areas that can be explored by therapists to increase their effectiveness in facilitating therapeutic growth of their clients.

The Use of Visual Inputs. This can range from something as simple as the use of a blackboard to the creative application of video tape. The blackboard can be used to illustrate visually the concepts we are trying to teach. The video tapes can be used to help the client see the main universal irrational concepts through the heightened and highly structured medium of tape. The client can *see* the principles working, as a viewer, before going on to the more difficult process of becoming a participant.

Bibliotherapy. Although for some a picture may be worth a thousand words, there are others for whom the printed word means much more. And this can range from books directly dealing with the concepts of RET to general literary works through which we can illustrate those same notions.

Tape Recordings of Sessions. When clients are in the midst of their sessions they may be so upset or distracted that they do not really listen to what they say or to what the therapist is saying. When such a client hears the session at a less stressful moment, he or she is more apt to get a better perspective and awareness about the interaction that took place with the therapist.

This can work to get clients to really hear not only their self-defeating ideas, but also evidence of improvement over the months. A chronic complainer can hear his or her constant complaints. And that client can also hear the diminution of that pattern at a later date in the therapy. This can be very encouraging — as well as reinforcing — to the client.

Word Association. For the client who is hostile, has mental blocks, or cannot readily articulate thoughts and feelings, the relatively simple process of word association can aid both therapist and client in getting at the main universal irrational concepts. Starting with one word, we ask for an association or meaning to go with it, and then follow it down to the point where the client rates his "worth" as a person.

Let me give you an example of this process. I had a client who had an extreme anxiety about night driving because she was afraid of getting lost. Because of her inability to articulate her concern about stressful situations, it was not possible to obtain much information by direct questions. Instead, I first focused on the word "lost." Then I kept asking her to give me another word or phrase that she associated with the previous one. Her association of words and phrases went something like this: lost — not to know — to be unaware — to be taken advantage of — to be vulnerable — to be hurt — to run away — to be alone — not to be wanted — to be undesirable — to *be NO GOOD.* In this case, through the use of word association, we had an inarticulate person actually seeing and making the connection between her extreme fear of being lost, what it meant to her, how she protected herself, and what she thought about herself. I find this a good way to get information and to challenge irrational concepts.

The following suggestions help get clients to remember what you say in other than just psychological terms.

Poetry. There are many poems that reflect much wisdom in ways that might be more acceptable to the client. The therapist might recommend poems, or poets, whether it is to see the rational concepts in them, or to have the clients see irrational ideas in a different setting. As only one example, I sometimes use Kahlil Gibran's *The Prophet,* which has some fine prose and meanings with regard to closeness, friendship, marriage, and love — most of it presented in a very philosophically rational and beautiful manner.

Plays and Films. These are good sources for the client to review. It is sometimes easier for the client to identify with a character or to see irrational character traits, since works of art have some degree of depersonalization — we are viewers, not participants.

A play like *Death of a Salesman* might be used to point out the universal irrational idea of the need for success. A film like *One Flew Over the Cuckoo's Nest* gives us food for thought. Who is really rational? Who is really irrational? Are people necessarily psychotic because they are different? Is conformity necessarily rational and sane?

Books. These can have a tremendous impact. Carlos Castaneda's books contain a great deal of wisdom from which to draw. I am paraphrasing, but I might ask clients to interpret for themselves what is meant by: When man lives, he lives with only a fraction of his potential, but when he dies, all of him dies, so why is it that man does not live with all of his potential? Or: I am a warrior and you are a pimp. I am a warrior because I learn about life by experiencing it. You are a pimp because you want to know about life by asking me.

Jokes. Jokes are very important because you can get meaning and profound ideas in a light vein, thereby helping clients to avoid getting locked into thinking that getting better is always a "heavy number" — to perceive instead that at times it is even pleasurable. Jokes can also be used to point out the absurd or irrational concepts we take too seriously.

Epigrams with Meaning. I enjoy using these: "When you walk around in circles, you can't get lost but you don't go anywhere either." For some clients there is a direct analogy with their staying at home rather than going out into the world. Sayings can get the client thinking.

Role Playing. Role playing with clients helps them to sense what a given situation might be like, to develop skills, to understand what possible responses they might encounter, and to develop confidence in dealing with such a situation in the future. It also allows clients to have experiences with someone who is accepting of them and who can give them some honest feedback on what they are doing.

Within professional and ethical boundaries, whatever works to assist the client to learn rational concepts is valid.

Experiential Homework Assignments. Homework assignments are at the core of the therapy. They construct the bridge between theory and practice. One of the most important aspects of therapy is what the client does *between* therapy sessions, as well as in the sessions themselves. The sessions may be the classroom, but life experience is the laboratory work.

These homework assignments may be done in several different ways. They may be thinking types of assignments, where clients are asked to challenge their irrational ideas. They may be experiencing kinds of assignments, where clients are asked to evaluate what kind of emotional experiences they have derived from the things that you got them to do. Or they may be "doing" assignments, where you actually ask the client to do something in order to develop skills. Homework may be assigned to get clients to deal with their lack of assertiveness, feelings they may have about shame, interpersonal relationships, tolerating anxiety levels, or just the clarification and understanding of ideas. The assignments may also ask clients to challenge some of their distortions about reality. In any case, homework assignments are the battlegrounds where theory comes to life.

Knowing the person with whom you are working will allow you to find the combination and blend of techniques that will help best. Knowing that person "conceptually," as well as rationally, will be facilitated if we stress the "E's" in RET — Empathy, Emotion, and Experience — and clinically understand the four main universal irrational concepts.

A Concluding Word

Regardless of how clever we become at the use of words to

describe what we do, our main goal is triangular: to help people to think rationally, to feel emotionally freer and stronger, and to behave constructively. We do this, in part, by emphasizing the value of being able to endure feeling bad. By developing "emotional muscle" people will, in fact, live fuller, freer, and more fulfilling lives devoid of compulsive and self-defeating behavior. Perhaps it would be more appropriate to think of the "E" in RET as an Emotional Self-Support System, rather than as Efficiency. A more comprehensive label for our method might be RATIONAL-EMOTIONAL SELF-SUPPORT SYSTEM THERAPY. We have a great theoretical construct at our disposal. Let's use it wisely, rationally, and emotionally.

The Evolution of Rational Behavior Therapy

MAXIE C. MAULTSBY, JR., M.D.

Department of Psychiatry, University of Kentucky Medical Center

© Maxie C. Maultsby, Jr., M.D.

Introduction

When Albert Ellis formulated the theory and technique of rational-emotive therapy in the late fifties, it (like most new theories of psychotherapy) did not cover every aspect of psychotherapeutic change. But Ellis's theory proved to be scientifically valid as well as logically consistent. That made it relatively easy to make useful and valid deductive additions and inductive extensions of basic RET theory and technique. Rational behavior therapy (RBT) is RET as Ellis originally described it (Ellis, 1962) plus the additions and extensions I made to it between 1967 and 1974.

I first influenced RET theory and technique in 1967, when I extended the Ellis concept of therapeutic homework (Maultsby, 1971g). Prior to 1967, RET homework merely consisted of certain therapeutic tasks. For example: An unassertive housewife might be told to tell her husband No at least once before the next therapy session and not feel guilty about having done it. An irrationally shy male might be told to go to a singles bar and talk to a female stranger every night until the next therapy session.

The Birth of Rational Self-Analysis or Written Homework

When I used the above type of practical homework assignments,

I found that, more often than I was willing to ignore, some patients refused to carry out their assignments. They protested, "It's too threatening. It's too hard for me." And I'd calmly (sometimes not so calmly) explain, "But it's not IT, the situation at A, that frightens you; it's B, your beliefs (about the situation at A), that makes you afraid at C. Now you need to stop doing that if you're to get rid of this emotional problem."

Midway through one of my explanations that "IT" never does anything — it's your beliefs that do everything — one of my patients said, "I believe that, but how do you get my gut to believe it?" That stumped me. Then I realized that Albert Ellis had not said it all; he had overlooked a very important detail — how to get the gut to accept what the brain knows is true. I recovered sufficiently to paraphrase basic RET theory with, "It's your job to get your gut to believe it. The only gut I can control is my own."

But the patient persisted, "How do you convince your gut?"

I said, "With the A-B-C's of human emotions. You have got to tell your gut that it's not A, the situation, but B, your belief, that's making you afraid at C."

"How do you stop your beliefs?"

"You just stop," I said.

"But *how?*"

"That's a good question," I said. "I suggest that when you get home, you take a pencil and paper and write out a plan."

"What will I say?"

"Write out your A-B-C's," I said. "At the top of the page write the letter A. Under it write, 'There I am in a singles bar and I see this attractive woman.' Then at the bottom of the page write the letter C and under it, 'I'm scared.' In the middle of the page write the letter B for beliefs; then under it write, 'It's not A, the situation, that makes me scared at C, it's B, my irrational belief. But I don't believe in that belief any more. So I refuse to be afraid without a rational reason.'"

And with that session, the new RET technique, the A-B-C's of written *rational self-analysis* (RSA), was born (Maultsby, 1971e).

The Birth of a Mentally Healthy Definition of Rational

After I had spent only two or three weeks of teaching the A-B-C's of rational self-analysis to college-student patients, a somewhat skeptical student-patient whose problem was pre-exam anxiety said to me, "I can see that I panic before exams because of the irrational things I'm telling myself, but those are the only thoughts I've ever had about exams. What I need now is for you to tell me how to get more rational thoughts." That's when I became aware of a theoretical oversight. Nowhere had Ellis made a clear objective distinction between what is rational thinking and what isn't. Yet this patient clearly needed a practical way of making that distinction.

I reasoned that what's rational would have to be based on rational scientific theory. I remembered my basic RET theory and began to think my way through my patient's potential therapeutic dead end.

"It's really quite simple," I said, "if you keep in mind the basic facts about human emotions. First, it's not the facts of your situation that upset you, but your irrational beliefs about the situation."

"I know that," said my patient, "but what I don't know is what I should change my beliefs to."

I said, "Change them to statements of facts. For example, when you tell yourself you can't stand to flunk a test, that's a lie. You have flunked tests and you survived. That proves you can stand them. So by telling yourself you can't, you just force yourself to feel bad in spite of the fact that flunking an occasional test really isn't that bad or even that inconvenient. I mean, you've always managed to make up your flunked exams enough to keep your grades to at least a B level. Right?"

"Right."

"Well then, for starters make your beliefs more rational by basing them on objective fact."

Then, fortunately, I glanced at my session timer. "Well, I see our time is up. We'll have to stop here. You just keep applying that one insight until I see you next week. Then we'll go over the second rule for rational."

Before the next therapy session, I read many definitions of rational, but none made any useful sense to me. I then decided that, since I was a rational-emotive therapist, a therapeutically useful concept of rational would be consistent with, if not defined by, optimum emotional health. Conversely, a therapeutically useful concept of irrational would indicate evidence of the lack of optimal emotional health.

So I read numerous descriptions of emotional health. No single one seemed comprehensive yet practical enough for everyday use. But when I combined the three most practical-sounding definitions, they implied that emotionally healthy people are reality-oriented and committed to living productive lives with maximum personal and social approval. I then tried to put those ideas into four practical rules for rational thinking and behavior in everyday life.

My first formulation read (Maultsby, 1971b):

1. What's rational is based on as nearly accurate a description of objective reality as is currently possible.

2. Regardless of the circumstances, what's rational is most likely to preserve your life.

3. What's rational enables you to most efficiently achieve your personal goals.

4. What's rational is least likely to result in your having either significant emotional conflict or significant environmental conflict.

These four rules served their purpose well until an obsessive-compulsive patient asked me these three questions:

1. What if your behavior is irrelevant to one of the four rules for rational but obeys the other three? Is it then rational or not?

2. What if you are not having significant conflict but you cause significant conflict for other people? Are you being irrational or not?

3. How much conflict is significant?

Again, I made rational use of my session timer by noting that the time was up. But I assured the patient that we would discuss each question in detail at the next session.

By rethinking basic RET theory, I saw how I could make therapeutic use of the RET assumption that all human beings are fallible — that they have an incurable error-making tendency and that's why it's irrational to try to be perfect. The only thing a fallible human being can do perfectly is die, and with advances in heart and other vital organ transplants, even that is becoming difficult to do. But one could be sure that no one could ever behave in a perfectly rational way all the time. Any useful concept of a type of human behavior necessarily has to be formulated in relative rather than absolute terms. Therefore, rational behavior has to mean relatively rational behavior to be useful. That logic led to the insight that any thought, attitude, belief, emotive feeling, or physical action would be more rational than irrational if it obeyed three of the four rational rules (Maultsby, 1975a). Conversely, relatively irrational thoughts, attitudes, beliefs, emotive feelings, or physical actions would not obey at least three of the four rational rules. At the next session, therefore, I said: "Yes, behavior can be called rational if it obeys only three of the rational rules."

Then to make clear that people can *rationally* cause significant environmental conflict for others without causing significant conflict for themselves (as for example, leading protest marches),

I separated rational rule number four into two rules. That made a total of five rational rules which I rewrote, using the simplest wording I could think of. They now read:

RATIONAL BEHAVIOR

1. Is based on objective reality.
2. Is self-protective.
3. Enables you to achieve your goal efficiently.
4. Prevents significant conflict with others.
5. Prevents significant personal emotional conflict.

I defined significant conflict as "the conflict that each person dislikes enough to work to avoid." That definition of significant made two other important therapeutic facts more obvious than they seemed to be before: What's rational for one person may not be rational for another. What's rational at one time or in one situation may not be rational at another time or in another situation. (In *Help Yourself to Happiness* (1975a), I described in detail those as well as my most recent additions to RET theory.)

My Most Recent Additions to RET Theory

After I passed the milestones of rational self-analysis and the definition of rational, RET worked well for me for two years. Then I noticed that patients who had longstanding problems would work at therapy and make rapid progress for a while. Eventually, though, they would arbitrarily stop working at therapy and, of course, stop progressing, but they would still keep their therapy appointments.

By questioning those patients thoroughly, I made a surprising discovery: They had stopped working at therapy because they were *afraid* to progress any farther. They had become so accustomed to structuring their daily lives around their emotional problems that they had lost any personally meaningful concept of what their lives would be like without their problems. They were merely reacting logically to the most potent human fear of all — fear of the unknown. One patient neatly summarized the problem: "I just wouldn't know what to do with myself if I didn't have any depression at all."

To help those patients over the therapeutic barrier, I again began to rethink RET theory. The basic assumption that human emotions are auto-conditioned by repetitive thought led me to review the work of Mary Colver Jones (1924) and Arnold Lazarus (1962). That review enabled me to formulate the techniques of rational-emotive imagery (REI) with its instant better-feeling maneuver (Maultsby, 1971d).

Systematic REI speeds up the emotional-change process. That was a therapeutic plus for most patients. But rapid therapeutic change in one's gut feelings always follows therapeutic changes in one's thoughts. Most patients, however, come to therapy expecting just the opposite. They want to feel better without thinking better. Consequently, some of my patients began to complain that rational thinking didn't do any good because they continued to have their old irrational feelings. Some other patients complained that rational behavior felt abnormal . . . unnatural . . . like they were playing games. Or worse, being phony. A few got so confused they dropped out of therapy.

To help patients deal more rationally with these normal aspects of rapid psychotherapeutic change, I combined my medical training in anatomy and neurophysiology with basic RET theory. The rational concept of cognitive dissonance and its physiologic basis resulted (Maultsby, 1972). That led to my theory of the psychology of words, which made it obvious to me why it makes a psychosomatic difference what you say to yourself. That insight led to my research study, which implied that RBT and RET may be the most logical psychotherapies for psychosomatic disorders (Maultsby, 1974d).

My last addition to RET theory is a clinically useful description of the five stages of emotional reeducation (Maultsby, 1975a). I normally describe the process of emotional reeducation to patients after they have done their first acceptable rational self-analysis. That's the point where patients must take their most important and confusing therapeutic steps. Having the whole process clearly explained to them then is both reassuring and helpful in maintaining appropriate therapeutic motivation.

RET and RBT: Are They Interchangeable Terms?

In the middle of making those extensions and additions to RET theory, I discovered these two facts: First, behavior therapy means human-behavior-modifying techniques that are based on learning theories of human behavior (Hilgard, 1967, p. 556). That meant RET is really a behavior therapy. Second, Eysenck had already listed RET among the behavior therapies. When I added those facts to the fact that RET deals therapeutically with cognitive behavior, emotive behavior, and physical behavior, it was clear to me that RET is the most comprehensive of all the behavior therapies. Furthermore, the name rational behavior therapy is probably a more accurate, as well as a more easily understandable, designation of what psychotherapists do, after they have been trained or otherwise influenced by Albert Ellis at the Institute for Advanced Study in Rational Psychotherapy in New York City or by Maxie C. Maultsby, M.D., at the Psychiatry Department, University of Kentucky Medical Center, Lexington, Kentucky. That's why I began to say RBT or rational behavior therapy instead of RET or rational-emotive therapy. But, since there is not now and never has been any conflict between Albert Ellis and Maxie C. Maultsby and since Albert Ellis has approved of, uses, and teaches all the therapeutic techniques and theoretical extensions and additions I have made to RET, you may accurately use the names RET and RBT interchangeably. RET really does mean RBT and vice versa.

Rational Stage Directed Therapy

DONALD J. TOSI, Ph.D.

Associate Professor, Faculty of Special Services,
The Ohio State University

J. NICK MARZELLA, Ph.D.

Director of Consultation and Education, North Central Mental
Health Services, Columbus, Ohio

Rational stage directed therapy (RSDT) is a didactic-experiential, cognitive-behavioral intervention designed to guide or direct the client through various stages. RSDT begins with *awareness* of self and situation and proceeds through self-and-situational *exploration, commitment* to rational thinking and acting, *implementation* of rational thinking and acting, *internalization* of rational thinking and acting, on through *change* and *redirection*. RSDT may focus on one problematic area or a set of related problems. The modality of RSDT, being an extension of standard cognitive behavior therapy, consists of vivid cognitive-emotive imagery under varying degrees of relaxation induced through any of the standard relaxation procedures, or hypnosis. Unlike other cognitive desensitization techniques that employ hypnosis or other relaxation procedures, RSDT is stage directed and places major emphasis on high-level cognitive control over emotive and behavioral and situational conditions. Through these various stages, the client using cognitive-restructuring intervention, specifically Ellis's A-B-C self-analysis, encounters directly (via imagery) external or internal events that serve to activate the irrational cognitions underlying affective/physiological/behavioral disorders.

In the first stages of RSDT, the client is exposed to the cognitive or rational restructuring technique and begins to develop a high-level skill in its use. Cognitive restructuring skills, a logical-critical thinking about disturbing internal or external events associated with emotional disturbance, are developed, reinforced, and implemented while the client is relaxed or in a hypnotic trance. RSDT is then augmented with "in vivo" behavioral tasks corresponding closely to imagery content.

Basic to RSDT is its potential for developing, reinforcing, and maintaining logical-critical thinking relative to affective, physiological, behavioral, and situational processes. Quite specifically RSDT is designed to dislodge, minimize, or eliminate internalized beliefs, attitudes, and emotions that are self-defeating in nature. RSDT assumes that individuals have a consciousness of self — an ability to think in constructive ways about themselves — and that they have the capacity to reconstruct, reevaluate, and ascribe new meanings to past, present, and future events and projections, thereby controlling their own destiny.

RSDT may be considered as an inclusive rubric for a rational stage directed hypnotherapy (RSDH) and a rational stage directed imagery (RSDI). RSDH should be practiced by therapists trained professionally in hypnosis. RSDI does not require hypnotic training but does require the therapist to be familiar with standard relaxation-imagery techniques.

The Time Dimension in RSDT

The time dimension is extremely important in RSDT. The origins, the development, and the maintenance of self-defeating cognitive-affective physiological-behavior motoric responses (attitudes) that may be suppressed — or repressed — are to enter the client's awareness. The intricate relationships between past, present, and projected future events contributing to emotional disturbance are discovered, described, analyzed, confronted, challenged, and finally reconstructed. The transition from imagery content to real-life situations is then made. The client is to apply the new learnings derived from her or his expanded awareness to the outside world.

Projections of the client into present and future events become a major focus of rational analysis. Essentially, the internalized symbolic meanings projected by the client into another person are examined. The irrational nature of projection is uncovered and isolated for the client to observe and thus objectively to confront subjective reality. It becomes difficult for the client to deny, repress, suppress, or distort experiencing of self. The therapist helps the client work through present, past, and future emotive-imagery associations in progressive stages using rational analysis and confrontation.

Self Processes in RSDT

The self consists of an elaborate set of cognitive, affective, physiological, and behavioral-motoric processes operating in a unitary fashion in transaction with the environment (see Figure 1). The self-processes are the object of RSDT when it is apparent that certain cognitive/affective/physiological and behavioral-motoric processes appear to be having a deleterious effect upon the person's well-being.

Technically, emotional/behavioral disturbances involve the action of various neuro-physiological phenomena. Cognitive events involving judgments and appraisal of stimuli that are external, or represented symbolically, activate other cortical and subcortical centers of the brain such as the hypothalamus and limbic system. Physiological and motoric processes are activated by such judgments and so become our emotions. What are generally experienced as emotions are changes in bodily states resulting from the activity of the endocrine system and the parasympathetic and sympathetic nervous systems. Cognitive events activating emotive-physiological processes occur so rapidly that they often escape awareness. Thus, they go unrecognized as if they do not exist. Therefore, it is quite natural to expect that, when an individual is experiencing intense affect, he may relate that experience to an identifiable external condition and ignore completely the mediating cognitive variable of judgment in the causal chain of event-judgment-affect.

Fig. 1. A self-in-situation model.

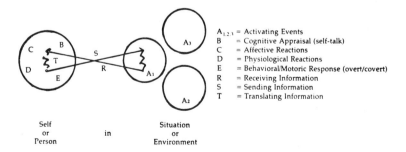

$A_{1,2,3}$ = Activating Events
B = Cognitive Appraisal (self-talk)
C = Affective Reactions
D = Physiological Reactions
E = Behavioral/Motoric Response (overt/covert)
R = Receiving Information
S = Sending Information
T = Translating Information

Self or Person   in   Situation or Environment

In RSDT, the clients' self-processes are explicated and explored. They are guided by the therapist to go deeper and deeper into relaxation, imagery, and/or hypnotic trance. The therapist guides clients through the stages so they may become more and more aware of, and explore, self-defeating internalized attitudes, beliefs, and perceptions of meaningful past, present, or future events. Clients are asked to imagine observing themselves — being conscious of their thinking (cognitive awareness), their emotions (affective awareness), their physical processes (bodily and sensory awareness), their actions (behavioral awareness), and their interactions with the environment (environmental awareness).

Ultimately the therapist guides the client's self-processes and assists in the development of more reasonable modes of thinking, feeling, and behaving — that is, the moving beyond awareness and exploration into the acquisition of self-directed rational activity. Through the therapist's technology, the therapist assists the client to expand awareness and explore new and constructive possibilities. The therapist then assists the client to commit the self to constructive/rational action, to implement this action, and finally to internalize new and growth-enhancing attitudes or modes of personal functioning.

The Growth Stages

In counseling and psychotherapy, we have observed that in the development and growth of the person in the environment, the individual acquires skills and competencies in rational self-management. In so doing, the person progresses through various stages. These growth stages are *self in-situational awareness, exploration, commitment* to rational constructive action, the *implementation* of rational action, the *internalization* of rational action, and *change and redirection*. Rational action implies not only behavior but thinking and feeling as well. The subject's progress through these stages is noted not only in the therapeutic context, but in real-life situations.

In each stage, clients acquire, develop, and refine behavior-modifying skills. In the awareness stage, clients learn self-monitoring and observational skills. As they move into the exploration stage, they develop logical-experimental and hypothesis-testing skills. They develop cognitive restructuring skills through practice and testing. The commitment stage forces clients into decision-making or choice. They acquire skill in using their learnings to make difficult choices. In the implementation stage, clients move from the safety of the therapy context to real-life situations, using their therapeutic skill in the real-life environment. As they internalize new and more effective approaches to life, they continue refining these approaches.

On What Is Rational

Rational means logically correct thinking relative to available or existing data or facts — whether these data be subjective or objective, inner or outer — and their connections according to commonly accepted rules. Rationality or rational thinking does not avoid or deny the existence of subjective or objective states but gives full consideration to them, in thinking and action (Hartman, 1968). Rationality does not attempt to deny reality; it is a *method* to deal with inner/outer reality as one pursues life goals (Sperry, 1974).

Persons who decide to enter a counseling or a psychotherapy relationship also have definite goals as fundamental as minimizing feelings of anxiety, depression, guilt, hostility, and worthlessness. Rationality, implying logical thinking and behaving, then is simply a means of achieving effectively one's goals. A person who acts purposively and rationally directs his or her thoughts, feelings, and behavior in a way that considers ends, means, and consequences by balancing, weighing, posing, and relating ends, means, and consequences against one another.

Criteria for Rational Thinking

The following criteria are useful guidelines for determining whether one's thinking and acting approximate "rational" (Maultsby, 1971a).

Thinking and acting are rational when

1. These behavioral processes consider objective and subjective reality — the facts — whether these data be environmental, cognitive, affective, physiological, and/or behavioral motoric.

2. These behavioral processes contribute to the preservation and enhancement of life.

3. These behavioral processes contribute to the achievement of one's immediate and long-term life goals (self-knowledge, self-acceptance, self-affirmation).

4. These behavioral processes minimize personal and environmental stress.

In the determination of rational thinking and acting, each of the above criteria needs to be considered. Obviously, self-deceptive strategies may serve one by giving the appearance that one is thinking and acting rationally — but often the careful observation of subtle affective-physiological processes in the form of psychosomatic symptoms may uncover the existence of underlying irrational thinking or meta-thoughts of an irrational nature. One's meta-thinking may not fit all of the above criteria even though one may at a conscious level assert that her or his thinking and acting meet the above criteria.

Example of Pseudo-Rationality

Joe S. is a brilliant attorney who has made a careful study of rational psychotherapy. He reports that he has few psychological difficulties. He says he has been able as a result of rational self-analysis to reduce substantially his blood pressure and interpersonal difficulties with his wife. As far as he is concerned, he has mastered the rudiments of rational therapy and is uncommonly articulate on the subject.

During a therapy session Joe calmly and undramatically tries to convince the therapist of his unusual progress. He does, however, complain of tingling sensations in his right hand and foot as well as back pain. When the therapist inquires about Joe's condition, Joe quickly says this is a physical condition for which he is having elaborate tests conducted by a neurologist. The therapist hypothesizes that such reaction may be related to underlying feelings of hostility that the client may feel toward his wife, who still seems to pose obstacles to his grandiose goals for his sex life. The therapist hypothesizes a close relationship between frustrated sexual activity and the client's physical reactions. The therapist confronts the client with this hypothesis. The client rejects the confrontation. The therapist patiently awaits the results of the neurological tests. The results show nothing of a physiological nature. The therapist confronts the client once again. The client will now consider denied meanings or thoughts possibly associated with or causing the hostility and the physical symptoms. He realizes his self-deception and poses it against the criteria for rational thinking.

Cognitive Restructuring

The use of cognitive-restructuring techniques in counseling, psychotherapy, or other helping relationships presupposes that attitudes, beliefs, values, and perceptions are amenable to modification through the cognitive process — the same cognitive processes involved in learning, internalizing, and maintaining attitudes. The learning and the unlearning of attitudes involves the same fundamental principles of conditioning, discrimination, acquisition, extinction, and reinforcement (external or internal). The cognitive processes involve memory, awareness, divergence (abstract/creative thinking), convergence (concrete, critical problem-solving thinking), and evaluative thinking. Evaluative thinking, whether based on scientific/experimental methods or noncritical or unscientific methods (unconscious indoctrination), is regarded as the primary component of an attitude — the component that determines resultant affective/physiological and behavioral-motoric responses (tendencies to approach or to avoid situations).

Social psychologists in general agree that an attitude can be defined as a strong and persistent tendency to approach or to avoid an object or situation that is judged or evaluated as suitable or unsuitable, which is reinforced by bodily changes (emotional states) and/or environmental consequences. The evaluative or cognitive aspect of an attitude is given special significance — although the emotive/physiological/behavioral components also have great import. Too, it is apparent that "attitude" suggests a unitary process involving people's interaction with themselves and with their environment.

Related sets of attitudes form belief-value systems (Rokeach, 1968) which may be ordered from simple structures to very complex structures, depending on a person's experiences. Fundamentally, the attitude is the prime unit to be understood in relation to classes of attitudes which form beliefs.

Thus, the attitude is pictured as a phenomenon involving (1) an object or situation that may be real or imagined, (2) an evaluation, judgment, or appraisal of the object or situation, (3) a feeling, emotion, or affective concomitant or resultant state, (4) a physiological reaction, and (5) a stable behavioral or transactional response toward or away from the object depending on how it is evaluated.

In traditional rational-emotive psychotherapy those attitudes that support, give rise to, or stimulate self-defeating activity over a prolonged period of time are called into question, examined, clarified, challenged, and ultimately replaced with more self-enhancing appraisals and judgments or "in general" a set of rational attitudes. (See Figure 2.)

Consider the following illustration of an irrational or self-defeating attitude:

A	Event	John is standing on the street corner and calls Bill a dirty name (objective event).
B	Cognitive Appraisal or Judgment	Bill tells himself consciously or unconsciously: "John is at it again. He tries to put me down most times I see him [appraisal is accurate]." "That John is a no-good louse [perceptions of John now becoming distorted]. He shouldn't act the way he does, and I can't stand his actions. He makes me look bad in front of others, and that's terrible. He should have his teeth bashed in for being such a SOB. But I'm afraid of him so I won't say anything."
C	Affective State	Deep frustration/anger.
D	Physiological Reactions	Increase in muscle tension, gastric secretion, and heart rate.
E	Motoric Response	Avoidance or becoming excessively irate, hostile, and attacking.

Assuming that Bill's reaction to similar situations is about the same, we would say that he has a definite attitude or orientation that may be quite self-defeating.

Consider the same situation but an approach illustrating a more rational or self-enhancing attitude.

A	Event	John is standing on the street corner and calls Bill a dirty name.
B	Cognitive Appraisal or Judgment	Bill tells himself consciously or unconsciously, "John is at it again. He tries to put me down most times I see him. Well, that's the way he tends to act in general toward me. I don't like it, but the names he calls me don't reflect what I really am. This does get embarrassing but it's hardly a catastrophe. I would be happier if John did not say these words, but that's not the way it is. Too bad! This causes me some inconvenience."
C	Affective State	Mild frustration/anger leading to eventual calm/relaxed state.

D	Physiological Reactions	Small amounts of muscle tension and gastric secretion, and decreased heart rate.
E	Motoric Response	Ignoring John or calmly approaching John and confronting him.

Initiating the Essential Techniques of RSDT, Including RSDH and RSDI

The technique of RSDT involves (1) a deep relaxation or hypnotic trance state: (2) vivid imagery of self-defeating thoughts, emotions, and behaviors; (3) cognitive restructuring of irrational attitudes — the challenging and confronting of self-defeating attitudes, thoughts, feelings, and behaviors and replacing them with more self-enhancing (rational) thinking, feeling, and behaving; and (4) directing these processes through the stages of awareness, exploration, commitment, implementation, internalization, and change. Initiate RSDT in the following manner (see also Figures 2 and 3):

Fig. 2. Client-therapist in RSDT situation.

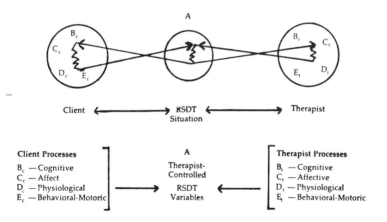

Phase I (Relaxation/Hypnosis). The first phase of RSDT is a four-part relaxation/hypnotic induction. The client is asked to sit in a comfortable chair, close the eyes, and begin taking slow, deep breaths. The deep breathing is continued until the client begins to visibly relax. He or she then is guided by the therapist through a systematic relaxing of all the muscles in the body.

Fig. 3. Counselor-client variables in RSDT.

A Therapist-Controlled Variables in Induction Procedures	B Client Mediating or Cognitive Variables	C Client Affect or Emotive Variables	D Client Physiological Variables	E Client Behavioral-Motoric Variables
A₁ Defining situation as RSDT — a combination of rational/cognitive restructuring and hypnosis or relaxation directed through stages — RSDH or RSDI	B₁ Receiving and translating transmission of A's	C₁ Experiencing suggested affective states	D₁ Bodily changes occur in relationship to specific attitudes, expectancies, and emotional states (heart rate, respiration, sweating, skin temperature, relaxation)	E₁ Overt or covert responses to therapist's suggestions (using hypnosis, arm levitation, limb or body rigidity, expresses age regression, amnesia) — RSDH only. Engaging in desirable behavioral motoric activity (in vivo or via imagery) — RSDH or RSDI
A₂ Minimizing fears and misconceptions	B₂ Developing positive expectations and commitment to RSDT	C₂ Minimizing resistance		
A₃ Seeking client cooperation	B₃ Thinking and focusing on and about suggested effects	C₃ Increasing commitment		
A₄ Asking client to keep eyes closed	B₄ Engaging in vivid imagery			
A₅ Suggesting relaxation only, or relaxation, sleep, and hypnosis (if preferred modality)	B₅ Using cognitive restructuring			
A₆ Maximizing precision in wording of suggestions, phrasing, and vocalizations of suggestions				
A₇ Coupling suggestions with naturally occurring events				
A₈ Stimulating goal-directed imagining				
A₉ Preventing or reinterpreting the failure of suggestions				

Unlike Jacobsen's relaxation procedures, the muscle relaxation is conducted on a cognitive-imaginal level and does not pit muscle tension against relaxation. The third step of relaxation uses imagery, wherein the client is asked to imagine specific relaxing scenes. The fourth stage (optional) is the utilization of any one of a number of standard "deepening" techniques to produce more intense relaxation or hypnotic trance. (See Kroger, 1963, and Erickson, 1967, for methods of deepening hypnosis.)

Phase II (Identification of Irrational Attitudes). When the first phase of RSDT is completed and the client is deeply relaxed, the therapist asks the subject to imagine reliving a previously discussed real-life situation in which he or she had exhibited self-defeating behavior. The scene is described in detail and each attitudinal component is labeled (A, B, C, D, E). The therapist instructs the client to experience as much negative affect as appropriate.

The client is then directed to experience the negative emotions and to observe the self acting ineffectively and to identify any irrational thoughts that may have occurred prior to the onset of the emotion. The therapist negatively reinforces this last sequence by repeating such phrases as, "Notice how uncomfortable and anxious you become when you keep telling yourself how awful it would be if you were not loved by virtually every significant person in your life." The client is asked to specify and describe each component of the irrational attitude in A, B, C, D, E symbols. The therapist then instructs the client to stop imagining the scene.

Phase III (Cognitive Restructuring). After identifying specific irrational attitudinal components, the therapist asks the client to imagine the same situation, but this time instructs the client to replace the heretofore irrational thoughts with more self-enhancing ones. For example, "Even if I am not loved by everyone, I am not a failure as a person. I still have value to myself." The therapist instructs the client to imagine experiencing more desirable emotions and engaging in more effective behavior. The therapist then labels each component of the rational attitude. This process is repeated relative to other significant problematic situations until the client masters the rudiments of the technique and is able to engage in it effectively outside of therapy.

In standard rational-emotive counseling and psychotherapy, the therapist helps the client challenge and confront her or his irrational assumptions and philosophies in a natural waking state. In RSDT the client engages in the same process but while in a deeply relaxed or hypnotic state.

Gregory and Diamond (1972) and Palmer and Field (1968) have shown that persons are more susceptible to suggestions while in highly relaxed states. Therefore, the hypnotic induction or relaxation procedure occurs prior to cognitive restructuring, allowing it to become more vivid to the client. Kroger (1963) cites as one of three "laws of suggestion" the law of concentration attention. Whenever attention is concentrated on a single event over and over again, it spontaneously tends to realize itself. This is not to imply that realization of the event takes place through some magical-mystical process. In RSDT it is only much practice that allows one to ultimately substitute rational cognitions for irrational ones. Since the behavior of subjects in hypnotic states is to a great extent a function of how one construes the hypnotic situation, the following ideas need to be considered:

1. There must be some willingness of the subject to explore the possibility of a more rational way of life.

2. The subject must perceive the therapist's suggestions as reasonable.

If the client meets these two criteria, she or he may be a good candidate for RSDT.

Summary

RSDT is based upon deep relaxation and/or hypnosis prior to employing the technique of cognitive restructuring. Recall that the basic techniques of RSDT occur within definite stages. Although the client experiences cognitive restructuring in the early stages of RSDT, it is generally only at an awareness level. Such awareness is unlikely to produce substantive behavioral change until the client has had many opportunities to explore cognitive restructuring over and over again relative to many different problematic situations and, based on the new data gathered by those explorations, is able to commit the self to the development, implementation, and internalization of the basic skills of cognitive restructuring in particular and RSDT in general.

An Example of RSDT

An A-B-C-D-E model will be utilized in rational stage directed hypnotherapy while processing the client through stages of *awareness, exploration, commitment to rational action, internalization,* and *change.* Prior to the hypnotic induction procedure, the therapist will guide the client through each of the six stages delineating rational parameters concomitantly. During the initial sessions, the therapist will have the client focus on the awareness and exploration of rational and irrational ideas. As the counseling progresses, the therapist guides the client through the rest of the stages, focusing on each one and concentrating on the particular characteristics contained in each stage. The therapist and the client decide together when to progress to the next stage.

After practicing and understanding the RSDH process, the client undergoes the hypnotic induction and the therapist guides the client through the entire stage-directed approach. The following is an example of the process, concentrating on the awareness and exploration stages. The therapist begins in this vein:

I want you to focus on the specific events or situations that you have determined to be disturbing. [Describe a client-identified specific event such as:] Imagine that you are at a party and you want to meet new people, but find yourself avoiding people you don't know. If you can imagine this event, please use your right index finger. [If ideomotor response is elicited, proceed to the next phase; if it isn't, ask the client to relax and to go deeper into relaxation, then repeat the suggestion.]

[Specify the emotion triggered by the client-identified specific event. In this example it is anxiety.] Allow yourself to feel the anxiety in conjunction with this situation. Notice how uncomfortable it is and realize how self-defeating this emotion is in this particular instance. Describe to yourself the ways in which these emotions are preventing you from experiencing or acting in ways that you would like. What about the situation would you like to change? Now concentrate on the thoughts you are associating with this event. Concentrate on specific irrational thoughts. Imagine saying to yourself [here state the applicable specific irrational idea], "If I attempt to make new friends, they will most surely reject me and, if they reject me, that is terrible and horrible. Not only is that terrible, but if they don't like me, then how can I possibly be of any value? I must be totally worthless." Continue to concentrate on those irrational self-verbalizations, and notice how you tend to become more anxious.

As you continue to see those thoughts in your mind, allow yourself to experience the emotional discomfort. The more you continue to tell yourself irrational, self-defeating thoughts, the more you will tend to feel these negative emotions. Continue to concentrate on those irrational self-defeating thoughts and notice how you tend to become even more anxious.

You can very clearly understand how those irrational thoughts are causing you to upset yourself. Now, I want you to tell yourself to stop thinking those irrational thoughts and we will begin to explore and become aware of more rational ways of thinking.

Let yourself imagine that you are thinking rational thoughts in conjunction with the same situation as before. Explore the rational thoughts. Become aware that you are thinking [here state the specific applicable rational thoughts]: "Even if those people do reject me, their rejection doesn't mean I'm a terrible, worthless, stupid person. It simply means that they may not like me. Since I realize I cannot and do not need the love and approval of every person that I meet, at most the situation is merely inconvenient. Simply because they rejected me doesn't mean that I'll be rejected by everyone all of the time."

Think those rational thoughts. Explore them and become aware of your feelings when you tell yourself these rational conclusions. Notice how your negative emotions tend to subside. As the negative emotion (in this case, anxiety) subsides, picture yourself in your mind engaging in rational actions and behaviors in conjunction with your rational thinking and feeling. Notice yourself becoming more effective when you think rationally. Explore new behaviors. Think of new ways of acting in these situations, and continue to think rationally about them. [Allow the client a few moments to consider some of the more rational behaviors that you have previously outlined with him. You may wish to discuss rational exploration at length.]

Now, I want you to allow yourself to relax very deeply . . . clear your mind and return to a nice comfortable relaxing scene . . . go deeper and deeper into relaxation. Allow yourself to relax completely, and concentrate on what I am saying to you. Between now and the next time we meet, I want you to allow yourself to practice this entire method of relaxation and rational thinking (the A-B-C-D-E method). Allow yourself to practice the relaxation and the A-B-C-D-E procedure at least three times a week for fifteen minutes each time.

Once more, relax . . . I am going to count to five, and when I reach the number five, you will be wide awake, feeling very refreshed and very alert. You may not remember everything we have talked about immediately; however, as the week progresses, you will remember everything you need to know. When I reach the number five, you will feel very refreshed and very alert. 1-2-3-4-5.

During later sessions the process is very much the same, but the focus is on higher-level stages. After the therapist and the client feel they have sufficiently explored and have become aware of both irrational and rational ideas and behaviors, the client is guided into the third and fourth stages of rational stage directed hypnotherapy: commitment to rational action and implementation. The commitment stage involves the client's imagining being publicly and privately committed to more rational ways of thinking and acting. A deeply relaxed or hypnotic state often permits the lessening of resistance inhibiting commitment.

The implementation stage implies that the client is to actively engage in the newly acquired skills to which there is now a commitment. The therapist asks the client to imagine actively participating in heretofore problematic situations in a more rational, self-enhancing manner. The implementation stage is the testing ground for the client's new behaviors. The therapist encourages and reinforces the client's applying what has been learned in the therapy session to situations outside of therapy by talking along these lines:

> I want you to concentrate only on the rational thoughts you have recently become aware of and have explored. Focus on these rational thoughts [identify specific thoughts] and images in your mind. You are committed toward acting, thinking, and feeling in more rational ways. For example, imagine that you are at a party and, rather than avoiding people, you have committed yourself to actively seeking out others.
> Notice how you are becoming increasingly committed toward acting in a more self-enhancing way. As you become committed toward thinking more rationally you find yourself more in control of your emotions and your behaviors. As you act in more rational ways and are able to assess your life's situations more effectively, you become increasingly committed to rational action.
> Now imagine that you are actually implementing the rational thoughts, feelings, and actions that you have committed yourself to. Notice how much more self-enhancing it is to act in rational manners and how pleasant it is to control your own behavior and emotions.
> Recall some of the different ways of acting rationally that we earlier explored. In your mind implement these ways of behaving: Test them out. You will find them easier to transfer outside the sessions after you have practiced implementing them here.

Once committed to rational action and implementation of more self-enhancing thinking, feeling, and behaving, the client may then be ready to proceed to the internalization stage.

Internalization is a logical progression from the preceding stages. Having implemented more self-enhancing thinking, feeling, and behaving, the client is more likely to internalize these. The therapist now essentially says this:

> Once you have committed yourself to acting, feeling, and thinking more rationally and have actually implemented all of the processes [therapist may outline specific self-enhancing situations] you find it much easier to internalize the process.

You can now imagine that you are in the act of internalizing a process of rational thinking and acting as well as desirable feelings. As you continue to think more rationally, you will further internalize a more self-enhancing way of perceiving, feeling, acting, and interacting.

Finally the client reaches the final stage of RSDH, the stage of change and redirection. Now the therapist observes the client engaging in self-directed activity and assuming responsibility for his or her behavior. The therapist reinforces the striving toward change, encouraging the client to generalize the newly acquired ideas for effective living to other problematic situations. If the counseling requirement was for minimum change and was limited to one specific client concern, it could be terminated at this point. Should the subject desire to continue therapy to work on problems, the therapist redirects the client through the entire process once more, focusing on the particular stage where there is difficulty.

Note that all stages are reviewed in each session and all stages are contained within each other. While exploring new rational thoughts, the client is also becoming more aware of them. As awareness of rational thoughts increases, the client can more easily become committed to them, and so on.

The stages present a specific, logical problem-solving progression through which the therapist guides the client. As the therapist outlines the purpose of each stage, the client can concretely focus on his or her problems and improve in resolving them.

Following is a brief outline of a six-session Rational Stage Directed Hypnotherapy Treatment Plan. Preliminary sessions may be required to acquaint the client with the theoretical process, as the client should have a basic understanding of RET prior to these six sessions.

RSDH: Six Sessions

Session 1

    A. Review A-B-C-D-E approach to behavior change, utilizing the self-directed behavior-change instrument or rational self-analysis

    B. Identify the problematic concerns and troublesome areas to be encountered in treatment

Session 2

   A. Explain hypnosis

      1. method of gaining more self-control
      2. state of concentrated attention
      3. more able to obtain and intensify relaxation
      4. dispel old myths of loss of control, sleep state, weak-mindedness, etc.

   B. Explain stage directed approach

      1. Awareness
      2. Exploration
      3. Commitment to rational action
      4. Implementation
      5. Internalization
      6. Redirection or change

   C. Present induction process didactically

      1. deep breathing
      2. cognitive muscle relaxation
      3. relaxing scene
      4. deepening by counting
      5. working stage (explain how stage directed approach will be used here — that the client will be put through the stages while under hypnosis to intensify experiences, and that the stages will be separately focused on)

   D. Put subject through the hypnotic induction up to working stage only

      1. allow subject to dream or relax for a minute or two
      2. bring out of dreaming or relaxation stage by counting to five

   E. Discuss reactions and clarify process

Session 3

   A. Review problems identified in Session 1 using the self-directed behavior change instrument or rational self-analysis

   B. Outline problems and process through the six stages

      1. Concentrate on awareness and exploration stages

    2. Identify appropriate irrational and rational ideas

    3. Emphasize the more rational thoughts, emotions, and behaviors

    4. Instruct subject that, once hypnosis is induced, you will guide her or him through all the stages once more, concentrating especially on the awareness and exploration of rational thoughts

C. Induce hypnosis

    1. Work on problems, concentrating on awareness and exploration stages

    2. Give posthypnotic suggestion that client will practice at home three times per week for fifteen-minute intervals

    3. Dehypnotize subject

    4. Obtain self-report of depth of hypnosis

Session 4

A. Record the number of times the client practiced

B. Review problems, processing the client through all stages, but concentrating on the commitment to rational action and implementation stages

C. Induce hypnosis

    1. Have the client work on problems, concentrating on the commitment to rational action and implementation stages

    2. Give posthypnotic suggestion regarding practice

    3. Dehypnotize the subject

    4. Obtain self-report of depth of hypnosis

Session 5

Same as Session 4, only concentrate on internalization and redirection or change stages

Session 6

Same as above sessions; give equal weight to each stage

Following is a brief outline of a six-session Rational Stage

Directed Imagery Treatment Plan. After acquainting the client with the rudiments of RET, treatment may be as follows:

RSDI: Six Sessions

Session 1

    A. Review A-B-C-D-E approach to behavior change, utilizing the self-directed behavior-change instrument or rational self-analysis

    B. Identify specific problems or areas to focus upon intensely

Session 2

    A. Explain stage directed approach

        1. Awareness
        2. Exploration
        3. Commitment to rational action
        4. Implementation
        5. Internalization
        6. Redirection or change

    B. Put subject through RSDI using his or her examples

        1. Ask subject to close eyes and imagine self at each stage
        2. Concentrate on awareness and exploration

Session 3

    A. Review problems identified in Session 1 using the self-directed behavior change instrument or rational self-analysis

    B. Outline problems and process through the six stages

        1. Ask client to imagine the self in processing each stage
        2. Concentrate on awareness and exploration stages
        3. Identify appropriate irrational and rational ideas
        4. Emphasize the more rational thoughts, emotions, and behaviors

    C. Ask client to practice imagery at home three times per week for fifteen-minute intervals

Session 4

A. Record the number of times client practiced

B. Review problems; process through all stages, concentrating on the commitment to rational action and implementation stages

C. Ask client to imagine concentrating on the commitment to rational action and implementation stages

D. Ask client to practice imagery at home three times per week for fifteen-minute intervals

Session 5

A. Same as Session 4, only concentrate on internalization and redirection or change stages

Session 6

A. Same as above sessions; give equal weight to each stage

A Three-Factored Theory of Depression

PAUL A. HAUCK, Ph.D.

Depression is among the most common and painful of emotional disturbances. It was conceived by Sigmund Freud as a complex interrelationship of frustrated dependency strivings in a demanding and grandiose personality. As one's needs are left ungratified, anger is directed toward the frustrator. But this involves a difficulty. The person capable of providing love cannot be sacrificed to one's anger. In addition, turning hostility onto a loved object, such as a parent, results in guilt. To avoid this uncomfortable condition the hostility must be reflected back upon the self, thereby achieving two important goals: (1) punishment of the aggressor, and (2) hiding the hostility from the loved one so that future gratification will not be withheld (Freud, 1950; Fenichel, 1945, pp. 387-90).

An analysis of the Freudian view of depression reveals a dynamic structure which easily accounts for some causes of guilt and explains self-pity. It is not clear how pity for others fits into Freud's scheme. As a result, therapy for depression, à la Freud, focuses on relieving the subject of crushing guilt by encouraging the expression of his or her hatred. In the mature light of his or her present understanding it is hoped the sufferer can be made to forgive himself or herself for the past evil wishes and deeds. The analyst tries to comfort the depressive by reassurance that his or her demands were the product of youthful ego and that self-blame today is pointless for behaviors arising out of the work of an infantile upbringing.

Those of us who followed this model know only too well how inadequate it is therapeutically. (It makes a great deal more sense theoretically, incidentally, than it does therapeutically.) One cannot quarrel with Freud's observation that depressives often suffer from guilt and that this arises from unacceptable hostile feelings toward loved objects. One also cannot seriously question the oral-dependent make-up of depressives who easily slip into self-pity when their goals are thwarted. Even though Freud was not very clear in his separation of these states, he knew of them. It is his therapeutic system which has been proved to be unacceptable, for the following reasons:

1. Freud's language, though possessing a literary beauty, is so complex and erudite in exposition that the message easily gets lost, even for the professional. The esoteric nature of analytic writings is perhaps exemplified in the works of Otto Fenichel (1945). Whatever such a style attempts to communicate, it suffers from lack of that rare virtue among writers: simplicity.

2. A more important criticism of the Freudian position on depression comes out of his misunderstanding of guilt. He never chose to distinguish between *feeling* guilt about oneself (being a bad and worthless person) and *being* guilty over a regrettable act (but still having the moral right not to damn oneself.) This means that Freudian therapists who attempt to deal with clients who suffer from guilt usually do so on a very selective basis. They see guilt as a valid construct and are horrified at the suggestion that no one needs to feel guilty about anything at any time. Yet, each time they work with a depressive suffering from guilt, they make an exception in that case and encourage him or her not to feel guilty any longer, to forgive the guilty self, and to understand how the errant behavior arose quite naturally from the set of factors he or she was conditioned to. It would be interesting to guess at how many exceptions an analyst would have to make before the truth dawned that he or she might just as well urge everyone to forgive the self for every single wrong act. To my knowledge this insight never appeared in print until Albert Ellis presented it more than twenty years ago (1962).

3. It is a cumbersome system wholly unsuited for the therapist who is talking to a depressed man who lost his job, or to a woman who feels guilty over yelling at her children. (These everyday, temporary events require quick solutions which not only teach the client the causes of that depression but how to avoid all depressions. This is accomplished only by undermining the philosophical tenets supporting the depressive structure.) Analysis is usually focused on the specific symptom and its alleviation, but makes no serious attempt to influence the cognitions affecting all depressions at the same time. It is perfectly feasible for a client in analysis to be relieved of guilt over wanting to reject his or her children but to return in a few years because of guilt over wanting to abscond with the company's funds.

4. It is difficult to know where to start in helping a depressive using analysis. Since the theory is not clear-cut and simple, it leaves the starting point for therapy rather vague. (A proper theory makes the therapist immediately comfortable with this condition and, after listening to the depressive for the first fifteen minutes, he or she can easily see the probable cause and how to attack the problem.)

These are among the main objections and difficulties I found with Freud's view of depression. The first helpful light on this problem was shed by Aaron T. Beck (1967). What immediately caught my attention with his formulation was the possession of precisely some of those characteristics the analytic model lacked: simplicity of structure, clear language unencumbered by abstraction upon abstraction, and a readily identifiable starting point. He neatly divided the causes of depression into a pessimistic view of (1) the world or (2) the self or (3) the future. Incidentally, he posited that manic behavior results from the opposite viewpoint: an overly optimistic view of the world or the self or the future.

Beck is a cognitivist, which immediately makes him acceptable to those in the rational-emotive camp. He achieves relief for depression exactly as one would suspect once the primacy of thinking is accepted in the etiology of depression — by debating one's pessimism through questioning the extent that one is truly in a bad way; by assessing one's life's problems with great care instead of with emotional haste. The client is helped to see that things are not as bad with the world, the self, or the future as he imagines. And when this can indeed be demonstrated, relief from depression follows.

I found the neatness of his system most appealing. It has the advantage of being easily understood, it has ready applicability to everyday and temporary situations, and (one of its strongest features) it follows a cognitive method.

But one criticism repeatedly gnawed at me. I objected to the view that a pessimistic view of the world, the self, or the future of necessity must lead to depression. In fact, I began to reason that such a view was sometimes the result of good reality testing and emanated from a mature personality. In short, being pessimistic about one's ability to climb a mountain or hold down a job could just as easily be the product of health as of neurosis. Believing that our country is going to the dogs and will never regain leadership and respect for many years to come could also be an accurate appraisal. It is not the pessimistic view itself, I reasoned, which causes depression but the *additional* act of blaming ourselves, feeling sorry for ourselves, or feeling sorry for others over the accurately or inaccurately assessed self, world, or future. From this point it was a simple step to translate Beck's three-factored theory of depression into a modified three-factor theory which held self-blame, self-pity, and other-pity to be responsible for any and all psychological depressions.

I have worked with this new formulation for the past half dozen years and have not encountered a single case of psychological depression which did not arise out of one or a combination of these three conditions (Hauck, 1973).

Now, instead of being uncomfortable wondering where I'm supposed to start, I find the only dilemma left is knowing for certain if the depression is functional or organic. I tend toward the following procedure in making this determination, acknowledging fully the leeway for error which obviously exists. If the client can readily focus on, or with some help can point to, an event in his or her life which is significantly frustrating and which is resulting in self-blame, self-pity, or pity for someone else, then I'm prepared to proceed on the assumption that the condition is functional.

If the client can describe no untoward event in his or her current life — insisting that life should be beautiful because there is enough money, everyone is healthy, the job is fine — then an organic condition must be considered. Hypoglycemia is one such condition but it is by no means the only one. For this reason referral to a medical doctor is mandatory.

Upon commencing therapy with a depressive, I usually proceed as follows: I listen for a quarter of an hour to get an inkling of what kind of disturbance the client presents. If it is a depression, I then formulate which method or methods the client is using to bring on this morbid condition. When I am satisfied that I have my general bearings, I proceed to teach the subject in the remaining fifteen minutes what he or she will have to know to bring on relief. But first I must know what the client thinks the trouble is.

I therefore proceed to describe briefly the three ways one gets depressed: self-blame, self-pity, or other-pity. I then ask which of those ways the client is using to get depressed. If we two agree I proceed to identify the client's irrational beliefs and show how to combat them. If we disagree as to the manner in which he or she is bringing on the depression, then I try to probe a bit further to determine if we are using different definitions, or if I have misjudged. In any event, I usually take the client's word for it and proceed from his or her premise. (I do not forget my initial impression, of course, and in all likelihood return to it at a later period.)

I find that strong language and a very directive approach are often quite helpful in relieving a person of self-blame or other-pity. But I have learned through hard experience that self-pity requires utmost tact and discretion. Haste and eagerness — even directiveness — initially send the hurt client scurrying for a client-centered therapist. So many of these people are more interested in *talking* about their *grievances* than in *learning* about their *depressions.* So it behooves us to make haste slowly, to lean back in the chair and let the troubled soul unburden all the gripes. Then, if you still remain gentle, you can proceed with the business of challenging his or her irrational beliefs. There are, of course, many self-pitiers who do not need to be treated with kid gloves, and our clinical experience and intuition help in making that decision. To be on the safe side, though, I advise caution.

Beyond these observations I would proceed with correcting the depressive in the same way we work with other neurotics: uncover the irrational beliefs, get the client to question them, then act according to these new insights. The improvement in recovery rate over other therapeutic approaches will speak for itself.

Four Types of Depression: A Cognitive-Behavioral Approach

BARRY M. BROWN, M.D.

Department of Psychiatry, University of Texas School of Medicine at Houston

During my eleven years of dealing with patients suffering from depression (as well as observing my own mood changes), I have found it useful to classify clinical depressions into four categories. Depression has been categorized many ways since it was first recognized by the ancient Greeks (Hippocrates, 4th century B.C.). The hope of understanding and treating depression successfully has motivated classification over the years. The categories I want to discuss are the ones that are clinically the most meaningful and workable to me. I see most depressions as being one of four types. *overresponsibility, indecision, self-criticism,* and *understimulation.* Each type gets its name from the theme that is part of the activating event — A in RET terminology — sometimes being the start of the chain and other times being brought on by prior events. The important thing is that a therapist can recognize these themes somewhere in his early history-taking and then deal with each appropriately according to certain specific techniques.

The following case histories are described only briefly, emphasizing specific data that I found important for the understanding and treatment of that particular case. The treatment descriptions are divided into RET procedures and non-RET procedures — the latter coming from cognitive therapy in general and broad-spectrum behavior therapy.

The Overresponsibility Depression

The overresponsibility depression occurs in perfectionistic, hard-driving people who usually function extremely well. These people get into difficulty when they take on extra responsibilities and expect themselves to do a perfect job at them. They find themselves short on time, rushing around frantically to get things done, neglecting relaxing, passive, pleasurable activities and having little time to think, plan, and fantasize. They come to the therapist feeling confused, apathetic, depressed, tense, and complaining of inability to enjoy any of their activities.

Case 1

A 21-year-old college senior with an almost all A record and an acceptance to medical school, but taking six major courses and playing in the two college bands so he could "get the most out of college." He had become tense, depressed and apathetic to the degree where he could not study. He had heard it was too late to drop courses, but never checked this out with school officials.

Irrational Beliefs

"I've got to do well in school."

"I can't miss any band practices."

"I must continue to do my school work thoroughly so I will get good grades."

"I really don't have time to do all this work completely, but it would be awful if I missed band rehearsal or cut corners in my studies and got poor marks."

"I've got all this work to do, I'll never get it all done."

Treatment

(In order of treating patient)

Advice — "Try to drop two courses. If this can't be done, talk to the dean and your teachers and tell them what has happened and see if they can help you decrease your work load."
(Assertive training)

RET — "Why must you do well in school? Why would it be so awful if you missed occasional band rehearsals or did your studies less completely? Would it really be catastrophic if you got a C or a D in a course?"

Cognitive Modeling — "I'd like to do well in my studies, but I really don't have to. And even if my marks go down, I'm still in medical school, and lower marks for one semester are no real catastrophe."

Advice — "Do one thing at a time and try not to think of all you have left to do."

Case 2

A 50-year-old white male owner of an automobile dealership comes in depressed, upset, tense. Exploratory procedures reveal that he is taking care of the needs of his elderly parents who are in nursing homes, constantly getting his sociopathic sister out of trouble, and helping his sickly wife, retarded stepson, and divorced stepdaughter. He is very involved with doing things for all these people. He can never refuse their requests. He is afraid to go on vacations for fear someone will need him.

This patient did develop some self-centeredness and took a week's vacation to Australia. He enjoyed the trip immensely and functioned in good spirits for two months after returning. Other problems began to develop and five months after his Australian trip he came in complaining of feelings of depression and tension relative to difficulties in his automotive business. He was still doing too much for his relatives but, in addition, feared financial loss and felt obligated to his employees because the business wasn't going well. He felt that none of his employees was capable of taking over some of his responsibilities. He mentioned that his wife had quite a bit of money from her first marriage but she wanted that kept for her children and he understood her feelings.

Irrational Beliefs

"If I went on vacation and someone needed me, I'd really feel like a heel, like I was really letting people down."

"If I'm not available for these people they wouldn't love me and that would be awful."

"If I let anyone down, it would prove I'm worthless."

"Wouldn't it be awful if I lost my money!"

"I couldn't live if I lost my money."

"I'm really letting those guys at work down. I should be able to do something to help the business and to help them."

"I've got to handle all the business matters. I can't let the managers handle things and take off from work more often leaving them in charge. If they don't do things as well as I do, the business might fail."

"I can't ask my wife for financial help — I should be able to handle this situation."

Treatment

Clarify what treatment needs his dependents might run into and ask a friend, or pay someone to handle those when he is out of town.

RET — "Why would it be so awful if your sister got in trouble with the law? Why should you have to protect and defend her?"

"Can't some of your family's needs be met by others?"

"Why do you believe you are irreplaceable?"

"What if your sister withdrew her love? Why would that be so awful?"

Self-Centeredness Training — "There's a long pattern here of your putting others first and not meeting your own needs. You've had no time to do what *you* want. That's why you're depressed. For you to start getting more out of life, you've got to make yourself Number 1. It's been all give and no receive. The fantasy that relaxes you and relieves your depression is taking a trip to Australia. Why not do that?"

Exploration with patient of all possible practical solutions to his realistic business problems: Get someone else to help manage the business, sell the business, etc.

RET — "Let's assume the worst: What if you lost every last cent you had? Would that be the end of the world?"

"If you got away from business and all the phone calls, complaints, and problems, would your assistant manager really mess up things to the point of ruination of your business?"

"Why do you hold yourself responsible for business being poor and the happiness and success of your employees? Are you responsible for how your employees feel?"

Self-Centeredness and Assertiveness Training — "You've done plenty for your wife and her children. Why can't you tell her of your difficulties and ask her to help you financially? You have a good marriage and she knows you're a good businessman. If you handle her tactfully, it sounds as if she'd let you use her money to help your business or start in another field."

The Indecision Depression

This arises when people begin to question whether to remain in a situation, such as a job or a marriage, in which they feel unhappy. Such patients may stay indecisive and in limbo because the arguments for staying in the situation are no stronger than those for leaving. They find this particular decision, in comparison with others they've been faced with, exceptionally hard to make. The indecision is not a symptom of being depressed. The indecision *is the* major activating event of the depression. Such a patient does not get depressed until beginning to obsess over which choice to make.

Case

A 25-year-old white female married five years begins considering divorce because she is feeling unhappy in her marriage. She feels she loves her husband, they enjoy doing many things together, and there are no major problem areas. Her only complaints are that her husband likes being with her all the time they are not at work. At home he gives her no time to be alone. She also feels that because she is married she can't get to know other men better. She has this feeling, even though her husband shows no jealousy when they are in the company of other men.

Irrational Beliefs

"My marriage is good but it should be better."

"I can't be happy unless I have what I want."

"He should leave me alone more."

"He should realize I want to be alone more."

"He should encourage me to talk to other men."

"I'd like to leave him and find a more perfect situation but he is a good husband in many ways and, if I leave and don't find someone as good or better, that would be catastrophic, awful."

Treatment

Assertiveness Training — "Tell your husband you like the marriage but feel it would be better for you if you had more time alone."

Contract Negotiations — Therapy sessions where each discusses what each wants and is not getting. Make a new contract such as an open marriage.

RET — "Even if your marriage can't be made better, why should you be 100% happy?"

"Why should he be what you demand him to be?"

"Even if you decided to divorce and later felt it was a mistake, why would that be catastrophic?"

The Self-Critical Depression

The self-critical depression is usually precipitated by a real or perceived rejection, a poor mark in school, a poor job report, a neutral response when a positive one is expected, or the thought that one has acted in a way that he feels is morally wrong (guilt). The self-critical depression is the type usually referred to in the writings of Dr. Albert Ellis.

Case 1

A young psychiatrist telephoned an ex-patient to find out how the patient was doing. The patient was pleasant but revealed she was in therapy with another psychiatrist.

Irrational Beliefs

"I must have done something wrong."

"I guess I'm not a good therapist."

"I'll probably lose a lot of patients."

"Word will get around that I'm no good and my practice will dwindle to nothing."

Treatment

General Cognitive — Therapist asks patient, "How many patients have you actually lost to other doctors or found out were dissatisfied?"

"What are the probabilities that you would actually lose most of your patients?"

"Aren't there other reasons the patient changed doctors that have nothing to do with your ability?"

RET — "Why should you expect yourself to be successful with all your patients?"

"Even if you did poorly with most of your patients, would that make you worthless?"

"Why rate yourself?"

Thought Distraction — Patients in this type of depression frequently can't talk themselves out of it, so I have them repeatedly think the words "STOP THINK" or concentrate on a pleasant scene or the color blue. Muscle relaxation, which is in part a thought distraction process, can also be used. Repetition of the words, scenes, colors, or feelings over a period of five or ten minutes seems to interrupt obsessing or irrational beliefs and leaves the patient in a less-depressed state.

Case 2

A 32-year-old white female married for 16 years, who, though she was brought up to believe that sex was bad and was never well handled by her husband sexually, learned to enjoy sex once she was urged into it and was even orgasmic 50% of the time. She never desires sex, however, and her husband pushes for it daily and then sulks if she refuses or is not responsive during intercourse. She accepts his blame and comes to therapy in hope of developing sexual desire and/or to learn to "try harder" to respond to her husband's sexual advances.

Irrational Beliefs

"I'm not pleasing my husband. I should work harder at liking sex so he'll be happy."

"I must keep my husband happy. It's a wife's duty."

"If he sulks, it must mean I'm doing a poor job as a wife and that's awful."

"I must meet all his needs all the time or I'm not a good wife."

"There must be something wrong with me since I don't desire sex."

Treatment

Advice — Education that for relationships to be satisfactory each person usually gives something. "It sounds like your husband doesn't try at all to please you, isn't romantic, practices no foreplay, and in general just uses you."

Praise that she has tolerated this man so long and that she has talked herself into learning to enjoy sex.

RET — "Why should a wife meet her husband's every demand?"

"If he sulks, why do you have to blame yourself and consider yourself a failure?"

"Why should you desire sex?"

Self-Centeredness Training — "You're 50% of this marriage, what do *you* want? How do *you* want things to be?"

Assertiveness Training — "Start telling him what your needs are."

(Communication is discussed and practiced.)

Case 3

A 28-year-old college professor divorced one time is extremely sensitive to perceived rejections from women. Frequent recurring depressions usually precipitated by perceived rejections.

Irrational Beliefs

"I failed in my marriage and I keep failing in all my relationships with women. I'll never be able to succeed and have a long-term relationship, and that would be awful."

"Since Jane couldn't go out with me Saturday night, I'm sure she doesn't care for me."

"When I go to bars, the girls talk to other guys but not to me."

Treatment

General Cognitive — "It seems many marriages are failing these days and that fewer people are able to have long-term relationships. You seem to think you're the only one."

"You assume, if a girl doesn't smile at you, she doesn't like you. Aren't there other alternatives, like she's shy or has a boyfriend? From the history, it sounds like many girls liked you."

RET — "Why does getting a divorce mean you're a failure?"

"Even if you failed in your marriage, why does that mean you'll do poorly in all future relationships with women?"

"Let's assume the worst — that *no* girl wanted to even talk to you. Would that mean the end of your life?"

Assertiveness Training — "You expect girls to come to you. We can practice ways of meeting girls and communicating effectively so that you can approach and get along with them."

Homework — "Go out and talk to all the girls you can. Think of all the assertive techniques we've discussed and practiced. Some of these girls, no matter how well you do, will reject you. Their rejections will give you an opportunity to talk yourself out of feeling hurt."

The Understimulation Depression

The understimulation depression encompasses many depressive states from mild to severe and seems related to a certain optimal level of stimulation that differs from person to person. Some people function well on low stimulation levels, while others seem to function best on higher levels. Depression occurs frequently when there is a drop in a person's perceived stimulation or a prediction of future lowering of stimulation. By stimulation I mean those people, events, or any other cues, that a person finds meaningful or exciting. One may take the example of a person who, on learning that a good friend is moving away, experiences mild to severe depressed feelings. Another example of this phenomenon is the man who leads a highly stimulating business and professional life, receiving many phone calls, meeting many people who are challenging, interesting, and educating, and receiving much gratification both monetarily and in self-esteem. When he arrives home, where there may be comparatively little stimulation, he may become depressed. Other men come home and relish the decreased stimulation. One of my peers went into a four-day depression after returning from a psychology convention in San Francisco where he went to many excellent seminars and workshops, saw many old friends, made many new ones, talked with stimulating people into the early hours of the morning, and visited many interesting and exciting areas along the whole West Coast. His depression began on returning home to his ordinary routine military existence.

My hypothesis is that the drop in level of stimulation or the prediction of a drop occurring is a very common cause of depression. Because of this belief, my history-taking from patients showing any degree of depression includes extensive probing into what things they have found stimulating and what their relationship with those stimuli is at present.

Again, as in the indecision depression, I do not see the lack of stimulation as a symptom of depression but as a precipitating event. However, I would not dispute that, once people are depressed — no matter what the cause — it is difficult to get them to seek stimulation.

Case

A 50-year-old married mother of two children in their early twenties moved to Houston with her husband and daughter two years ago after living in Connecticut for 13 years. Her depression started nine months ago and has become progressively deeper. She blamed her depression on living in Houston, "a city with no hills," "hot weather all year around," and "nothing to do — as compared to New Haven with its hills, four seasons, and many activities." She knew she would probably have to stay in Houston because her husband's firm transferred him there. The husband liked Houston but agreed to try to get transferred back East for his wife's sake. However, this could not be done and his attempts to find his type of work in the East were to no avail. There was no history of marital problems or family disharmony.

Irrational Beliefs

"I can't stand Houston. It's so hot here and no one is on the streets. There are no hills to hike on."

"Life should be the way I want it to be."

"My husband should realize how unhappy I am here."

"Life will be empty with everyone gone. I won't be able to stand it."

"I need my family to get any pleasure from life."

"If I introduce myself to my neighbors, they may reject me and that would be awful!"

"What if the church here does things differently and doesn't like our ways? We might not be accepted."

Treatment

A. *Data Collection*

The patient was very verbal and much data was gathered from her, her daughter, and her husband. Two main themes emerged from the data: (1) The patient was at first content with Houston but began getting depressed when her son decided not to transfer to a Texas college as he had planned to do, her daughter began talking of moving to Ohio to live with a girlfriend, and some close relatives who had lived with the patient and her family for the last four months moved to Alaska. (2) The patient has always been slow to adapt to new situations, especially moving from one city to another. Her husband claimed that it took five years before she began to feel comfortable and enjoy New Haven.

B. *General Cognitive and RET*

1. *General Cognitive* — Emphasis was continually put on the belief that people's feelings have more to do with other people than with geographical locations.

RET — "You may not like it here, but surely you can stand it. No place is perfect, even New Haven. Why should life be the way you want it to be? It would be nice if life were as you wanted it, but why *should* it be that way?"

2. *General Cognitive* — The patient was told that it sounded like she was content in Houston until three disappointments arose in her life — her son's deciding not to move here, her daughter's thought of leaving, and the actual loss of the relatives. The therapist pointed out to her that these family members were sources of great stimulation to her and their loss meant less stimulation for her and that was the real precipitant of the depression.

RET — "It's true you will miss these people and life may be hard, but not impossible. You may not like it, but you can stand it."

"It would be desirable to have your family here for stimulation, but you don't *need* them. There are other sources of stimulation in Houston and, even if you're only 25 or 50% stimulated, why will that be awful?"

3. *General Cognitive* — "Adapting to new places has always been hard for you even when the family was with you. Adaptation involves fear of people — what they will think of you and how they will act toward you."

RET — "It would be unfortunate if neighbors didn't care for you, but why would it be awful?"

"Even if church life here isn't what you're accustomed to, why is that a catastrophe? Assuming the worst — that no one in church accepts you — is that the end of the world?"

Advice, Education, and Assertiveness Training —
"Get involved with new things."

"It's a fact of life that children grow up and leave home."

"It's difficult to get used to, but not impossible."

"Let's practice how you'll introduce yourself to neighbors and the minister."

"Ask your husband if you can join him at the balloon races."

Conclusion

I have tried to categorize the depressions that I have treated into four types so other therapists may quickly recognize them and implement the cognitive and behavioral techniques discussed. Use of these techniques should not only help patients in the therapist's office but enable them to exercise some control over their depressions when on their own.

The techniques discussed may not work in depressions of severely retarded persons or in depressed people who are unable to verbalize well. For these patients I advise the use of antidepressant medication. Even if I have a depressed patient who verbalizes well and discusses precipitating events likely to lead to depression, failure to show significant improvement in from four to six therapy sessions is an indication to me that biochemical factors are involved and that antidepressants should be used.

The categorization of depression into four types is undoubtedly not a complete one and I would welcome additional categories from other therapists so that we may continue to improve the management of this, the most ubiquitous of emotional disorders.

Religion as Rational

ALBERT F. GRAU, S.J., Ph.D.

Professor Emeritus of Psychology and Consultant to the Counseling Center, Loyola College, Baltimore, Maryland

"Religion" can be defined as a personal or institutionalized system of beliefs relating to God, to the divine or supernatural, or to that which is held to be of ultimate importance.*

What is meant by "religion" here can be distinguished on the one hand from "religiosity" (excessively, obtrusively or sentimentally religious), and on the other hand from "superstition" (a belief or practice resulting from ignorance, fear of the unknown or trust in magic or chance).

It would seem that the notion of "religion" involves the triad of human experience simplistically summarized as thinking-feeling-behaving. In addition to religious belief *(thinking)*, implied at least are religious *feelings* and religious *behavior:* Belief generates feeling, and feeling is usually, albeit not always, expressed in behaviors consistent with or appropriate to the way we feel.

When we refer or relate to the "divine" or the "supernatural" we are referring "to an order of existence beyond the visible, observable universe" — beyond the *comprehending* ability of the mind, not necessarily beyond the perceiving ability of the mind. In this sense, the notion of the "supernatural" is *supra-rational*, not anti-rational. Religion may be *in se* nonrational; it is not *in se* irrational.

When is religion irrational or anti-rational? It is so when it cannot in any component of the triad of human experiencing correspond to the criteria for "rational."

---

* All definitions in this paper have been drawn or adapted from *Webster's Seventh New Collegiate Dictionary* (Springfield, Massachusetts: G. & C. Merriam Company).

Maultsby proposes five criteria that are necessary to validate behavior as "rational." The following list, except for some minor modifications, corresponds to Maultsby's criteria. The behavior

1. must be based on verifiable reality
2. is integrative of the self, perfective of the self, of the total self
3. is productive of personal goals or fulfilling of personal values
4. eliminates and/or prevents significant personal conflict (affects the "within")
5. eliminates and/or prevents significant environmental conflict (affects the "without")

I see the notion of *conflict* as fundamental to these criteria. If the religious person is in any area of his human experiencing (thinking-feeling-behaving) in conflict

1. with verifiable reality
2. with the process of self-integration
3. with his goals
4. with his inner serenity
5. with his environment

then he is irrationally religious.

Let us suppose that the religious person is practicing "humility." He can do this rationally or irrationally.

Rationally, he could think-feel-behave in a submissive, deferential manner.

1. Can this be based on verifiable reality? Is he justified in deferring? (Maybe he is inferior in this or that respect.)
2. Is it self-integrative? (It reduces his arrogance, makes his self-concept more realistic, etc.)
3. Is it goal-productive? (Could be, depending on what his goals are: to be a better co-worker, to help the self-enhancement of others, etc.)
4. Does it abet inner serenity and peace? (He sees others as deferrable to, because of some attributes they have; it gets others in clearer perspective, etc.)
5. Does it eliminate environmental conflict? (He may become more likable in eyes of others, has dropped his one upmanship, etc.)

Irrationally, he could think-feel-behave in the same way, but

1. He professes, "I am the dumbest man in the world." (He has a Ph.D.)
2. He becomes proud of his humility.

3. His deference may be inappropriate (for example, in *his* work situation as a supervisor or director).
4. His deferring could cause his anguish. ("Why don't they reciprocate?")
5. He may be shirking his responsibility which may exclude deference as a viable manner. Work disintegrates.

A pertinent observation: Even *bona fide* religiousness is a process, a continuation — not a final once-for-all act. It can happen that what was originally authentically "religious" in an individual deteriorates into neuroticism by processing religious ideals through the irrationality of various ideas and belief which Ellis has outlined. To illustrate what *can* happen, I have worked out a schema around Ellis's theories concerning irrational ideas to indicate some sample ideals deteriorating into some sample neuroticisms.

Sample Religious Ideals	Irrational Ideas	Sample Defenses and Neuroticisms
Good Reputation	1. The idea that it is a dire necessity for an adult human being to be loved or approved by virtually every significant other person in his community.	Compensation
Good Religious Subject	2. The idea that one should be thoroughly competent, adequate, and achieving in all possible respects if one is to consider oneself worthwhile.	Hypocrisy
Orthodoxy	3. The idea that anyone who does not measure up to my standards of "goodness" is therefore "bad," and is thereby my opponent to be scorned, rejected, or anathematized.	Displacement (Righteousness)
Idealism	4. The idea that it is awful and catastrophic when things are not the way one would very much like them to be.	Denial of Reality
Indifference, Humility	5. The idea that human unhappiness is externally caused and that people have little or no ability to control their sorrows and disturbances.	Projection, Hypercriticism

Sample Religious Ideals	Irrational Ideas	Sample Defenses and Neuroticisms
Abnegation	6. The idea that, if something is or may be dangerous or fearsome, one should be terribly concerned about it and should keep dwelling on the possibility of its occurring.	Inadequacy, Catastrophizing
Detachment	7. The idea that it is easier to avoid than to face certain life difficulties and self-responsibilities.	Rationalization
Obedience	8. The idea that one should be dependent on others and needs someone stronger than oneself on whom to rely.	Abject Conformity
Resignation to God's Will	9. The idea that one's past history is an all-important determiner of one's present behavior, and that, because something once strongly affected one's life, it should indefinitely have a similar effect.	Pathological Passivity
Charity, Solicitude	10. The idea that one should become quite upset over other people's problems and disturbances.	Identification
Religious Perfection	11. The idea that there is invariably a right, precise, and perfect solution to human problems, and that it is catastrophic if this perfect solution is not found.	Obsessive Compulsiveness
Institutional Loyalty	12. The idea that the "image" of the institution, system, or establishment must be kept enhanced at *any* cost.	Scapegoating

Let me expatiate on only one or two items as an example:First, let's consider *detachment*. In the language of religious asceticism, detachment means "indifference to worldly concerns." An erstwhile religious person may be so "detached" from success and praise that he or she does not make any genuine effort in his or her work (which may bring success and praise), and then rationalizes this lack of effort as practicing "detachment." Another example: *resignation to God's will*. In ascetic terms, this would mean that, while making all reasonable efforts to accomplish a particular task, one accepts the outcome as being a disposition of Divine Providence. The so-called religious person could sit on his or her duff, do little or nothing to (for example) overcome a handicap, and, in this state of passivity, justify being "resigned."

Similarly the reader can "think through" other items.

In virtually every instance where one observes "religion" as similar to or identical with "superstition" or "religiosity," one can, upon thorough investigation, discover a basic irrationality in some aspect of the thinking-feeling-behavior triad.

In summary, any religious experience which avoids the conflict precluded by Maultsby criteria, or which eschews the irrational ideas articulated by Ellis, is basically a rational experience.

Three Forms of Rational-Emotive Meditation

KENNETH PEISER, Ph.D.

Chicago Institute for Rational Living

It is assumed in the following presentation that differer.
therapeutic techniques vary in their effectiveness with different
clients and different kinds of problems. Three new techniques
will be presented here with some suggestions as to their possible
relative effectiveness in various situations. It will first be noted
that there are various dimensions of personality and psychopathology and that it is likely that these dimensions affect
psychotherapy requirements.

Dimensions of Personality and Psychopathology

A. One major personality dimension is extroversion-
introversion.

1. One aspect of this dimension seems to be external versus
internal locus of control and, since rational-emotive behavior
therapy (REBT) emphasizes internal locus of control, one
would expect more-introverted clients to catch on more readily
and therefore do better in learning emotional control in the
early stages of therapy, although in the long run more-
extroverted clients might compensate by greater willingness
to put their insights into action. Obviously these differences
could affect the emphases and procedures in optimally effective therapy.

2. Another possible difference between more extroverted
and more introverted clients seems, from clinical experience,
to be a relatively greater emphasis by the former on the irra-

tional "need" for love and approval and by the latter on the irrational "need" for achievement and success. Again, this difference is likely to require somewhat different approaches for the therapist seeking greater efficiency.

B. Another possible dimension could be called "chronicity-defendedness" versus "acuteness-fragility."

1. The client who is "normally" neurotic but suffering excessive stress in reaction to what he or she sees as overwhelming current environmental pressures (for example, divorce or final exams) often benefits more from a relatively more empathic-supportive approach and frequently rebels, because of the disorganizing effects of unusually high anxiety, against excessively early and strong confrontation.

2. The chronic well-defended client, on the other hand, can wallow for years in Rogerian or supportive therapy with little or no progress and seems to respond better to a highly confronting and challenging approach which helps to break through cognitive-behavioral patterns which are years old and highly repetitious.

C. Intelligence, defined in this case as learning and problem-solving capacity, most probably also affects the efficient therapist's approach as, for example, in emphasizing more abstract philosophic concerns for the more intelligent and more operant conditioning and modeling techniques for the less intelligent client.

D. Much evidence has been accumulated that indicates a dimension of thinking style related to frequency and amplitude of brain waves and/or cerebral hemisphere use.

1. What I will call Type I thinking, related to slower, higher-amplitude brain waves and right-hemisphere functions, is more intuitive, inductive, generalizing, and concrete. Disruptions in this kind of thinking result in more bizarre symptoms (such as hallucinations) and probably involve more general, more primitive, and less easily verbalizable irrational ideas, thus calling for the therapist to spend more time helping the client to put into words what he or she is thinking.

2. Type II thinking, related to faster, lower-amplitude brain waves and left-hemisphere functions, is more conceptual, deductive, discriminating, and abstract. Disruptions in this kind of thinking result in the more ordinary symptoms (such as

obsessive worrying) and probably involve more specific, more sophisticated, and more easily verbalizable irrational ideas, thus responding more readily to the REB therapist's, "What are you telling yourself?"

E. Another dimension along which clients vary significantly is simply the degree of psychopathology or degree of anxiety-irrationality as influenced by genetic predispositions and environmental factors including prior exposure to effective psychotherapy.

1. At the lowest level is the client who chronically (or only temporarily) displays little or no contact with rationality. This is the client with little psychological insight (at least at the moment) whose every sentence is of such an irrational nature that the therapist hardly knows where to begin.

2. In the middle is the typical client seen in private practice who displays a certain amount of rationality, a certain amount of objectivity and self-correction, but who is confused about which values, feelings, and acts are rational and which are self-defeating. This is the client who rather frequently gets upset but who then in an hour or a day recoups and goes on with life until the next "catastrophe."

3. At the highest level is the sophisticated client who works well and rather regularly on his or her disturbances, who is insightful and has a deep sense of what is rational or irrational. This client (who, in my experience, is often a professional counselor or therapist) for the most part just wants confirmation that he or she is moving in the right direction, plus a somewhat different perspective from time to time.

Techniques

Rational-emotive meditation (REM) is a set of techniques, devised by me with Kathy Thome of the Chicago Institute for Rational Living, which can be used in individual or group psychotherapy, workshops, or as "homework" assignments. There are three forms, varying in degree of structure provided and in degree of self-awareness which they elicit and require. Clients varying on the above-mentioned dimensions and on others as well can be expected to benefit more from one REM technique than another, and the degree of benefit can be expected to change as therapy progresses, thus making one technique more valuable at first, another later. Given the dictionary definition of meditation as "deep thinking," the three forms of REM qualify as genuine meditative exercises. More importantly, they share with most forms of standard meditation the goal of loosening up and weakening the effects of entrenched systems of conceptualization which blind one to reality. Each step of each technique is described below with a fictitious but realistic and fairly typical example (underachievement — fear of failure) of the verbalizations or verbal formulas appropriate to that step of the exercise.

A. *Reprogramming* is probably most useful (at least initially) for the client with more external locus of control, for the acutely disturbed or overwhelmed client, for the less intelligent client, for the client with underdeveloped Type II thinking, and especially for the client described in E1 above who is constantly "meditating" on irrational *mantras* (for example, "I can't do it," "I'm no good," "It's awful"). This form of REM has, at least superficially, some similarities to certain forms of Tantric mantra repetition, especially those forms in which the meaning is to be deeply contemplated. Reprogramming also seems similar in certain regards to some forms of Jewish, Christian, and Muslim prayer that have a meditative aspect. The procedure is as follows:

1. Select a relatively complex irrational idea (this often requires the therapist's help): "I must pass this course because, if I don't, it will prove that I'm a total failure."

2. Formulate a rational contradiction to that idea (again, at this level, the therapist's help is usually important): "I don't have to pass this course and even a large number of failures can't make me a total failure."

3. Repeat (usually aloud) that rational idea several times until it is memorized verbatim.

4. Then repeat it several times with as much emotion as possible. This is aided by saying it with different vocal stresses and inflections each time. Really get into it! *Chew it over!*

5. Next, with deep feeling as above, repeat the same concept paraphrased in several different ways:
"It is not necessary to pass this course, because I can't be a total failure if I succeed at anything even once."
"One or even many failures can't prove that I'm totally worthless and therefore I don't need success in this case."
"Failing this course is possible. It wouldn't mean I'm a

complete failure and would simply be inconvenient."

6. Finally, repeat with deep feeling several related but not ideational rational ideas in order to generalize further the rational thinking and link the new idea with other memory traces for improved "storage":

"Failure is frustrating but not shameful or awful."

"My value as a person is not determined by my achievements."

"The less I demand perfection the easier it will be to study."

7. A common immediate effect of reprogramming is an increased sense of determination, confidence, and "will power." There is a feeling that one can handle these problems — that one need not be stuck or trapped in one's erroneous thinking. This is perhaps especially true for depressive states or anxiety with the quality of timidity and avoidance. Perhaps this effect is related to the effects of "pep talks," rousing political speeches, positive thinking, hypnosis, and the like.

B. *Careful thinking* is the intermediate method and is very much like the verbal interaction in a typical rational therapy session in which statements are constantly corrected and refined. Its intent is to train one to think in a different way rather than just to think different thoughts. It leaves more room than reprogramming does for clients to have insights or *aha* experiences and to do their own thinking. It thus requires somewhat more internal locus of control, somewhat more intelligence, a combination of Type I and relatively adequate Type II thinking, and is especially appropriate for the typical client (see E2 above) who is already capable of self-corrective thinking but who could use more rigorous practice. This is a contemplative form of thinking — familiar, in essence, to the serious student of any religious tradition, but even more typical of creative scientific and literary production. The procedure is as follows:

1. Select a problem area in which thinking is partly irrational, somewhat confused, and ignores certain relevant facts, and describe the problem in this way: "I am excessively afraid of failing this course because I don't want to be a failure and it is terribly important for me to pass."

2. Translate this description into irrational ideas, with the therapist's help when necessary, and take responsibility for the irrationalities: "I am erroneously telling myself that failing this course will make me a total failure and that, therefore, I have to pass it."

3. Translate such irrational idea into a contradictory rational idea: "What in fact is true is that one or even many failures only make me a partial failure and therefore I don't have to pass this course."

4. Proceed to successively refine this idea, making it more complete, more accurate, more scientifically qualified: "It is perhaps true that some failures, according to some value systems, make me a partial failure (or, better, one who has failed in certain instances) but that does not make it necessary for me to pass, even though that might be best for me in the long run."

5. Continue this process until a very careful, relatively complete rational paragraph has been composed which emphasizes probabilistic thinking, reduces dichotomies and overgeneralizations and is as free as possible of logical and factual fallacies. Carry out these successive revisions slowly and thoughtfully as if formulating and reformulating a scientific or philosophic essay: "Some failures probably have disadvantages, although this potential failure might even have some advantages, and I do not need to adopt a value system that, by definition, evaluates me as a total person based on my success or lack thereof in any particular task. Therefore, nothing necessitates my passing this or any other course and, therefore, neither terror, horror, nor shame need precede or follow failure in this case, although concern and determined efforts could well yield certain practical benefits."

6. There are two frequent effects of careful thinking: One is a feeling of relief and release, an increased sense of freedom from unnecessary burdens and troubles, a sense of lightness and even some sense of humor about the previously sticky, confusing issue. The other is a feeling of boredom or mild irritation with the problem: "Isn't this ridiculous? What have I been wasting my time for? Why keep hassling? What can I do now that's productive?"

C. *Socratic meditation* (so designated by Kathy Thome) is the most demanding of reliance on self, intelligence, insight, and awareness. It requires excellent Type II thinking but also stimulates and develops Type I thinking and is most suited for the relatively independent client (see E3 above). It bears some resemblance in both form and intent to Zen koan meditation, although there are some serious differences. Since it is rather specifically geared to stimulate rational Type I thinking, it comes closest to the aims of many orthodox forms of meditation and contemplation. The procedure is as follows:

1. Select an area in which one wants to deepen understanding of, and belief in, certain rational ideas, or especially in which one wants to uproot and destroy the impact of certain irrational ideas, and formulate one most basic irrational concept: "I must pass this course."

2. Question that concept and search for the underlying irrational idea: "Why must I pass this course? Because it would be shameful to fail."

3. Continue to question each irrational idea as it occurs, being careful not to "cover up" a still-present irrational idea by simply mouthing a textbookish rational idea, until a genuine shift in feeling occurs and the most deeply felt answer is a rational one:

"Why would it be shameful to fail? Because I worked so hard."

"How does unsuccessful hard work warrant shame? It proves I'm stupid."

"How does one failure prove I'm stupid? Oh, it doesn't, really. It's just a big fat disappointment. But then, maybe I'd learn something from this failure so, in a sense, it could even be a good experience."

"Is there any other nonsense still there? For example, would it be shameful if I were really stupid? No, not really — I could adjust to that by simply not demanding performance beyond my capacity."

4. The actual process, of course, will take longer than the above example and, when seriously done, requires much self-honesty and insightful awareness and is deeply emotional. The questions at their best are maximally intuitively probing and self-confronting and, as noted above, require more than most clients are initially (if ever) prepared for. The immediate effect of serious participation in this process is an emotionally intense turnaround in one's thinking about the perception of the problematic situation and emotional sense of relief and power (a blend of the effects of reprogramming and careful thinking) with the confidence that one can really handle things well.

Interrelationships

It is tempting to speculate — and I will not resist — about the interrelationships among the three forms of REM, brain waves, cerebral hemispheres, and psychological functions.

A. Evidence from recent research on hemispheric differences in psychological functions, meditation, and brain waves, and from ancient Oriental practices can be interpreted to mean that:

1. Neurotic-like disturbances involve excessive and anxious, distorted Type II (fast brain wave, left hemisphere) thinking which blocks intuitive or Type I thinking (slow brain wave, right hemisphere). Example: obsessive worrying.

2. Psychotic-like disturbances involve underdeveloped Type II thinking and anxious, distorted Type I thinking. Example: delusions and hallucinations.

B. The three forms of REM would seem to be capable of somewhat selectively correcting different aspects of these two kinds of disturbances.

1. *Reprogramming* seems to focus primarily on developing rational Type II thinking. This could provide a heretofore missing cognitive structure to act as a basis for reevaluating distorted Type I intuitions (delusions) but it does not directly work on or with Type I thinking. It can also be seen as a tool for interfering with or "drowning out" obsessive Type II thinking which might then, as a secondary benefit, free the Type I capacities which up to that time have been inhibited or blocked.

2. *Careful thinking* can be used only after there is a sufficient base or store of rational Type II concepts, and refines and integrates these while, at the same time, it intentionally gives play to Type I intuitions. It thus helps to liberate intuitive thinking, while maintaining a constant critical check by logical reality-oriented Type II conceptualization.

3. *Socratic meditation* assumes adequate, integrated Type II thinking — that is, it assumes the presence of a well-developed philosophy of life which is not necessarily fully incorporated at the Type I thought level. The emphasis, therefore, is on revealing the Type I errors on the assumption that, as these "surface" in the light of a rational cognitive superstructure, they will be transformed into or yield to reality-oriented and accurate holistic Type I intuitions.

C. Whether or not some of the above relationships hold, on the basis of clinical and workshop experience so far, the three REM techniques and various modifications thereof appear to be useful tools which, together with methods such as the two forms of rational-emotive imagery, the Homework Form, and DESIBELS, enrich, deepen, and broaden the scope of cognitive-behavior modification therapy. We hope others will explore the above ideas and methods and provide us with feedback.

Comments by Jeffrey M. Brandsma, Ph.D.

I would like to compliment Dr. Peiser and his colleagues on working out a concrete program of meditation techniques. This ability to make things usable by most people is a strength inherent in RBT theory and exhibited by most of its practitioners.

As most of you are aware, what we currently call rational thinking is a highly evolved and sophisticated product of Western culture with an emphasis on empiricism, logic, and the values of science. In the West there has always been a tremendous emphasis on doing, on manipulating reality, and achieving, in contrast to the Eastern cultural set toward acceptance of one's being and all other forms of being.

Rational thinkers and therapists as currently constituted are deeply a part of Western culture and have emphasized the organism's relationship to objective reality. At times you would think that achievement and sex are the only categories of good experience — and thus, as an example, even REI is reality-oriented, problem-solving, goal-producing, and of course, scheduled. But in the rational therapy movement there has been little emphasis on "recreational thinking" (fantasy) or nonproblem-oriented or behaviorally oriented thinking. I think this is a mistake — a narrowing of our brain's potential and our personal satisfaction possibilities — and I believe that the various forms of Eastern meditation could provide techniques that could be integrated with rational thinking.

The brain's main function is as a reducing valve to shut out the totality of experiencing so that man can do what is in front of him. Meditative techniques are geared, it seems to me, to open the brain more flexibly to what is usually unconscious or preconscious.

As I have briefly read the research literature on meditation, I think it can be said that it has documentable physiological changes which make it different from sleeping or a trance. Depending partly on the type of meditation, it can be stated that oxygen consumption and breathing decrease, as does heart rate, while there is a corresponding increase in galvanic skin response and alpha. Obviously it is very relaxing but it also seems to generalize and decrease anxiety as a trait and decrease dependence on drugs.

Now to get to specifics: I, like Dr. Peiser, have been primarily interested in getting people to what he conceptualizes as Socratic meditation. But I think that, when they get there, this level of functioning allows for a lot of new techniques — self-exploratory techniques to plumb the uniqueness of the billions of experiences which make up any self. This is an area that needs exploration and integration with rational living. I suspect we must be somewhat selective here because there are different systems of meditation. For example, the Zen philosophy emphasizes detached, yet precise, perception of inner and outer stimuli — something rational thinking values. However, Yogic forms emphasize noninvolvement in the world and attempt to block awareness of external events. We must look closely at our purposes and goals before we choose a technique. Let me emphasize that these techniques could be useful for all people — some with the help of a therapist, others by themselves. Without any data to refer to, I would suspect that introspective people and those who have had early experiences of pleasant aloneness in their childhood would have an easier time learning these techniques. Hard-driving executive types would have a hard time learning them, but probably would increase their life span if they learned some form of relaxing meditation.

The "reprogramming" idea comes from the current fascination with computers, and the techniques are good. I would like to point out that many Eastern meditative systems use *mantras,* or little sayings that its adherents repeat over and over to themselves, especially when relaxing. I would encourage clients to devise their own mantras based on their individual life experiences.

I endorse the Socratic procedures of "listening for the most deeply felt answer." I think the idea of slowing down and becoming aware of internal processes is crucial for all forms of successful therapy and living. Therapy is a process of retraining the brain to be constantly observing behavior and internal reactions, discovering motivations, and learning to enjoy the process.

My only criticism is perhaps partly a semantic one: Like most rational thinkers, Dr. Peiser tends to "cognize" almost everything and thus calls meditation "deep thinking." I think what he means to get at is deep *experiencing.* I don't think this is *just* semantic because one of the purposes of meditation is to inte-

grate the frontal cortex with all the other areas of the brain —
emotions, autonomic processes, memory, and so on — parts that
are usually less than conscious.

I would like to offer you a few remarks as to how meditative
techniques can be useful in developing a rational self-concept.
I'd like to see someone explore and extend these ideas with
regard to sensual awareness and sexual problems. As you know,
rational theory emphasizes unconditional self-acceptance; yet
we need specific, widely usable techniques for applying and
practicing these insights — to change the postulates of one's
self-theory, as well as the superficial self-concept.

In order to work at changing one's self-concept or self-theory,
it is helpful for a person to have a rational understanding of the
self — but not of an adolescent variety which talks about the
"real" self or the "good" self. A self, simply defined, is the sum
total of all experiences encountered by an organism inside and
outside its skin during its existence. Thus, the data base for a self
is a very large and unique set of experiences. To make contact
with a broad sample of these, one must suspend the usual cognitive filters and put aside the overlearned process of evaluation. I
would encourage people to develop a sense of detachment and
acceptance similar to what might be attributed to a god. The
basis for this stance is that it is humanly impossible to rate all the
pieces of the self — or to come up with a summary rating — so
don't try.

If bad feelings arise during these exercises (memories and so
on), one would know that an evaluation is taking place. Here it
would be advisable to stop and do a rational self-analysis. The
outcome of a meditative session is to feel calmness or mild
pleasantness — perhaps a "tingly" feeling.

A logical starting point would be with one's only given — the
body and its many varied but usually ignored sensations. This
might later be extended into sensual capacities, fantasies, and
then into sexual functioning.

As you can probably tell, I am not very concrete yet in terms of
techniques and steps, but I have some ideas as to desired outcome. It seems that this kind of practice would lead to a more
centered, inviolate self with good integration of experience into
one's self-theory and daily existence. The process implicitly attributes value to the self, and teaches forgiveness, detachment,
and flexibility of consciousness.

A lot of work remains to be done here but, armed with flexible
rational thinking, I believe a productive interchange can occur
between East and West.

The Rational-Emotive Approach to Marriage Counseling

BEN N. ARD, JR., Ph.D

Professor of Counseling, San Francisco State University; Clinical Director, Institute for Rational Living, San Francisco

Mark Twain, that perceptive observer of human beings, once said, "we all do no end of *feeling* and mistake it for *thinking*." Throughout the history of counseling and psychotherapy, from Sigmund Freud to Carl Rogers, the major emphasis has been on clients' irrational impulses and *feelings*, rather than on what they *think*. However, there has developed a new approach in counseling and psychotherapy which goes against this trend.

One of the most provocative and challenging developments in marriage counseling of recent years is the rational-emotive approach originated by psychologist and marriage counselor Albert Ellis, who is Executive Director of the Institute for Advanced Study in Rational Psychotherapy in New York City. Other contributors to this developing approach have been Robert A. Harper (1960), Ben Ard (1967, 1969, 1971, 1974), Virginia Anne Church (1974), and Leonard Diamond and Eleanor Songor (1972), to mention just a few.

In considering the kinds of problems marital partners face, we may divide the reasons for unhappy marriages into two main causes: (1) real incompatibility between the spouses, and (2) neurotic disturbances on the part of either or both the husband and wife which make them think and act so that there *appear* to be fundamental incompatibilities between them (Ellis and Harper, 1973). By *incompatibility* we mean truly irreconcilable differences in the basic attitudes, ideas, values, and interests of the marital partners. The main remedies here consist essentially of striving for mutual interests. This is often quite difficult, and sometimes the differences are irreconcilable. Then the realistic alternative is divorce (Ellis and Harper, 1973). A rational approach in this latter instance is for the marriage counselor to help his clients get though the divorce without unnecessary feelings of bitterness, resentment, failure, and guilt.

But what is a rational approach to marriage counseling for couples who do not have irreconcilable differences but whose neurotic disturbances are affecting their marriages? Rational-emotive therapy (RET) is well suited to couples who do not believe that they are emotionally disturbed but who know that they are not functioning adequately in some specific area of life, such as their marriage. Possibly most of these troubled people should seek intensive, long-term psychotherapy rather than marriage counseling, but the fact is that they do not (Harper, 1960). It therefore behooves the marriage counselor to be enough of a trained and experienced psychotherapist to deal adequately with the people who come for help (Ellis, 1956). If the marriage counselor knows and practices the essentials of RET, he or she will be well prepared in this regard (Ellis, 1962).

Most couples who come for marriage counseling are victims of what has been called "neurotic interaction" in marriage (Ellis, 1958a.) Such "neurotics" are individuals who are not intrinsically stupid and inept — but who *needlessly* suffer from intense and sustained anxiety, hostility, guilt, or depression. Neurotic interaction in marriage arises when a theoretically capable husband and wife behave in an irrational, marriage-defeating (and self-defeating) way with each other. If the theses of RET are correct, the marital neurotic interaction arises from *unrealistic* and *irrational ideas, beliefs,* or *value systems* of one or both of the marriage partners; and it is these beliefs and value systems which therefore must be concertedly *confronted, challenged,* and *changed,* if neurotic interaction is to cease.

What are some of these basic irrational ideas or beliefs that are common among clients of marriage counselors? One of the main irrational beliefs that people use to upset themselves is the notion that it is a *dire necessity* for an adult human being to be *approved* or *loved* by almost all the significant other people he or she encounters; that what *others* think of the person is most important instead of what the *person* thinks of ...elf or herself. The ancient Greek Stoic philosopher Epictetus once gave us some words of wisdom that are relevant here: "If any one trusts your body to the first man he met, you would be indignant, but yet you trust your mind to the chance comer, and allow it to be disturbed and confounded if he revile you; are you not ashamed to do so?" (quoted in Oates, 1940, p. 475).

Applied to marriage, this irrational idea means the "neurotic" male firmly believes that, no matter how he behaves, his mate, just because she *is* his mate, *should* love him; that if she does not respect him, life is a catastrophe; and that her main role as a wife is to help, aid, and succor *him*, rather than to be an individual in her own right. The "neurotic" female would hold similar irrational ideas about her mate. This leads to obvious conflicts in marital relationships.

The second major irrational belief which most "neurotics" in our society seem to hold is that a human being *should* or *must* be *perfectly* competent, adequate, talented, and intelligent — and is utterly *worthless* if incompetent in any significant way. Perfectionism and striving constantly for "success" are rampant in our society.

A third irrational assumption of the majority of "neurotics" in our culture is that they *should* severely *blame* themselves and others for mistakes and wrongdoings; and that punishing themselves or others will help prevent future mistakes. The concept of sin runs very deep in our culture. Many people upset themselves because of the behavior of other people — even when that behavior does not needlessly or gratuitously harm them. We need to return once again to the wisdom of Epictetus: "For no one shall harm you, without your consent; you will only be harmed, when you think that you are harmed" (Oates, 1940, p. 476).

A fourth irrational assumption which underlies and causes emotional disturbance is the notion that it is horrible, terrible, and catastrophic when things are not the way one would like them to be, and that one should not have to put off present pleasures for future gains. These ideas cause untold havoc in many marriages.

A fifth and final irrational belief which we shall consider here is the mythical supposition that most human unhappiness is *externally* caused or forced on one by outside people and events, and that one has virtually no control over one's emotions and cannot help feeling badly on many occasions. Actually, virtually all human unhappiness is *self*-caused and results from unjustified assumptions and internalized sentences stemming from these assumptions, such as some of the beliefs noted above. Another Stoic philosopher, Marcus Aurelius, has put the matter succinctly with regard to this last irrational idea: "If thou art pained by any external thing, it is not this thing that disturbs thee, but thy own judgment about it. And it is in thy power to wipe out this judgment now" (Oates, 1940, p. 550).

It is a staunch contention of Albert Ellis, then, that a seriously "neurotic" individual possesses, almost by definition, a set of basic postulates which are distinctly unrealistic, biased, and illogical (Ellis, 1975). These ideas or beliefs are implicit if not explicit in the person's behavior.

If what has been said so far is reasonably accurate, then the solution to the problem of treating "neurotic" interaction in marriage would appear to be fairly obvious (Ellis and Harper, 1973). If "neurotics" have basically irrational assumptions or value systems, and if these assumptions lead them to interact self-defeatingly with their mates, then the marriage counselor's function is to tackle not the problem of the marriage, or the neurotic interaction that exists between the marital partners, but the problem of the irrational ideas or beliefs that *cause* this neurosis. This consists largely of showing each of the marital partners who is neurotically interacting (1) that he or she has some basic irrational assumptions, (2) precisely what these assumptions are, (3) how they originally arose, (4) how they currently are being sustained by continual unconscious self-indoctrination, and (5) how they can be replaced with much more rational, less self-defeating philosophies (Ellis and Harper 1973).

In the rational-emotive aproach to marriage counseling (as opposed to other aproaches), there is an attempt to help the disturbed individuals acquire *three levels of insight* (Ellis, 1962). Insight Number 1 is the usual kind of understanding that the Freudians make much of — the individual's seeing that his or her *present* actions have a *prior* or *antecedent cause.*

An additional and unique contribution of RET, however, is that rational-emotive therapy does not stop there. It offers Insight Number 2 — the understanding that the irrational ideas acquired by the individual in the past are *still existent,* and that they largely exist today because *the individual keeps reindoctrinating himself or herself* with these ideas, consciously or unconsciously.

And, finally, Insight Number 3 is the full understanding by the disturbed individual that *he or she simply has got to change his or her erroneous and illogical thinking* in order to get better. Unless the client, after acquiring Insights Number 1 and 2, fully sees and accepts the fact that *there is no way* to get better except to forcefully and consistently attack his or her early-acquired and still firmly held irrational ideas, that client will not overcome his or her emotional disturbance.

The rational-emotive therapist, then, adds to the marriage counselor's other methods the more direct techniques of *confrontation, confutation, deindoctrination,* and *reeducation,* as well as a unique contribution known as *homework assignments.*

These techniques, while they may go against the teachings of some other approaches, probably account for the effectiveness and elegant solutions arrived at through the rational-emotive approach.

Confrontation means facing the client with the self-defeating irrational ideas, premises, or assumptions which are implicit in the client's behavior. The marriage counselor needs to be well trained and experienced in what has been called the Socratic dialogue. That is, the counselor needs to know how to ask questions that get at the philosophical assumptions of the clients.

Confutation means that the marriage counselor needs to have the question-asking skills of a good Philadelphia lawyer as well as sound training in logic and the scientific approach. He needs to be able to show the client where the client is mistaken in his or her assumptions, premises, or basic values, and particularly in the client's illogical thinking and overgeneralizations.

Deindoctrination means that the counselor needs to help the client get rid of the irrational assumptions, ideas, and conclusions previously indoctrinated in him or her by parents and the unquestioned assumptions of much of human society. This is hard work. It takes time. It is difficult but it is not impossible.

Reeducation is the final or ultimate technique the marriage counselor uses to help the client develop a more rational philosophy of life — one less self-defeating than what has guided the life-decisions previously made. This is the basic function of psychotherapy: reeducation.

Homework assignments are perhaps the fundamental tool or technique that the rational-emotive approach relies upon to get clients to question and challenge and change their self-defeating philosophies. Clients, if they are going to *get better* rather than just temporarily *feel* better in the therapeutic hour, need to risk themselves during the other hours of the week and try out what they are learning in therapy. The client's homework assignments can involve actually trying out new behavior, checking out self-talk by preparing homework assignment sheets about critical events and his or her reactions to them, and reading books that may help him or her move faster and more efficiently through problems (bibliotherapy).

Skilled therapists have written a whole series of books to help clients look at their problems and learn more effective ways of dealing with them. Ellis and Harper wrote *A Guide to Successful Marriage* (1973), a very helpful tool in marriage counseling. Ellis has also written books designed to help in specific areas — for example, clients who are single again (1963a, 1963b, 1970), who are having sexual problems (1960), or who decide to stay married to a "neurotic" partner (1975). Ard's book on treating psychosexual dysfunction (1974) is intended to help the intelligent lay person clear up some misunderstandings in the sexual area.

More concretely, rational-emotive therapy applied to marriage counseling shows each spouse that his or her disturbed behavior arises largely from underlying unrealistic beliefs; that these beliefs may have originally been learned from early familial and other environmental influences but that they are now being maintained by *internal verbalizations (self-talk)*; that the marriage partner, in consequence, is rarely the real cause of the problems; that the individual himself or herself is actually now creating and perpetuating these problems; that only by learning to observe carefully, to question, to think about, and to reformulate one's basic assumptions can one hope to understand the mate and oneself and to stop being unilaterally and interactionally "neurotic" (Ellis, 1962, p. 211).

Whenever marriage-counseling clients can be induced to *work* at changing their underlying neurosis-creating assumptions, significant personality changes ensue, and their interactions with their mates, families, or other intimate associates almost always improve. More specifically, this work usually consists of their (1) fully facing the fact that they themselves are doing something erroneously, however mistaken their intimates may *also* be; (2) seeing clearly that behind their "neurotic" mistakes and inefficiencies there are important irrational, unrealistic *philosophic assumptions; (3) vigorously and continually challenging* and *questioning* these assumptions by critically examining them and actively proving they are unfounded (i.e., doing homework assignments); (4) making due allowances for the intrinsic differences and frustrations of certain human relationships such as monogamous marriage; (5) learning to keep their mouths shut when one of their close associates is behaving badly, or else to objectively and *unblamefully* point out the other's mistakes while constructively trying to show him or her how to correct them in the future; and (6) above all, continually keeping in mind the fact that a relationship *is* a relationship, that it rarely can spontaneously progress in a supersmooth manner, and that it must often be actively worked at to recreate and maintain the honest affection with which it probably started.

While the rational-emotive approach is considered heretical by many in the field of marriage counseling who emphasize the importance of *expressing feelings* rather than *thinking rationally,* we may turn one final time to the ancient Greek philosopher of Stoicism, Epictetus, who as usual gets to the crux of the matter very quickly: "What disturbs men's minds is not events but their judgments on events. . . . And so when we are hindered, or disturbed, or distressed, let us never lay the blame on others, but on ourselves, that is, on our own judgments. To accuse others for one's own misfortunes is a sign of want of education; to accuse oneself shows that one's education has begun; to accuse neither oneself nor others shows that one's education is complete" (Oates, 1940, p. 469).

Put in simple A-B-C terms, it is rarely the external stimulus situation, A, which gives rise directly to an emotional reaction, C. Rather, it is almost always B (the individual's beliefs regarding, attitudes toward, or interpretation of A) which actually leads to his reaction, C.

Our job as marriage counselors, then, is to help clients see for themselves that it is necessary for them to work on the B step (their assumptions or internalized sentences) rather than rail at the external past situation (A), or wallow in their miseries at C. If we can get our clients to work on their assumptions and challenge their self-defeating values, they can develop more rational and therefore more self-satisfying philosophies and lives.

The Rational-Emotive Technique in Counseling Married Couples in Legal Crisis Settings

VIRGINIA ANNE CHURCH, J.D., Ph.D.

Former Dean of Lewis University College of Law, now Executive Director, Institute for Rational Living, San Francisco Branch

Dr. Ard has given you a very good overview of use of marriage-counseling techniques based on rational-emotive therapy. I want to confine my remarks to explaining the quasi-legal settings in which lawyers, conciliation court workers, and others working with people thinking of or intent upon divorce see their clients. I had been doing this kind of marriage counseling for over ten years before coming to Lewis [Lewis University College of Law] to train law students in marriage-crisis counseling techniques.

The first thing I identify as needing examination by counselor and client is the "twelfth irrational belief" (as I term it) that *the world should be fair and that mercy and justice must triumph.* Very few people, including lawyers, believe that statement represents an irrational belief — yet it is. Let me read you an article I recently completed called "Why the World Should Not Be Fair."

Judge Justice had always believed the world should be fair, and justice (or mercy) must triumph. This was his slogan, in fact, during his election campaign. The first day on the bench, Judge Justice discovered a problem with that concept. After two days on the bench he, being a rather open-minded, realistic sort of person, discovered that there was, literally, no such thing as fair!

Martin and Marjorie had been married for ten years and had four children, two under four years of age. The couple had many problems, money among them. They decided to get a divorce in Judge Justice's no-fault state.

Martin commuted long hours to work in Center City. He earned $125 a week. Marjorie had never worked and had not completed high school. None of the children was over eight years old. Her, and their, living expenses ran $125 per week. Martin, having left Marjorie, now had living expenses of his own. Neither had parents able to care for the kids.

The judge's problem was the usual "simple" one of deciding how much money to give Marjorie and for how long. He had only to be "fair."

But was it so simple? How do you decide what is fair? "Well," he thought, "dividing the income and assets in half, *that* would be fair."

It developed the couple owned nothing but bills and the secondhand furniture — just enough beds and chairs to provide the wife and children with minimal living facilities.

"Besides," Marjorie's lawyer pointed out reasonably enough, "how could the judge even consider expecting five people to live on the same amount as one person — fair?"

Judge Justice hadn't thought of it that way. "Well, then," he said (he really wanted awfully badly to be "fair"). "Well, then, we'll do it mathematically. Nothing could be fairer than that!" And so, he announced that he would give Marjorie five-sixths and Martin one-sixth — $104.16 to Marjorie — and, let's see — $20.84 to Martin each week. At this, Martin's lawyer rose to his feet bellowing, "That's not fair!" When he had calmed down a little, he explained, "Martin makes *all* the money. He can't live on $20.84 a week. That wouldn't even rent him a room, much less buy him food and clothes, operate his car. If he has no car, he can't get to work. The family will earn nothing!"

And so it went — for hours. "Fair" kept eluding the good Judge Justice. At the end of that first day, under the press of other business, he went ahead and made his first "unfair" decision.

The sad plight of the would-be-fair judge is not really a fairy tale. It happens all the time all over the world, and especially in America, where we have what amounts to a cultural hang-up about being "fair"! That "fair" cannot be determined — except from a particular view or bias — never seems to be considered by people demanding it.

In 1973, I gave a simple rating scale questionnaire to a group of dedicated family-law attorneys gathered in national conclave in Washington. The test required that the lawyers rate each of Albert Ellis's "common rational beliefs" on a five-point scale from "certainly true" to "never true." To check out my own speculation that even those who dealt most closely with the administration of justice would not realize "there was no fair" . . . and that justice was merely a construct which was in no way absolute . . . I added to the bottom of Ellis's list a twelfth "irrational belief":

> That the world (and especially other people) should be fair, and that justice (or mercy) must triumph!

Interestingly (especially to the many anti-lawyer laymen with whom I associate), almost everyone in the room marked that particular belief as "certainly true." The judges in the room *all* did so.

Yet, each of them had firsthand knowledge that there was no such thing as fair. They lived with it every day. Maxie Maultsby has said, without fear of refutation — "What *should* happen *does* happen" — meaning that whatever happens only does so after all of the objective prerequisites for its happening have occurred. Had they not so occurred, then something else would have happened instead of what did.

Yet, people continue to speak of "fairness" and justice as if it could be accomplished in every case if people only would do as they *should* do!

Think about it. When we say the world *should* be fair, don't we really mean "fair to us" — or "to our side"? The best way to ferret this out is usually to suggest that the winner in a lawsuit divide the gain with the loser, or (even more radical) that the loser *voluntarily* pay the costs of the winner's action against him. (That happens frequently enough by order, but never, to my knowledge, voluntarily and not even without a great deal of consternation and screams of "unfair"!) So, we really seem to mean "other people *should* be fair to me."

Usually. Of course, there are those who really do believe the world, and especially they, themselves, *should* do what is just even when it works against them. But they are operating on a "biblical" belief the Bible never really promised — "if you do unto others fairly, they will also do so unto you fairly." How do I know that is what they think? Well, of course, I don't know. But I can infer it from long years of professional experience with such people's outrage and resentment when they are not, in fact, treated fairly in return! My experience both as a lawyer and as a rational therapist has led me to observe that people only become angry about violations of their own irrational beliefs, not about things they have no firm belief about.

"O.K., then," someone usually says in my group when I

introduce Belief #12. "What about those people who really are fair, even though they are always getting it in the neck?"

"Oh, I agree," I say. "My father, for instance, always fed the parking meter whatever time he was overparked before he drove off — even when there was no cop in sight. Now, that's fair. Render unto Caesar, etc."

"That's not fair — that's stupid!" many people will declare. "There's no need to be *that* kind of fair." Well — I try again —

> How about the mother who has $100 and three children to divide it between? The eldest child has been lying around not working and smoking pot all summer. The middle child, on the other hand, has worked downtown as a delivery boy, making $100 a week in tips. The youngest child has remained at home, caring for the house, watching the children of her mother's sister, and generally tying herself down serving the family.
>
> What's the mother to do? Justice would require an equal division . . . three children . . . $33.33 each. Mercy or equity might recommend another division . . . and practicality of who needed money, who had access to making it might be quite different. My point is, of course, that whatever the mother did, she could be accused (and correctly from *each* point of view) and making an "unfair" decision.

The justice lovers normally want justice softened to "mercy" when it is directed at them, and kept to strict justice when directed at those who have injured them. A rapist who has "ravished" a young girl (meaning he had sexual intercourse with her against her wishes) *should* be killed — according to justice (the laws in our state). If the girl was your young daughter who you believe (and want everyone else to believe) is a virgin, you will likely feel quite justified in demanding the penalty, especially if statistics show there is too much of this attacking going on and people are not "safe in the local streets." If, on the other hand, the young rapist is your young son — the chances are you'll be screaming "mitigating circumstances" — the girl was unchaste, she tantalized or seduced him, he's never done any such thing before. You would likely say and believe "she must have brought it on herself — the law is too strict, too harsh — justice must be tempered with mercy."

When all the verbiage is removed you come down to the unavoidable truth: two peoples' ideas of fair are, as usual, quite different . . . justice for one, mercy for the other. In one case the man lives to repent (or not to) and in the other he dies (whether or not he repents).

Justice is a harsh concept: an eye for an eye and a tooth for a tooth. Publicly, we no longer believe in that kind of justice. Or if we do, we will be daily disappointed and enraged (as, indeed, many of us are!). Mercy, on the other hand is, indeed, like the "gentle dew that droppeth down from heaven." It is just as hard to catch and hold.

The reason these are not merely interesting observations on human behavior, rather than a proposed #12 irrational belief, is just this common acceptance that things *should* be a way we all can tell (after a little reflection or in vivo testing) they cannot, in fact, be.

If the world were to be "fair" it could only be accomplished by legislating what is "fair," and then requiring everyone to follow that rule without exception. We don't want that! We want, I venture to suggest, something quite different. We want and prefer actions toward us and toward others that, as near as possible are in keeping with our best interests first, and their best interests (unless they strongly invade ours) a close second. We want to weigh and judge each situation on its own merits, and then we want to do an imperfect best. This best will be based on the situation as we understand it at the time we are making the decision. That is what we and our courts do most of the time when trying to arrive at "fair," so that is likely to be a practical approach.

Why should we give up the notion that "fair" can actually be determined and achieved? First, because it can't be! Setting an impossible goal as one we *must* achieve, leads to poor emotional consequences. We will be likely to upset ourselves unreasonably, to gnash our teeth (bad for the enamel as well as for the neck and jaw muscles), give ourselves headaches, ulcers, hypertension, and colitis . . . and for what? Because we *choose* to hold this "impossible dream" favored by Don Quixote and Diogenes as a fool's quest so long ago.

We can, however, idealistically continue to "prefer" more "fair" behavior than "unfair" behavior. We can *strongly prefer and seek to achieve this*. This whole system for the administration of justice is dedicated to so doing. These are worthy ends. But, we would better give up the notion of absolutes . . . absolute mercy and absolute fairness! These do not exist. They are beyond the grasp or even reckoning of fallible human beings. What we can do is do the best we can to consider our own and other people's best interests, and to behave rationally in accordance with them. That is enough of a chore without requiring magical infallible behavior of us all. Man is not God, and Unfairness *is* reality. Therefore, the World should not be fair, and indeed that is a true fact — objectively determined — for *it is not*. ■

That article accurately presents the dilemma of the bench and bar and of people seeking "fairness" as an ideal disguising the usual fallible self-seeking that we all rationally engage in, when dealing nonmagically.

How does one counsel with such people? My technique is very directive and largely didactic. Open with something like, "I'll bet you don't know where your feeling [the one he or she was just talking about and putting off on the spouse] actually comes from! I find many or even most people have very little understanding of how their brains work to create their emotions. For example, many people believe, as you seem to, that what he or she does to you, or just 'does' *causes* you to feel some particular way." I stop to allow input, then go on to explain the A-B-C's of RET. In doing this I usually refer to the graphics which you see here on the stand — the RET posters which I have hanging around my office or group room.

This technique of using eye as well as ear is often further buttressed by teaching the client to do Maxie Maultsby's RSA's (rational self-analyses) in writing on the particular issue under discussion. This adds hand to eye and ear and, when buttressed even further by tape-recording the session for the client's later review, you have maximized the possibility of the client's learning something different and retaining at least some of it.

My experience with this first intensive treatment session is that it runs a good hour and a half. That is not unusual in legal settings, where intake interviews are expected to take one to two hours. It is less usual in psychological settings — especially in RET ones, where the interview usually is expected to take thirty minutes. However, I stick rationally to the method as I have secured rather consistently good results from it, which reenforce my continuance. Moreover I am tending to believe that an intensive week with the couple working three to eight hours and more a day with a variety of modalities and interactions would be even better to break through the crisis state of projection, blaming, resentment, anger, and/or depression that is usually brought to the law office obscuring real issues and rational solutions.

Subsequent sessions allow the client more opportunity to talk and express their "feelings," but are always controlled within the RET model so that the client does not leave with any stated projections intact (or at least with as few as possible). Many will not have been elegantly dealt with, but a self-treatment plan emerges early in the sessions and is modified (usually expanded) as the sessions go on.

The usual number of sessions varies from six to perhaps twelve or more. I like to include the people in a same-sex group of other people going through the same kind of decision-making with different values and learning backgrounds. I have described those groups in the pamphlets the Institute for Rational Living puts out as "Rational Counseling in a Legal Setting."

Usually we can establish some goals after two or three sessions, and often it becomes possible at about that point to involve the other partner in reading some of the RET materials. *How to Live with a "Neurotic"* (Ellis, 1975) and *Overcoming Depression* (Hauck, 1973) are the two books I hand out besides the standard *A New Guide to Rational Living* (Ellis and Harper, 1975). *How to Live with a "Neurotic"* is quite popular in this setting, as the client I get always believes (at least initially) that the other is the neurotic, and takes the book home almost licking his or her chops at the prospect of reading all about that "evil" other. The usual result is that they come in somewhat sheepishly for the next visit admitting they found not only the spouse but themselves in that category. One client so disturbed herself at discovering for the first time that her husband had been living for years with a neurotic — and much more placidly and uncomplainingly than she had — that my next offering was *Overcoming Depression!*

My experience with this directive teaching technique has been good. How much of the success rate is due to its use within a last-ditch, rather authoritative setting, I can't say. However, most other legal counselors seem to feel the law-office setting contraindicates conciliation because people have made an investment in their decision to divorce. That may be true — at least for them. It may well be that those first few "teaching" sessions whereby I help them reprogram their "okayness" to permit a relook at a mistake or possible poor solution, relabeling it as a reasonable or at least logical act based on circumstances as they then were (including self-understanding as it then was), produce the different result. That fits into what you've been hearing elsewhere with Maxie Maultsby, Albert Ellis, and others saying "everything happens as it should have happened" because all the prerequisites for its happening that way have occurred. I remind my clients that 20-20 hindsight is easy, but to broaden it to recognition that the best reason any of us ever did anything stupid or with any kind of poor results is actually because *at the time* it seemed like a good idea and that only subsequent learning has shown us it wasn't!

I lay considerable emphasis on the irrational beliefs (as a teaching device, I also use the three whines in therapy as simpler and all-inclusive) and my clients in legal counseling groups will remind themselves that they are sounding just like number 2 or number 1 or whichever. We talk a lot about changing behavior and how the first step to doing that is recognizing that old habits and the feelings supporting them can be changed. The second step is learning to get a "red flag" up to interrupt the nearly automatic old behavior and feelings combo. Dr. Lazarus talks a good bit about these interruptions, and you might profit from reviewing his work.

Joint sessions are good, but I tend to use them much further along than most family therapists. I agree to see people jointly the first time (if they want and to give myself a view of the interaction). Then I insist on seeing them individually and in same-sex groups where possible, to allow for quickest learning of new attitudes and challenging the old beliefs out of the presence of the other partner (before whom "face" might make open learning difficult because of the investment in the previously held position). Once the new RET outlook is trained in and made a part of the client's thinking, joint sessions can be remarkably productive. Before that they tend to reinforce old wounds.

In summary, my marriage counseling approach deals with crisis intervention on a time-limited basis with people who "think" they want a divorce. The important goal is to interrupt the attitudinal supports for these negative feelings, and to teach that emotional responses can be changed and how to change them to produce more goal-directed and satisfying feeling responses to previously disturbing or disappointing situations.

There follows retraining of adaptive and happiness-producing communication techniques and new ways of interpreting events and other people's behaviors. This is followed by goal-setting conferences in which the couple (or the individual with whom the techniques are being used) rethinks the marriage problems, takes responsibility for the various portions of the nonsatisfying results, and for a self-treatment plan to change those attitudes, behaviors, and feelings which are presently interfering with their own and each other's enjoyment of the marriage.

The effectiveness of this program is linked strongly to use of the bibliotherapy and graphic aids available through the rational network, and I use my own copy of the Family game — *Play Yourself Free* – in working with families by indirection.

Ten Heavy Facts About Sex

SOL GORDON, Ph.D.

Syracuse University

Not too long ago I was on a television program with a leading reactionary. He looked up at me and he said, "It's *you*! It's people like you that are responsible for all the venereal disease in Syracuse!" I didn't know whether to be proud . . . or . . . . He went on to say, "Back in the good old days, we didn't have people like you, and sex and love were marvelous . . . . " I recovered, of course, and I said, "Come on, you and I are the same age. What are you talking about? Look at all the people who are getting divorced! Look at all the people we know who have sexual problems! Look at all the wars we started!" And he looked up at me, and he said, "Don't you dare spoil the good old days for me!"

Well, my main message is . . . you have to be the sex educators of your own children. Some of you are already married. Most all of the rest of you will marry whether you like it or not. You'll have 1.8 children, a color television, a dog, and a gerbil, and you'll have an All-American family. And what I'm saying to you is that you need to be the sex educators of your children. But first you need to become a little more comfortable with your own sexuality, and for the next thirty-five minutes I'm going to help you become comfortable with your sexuality. That's about how long it takes.

The first thing you need to know about is masturbation. As you know, it's the latest thing — everybody's into it these days. When I was growing up, there was no problem. You got from masturbation tired blood, mental illness, blindness (that's why I wear glasses). But we were pioneers in those days! Now, of course, the modern mother says to the modern child, "Honey, it's okay to masturbate." Then she pauses, and she says, "It's okay, if you don't do it too much." And nobody in the United States knows HOW MUCH IS TOO MUCH. That's the All-American dilemma! How much is too much! Once a year, twice a week, after every meal . . . nobody knows!

Oh, you read in the medical literature, "We doctors, of course, know that masturbation is a normal expression of sexuality, but if you do it too much, you have a tendency to be shy, retiring, narcissistic, and you have no friends." Now I'm asking you, how long does it take to masturbate? Why should it interfere with friendships? Some of my best friends are masturbators! And some people I know never masturbate and they have no friends. Masturbation is a normal expression of sexuality at any age, at any time. ONCE is too much if you don't like it. If you don't like it, don't do it. That's all there is to it. Some women achieve their only orgasms by masturbation. And some women begin to introduce themselves to their own bodies that way.

Now the next thing we need to understand, of course, is the female orgasm. Everybody's into the female orgasm these days. You cannot read any woman's magazine without something about the female orgasm. It's reached the point that women are so insecure that unless they have a Good Housekeeping Seal they don't even know if they're having one. Or they consult their doctors — and, of course, the doctors know less about it than they do. And the women say, "Doctor, how do I know if I have one?" And he responds in all his wisdom, "If you had one, you would *know* it."

Men and women have sex these days. The first thing he says to her is, "Did you have one?" What kind of conversation is that? Is there no tomorrow?

You know, before Freud, women weren't even supposed to have any. Freud came along, and he said, "You women can have vaginal ones," and the women were satisfied with vaginal orgasms for fifty years. And then Masters and Johnson came along and said, "Those vaginal ones aren't good enough! You need clitoral ones now." And *now!* Those clitoral ones are not good enough. Because you have to have MULTIPLE ones and SIMULTANEOUSLY! They don't want to leave women alone! I predict in five years' time the orgasm is going to be titular. We're moving up!

What has happened in the field of human sexuality is that it has become like gymnastics — the pursuit of the ultimate, multiple, simultaneous orgasm. Where is love? Where is caring for another human being? The ultimate arousal is getting to know another human being. Some of the most bored, alienated, unhappy people I know are sexually "liberated." The All-American guy is the guy on the make. You know, a guy who's on the make hates women. He might as well put his prick in a knothole for all it's worth. Because he abandons each woman as he goes along. We have to introduce the concept of love and caring for another human being as part of our sexuality. Sexual intercourse is only a small component of an intimate relationship.

I'm now going to reveal something that no male has ever revealed in Illinois before, at least not standing up. I don't know if you're ready for this, but it is *heavy*. You see, everybody's talking about the female orgasm, but nobody is paying any attention to the male orgasm. The reason nobody's paying any attention to the male orgasm is that males have been faking it for centuries. I'm going to now destroy the last vestige of male supremacy that exists. You see, women are supposed to have orgasms only when they're emotionally ready or if they've had certain kinds of parents. But males: *animals.* They have an ejaculation . . . pschewww . . . orgasm. That's what they would like you to think. Even males think that sometimes because they've been so brainwashed. As a matter of fact, a male can have an ejaculation and feel NOTHING AT ALL, or feel a little bitty thing, or feel WOW! The male orgasm is just as psychological as the female's. And I want you women to ask your friends tonight or tomorrow. Ask them about their orgasms, and if a man denies what I have revealed, he's either not telling the truth or he can't be trusted. Would any male like to contradict what I've just said? Stand up. You see? THAT'S RESEARCH!

Now. We're getting somewhere, aren't we? As a matter of fact, much of the work in the field of human sexuality is based on a series of false assumptions documented by research. Listen. Pay attention. *Much of the work in the field of human sexuality is based on a series of false assumptions documented by research.* Got it now? All right. I'll explain it.

They say that a male reaches his peak at age nineteen sexually. You read it in all the books. And the women, they have to wait until they're twenty-nine. Okay? How do they know that? Did they do a random sample of eighty-five-year-old men and women and ask them when they reached their peak? I thought I'd reached my prime twenty years ago until the other night.

A kid came to my office and he said he's twenty years old . . . he's past his prime, and he hasn't even started yet! Where do we get nonsense like that? Or they say the average couple has 2.2 outlets a week. (You get points for "perversions.") Well, how do they get this information? A psychologist goes to the home of a couple, and asks the couple, "How many outlets do you have?" Of course the couple thinks, "Electrical outlets . . . " But finally they get it clarified that they're talking about SEX. And, of course, what happens is that the couple lies. Have you ever heard of any couple who tells the truth about their outlets? The couple lies, the psychologist copies down the lies, averages up all the lies, and comes out with 2.2, and everybody in America feels inferior.

You women don't know this, but when men go to the bathroom . . . they go to their own separate little urinal. And there may be six or eight urinals. And the men, they stand up and they're supposed to go look in their own urinal. But they don't. No! They're looking for a penis that's smaller than theirs. It's a lifelong pursuit! And what the male doesn't know and understand — nor the female — is that you cannot tell the size of the penis from observing its nonerect state. There's *no way* you can judge the size of the penis from looking at its nonerect state. There are some men that have little bitty penises, that hang real small . . . you've seen 'em. And there are some men who have penises that hang long . . . you've seen those, too. Especially the big ones, because they're boasting all the time. But, you see, the man who has that little bitty one there, when he has an erection, it could be six or seven inches. And his fantasy is that, if his little bitty one extends to six or seven inches, then the ones that hang long must be something like a couple of feet. But the plain fact is that some of those little bitty ones extend *longer* than some of those that hang long. So some of you men who've been boasting about your big ones, forget about it.

Besides, size doesn't matter. There's no way anybody can say that the larger the penis the more satisfaction. It's simply not true.

Then there are the women who worry about the size of their vaginas. They think they're too small. Very interesting! Because they hear about these enormous penises. And they start worrying that maybe they're too small. But you *know*, a BABY comes out of that place. I don't know if you realize it — even the smallest baby is this big — and there's no penis that big in the whole *world!* You can be psychologically tight, but you can't be physically too small.

And there are just a few more things you need to know.

A young man came to see me, and he was very anxious to talk to me. He said, "I heard you speak, and I have to talk to you. Can I trust you?"

I replied, "No . . . "

He said, "Why? You're a psychologist. You're supposed to be trusted!"

I said, "Me, you can't trust."

"How come?"

I said, "I don't even know you! I don't even know if I'm gonna like you. And the same is the other way around. Trust comes at the end, not at the beginning. All meaningful relationships involve risk . . . without risk, nothing happens in life. If you're going to operate on the assumption that if you tell people something about yourself, they'll take advantage of you, so you won't tell . . . then you're stuck. You have to take the risk, the possibility that somebody will like you, somebody will hate you, somebody will take advantage of you, somebody will exploit you. Without risk, nothing happens in life."

So he said, "Okay, I'll risk it." He said, "I don't know how to tell you, though."

I said, "Tell me, already." (I don't fool around.)

He said, "I'm a homosexual."

I said, "Well, have you ever had any homosexual experiences?"

He said, "Omigod, of course not. What do you take me for?"

I said, "I don't *know* yet. Have you ever had any heterosexual experiences?"

He said, "Certainly not! I'm a homosexual."

I said, "So far, the diagnosis is 'antisexual.' " Then I said, "Okay, tell me your life history; you have five minutes."

And he said, "When I was thirteen years old, I started to have these homosexual dreams, I started to get turned on by other guys . . . ."

I said, "Stop already, I know the rest of your life history. You didn't know that all thoughts, all fantasies, all dreams, all wishes are normal. If you feel guilty about a thought, you'll have that thought over and over again. It becomes a self-fulfilling prophecy."

The more guilt you feel about a thought, the more you'll have them, and the more compelling those thoughts are. It's one of the most dynamic concepts in all of sexuality. The more you think about something, and the more guilty you feel, the more you have these thoughts! We have to somehow get across the message that all thoughts, all dreams, all wishes, all fantasies are normal! Behavior can be immoral or abnormal, but not thoughts. I walk down the street and I see a pretty girl, I rape her. The girl doesn't know about it; my wife doesn't know about it; and I enjoy my walk. Now, I don't want to give you the impression that that's my total repertoire . . . but I enjoy walks!

All thoughts are normal. And if you have a thought that's unacceptable to you, if you know that it was normal, it will pass. And nothing will happen.

A kid sees his sister in the nude and thinks about having sex with her. If he knows that all thoughts are normal, it'll pass and nothing will happen. If he feels guilty about the thought, he'll have that thought over and over again; it'll preoccupy this kid, and sometimes he will repress it and develop symptoms as a result. It can have a *devastating* effect on the personality.

So what does an intellectually minded kid do? Where does he go to find his identity? He goes to a psychiatric textbook, looks up homosexuality in the index . . . and it doesn't exactly fit because he's never had any homosexual experiences, and then he goes to an advanced psychiatric textbook, and he finds . . . what? *Latent homosexuality.*

There he is. He's latent. He's identified, diagnosed, and *finished* for the rest of his life. And he hasn't even done anything yet. Latent is something you're supposed to have within you. You might as well say all women are latently pregnant. Latency is a figment of the psychiatric imagination. The psychiatrists have made it up as a weapon against all of you. When I was growing up, "everybody" was a latent psychopath. Anybody we didn't like, didn't enjoy, wanted institutionalized, or didn't understand was a psychopath. Latent. And the fashionable latency is now what? You're either a latent schizophrenic or a latent homosexual.

You know what Thomas Szasz says about schizophrenia? You talk to God, you're religious . . . but if God talks back to you, you're schizophrenic.

Hear me now. There are twenty people in this room who are nothing but latent. Nobody knows or understands you; latency means potential creativity. That's all. Don't let anybody make a diagnosis out of you. Maybe tomorrow, maybe the next day after tomorrow, you won't be latent any more. But there are twenty of you who have just nothing going for you except your latencies. And do express yourself soon, because you don't want to be too late(nt). Listen. We are all latent everything there is. We're all latent homosexuals, we'll all latent heterosexuals, we're all latent bisexuals, and we're even all latent trisexuals. Would you like to know what a trisexual is? A trisexual is somebody who tries everything.

We have to understand that there's only one definition of a homosexual and that is a person in his or her adult life who has and prefers relations with members of the same sex. A few homosexual experiences don't make a person homosexual, any more than a few drinks make a person alcoholic. Thoughts, dreams, fantasies of homosexuality don't make a person a homosexual. I can tell you that every time I make that statement on television or radio, somebody will call me up and say, "I can't tell you how thrilled I am! When I was thirteen years old I had this homosexual experience; I thought I would be homosexual the rest of my life. And I even like girls, I want to get married. Now I'm going to marry."

And that wasn't five years of psychoanalysis . . . that was five minutes of Sol Gordon.

Or sometimes they say, "A guy who's frightened of homosexuals must be a latent homosexual." I have a message for you. A guy who's frightened of homosexuals is *frightened of homosexuals!* If you are afraid of dogs, does that make you a latent dog?

Now, I have something to report to you. Humor is very important. If you want to be a sex educator, you'd better have a sense of humor. Because humor relieves anxiety, and sexuality is a tremendous anxiety-provoking subject for everybody. That's why people find it so difficult to talk in a mature way about it. They have to jest. They have to joke. They have to tell obscene stories. So we need a little humor to relieve anxiety. If you don't have a sense of humor . . . develop one. And if you can't develop one, you can always become a supervisor.

Now, there are five people in this room who haven't cracked a smile yet. I want to tell you something about yourselves: You're in trouble. And you know who you are. See me after this session.

Without humor everything becomes a trauma. Your kid walks into the bedroom. You parents are having sex. What should you do? Just tell the kid to get the hell out . . . and in the morning you can apologize for not having said, "PLEASE get the hell out!" And then you can explain to the child what you were doing, and then the child will ask, "Can I watch next time?" Say No. You can help the child with his own concepts of privacy. And then there are some people who say, "Ho! The child has witnessed the primal thing! Five years of psychoanalysis *at least!* BULL-SHIT! Some hungry psychoanalyst made it up!

Not everything's a trauma. If you catch your children playing doctor, what should you do? Be careful if it's a girl, because we need more women doctors. Holy Jesus, it's not a tragedy! Not everything's a trauma. Two little girls were walking in the park, and along came this man with the proverbial raincoat. He stopped in front of them . . . and he opened up his coat and exposed himself. And one little girl said, "Ha! My father's got one of those!" And the other little girl said, "Ha! My dad's is bigger than yours!" The man fled in terror.

Not everything's a trauma! Why travel heavy if you can travel light? Write that down. Pass it along as a rumor. Because if you tell people it's the truth, nobody will believe you. We need more rumors.

They say the Women's Liberation Movement is the greatest

evil. "Women are aggressive these days . . . you know . . . " And because women are aggressive, you know what's happening to the men? Impotent. Some broken-down psychologist with nothing better to do reports in the literature that all the men he's been seeing lately . . . impotent. And who's responsible? Aggressive women! Well, I have news for you. For every man made impotent, ten thousand of us have become liberated as a result of the Women's Liberation Movement. And where did I get these facts? I made them up . . . because my made-up facts are just as good as their made-up facts. Well! The Women's Liberation Movement represents the greatest source of freedom and liberation for all of us for all times! Women are not aggressive; women are *assertive* . . . . Women are assertive, and if they don't get justice, they become aggressive. I personally hate housework. I can't stand housework! But I'm doing it now, because I have an assertive wife, and I don't want her to become aggressive.

And I have a warning for some of you women: If you're going to help your friend or spouse through medical school or law school, or whatever kind of schooling . . . be sure to sign a contract, so that when he finishes, *you'll* go. Or, better still, you go first. The Women's Liberation Movement cannot be defined in terms of its enemies. Women can be fully liberated and still be housewives. They still can have babies and take care of them! Liberation is in the mind; liberation has to do with equal opportunities and equal responsibilities, and equal respect for each other! It has nothing to do with the kind of work people do; but if you do the same work, then it has to do with equal pay. That's the Women's Liberation Movement. It has nothing to do with aggressivity, it has nothing to do with braless women. It has nothing to do with not having babies! Nothing! It has to do with having babies by choice by marrying people you love. One of the best things that is happening on the college campuses today is that people are relating to each other; because they love each other — they care about each other — for the first time in history, people are marrying because they *love* each other. And they're going to have the number of children they want and when they want them. This is unique in our history.

And the problem is, of course, that this movement has not extended to the high schools or the junior high schools yet. The guys still have lines. Girls don't have lines. I don't know why! How come only high school boys have lines? "Honey, if you really love me . . . you'll have sex with me." "Honey, . . . if I don't have sex, I'll become mentally ill." The girl must immediately respond that she never heard of a guy dying from an unrelieved erection. Or they want to have sex, and the guy says,

"Oh, honey . . . we have to have sex, because it's okay. . . ." The girl says, "But where's your condom?" The guy says, "Oh, honey, I get no *feelings* out of a condom." And the girl must immediately respond by saying, "All the other boys I know get plenty of feelings with condoms! What's the matter with you?"

The girls need to have some *lines,* because girls are still exploited. The birth rate is declining in every age group except among teen-agers. In 1975 there were a million pregnancies among teen-agers; 260,000 girls gave birth to babies out of wedlock; 320,000 or more gave birth but they married to cover up the pregnancy. About 70 percent of teen-age marriages break up, especially if they're covering up a pregnancy. And about 400,000 will have abortions. There were three million new cases of venereal disease last year; two-thirds of them were among young people under twenty-four years of age. The highest rate of increase, 150 percent, was in the age group between eleven and fifteen. We're in a lot of trouble. And they *say,* you know what they *say!* "IT'S THE PILL THAT'S MAKING GIRLS PROMISCUOUS!" You know that less than 20 percent of sexually active teen-age girls are regularly on the Pill! If only they would *use* the Pill, we wouldn't be in so much trouble. Or they say, "If you tell kids about sex, they'll do it." They're doin' it.

In the twenty-five years that I've been working, no kid has ever asked my permission for sex. Half of all the young people in high school today will have sexual relations, whether we like it or not, or whether *they like it or not.* But some kids ask me, "Is it normal to wait until marriage?" The pressure for sexual behavior is so great that they want to know from me if it's normal to wait. And I say, "Yes, it's normal to wait." And I could stop right there. But I add, "Listen, if you're gonna wait, I hope you don't expect a simultaneous orgasm on your wedding night. If you did, you might ask yourself, the question, 'For this I waited?' "

You know, the boys are still saying things like, "Oh, of course, I'm a boy. I'm gonna have sex. I'm a boy! But when I marry . . . I'm gonna marry a virgin." (If there are any left.) I say, "I hope you'll marry a person! Not a hymen."

Well, we've broken the spirit of one person, there are now only four people who haven't cracked a smile. One person . . . there's a little smile . . . couldn't help it, couldn't help it . . . somehow or other. . . . You know, there are these four people left who say, "He's a showman!" So . . . ? Why does sex education have to be boring? Or are you attacking me for being effective?

The lunatic fringe in this country very often says to me, "But you're a showman." So . . . ? Or they say, "Look how much harm you can do children . . . Johnnie asked his mother about where he came from and his mother gave him this long elaborate explanation, and Johnnie says, 'I didn't want to know that, I just wanted to know whether I came from Santa Monica or not.' " So . . . ? Now Johnnie knows that he came from Santa Monica and how he got there. Why is that an attack on sex educators? Why is that an attack on the mother who gives information — more than what a child wants to know?

And by the way, one of the reasons parents aren't the sex educators of their own children is they're afraid they'll overstimulate their children with too much information. You *can't* tell an American child too much about anything. Have you ever tried? They'll turn you off, they'll be bored, whatever. You can't tell an American child too much about anything. And parents don't have to be supercomfortable. Who's comfortable about anything these days? You can just try to be comfortable, a little bit more comfortable, but you don't have to be supercomfortable to be the sex educator of your own children. When's the last time somebody said to you, "Don't worry!" and you stopped? You can't tell a child too much. You don't have to know that much in order to be the sex educators of your children . . . you simply have to be askable. If you bathe with the child, the child will ask you questions. The child will say, "How come you have one and I don't have any?" Or "How come you have two and I don't have any?" And you don't have to worry about parading around in the nude. Sometimes, at four or five, the child's own sense of modesty will tell you when to stop. The child will close the bathroom door . . . the child will want to dress alone. In this way she or he'll learn something about privacy. But if the child doesn't stop by twenty, you can stop.

And use the correct terminology! What is this "wee-wee" and "poo-poo" or "pee-wee"? A kid I knew thought he had a "dinga-ling" until he was ten years old. Use penis, use vagina. And if you can't *say it*, practice tonight! Everybody practice tonight, ten penises, ten vaginas! If you all do it at ten o'clock, Chicago will resound with penises and vaginas! And if your little honey comes in and says, "Hey, mom, fuck," what should you do? The average mother will slap the kid in the face and say, "Don't you ever say a word like that! Don't you ever think it!" And no wonder little honey stutters on the letter "f" for the rest of her life!

What should you do?

The thing a modern parent should do is say, "Listen, honey, fuck is another word for sexual intercourse. That's when your mommy and daddy or man and woman have sex, and the man puts his penis into the woman's vagina, sperm gets circulated around and reaches the egg and a baby gets started maybe, but you don't have to worry because we use birth control." The kid may not know what the fuck you're talking about. But it doesn't matter! Look what you have accomplished with one little obscenity! First of all, the child will never use that obscenity against you as a weapon. You have sensitized it. Secondly, you have become an askable parent. The child knows that he can ask you anything. What a fantastic achievement with just one little obscenity!

Be the sex educators of your own children. Be an askable parent. Don't be afraid to tell your children too much. Don't be afraid to initiate the conversation. Don't be afraid if you are teachers or in the helping professions to respond to children's questions. They are asking you because they can't ask their parents. And be ever alert to the lunatic fringe in this country that is saying that knowledge is harmful. All opposition to sex education in this country is based on the notion that knowledge is harmful. And if a subject is controversial, it's dangerous. They tell me, "We can't have sex education in the schools, because it's controversial!" So . . . ? If you're not controversial, you don't have anything to say! Let's spread that around as a rumor.

We have in this country a lunatic fringe that believes that, if we introduce sex education into the schools, it will be an introduction to Communism. If you think for one minute that I am making this up, I would like to read to you from an article that appeared recently in the *Kansas City Star* when some comic books that we have developed had just been banned from the Johnson County Health Department. One Johnson County organization thinks the material is not only pornographic, but Communist-inspired.

> " 'I believe, they're right!' says a member of the Concerned Citizens of Johnson County. 'But what are they educating them for? If the gals want to grow up to run a house of prostitution, they'll know exactly what supplies are needed. I think it's demoralizing promotion by Communism,' _____
> said. 'If they get the young people interested in sex, they can demoralize the country and just walk in and take it over.' And adds, 'That's the Communist procedure.' "

We developed comic books for teen-agers. The reason is that I have written numerous books in good taste — and those, only the librarians read. There are three hundred million comic books sold in this country, and most high school students read them exclusively, and college students read them secretly. And so we produced a comic book called, "Ten Heavy Facts About Sex." And we distributed them at a New York State Fair. One state senator looked at this comic book and he said, "Oh my God, this comic book puts ideas into the minds of teen-agers whose minds do not have them already." Obviously he's never been to a public-school bathroom. So he arranged for this comic book to be banned. And we were thrilled! As a result of the ban, thousands of people from all over the world wrote to us asking for copies of the comic books. Some wanted them in a plain brown wrapper. We had newspaper articles in the *New York Times* and in *Playboy* and *Time*. We had thousands of dollars' worth of free publicity. We were so grateful, we were so absolutely thrilled with the ban, that we dedicated the next edition of this comic book to that state senator.

We've sold millions of copies of that comic book. Then we put all the comic books in a book called, *YOU*. It's a very interesting book, because it's got the world's longest title. It's called, *YOU — The Psychology of Surviving and Enhancing Your Social Life, Love Life, Sex Life, School Life, Work Life, Home Life, Emotional Life, Creative Life, Spiritual Life, Style of Life Life*. And besides all the comic books it's got all of my schtick and slogans. And it's almost everything I've ever thought about. The main themes of this book are, "Nobody can make you feel inferior without your consent." And life is not a meaning, life is an opportunity. People go around saying, "Ha . . . ! Life has no meaning!" Schmuck! Of course life has no meaning! Life is not a meaning, life is an opportunity! You find the meaning of life at the *end* of life. For the going off to find yourselves . . . where're you going? You gotta find yourself right where you are. Maybe you're gonna go and take in some TM or yoga or masturbate a little bit, or play basketball, and you think you'll find the solution to life. You cannot find the solution to life, even if you find God; you have to test Him in your relationships to other human beings. And *that's* what it's all about.

I would like now to read to you, in conclusion, one of my favorite poems. It appears in my book *YOU* and it's called "On Being Intimate with a Chestnut."

Sometimes we talk about intimacy
We quickly agree that people can be sexual without being
　　intimate . . .
But, ah, can anybody be intimate without sex?
Perhaps.
But what about intimacy without touching?

We decide that there are many different levels and intensities
　　like in love, or enchantment

The intimacy we care about seems to be being at one with, or at
    any one moment in harmony with,
Another person, an imaginary friend,
God, Nature
A stuffed animal, a real dog
Your family
Your doll,
Jesus,
Your horse,
Your genitals
Your motorcycle, your blanket,
Grass,
Yourself,
and even a chestnut.

It's not easy, this intimacy business . . .
One thing we know for sure
Is that the path to its fulfillment can be
Treacherous.
First you must reveal yourself
But when you do
You risk
Humiliation
or betrayal

But you also have a chance of a response that you want
Intimacy means being responsive, not reactive . . .
A person falls in love with you.
God is revealed.
The motorcycle sends out vibrations.
Your doll, dog or horse listens to you as no one else has before
Or your music captures the soul . . .
Most people are afraid
Of being intimate.

Some people don't even know *how* to be.
What a pity.

How can you tell about intimacy?
It is joyous
And sad
It is sharing
And giving
And openended
And taking your mind off yourself
Momentarily.

Have you ever touched anyone with your body or mind
And then,
Someone talked about being intimate
With the chestnut.

For an entire summer
He fondled and confided in
and loved her
And the response
Of the chestnut
Was simply marvelous
To behold.

A Rational Approach to Treating Jealousy

ROBERT W. HIBBARD, M.D.

Director, Huntington Institute for Rational Living

Jealousy, an issue that occurs in most relationships, especially marriage, is experienced by nearly everyone in varying degrees and at various times. Hollywood has romanticized and novelists have idealized the intense "lover" who demonstrates the depth of his love through jealous outrage and emotional tantrums. This paper explores this type of jealousy and offers an alternative to the self-defeating feelings it engenders.

Albert Ellis (1972a) distinguishes two types of jealousy, rational and irrational. For example, what might a person think and feel if the spouse or lover were not with him or her and were in fact being physically and/or emotionally intimate with someone else? The rational person would likely use evaluating beliefs to this effect: "I wish he were with me so we could enjoy each other. I don't like it when he is not here when I want him to be." By employing only rational techniques the person avoids undue upset and feels only varying degrees of frustration or disappointment. Unfortunately, rational jealousy is seldom encountered, since very few people think rationally in their love relationships.

The other type of jealousy — irrational — is the one most frequently seen by psychiatrists. In the clinical practice of psychotherapy and counseling, jealous reactions are associated with anger, rage, depression, anxiety, divorce, and suicidal and homicidal acts. Fear and feelings of insecurity and inferiority create irrational perceptions and evaluating assumptions that lead to jealousy. People who feel insecure rely on others, especially the spouse, to define worth or "OK-ness." Thus, if an act or perception causes insecure persons to question whether or not their spouse still cares for them, a jealous reaction develops.

People who become irrationally jealous are the creators of their feelings. They use certain false and irrational techniques in evaluating events and their influence. The sequence of disturbed thinking or feeling that follows both real and imagined "unfaithful acts" often goes like this:

1. "If my spouse or lover is intimate with someone else, I might be compared with that person. I might not be considered as good a lover or as thoughtful or as understanding. That would be awful." This perception leads to self-induced anxiety.

2. "He or she might leave me or embarrass me, and others would find out. I would look foolish and would lose someone I want to keep. I could not stand that." Here the anxiety is further escalated by irrational beliefs.

3. The blame for the self-induced anxiety is now projected onto the unfaithful spouse or lover by such thoughts as, "You upset me. You make me unhappy and make me doubt myself. You have no right to do that."

The jealous person becomes angered or even enraged. He may then withdraw into self-blame or may attack his lover, vilifying and condemning the "unfaithful" party with such timeworn labels as worthless, slut, prostitute, and whore. In some instances, the jealous person resorts to physical violence against his lover or spouse. More often than not, vindictiveness enters the relationship.

4. Often the next step is depression, induced by such thoughts as "I'm unloveable," "I am a failure," or "I should have tried harder." These may be followed by "I'll get even," "I've got to get a divorce so that my integrity will not be compromised or cuckolded," and "I can't live without him."

The debilitating emotion, jealousy, can be understood and dealt with through rational-emotive therapy (RET). Through reprogramming and relearning, people can change the way they think and feel. Irrational jealousy can be converted to a less-destructive emotion, such as the annoyance of rational jealousy.

Through RET's direct, active approach, jealous persons encounter the basic concepts of rational emotional thinking and confront their irrational belief systems. They learn that by clinging to unfounded beliefs they are disturbing themselves and their desired relationship in a most self-defeating way. When they shed their irrational beliefs and think rationally about the spouse or lover's behavior, they ease their disturbed mental state.

The therapist continually confronts and challenges the client's irrational belief system. He or she demonstrates that one needn't disturb oneself over anything one doesn't like. If, for example, a male client says his spouse has been unfaithful and that means she doesn't love him, the therapist might quickly point out the error of this type of *non sequitur* thinking. Indeed the therapist might note that all that can be assumed is that the spouse was intimate with someone else at a given moment because that is what she wanted to do. If the client declares how awful it would be if he were negatively compared with his spouse's lover, the rational therapist would try to persuade him that "awful," "horrible," or "terrible" can exist only in his mind. These words represent subjective value judgments imposed by learned cultural myths. It would only be sad or unfortunate for the client if his spouse left because she liked the other person better.

The source of the client's anger and rage is handled by explaining the "should" concept, which merely states that *reality is always as it should be until it is changed.* The client's insistence that his spouse shouldn't have been unfaithful (reality) because he didn't like it is as absurd as saying one's bank balance shouldn't be five dollars because one doesn't like low bank balances. Neither a spouse's unfaithfulness nor a low bank balance need be cause for unreasonable upset. The client is taught to use rational evaluations about his spouse's behavior such as "I don't like that behavior," "I'll try to persuade her not to keep it up," or "I will not allow my perceptions and beliefs about her behavior to overwhelm me." These more rational thoughts might result in appropriate emotions of lesser import, such as irritation, annoyance, sadness, or regret.

If depression is brought on by such irrational thoughts as "It's terrible if he doesn't love me," these thoughts are challenged by such questions as "Where's the proof? Even if my spouse doesn't love me, it's not terrible but only sad and perhaps unfortunate for me at the moment. *Terrible* exists only in my mind." If self-blame is apparent, the therapist can point out — why blame yourself and feel guilty for anything you ever do? The therapist begins to point out more effective ways of changing the behavior that concerns the client and that he wants to alter.

Another example: A female client says she is embarrassed and humiliated by her mate's infidelity. Embarrassment is handled by encouraging the client to reveal the irrational fear that people will think she's inadequate. She couldn't stand for them to think of her that way. The RET therapist repeatedly points out that the client cannot know what others are thinking, and even if they did think negatively about her, she can withstand disapproval or rejection. She doesn't need the approval of everyone, and she cannot be inadequate as a person, even if she performs inadequately.

Emotional disturbance, such as anger, guilt, and depression, results from the labeling or condemning of another (or of oneself) as a person, rather than the labeling or condemning of certain behaviors.

Unfortunately, the majority of people view their jealousy and that of their mates as clear indication of love. In reality the intensity of their jealousy is directly proportionate to their capacity to misperceive and/or to think irrationally and upset themselves. I once saw in my practice a seventeen-year-old girl who had dated her boyfriend for only two weeks, but she kept saying she knew he really loved her. When asked for the source of her certainty, she replied that he had said he would kill anyone who looked at her. This statement only shows the boyfriend's potential for upsetting himself and gives no real indication of his feelings for the girl.

In our culture many nutty myths about love and jealousy flourish. In a popular magazine there recently appeared an article in defense of jealousy (Harrison, 1974). The author says that even God was jealous and that this means jealousy is OK for the rest of us. She also maintains she has never spoken to anyone who hasn't experienced jealousy. I contend her sample was too limited, because there are people who have escaped the social programming of jealousy. Why defend self-induced, painful, jealous disturbance as OK? Is jealousy profitable? Only rarely, and usually the profit is short-lived and produces no long-term changes.

Jealousy is a learned response based on irrational cultural and personal assumptions or beliefs. It leads to many overly strong, highly destructive emotions and to such behaviors as guilt, depression, anxiety, embarrassment, anger, rage, homicide, suicide, divorce, and revenge. In RET, irrational beliefs can be challenged and disproved. The jealous client can be taught to think rationally and to shed self-induced misery.

Several self-help techniques can be taught the jealous patient. Systematic written homework (Maultsby, 1971e) is an excellent way for the conscientious patient to reprogram the brain and reduce the frequency, intensity and duration of jealous reactions. The practice of rational emotive imagery for five to ten minutes two or three times a day rehearsing in fantasy the way you wish to think, feel, and behave is definitely helpful in reducing jealous reactions.

Finally patients are encouraged to confront themselves with this provocative question (and answer it): What difference does it *really* make what my spouse or lover does when he or she is not with me? The answer is usually none. However, realistic deprivation might merit consideration. If the spouse or lover is spending so much time in his or her sexual pursuits that the other is seriously deprived of companionship, sexual satisfaction, etc., a legitimate complaint may be in order. Rational negotiation between spouses or lovers can usually resolve this. Little difference does it make in the final analysis whether the spouse or lover's time is spent on golfing, fishing, or working. The important factor is that sometimes they are not with you at times when you would like them to be. This, alas, is but one of the many frustrations and disappointments of everyday life. With the rational approach these can be handled sanely and with minimum discomfort.

RET is based on learning theory that asks, "What incorrect (irrational) beliefs learned in the past can be replaced by rational and more positive beliefs about oneself and others?" As such it is one of the few therapies that can treat jealousy effectively so that immediate and long-term perception and evaluative beliefs become more rational and more satisfying.

Instant Replay: A Method of Counseling and Talking to Little (and Other) People

STEWART BEDFORD, Ph.D.

Private Practice, Chico, California

Introduction

This procedure offers the child and other interested people a new method of approaching problem situations and thinking and talking about problem situations. I take responsibility for the description, but it is not presented as a "new theory."

Significant other people who have influenced the evolution of these ideas are Albert Ellis and his rational-emotive psychotherapy, Virginia Satir and her method of family therapy, Maxie Maultsby and his theories of rational behavior therapy, and Ben Ard (who first asked me to present these ideas in a professional meeting). I have also been influenced by reading in the areas of behavior modification techniques and in Parent Effectiveness Training, developed by Thomas Gordon.

I have found that the method can be taught to parents and to children and that with the use of homework it can be successfully integrated with ongoing consultation and counseling. I think of the method as a tool which I include with other methods that I use in my work.

Setting

Child referrals that are made to me in my private practice of psychology are usually oriented on specific problem areas or behavior seen as unacceptable by parents or parental-authority figures. I therefore see families who are usually in some type of crisis situation. In my consultation with families, I find that I can introduce this method during the first interview, usually with children and parents participating together.

In the first part of the first interview I get some background information regarding the problem and the individuals in the family. Following this I try to get the family members (particularly the children) to talk about the "fun things" in their lives. This is usually followed by some description of "unfun things," which may or may not be a description of the problem as presented by the parents or the referral source. I usually choose one of the "unfun things" and label it as a "rough spot." Following this, I describe the system of Instant Replay briefly and we go through the method, usually with the child presenting information about the rough spot.

In the latter part of the first interview, while making homework assignments, I tell the family I want them to do Instant Replays on rough spots that occur between sessions. I ask them to keep track of these discussions and any problems that develop while trying to discuss the difficulties.

As noted above, I consider this method to be a tool and I use it with other methods while working with children and families. I find that it can be easily integrated with behavior modification techniques and it also fits in with some modified play therapy methods that I sometimes use while working with children and families. In addition to my office practice, I have demonstrated the method in workshops with parents, probation officers, protective service workers, and professional psychotherapists. In these demonstrations I have tried to use real families working on real problems and I have found that the method can fit into this type of workshop situation.

Procedures

Rough Spot. I label as rough spots the situations or events that result in unpleasant emotions (feelings). A situation or event is not necessarily labeled as a rough spot by both child and parent. In the procedure I have either a child or a parent label a situation as a rough spot, and then suggest that we do a "rerun" or "instant replay" of the situation that has been so labeled. In the labeling phase of the procedure, I'm not particularly interested in a lengthy discussion of the situation but I do want both the children and the parents to become aware and try to recall the situation being discussed (and labeled as a rough spot).

Feelings. Here, I attempt to get the children and parents to describe the feelings or emotions that each has had in relation to the rough spot. I ask them to describe and recall how they felt and I try to get them to focus their attention on the "body language" involved in the feelings they have had. After the feelings have been described, we label the feeling, trying to stay with the words used by the child and/or the parents. Here, an effort is made to become more aware of feelings and to get practice in putting feelings into words with statements that start with "I feel — ."

Instant Replay. This phase involves a more detailed description of the rough spots, including setting, time, preliminaries, what happened, and what was the end result. I compare this to a television instant replay (and most people, particularly children, know what these are). I usually have the child describe the situation first and then have the parents "tell it like they saw it." However, in some instances, the children prefer to have their parents describe the situation first, which is almost always followed by their own description of what they thought went on.

Psychroscope. Here, I ask the participants to tell me what their thoughts were about the situation (rough spot). I ask such questions as: "What did you tell yourself about the rough spot?" or, "What did you think to yourself when that happened?" or, "How did you read that?"

This follows Albert Ellis's rational-emotive therapy and his "A-B-C's" of perception. In this, A=the event, C=the reaction, and B=the person's interpretation of A.

This is an area that can be delved into more deeply by a trained therapist, but it is an area where some insights can be exchanged between parent and child without getting into any particular depth. This area gets into the inner communication that we all use in our daily living and is an area that in my work I sometimes label as "inner space."

Other Options. Here, I have the child try to think of as many alternate plans as he or she could have come up with at the time of deciding to do whatever he or she did. Anything goes here and this part of the session can be somewhat similar to "brainstorming." After the child runs out of ideas, the parents can throw in any ideas they have, and the counselor or other group participants can also contribute. (If the procedure is used in a group situation some wild ideas are usually brought up here.) Actions and behavior are not the only type of options considered — it is also possible for the person to consider other emotions they could have had. (I have found that this helps emphasize the part that our interpretations of events play in the emotional reactions that we have and helps people see their own methods of perception in operation.)

Consequences. After the options are listed (written down if possible), the child tries to think of various consequences that might have occurred in relation to any of the options that were considered. It is particularly important here to define consequences in terms that the child understands. (I have found that most younger children do not understand the word consequences, although they usually end up wanting to use the word themselves in this procedure.)

After the children have thought of as many consequences as they can, I encourage the parents or other participants in the session to think of as many possible consequences as they can, keeping in mind the options that have been listed. It is possible to have the children rate the various options at the end, but I have found that by the time we have gotten this far, most of the options have been more or less rated by all concerned.

Instant Replay: A Case Illustration

This is an example where a father's mind was really blown by a rough spot that occurred during the first session in some interviews that I had with a family. The family was referred because the son, age eleven, was having trouble with reading. An evaluation of his reading had been done at school and he had been assigned to special, remedial classes. In the process, the parents said that they had been told by the school that the boy had a "mental block." In the first interview, the boy was seen with both parents and with a younger sister — a good reader. In the first part of the session while the family were discussing the fun things they liked to do, the boy said he could not think of any fun things that he liked to do. The father was surprised and asked the boy if he didn't think that Little League was fun. When the boy decided to list this as an "unfun thing," the father had a rough spot right then and there. I suggested that the boy think of a specific instance in Little League and describe this (since Little League was more or less described as the "rough spot"). The boy did not do very well at describing his feelings after he had designated a situation where he was up at bat. He did say that he had "funny feelings inside" that were sometimes "like sick" and sometimes like "shaky."

In the instant replay he was more descriptive. He said, "There I am standing there at bat. Maybe there's two men on and two outs. I can hear dad up in the stands yelling at me and the pitcher and the umpire. Then I start to shake and I can't see the ball and I usually strike out."

In the psychroscope phase, he said he told himself that he guessed he was scared but that he had better not let his dad know that. He said, "I hate this, but I better not let dad know. He's going to give me a bad time as it is 'cause I'm going to strike out. Then he'll say I didn't try."

When asked what he told himself about his father yelling, he said, "I think he's mad at me and I think he don't like me 'cause I'm not good enough."

The boy didn't come up with much in the way of other options, but fortunately the father did. I had the father describe the rough spot he experienced when his son was talking. He was able to repeat most of what his boy had said in instant replay and he described feelings of shock within himself. He said he also felt some anger and then had "a sinking feeling in my stomach like I had just been hit in the guts by a line drive." (The father turned out to be a former semipro baseball player.)

In the psychroscope phase, the father saw himself as saying to himself, "I just can't believe what he's saying. Little League has to be the greatest thing that's ever happened to him, and he says he doesn't like it. I finally asked myself, 'Where did I go wrong?' "

When talking about other options, he described other ways he could change his approach and he focused on consequences that involved fun for his son rather than on the son's becoming a better ball player.

In this case, I saw the family for about five more visits. The boy's reading had not improved much at the end of these sessions, but his baseball had improved and the relationship between father and son had taken on new dimensions. In this case, the family were active in doing homework, and in further sessions the boy had a chance to talk about other rough spots that he had, including reading and competing with his sister. I felt that the sessions offered an opportunity for the family to expand their methods of communication and in this, instant replay (both in the office and in homework assignments) played what I considered to be a significant part.

Instant Replay in Psychotherapy

Using this procedure, the counselor or psychotherapist can go back and follow up on almost any phase of the operation by having individuals expand on their inner perceptions (what they told themselves about the situations they encountered, the feelings they had, or the consequences they anticipated). If irrational thinking exists (as it very likely does in persistent problem behavior and/or emotional disturbances), the counselor can use the option and consequence approach in having individuals consider other things that they might have told themselves or that they might have considered.

I have found that the method also works in group situations either of a classroom type or a group therapy type. I have found it particularly effective in going back over situations that have arisen, on the spot, in such groups and where many participants have had observations of and about the "rough spot."

As yet, I do not have statistical or experimental proof of the efficacy of the method but it has worked for me and the people with whom I have worked. It is a method that I enjoy using, particularly with children, and that is a significant factor for me.

Counseling Strategies with Working Class Adolescents

HOWARD YOUNG, M.S.W., A.C.S.W.

For the most part I will be discussing counseling strategies with adolescents who come from working class backgrounds. This category of teenagers includes those who possess average or less than average intelligence, read very little (if at all), are school dropouts or terminal high school students, usually obtain employment in the unskilled labor market, come from lower middle-income or welfare-supported families, and are frequently unmotivated for psychotherapy. Most of my suggestions can also be applied, with appropriate modifications, to normal, neurotic, delinquent, or psychotic adolescents. Further information on a behaviorally oriented approach to differential diagnosis is available in Dr. Maxie Maultsby's excellent article (1975c).

Although I do not deny the existence of such developmental issues as struggles with independence, sex role identity confusion, or parental separation problems, I shall not be discussing such general issues in this paper; for I believe that it is not the developmental struggles themselves which are the central issue, but rather the adolescents' *attitudes* about these problems which are the main concern, particularly when these attitudes are exaggerated, distorted, and otherwise inaccurate. In more simple terms, the primary problem in adolescence is cognitive misconceptions, and the task of therapy is correcting these misconceptions (Young, 1975).

With this introduction in mind, let me move directly into specific counseling tactics and strategies. Because adolescents are a difficult client group capable of a wide variety of resistant behaviors, perhaps the most sensible place to start is the establishment of a systematic, well-structured framework.

I generally follow these steps: (1) developing a relationship, (2) defining the problem, (3) teaching the principles of rational thinking, (4) encouraging change.

Of course, one need not necessarily hold to this particular order; it is understood that there may be overlapping. For instance, one could be developing a relationship while defining a problem or vice versa. Additionally, the therapist might want to concentrate on one area more than another. Nevertheless, I have found reliance on such a structured approach to be extremely productive in maintaining a therapeutic direction with adolescent clients.

Developing a Relationship

Although the importance of relationship-building is not necessarily emphasized in RET theory, I view it as a primary consideration in any attempt to practice RET with young people. The average adolescent often approaches counseling, if he approaches it at all, with anxiety, apathy, or defiance. Add this to what appears to be an almost universal distrust of adults, and you have a situation that is hardly conducive to the development of a therapeutic alliance.

It is, therefore, desirable and beneficial when working with an adolescent, to use various expressive techniques that will encourage a trusting, accepting interpersonal relationship. Though I place importance on relationship building, I do not view the relationship as the therapy itself, but rather as the medium in which growth and change can best take place.

It is on this point that RET appears to differ from many other systems of psychotherapy. For example, in a recent article (Lechnyr, 1975) student effectiveness in clinical training was determined by the therapists' abilities to establish empathy, warmth, and congruence with their clients. Nowhere in the article was any other goal, such as specific client change, suggested. The implication was that students would receive a passing grade and treatment outcome would be positive if, and only if, a proper relationship was established.

Relationship development as a goal in and of itself represents gross therapeutic misdirection. It is a little like a salesman who judges his performances according to how well liked he is by his customers, with little regard to sales outcome. Such a salesman would either be reprimanded by his employer for confusing means with ends, or fired.

A therapeutic relationship is no different or no more unique than any other form of human contact which aims at changing people. When we help our clients overcome their problems, we are using the same techniques that have been developed over thousands of years in law, politics, religion, education, commerce, and advertising.

In more simple terms, the purpose of a therapeutic relationship is to establish a position of authority and influence over a client. If such persuasive powers can be enhanced through empathy, caring, and concern, then we would better take advantage of such techniques. However, at the same time, we would better realize that a therapeutic relationship is a means toward an end — not an end in itself.

Here are some techniques and strategies I recommend for developing a responsive relationship with adolescents:

Allow long periods of uninterrupted listening. This is perhaps a departure from the more active, interventionist approach usually employed in RET. However, I have found that many adolescents have not had the opportunity to talk with an adult without some kind of admonishment or interruption. As a result, I tend to sometimes allow chatting or rapping in the interest of encouraging ease and comfort in the therapeutic situation.

Avoid silences. Especially with teenagers, silences are not particularly productive. With the exception of a client who is collecting his thoughts or pausing to come up with an answer to a question, I make every attempt to keep the conversation going. I find that most teenagers get very uncomfortable and self-conscious when silences are deliberately allowed to last.

Accept their reality perspective regardless of how distorted or limited it may be. If, for example, a young person decides his parents are "always on his back" (even though I know in many cases this is not true), I usually accept this conviction as fact. This is especially important with delinquent or anti-establishment adolescents. Instead of talking the client out of his faulty opinion right away, I allow it and proceed from there. This indicates that I am an ally rather than an opponent and often decreases defensiveness.

Discuss openly your own opinions and attitudes. I try to answer all questions casually and directly, including questions about my marriage, sexual attitudes, personal problems, and counseling experiences. I have found that I tend to be asked more personal questions by teenagers, and this is understandable since many of them are trying to find out what adulthood is all about. They usually do not have this opportunity with other adults, such as parents or teachers, who are often hidden behind moral or idealistic roles.

Allow a companion to sit in on the session. Quite often, letting a young person bring along a friend seems to relax the situation and pave the way for future progress. In fact, sometimes I use the companion to make a point or two. On more than one occasion I have found that the companion picked up the message quite clearly and was able to repeat it back to the primary client, thus facilitating the therapy. I have also used this same approach with good results by allowing a pet to join us for a session or two. I have shared encounters with dogs, hamsters, cats, mice, turtles, birds, and ants (but turned down a pony).

Ask questions that can be easily answered. I usually begin the interview with a biographical data sheet. This includes the usual name, age, school, grade, and parents' occupation type of information. Often the client feels more comfortable when I begin with questions that can be easily answered. Along the same lines, I will ask questions about their favorite movies, TV shows, hamburger hangouts, friends, and enemies. Since parents and teachers often concentrate on what's wrong with these interests, many young people will open up and talk more easily when I show positive regard for their activities.

See the adolescent first. When a teenager is brought in by his parents, and they are registering the complaint and asking for therapy, I very frequently see the teenager first. This can sometimes give the impression I am willing to listen to him and respect his point of view, and helps lessen his concern that I am collaborating with his parents.

Get the parents to make an initial concession. With strict or overprotective parents, I sometimes make an effort to get them to give in on some of their demands. Increasing an allowance, extending curfews, or reducing house or yardwork commitments are good examples. This gives the teenager the idea that I have influence over the parents, a previously unthought of idea, and often paves the way to a more responsive relationship.

Make the youngster feel he is special. With certain teenagers I make a deliberate but prearranged point to forcefully tell my secretary, "Absolutely no phone calls while so-and-so is in my office," or words to that effect. Such a technique, when used appropriately, can go far in encouraging a young client to think what he has to say is very important.

Show positive regard for the young person. Although many

other variables, both planned and unplanned, could rightfully be included in successful relationship building, it is my opinion that a positive interest in young people is very important in developing a trusting relationship with an adolescent.

Defining the Problem

With an adult client, "problem defining" might not necessarily receive special or undue attention. RET is a problem-oriented approach anyway, and most adults are able to focus fairly quickly on what or who is bothering them. I have not found this to be the case with adolescents — especially those who are unmotivated because they have come for counseling against their wishes. It is not unusual to find young clients to be vague, evasive, defensive, or downright defiant when asked why they have come for help.

Even after a problem area has been successfully defined, adolescents seem to wander off easily into tangents, get wrapped up in the details of their volatile life experiences, or become lost in meaningless philosophy-of-life excursions. Sometimes I permit such wanderings in the interest of relationship building, but usually I make an effort to encourage young people to become problem-focused.

Sometimes matters can get complicated. Often the young client is referred and brought to the counseling session by someone other than himself. The referral source and the young person often see a different problem area. For instance, a parent might see smoking marijuana as a problem; the school might see underachievement as the problem; and the client might see difficulties with a boy or girl friend as the problem. When confronted with this kind of situation, I make every effort to get the adolescent's agreement on exactly what needs attention. If this means initially concentrating on a problem unrelated to the serious concerns of others, then I usually proceed with this problem, hoping to get back to the "serious concerns" later.

I might again emphasize that it is incredibly easy to get lost with teenagers. Despite what I think is a very admirable ability to "get down to business," I often find myself lost, wondering how the hell I got into talking about UFO's, ESP, the SLA, Vietnam, Billy Jack, and a host of other interesting but therapeutically irrelevant subjects. It is for this reason that I find the framework I outlined helpful in maintaining my own problem-focused direction, and often in the middle of a fascinating discussion of ancient astronauts, I will interject, "Now let's get back to that history test you are afraid to take."

Some of the principles I have found helpful in locating and maintaining a problem-focused direction are:

Define the problem.   As I mentioned, in many cases young people who come to my attention are initially referred by parents, schools, or police. Usually I have some knowledge of their difficulties beforehand, and a simple statement like, "I understand you are here because you ran away," leads to a lively problem-focused discussion.

Give a representative example out of the life of another young person.   By discussing a problem of another teenager I'm able to illustrate what I am looking for. This not only provides a sense of "at least I'm not the only one with problems," but offers a concrete example of the kind of subject matter discussed in counseling.

Give a problem example out of your own life.   This is especially effective if it deals with criticism, rejection, and failure — all common adolescent overconcerns. Not only do such admissions humanize the therapist, they also help the young person discover that such problems are inherent in human living.

Encourage a discussion about the problems of other people.   With a particularly anxious young person, I sometimes find it helpful to focus on the problems of friends, parents, or anyone else she or he cares to mention. Usually these problems are self-related and at least allow me to maintain a problem-solving direction.

Use visual aids.   I have found that the most effective tactic with the evasive or "problem-free" young person is to use wall posters that contain all the irrational ideas and many of their corollaries. I have the young person look at this list and see if he or she believes any of the ideas. This is a quick way to get a diagnostic impression of an adolescent's thinking, and can serve as a stepping stone to identifying a specific problem area.

Simplify the definition of a problem.   Many times young clients are afraid to reveal a problem because they feel they are supposed to tell their innermost fears, or that anyone with a problem is crazy. In order to overcome this attitude, I reduce a problem to one of three possibilities: not getting your own way, someone on your back, or any kind of hassle. Since I have yet to meet a teenager who doesn't complain about such areas, this technique usually gets a problem-facing process started.

Discuss bad feelings.   I will frequently tell a teenage client that a problem is "feeling bad." Although this is oversimplified, it often serves to encourage talk about emotions, upset, and the like.

End the interview. I have found with unmotivated adolescents who were forced to come in against their wishes, that once I feel I have established a positive relationship with them, I can suddenly end the interview by saying, "Well, I guess it's silly to continue. You don't have anything I can help you with." Then, with much sorrow and regret, I tell them that although I enjoyed rapping with them, I really have other things to do. In the majority of cases I get about a half-hour of uninterrupted problems. In fact, some of the best problem-defining has taken place on the way to the front door.

Teaching the Principles of Rational Thinking

A primary goal in RET is to help people recognize, challenge, and correct irrational attitudes that can lead to emotional unhappiness and self-defeating behavior. This remains so with the adolescent, but it is, I find, a more arduous task than with the adult.

This might be explained by the fact that the average adolescent has just reached (or is still in the process of reaching) mature cognitive development. In other words, adolescents are only beginners when it comes to manipulating thought and applying abstract concepts as principles with which to direct one's life (Piaget and Inhelder, 1969). It is also probably safe to assume there has been little attention, past or present, to the training or encouragement of the rational capacity toward logical and independent thinking. Thus, although rationality might now be available for service, it lacks adequate training and experience.

In my view, the primary role of the therapist in such circumstances is that of a teacher whose goal is to provide the emotional facts of life within a framework of reason and common sense. This might, at first, seem like an extremely difficult task. Let me assure you it is! However, I usually get somewhere when I observe the following guidelines:

Keep things as simple as possible. Because young people have difficulty with abstract philosophical concepts, I have found that it is wise to simplify, even oversimplify, in the interest of getting a point across. A simple but familiar statement such as "sticks and stones will break my bones, but words can never hurt me — unless I believe they can," or "happenings plus thoughts equal feelings," is an example of this approach.

Make liberal use of the A-B-C principle of understanding emotional upset. I use a poster to illustrate the A-B-C paradigm. The most successful poster design I have used to date is one that begins with a cartoon character who is wakened in the middle of the night by a loud noise. I have a series of posters that show how this noise could produce three separate emotional reactions (calmness, fear, and joy), depending upon three different interpretations of the noise.

Use visual aids. I have charts, drawings, and posters on the wall of my office. Often these get across a concept that verbal dialogue is unable to clarify. In addition, I have a small blackboard that I can hold in my lap. I will write or draw on the blackboard and get various points across in this way. This seems to make a greater impact on an adolescent than a straight talk session. Many times in subsequent interviews they will admit to remembering a point and applying it successfully because it was made more vivid through a visual experience.

Keep the instructive experience brief, dramatic, and full of impact. Though RET can be introduced in different ways, I find that a Socratic dialogue is often beyond the grasp of average adolescents. When they cannot answer questions effectively they often begin to feel inferior and tend to become less responsive. As a result, I find it very effective to stop the interview at a certain point and indicate that I would like to teach an idea or two that might be helpful. Thus, I will take a few minutes out to teach some of the rational-thinking principles, and then refer back to them, occasionally pointing out how to apply these principles as complaints or problems are brought up throughout the rest of the session.

Confront and explain the concepts of "should," "awful," and "can't stand." Since most adolescent problems stem from their demandingness and exaggeration of disappointments, I try to sensitize them to their use of "should," "awful," and "can't stand." Since understanding these words is a key to understanding rational thinking, I have used a number of techniques to help teenagers grasp their meaning. Some of the best ways I have found to explain the meaning of "should" are:

1. *Use "must" or "gotta" in place of "should."* Teenagers use the word "should" so frequently and indiscriminately that sometimes just getting them to change the word to "must" gets the imperative quality across. "I should get an A," makes sense to a lot of teenagers, but "I gotta get an A" often encourages them to see the error of believing in absolutes.

2. *Change the "should" concept to a "no right" concept.* Another method of getting across the absolutistic meaning of "should," especially with angry teenagers, is to change the "he shouldn't do that" to "he's got no right to do that." Explaining the irrationality of "he's got no right" is often easier for some teenagers to understand.

3. *Use the "want-need" concept.* Another way of getting teenagers to recognize and challenge their absolutes without using a "should" is to teach them the difference between wanting and needing. I have found that some of the most resistant and stubborn young people, especially those who are engaged in behavioral excesses, are quite capable of understanding the critical distinction between desires and necessities, and of using this insight productively.

4. *Teach that "should" equals "unbreakable law."* It is sometimes helpful with young clients who have difficulty understanding the absolutistic meaning of "shoulds" and "musts," to suggest that when they are upset in their tummy, they are making up unbreakable laws in their heads. "Debbie's Commandments," "Tom's turn to be God," or "Time for Bill to play judge and jury in his head" are examples of this approach. Once they understand what it means to be unrealistically demanding, I proceed to show them there is probably no such thing as unbreakable law that can be applied to human beings.

Now let me suggest some ways to get the concept of "awful" to teenagers:

1. *Substitute the words "disaster," "catastrophe," or "tragedy" for "awful," "terrible," or "horrible."* The words "awful," "terrible," and "horrible" are so much a part of the average teenager's working vocabulary, and have such a variety of meanings, that I have found it extremely difficult to define these words according to the *bad, all bad,* and *more than all bad* RET model. Instead, I will ask an emotionally distressed adolescent, "Well, was it a disaster?" This word has a more precise, concrete meaning and can be more easily confuted than "awful."

2. *Use the phrase "end of the world" in place of "awful."* Again, I find that asking "Would it be the end of the world?" usually gets an eye-rolling "Of course not" from most adolescents, and allows the next question, "Then exactly what would it be?" The answer is almost always in the realm of realistic

disadvantage and begins to teach a method of anti-awfulizing.

3. *Use the phrase, "A fate worse than death."* Once more, by substituting a more meaningful term, I find that adolescents can sometimes begin to understand that the excessive, disturbing feeling in their gut comes from an exaggerated nutty idea in their heads.

4. *Ask them, "What's the worst that could really happen?"* For anxiety-ridden teenagers, I avoid the word *awful* by getting them to focus on the most probable but worse outcome they can imagine. This forces them to stay away from possibilities and concentrate on actualities. In essence, they are learning to deal with the hassle and not the horror.

5. *Ask them, "Could it be any worse?"* Often they will exaggerate and consider a situation totally bad. By encouraging them to come up with something that could make it even worse, they sometimes see it is highly unlikely that any disadvantage is one hundred percent bad. Helping teenagers realize that something could be a lot worse often gets them to turn disasters back into disappointments.

Finally, I will mention a few methods I use to help teenagers comprehend the "can't stand" concept. This idea is ubiquitous in adolescent belief systems, but my experience shows that, for some reason, adolescents seem to grasp this concept and understand why it is irrational more quickly than other RET concepts. However, when I run into difficulty, I find the following usually gets results:

1. *Substitute "unbearable" or "intolerable" for "can't stand."* Often I am able to encourage a young client to realize how pernicious the "can't stand" concept is by getting him to realize it means the same as "unbearable." Many teenagers, after hearing it put this way, will say, "Well, it's not that bad. I mean, I can bear it."

2. *Ask them if they will "curl up and die."* Sometimes, asking if a problem is so bad that it will literally cause them to "curl up and die" gets the point across and shows them they are making matters worse than need be.

3. *Substitute "won't" for "can't."* Frequently when I hear the word "can't" I quickly substitute "won't." This is an immediate way of showing that it is one's *attitude,* which is under the individual's control, and not the *situation,* that is overwhelming.

4. *Explain "difficult" versus "impossible."*   Often the "can't stand" concept can be better understood by asking if a particular problem situation is impossible, or just difficult to tolerate. Even some of the most resistant teenagers can see this point and realize that just because something is a pain in the neck doesn't mean they can't put up with it.

5. *Give three "can't stand" situations.*   I will sometimes ask, "Suppose you were allowed to eliminate three of the biggest, most unbearable hassles of your life? Which three would you pick?" Often the answer fails to include the present problem and helps demonstrate that the young client can indeed stand the difficulty.

Show the client that overcoming emotional upset does not mean eliminating emotions. Teenagers, after hearing a little of the wisdom of RET, often become dismayed because they think rational thinking will convert them into robots or zombies. They are afraid if they learn to overcome emotional distress they will be left without any feelings or emotions. I usually handle this problem in the following ways:

1. *Ask them if they know anyone who is without emotions, who never feels anything.* I point out I am not talking about holding feelings inside or pretending not to feel certain emotions, but do they really know someone who literally cannot feel anything inside his gut? I've yet to get a yes on this.

2. *Use myself as an example.* I will ask if I look like I don't have any feelings. I point out that I'm a rational thinker a good part of the time, but add a variety of examples of different kinds of emotions I feel. I especially reveal those times I still get myself emotionally upset.

3. *Explain that rational thinking helps you get less angry and less worried.* Sometimes just using the word "less" in front of upsetting feelings helps some teenagers realize that I'm talking about a very reasonable goal. I let them know that the more they work at rational thinking, the less upset they will become; but that they will probably never eliminate emotions.

4. *Explain that bad emotions do not always equal upsetting emotions.* Along the same lines, I point out that when a disappointment occurs, rational thinking will probably still produce *bad* feelings, but not *disturbing* feelings. With somewhat brighter youngsters, I usually explain that upsetting feelings produce great pain, may overwhelm one, and lead one into trouble and

away from problem solving. I further explain that a bad but appropriate feeling produces tolerable pain, is controllable, and leads one away from trouble and toward the attainment of one's goals and desires.

5. *Use a visual aid.* The best way I have found to teach young clients that overcoming upset does not mean eliminating emotions is to use a feeling continuum. I will draw a vertical line on the blackboard and put "calm" at the bottom and "upset" at the top. In the middle I put annoyance, irritation, or some word describing emotional discomfort. I then tell them the goal of rational thinking is to get to the middle of the line, because this will help them produce manageable emotions that they can use to solve their problems.

Make every effort to teach the concept of self-acceptance. Self-acceptance, as you are probably aware, is unique to RET, and I consider it a concept that is most effective in helping overcome emotional upset. Unfortunately, I find this one of the most difficult ideas to get across to teenagers, and, I might add, to working class adults as well. Some of the explanations I have found successful include the following:

1. *Use a visual aid.* I draw a circle which I label "self." Next I put a series of smaller circles inside the self circle. These represent the traits, characteristics, and performances of the individual client. I pick out the particular trait area that is in question and put in even smaller circles to indicate specifics within that trait area. I use plusses and minuses to show success and failure. From here I try to show that, when one area of one trait goes bad, it does not make the entire circle (self) bad.

2. *The flat tire example.* Although there are a lot of examples that illustrate the illogic of overgeneralizing from an act to personhood, I have found that the flat tire example is the best for teenagers. This is the one where you ask if they would junk the whole car if they found it had a flat tire. The key word seems to be "junk." Once they pick up on this word-image, I use it when they put themselves down for mistakes or criticism by saying, "There you go again, junking yourself because you . . ."

3. *Show that although you are responsible for what you do, you are not the same as what you do.* This is sometimes a tricky concept to get adolescents to understand. They frequently argue that if they *do* something bad, *they* are bad. I use a cow example: If you go around town mooing like a cow, does that make you a

cow? I usually get a "no." Then I say, "But you did it, you're the one who is mooing." After a few examples like this they usually get the point and begin to learn how to separate what they do from who they are.

4. *Focus on "it" rather than "me."* Sometimes I get very good results by suggesting to teenagers when they fail at something or get criticized to forcefully tell themselves, "It's too bad," rather than the more pernicious "I'm bad!" This simple device often serves as a shortcut for getting adolescent clients to concentrate on problem-solving instead of self-rating.

5. *Teach the RET pleasure principle.* Lately I have been using a technique that has been quite successful in helping young people learn to separate intrinsic value from extrinsic accomplishments. I point out that success and approval are, in the final analysis, nothing more or less than pleasures. Seeking these pleasures is both sane and rational. However, using these same pleasures as ego boosters or for the sake of self-value is both insane and irrational. I use the following example to get the point across: If you go into an ice cream store, buy an ice cream cone, and eat it, you will feel pleasure. However, you wouldn't also conclude that because you had this pleasure you can now hold your head up high, you are a good person, and have self-respect. This would be idiotic because all that occurred is that you experienced pleasure. I further point out: If you go into the same ice cream store and discover they are out of ice cream, you will feel bad or deprived. You will lack pleasure. Again you probably wouldn't conclude that because you have been deprived of pleasure you are a louse, cannot hold your head up high, and have no self-respect. This would also be idiotic because all that happened is that you didn't experience the pleasure you desired. I then suggest that the client put the problem in place of the ice cream. Or I will suggest (when he or she does not get success or approval) that an appropriate statement would be: "So, I didn't get my ice cream cone — too bad!"

Encouraging Change

It comes as no secret that client change and growth are dependent largely on actively putting knowledge learned in therapy into practice in concrete and specific situations. This requires conscious effort and hard work. Unfortunately, these requirements are not high on the list of adolescent virtues. Young people are notoriously reluctant to apply themselves to any task that does not promise immediate results. This is understandable, since most adolescents have only recently emerged from a well-conditioned period of childhood dependency and security. Recognizing this as an unfortunate but unavoidable reality is the first step, not only in understanding young people but in recognizing that behavioral change may be a slow, frustrating process.

Although some adolescents learn and apply rational thinking principles on their own, most do not. As a result, additional efforts are usually necessary to encourage self-benefiting behavioral change. I have found these approaches and techniques helpful in promoting such change:

Develop an attitude of "total tolerance." The therapist would best view his own "shoulds" and "oughts" and remember realistically that an adolescent does not *have* to improve, change for the best, or follow a rational, constructive lifestyle. Another important therapist requirement is to avoid exaggerating or "awfulizing" adolescent complaints. Young people are able, seemingly quite easily, to get themselves into the most difficult situations. It is more productive for the adolescent to be able to discuss his harrowing experiences within the confines of a responsive but reality-oriented relationship.

Recognize that not all adolescent emotional complaints have a cognitive basis. Adolescence is a period of rapid physiological change that can sometimes bring about extreme bodily urges and sensations. Such feelings, if uncomfortable and intense, can be exacerbated by thinking the source is body tissue, and not *shoulds, awfuls,* and *can't stands.* Perhaps the best way to avoid chasing irrelevant emotional complaints is to tell the client that in all likelihood he is suffering from temporary "growing pains," and then to guide him into more appropriate emotional concerns.

Write out an A-B-C homework assignment. Although I am frequently successful in getting adolescents to understand why their thinking is irrational, I find it difficult to get them to practice challenging and correcting their irrational ideation outside the therapy session. The hard work involved in changing conditions usually begins and ends in the office. As a result I try to outline their problems on a blackboard or sheets of paper. I try to take them through at least one A-B-C paradigm per session. I also have them take their assignments home with them and refer to them during the week between sessions if the problem comes up again. I have not been particularly successful in encouraging adolescents to read the RET literature; no doubt reading and writing assignments are too closely associated with unpleasant school duties. I thus put more effort into the therapy session, and rely less on bibliotherapy, than I would with an adult client.

Combine thought change with behavior change. I almost always try, whenever appropriate, to combine rational thinking with assertive or goal-striving actions. For example, I not only help a shy adolescent boy understand the cognitive source of his shyness, but also get him to do something assertive like go to a party, ask a girl out, or maybe say "no" to someone he usually accommodates with a "yes." I have found that young people are more likely to accept some of the ideas of rational thinking after they have tested out emotionally provoking experiences in social situations. In this regard, it is important to remember that rational thinking is not necessarily an end in itself, but rather a means toward the end of problem solving and goal striving.

Tell adolescents what to think. I have found that, despite heroic efforts, some adolescents are simply not going to learn how to "reason things out." Either they lack intelligence or are unwilling to put in the effort. In this case, I simply give them the correct sentences to tell themselves. For instance, I might say, "Next time someone calls you an asshole, tell yourself: 'If they call me a finger it doesn't make me a finger, so why get upset over being called an asshole?' "

Teach the client to use a dictionary. Name-calling is a particular problem with young people. I have suggested that they stop each time they are called a name, and look up the name in a pocket dictionary. If they can prove they *are* the name, then they can feel miserable. If not, the name-calling proves nothing about them, but might just tell them something about the name-caller.

Tell the youngster what to do. Some adolescents do not respond to efforts to directly change their thinking, no matter what method I use or how simple I make things. In cases like these I concentrate on telling them how to do things in such a way they can enjoy themselves and yet keep out of trouble. This could include such things as how to creatively lie to their parents, how to cheat successfully in school, and how to handle the police. For instance, I suggested to a teenage girl on parole who consistently broke the rules of parole and was on the verge of being sent to a correctional school, that she cry in front of her parole officer. Her parole officer did not like the girl because she was defiant. The girl did cry, continued to break the rules, but was not incarcerated because she gained the good graces of her parole officer, who now thought she had finally gotten through to the girl. I recognize that when we correct behavior at the expense of appropriate cognitions, people often change, but for the wrong reasons. Unfortunately, we cannot always obtain the most elegant solution to emotional problems; and very often, especially when counseling teenagers, we would sometimes better take what we can get — as long as it relieves suffering and does not cause further difficulties. I might add that a lot of my RET counseling with teenagers follows this philosophy.

Go for the reduction of a behavior rather than its elimination. Sometimes with certain teenagers I am able to modify their behavior by getting them to cut down rather than cut out. In other words, I try to get them to pass just one of four subjects they are failing, or maybe to get them to smoke only outside their home. Sometimes a minor alteration will serve to satisfy parental or school pressures. (This, of course, will not work with drugs.)

Recommend the use of an appointment book. I try to encourage teenagers to buy an appointment book and get them to organize their time. This includes responsibilities like school work and household duties, and also their recreational activities. Teenagers are notoriously unorganized and forgetful. I have had considerable success with some school underachievers by just getting them to make a list of tests, papers, and other school requirements.

Make use of the relationship to encourage change. I find that, at least initially, many young people change because they want to please me. This is often enough to keep them working until they can experience the rewards of their own efforts, which thereafter can replace the relationship as a motivating factor. As I mentioned earlier, relationship development with adolescents is an integral part of RET, and may be the most significant factor influencing positive outcome. Although I could list a number of ways to use "friendship power" to encourage change, the most obvious is to tell them, "Do it for me!"

Use supportive coaching and positive reinforcement. I have found simple encouragement extremely helpful with young people. Counteracting their resistance and sense of hopelessness with, "Yes, you can, you just keep trying," "It will come after a while," and similar behavior-shaping comments can be highly useful. Many adolescents are accustomed to having their faults overemphasized and as a result are quite receptive to positive feedback when appropriate and not overdone.

The Fourth "R": A School Psychologist Takes RSC to School

DAVID A. BROWN, PH.D.

Director, Dunn Mental Health Center, Inc., Connorsville, Indiana

I have been using rational self-counseling (RSC) in seven Florida schools for the past year with great success. This was the first time RSC had been introduced into the schools and taught as a class. The process has met with great interest and support.

Training sessions in RSC for administrators, psychologists, counselors, social workers, teachers, and students have helped each individual to be more rational in his or her life. Many have also learned the technique well enough to share it with others.

These workshops and training sessions in RSC have produced such comments as, "Using objective reality in talking with another person is difficult and something few of us have done before." Other familiar comments from professionals include: "This seems to work far better than sitting and nodding my head as a student is telling me his or her problems." "I have learned a real way to teach people how not to be what they hate being," and "RSC has supplied me with concrete ways to help students. Not only that, but it's working for me!" At the conclusion of a recent training session, one counselor approached me and said, "I thought this was going to be just another workshop. But this is the most significant therapy I have ever encountered."

Perhaps the most exciting aspect of my work during this past year is that counselors and teachers report success from using RSC with students who had previously been the most difficult to reach and help. RBT has given these professionals a nonjudgmental, nonthreatening technique for helping students reach their goals. At the same time, those students learn to stop disrupting the system.

RSC in High School Psychology Classes

The easiest way I've found to introduce rational self-counseling into high schools was to get permission to teach it as a new theory of personal psychology in ongoing psychology classes. We told the students we had three goals: (1) to teach them the theory, (2) to see if they saw any value in the therapy for their lives, and (3) to see if the theory would stimulate them to learn and apply RSC in their daily lives.

When we started our first class in the first high school, we had no idea how it would be received. Soon, however, other classes in that school were requesting that we share our ideas with them. And before long, other high schools were requesting that we also work with their classes! Those requests were prompted by rumors they had heard of what was taking place in the classrooms and between students who were learning RSC.

Students Respond with New Behavior

As an example of the changes that have taken place without effort on my part, I'd like to relate this story of what happened in one class in the first high school into which we introduced RSC. I had given one of the psychology classes three 45-minute periods of instruction in the theory of RSC. A few days later, the regular teacher returned to the classroom in what his students called "a bad mood."

The teacher later told me that on such days he and the students would normally argue until he sent one or more of them to the dean's office for the rest of the period. But this particular morning was quite different. One of the usual "acting-out" students raised his hand and said, "You seem to be bothering yourself about something. I was wondering . . . is there something we could do to help?"

The teacher then told the class what had happened to him that morning before he came to work. He went on to explain what he was thinking and feeling at the time. He discussed his thoughts and feelings with the class for the remainder of the period. When he called me the next day to report what had happened, he questioned me about the strange new behavior of the students. Even though he didn't accomplish his assigned work during that period, he did feel a great deal better and somehow different about the attitudes of his students.

Hearing about such experiences has become ever more frequent as my teaching of RSC in the classroom increases. Students really like the idea that they control their own emotions. One boy had told me, "The dean of boys can make me angry whenever he wants to. And he can keep me mad for as long as he wants to." When this boy learned where his anger came from and who controlled it, he learned not to punish himself any longer. At that point, his relationship with the dean changed dramatically. The dean, in turn, commented to me about the "miracle" I had accomplished with that student. But what really had happened was the student had learned how to meet his needs and achieve his goals without inviting interference from the administration.

A New View of Students

The introduction of RSC causes school administrators to adopt a completely new way of viewing students. How often in the past have we heard, "This student cannot function in the system any longer!" When teachers pass such a judgment, they soon find a way to eliminate that student from the system. The system gets rid of the friction caused by the student, but the student receives no further education. That seems to me to be a bad bargain for the student.

Using RSC helps teachers redefine the problem. It is now stated as: "This student could function in the system if he knew how. Since it is my job to teach, I need to find out what he doesn't know and then teach it to him." In this way, the nonproductive elimination of the student is replaced by a productive effort to determine what education is needed and the best method for that education.

The worth of rational self-counseling has been clearly demonstrated in the schools I serve. Through RSC, teachers see the objective reality that students are only doing what they should be doing, given what they have learned. If they are doing inappropriate things, the teacher can choose to teach students how to do something else — something that will get them closer to educational goals with less conflict. Then both students and teachers benefit. The students benefit from increased education. The teachers benefit from seeing increased evidence that they are doing what they are paid to do: to educate students to care for themselves in a more rational manner.

The High School RSC Group

To help students who complain about "pressure building up" or "the system just gets to me," we established an RSC room in the school. This room is open ten hours a day, one day per week.

A student may come to the RSC room at the end of any class period and stay as long as he or she wishes. The only requirement is that the student read RSC material or do a rational self-analysis while there. The more advanced students teach RSC to new students.

To start this activity, we invited ten students to the first session. They had the option of leaving whenever they wished and not returning, or remaining and even inviting a friend to join them on their next visit. It was up to the students to publicize the RSC room, if they found it beneficial.

After two weeks, the original room was too small. More than forty students were attending each hour of the day! We found, however, that RSC discussions were not limited to the RSC room. Teachers began to hear talk about RSC in the hallways, in the gym, and in spontaneous small groups of students on the grounds of the high school.

I find that very exciting. A girl told me recently, "Now I only get angry with my parents when I want to — and that's never!" She used to spend a great deal of time getting angry at them because she believed they made her feel that way. Now that she understands that's impossible, she seldom makes herself angry.

RSC and Work-Study

In an effort to use RSC in every manner possible, I have introduced it into the work-study program in a junior high school. This program was set up for students "who have not made it in the regular program." They have been selected to attend school only part of the day. These students are taught to use rational self-counseling as part of their jobs.

One of the female students had such a problem with irrational anger she was about to get fired. She would get furious when customers changed their minds about their food orders. "They make me so mad when they change their minds!" she told me. After two weeks in her RSC class, she was successfully resisting getting angry at work when customers changed their minds. Her most helpful insight was that she was getting paid to serve the food the customers decided to pay for. Until the customers finally made up their minds, they had the right to change their selections as often as desired. It's significant that this student had been taught by her mother that it was bad to change one's mind. At home, she was punished for changing her mind.

Other students in that group have experienced similar success by rationally working on their problems with their employers as well as with their customers. Greater job satisfaction and performance have resulted.

The Use of RSC with Younger Students

Student groups who have benefited from learning RSC range from the sixth to the twelfth grade. These groups have been classified as "runaways," "aggressive," "acting-out students," "students who can't function in a regular school setting," "students who resent authority," "students who have no respect for themselves and others," etc., etc.

In the elementary schools, we find that the most efficient and helpful way to introduce RSC into the classroom is to teach the principles of rational self-counseling to the teachers first. That way the teachers can teach it to their students as well as demonstrate it to them by personal example.

Professional Involvement in RSC

We believe that it is helpful, but not necessary, for teachers to learn to apply RSC well in their own lives, as they teach it to students. Our best success usually comes when teachers and school administrators are interested in learning new ideas. We have now taught rational self-counseling to over a hundred professionals in our country. For the most part, we have achieved the same fine results with them as with the students.

Summary

Having read of our rational self-counseling projects and successes, I'm sure you can understand my enthusiasm about teaching this approach to personal growth in school systems. The success of my efforts to teach RSC to secondary students has demonstrated several things to me. First, RSC works well with secondary school age students. Second, students will choose to study and learn RSC if they are given the chance. And third, students do learn RSC well enough to reeducate themselves emotionally and live more rational lives.

It's clear to me that interested students and professionals find RSC more personally helpful than any other nonacademic technique they have tried in the past. That's why I am excited about the present as well as the future of RSC. It is also the best technique I have found to help myself to greater happiness.

Rational Skills for Business People

WILLIAM D. CRIDDLE, Ph.D.

Director of Training, Institute for Rational Living, N.W., Seattle, Washington

JAMES J. TRACY, Ph.D.

Beginnings of Criddle-Tracy Associates

In forming Criddle-Tracy Associates we were influenced by three factors. The first factor was our experience using rational-emotive therapy with business people on an individual therapy basis. It was our viewpoint that many of the problems brought to therapy by businessmen and women were concerns generated on the job. Of course, these concerns dovetailed with intrapersonal problems as well as with family difficulties. There seemed to be no doubt, however, that there were many problems with common denominators among business people which arose in their business life. Hence we concluded that we might appropriately develop an RET package geared especially for executives.

It was my experience (Tracy) that RET could be blended with actual management tasks. In working in a social service system, I was able to implement and carry out some of the behavioral techniques and RET methods discussed later in this paper.

Finally, we were aware that psychological principles were being applied in the business and management field by other practitioners. National Training Laboratories (NTL), for example, has for some time been very active. Although their impact may be waning, there are still a number from this group active in business management. In addition, transactional analysis (TA) is one of the hottest-selling products in business communities. It certainly has benefits, but they seem to be limited. TA is a convenient way of teaching people how to code communications, but if you are interested in production and behavior change and a number of other practical variables, TA does not seem to lend itself as directly to the problems that business people encounter as rational-emotive therapy.

Also, you have probably read articles in newspapers like the *New York Times* about the double-edged sword in management training. Sensational stories talk about outside consultants who turn people on to their wants with the result that some of the best executives leave a company and go to New Hampshire to start a commune. In our experience, this is not a major hazard.

In spite of the fact that there are a number of active consultants in the field and in spite of possible rejection by the business community, we believe the time is ripe for RET in business.

The Executive Effectiveness Program

We have developed three key areas in our Executive Effectiveness Program: goals, skills, and measurement. In addressing the first area, we have separated goals into personal goals for the business person and business goals. As we have been working with business people in therapy, many of them seem to have a vague dissatisfaction with life and very little motivation. They cannot identify the source of dissatisfaction and just feel as if they are wallowing around. In working with these individuals, it frequently seems that they don't have any specific ideas about what they really want in life or whether they are going toward what they want in life. Sometimes we discover in therapy that they really have some vague notion of an underlying value system as indicated by the direction of their behaviors and personal programs, but they never have *specified* these goals. Specifically, they have failed to sit down and take the time to figure out where they are and whether they really value the goals they apparently are working toward. They frequently begin to question whether they are just accepting the goals they have learned from society or from their boss or from their families or wherever. This is where we start with business people — teaching them skills to specify their personal goals.

We have searched for tools to use in goal specification. One effective tool appears in Alan Lakein's book, *How to Get Control of Your Time and Your Life.* He has a number of chapters on goal specification, where one writes down in a few minutes everything he or she would like to do within different periods of time. There are short-term goals and long-term goals. The time periods specified are "the rest of my life," "three years," and "if I was going to be killed by lightning in six months." After the goal specification, exercises are described to specify objectives, activities, and behaviors that one can do on a daily basis toward obtaining one's goals. When clients have completed these exercises, they report feeling more meaning in their lives and sensing that they really know where they are going.

We have two other tools for use with business people that we have used successfully with individual clients. One comes from Harry Browne's book, *How I Found Freedom in an Unfree World.* He outlines some imagery techniques such as instructing the individual to imagine starting over in life and just letting the imagination run completely free, and to do this repeatedly over a number of days and weeks. This helps one figure out what he or she would really like to do. Another tool is the "life inventory" technique, an NTL exercise. The individual sits down alone and writes down many answers to different personal questions, such as, "What do I do well?" "When do I feel really alive?" These questions help stimulate some serious thinking about what one is doing in life, what one is not doing in life, what one really wants to do, what one's values really are, what progress one is making toward these goals.

Business Goals

It is our assumption that a person will be more satisfied with a job and with life in general if there is some link between personal life goals and the goals an employer is asking him or her to pursue. On the basis of that assumption, we have a session which is entitled "What Business Wants of You." Now such a topic may seem strange in this day when corporations regularly hand out job descriptions and information on "the objectives of management." But when you gather a number of job descriptions together, you find them to be extremely vague. We have one from an international firm that is talking about the primary responsibilities of a power systems sales engineer. It appears that this person is responsible for sales and for organizational effectiveness. He is asked to specify "sales which includes pricing, sales planning, sales organization, effectiveness, proposals, and self-development." One does not need much behavioral training to see that job description as one large abstraction followed by a series of other abstractions. Small businesses, as opposed to large businesses, are even less precise in articulating in written form what they want a particular executive to do.

This lack of specificity in job description and in what business wants from its people often leads to an "existential crisis" or — a term now developing in management — "middle-management malaise." The latter seems to be a sort of "blahs."

One of the things we do in our pre-sessions — before we offer a workshop — is to approach the company and find out what they want an executive to learn from the seminar. We do not believe it is a good idea to bring top- and middle-level executives together because then one can get caught in hidden agenda problems. Initially we prefer to talk to higher levels of management, asking them what they really want, and then separately to talk to the executives, asking, "What do you really want?" We then attempt to appropriately modify and adapt their wants and preferences.

Many times we find that vagueness in job descriptions is not a bad thing. We believe that executives, especially middle-management executives, are making themselves anxious and nervous about what it is they "should be doing." The fact may be that the executives at the next higher level really don't know, but are hoping their lieutenants will take the abstract job description and do something with it. Many times, unfortunately, upper-level management people are not straightforward in sharing their own quandaries and ignorance.

As an exercise then, we ask executives to gather together all the memos they have describing their jobs and bring them to the workshop. This is part of the behavioral homework they actually do in a workshop. When they bring in goals that have been suggested or put upon them by business or corporations, we have exercises in which they operationalize or behaviorally define (as best they can) what it is that will be demanded. For example, if a person is responsible for proposals in the sales section of a job, we ask him or her, "What does that mean?" "Does that mean you have to generate a number of proposals?" "Does it mean that you have to get a certain number of proposals accepted?"

In general, it seems to us that everyone, whether involved in social services or in the business community, had best carefully read what is presented in terms of requests, demands, or job descriptions. In addition, it would be in people's best interest to observe their environment, including themselves and what they want, and then to make a good behavioral definition of the various responsibilities. With these goals in mind, one can start to move rationally into the specifics of integrating one's personal preferences and one's job demands.

Self-Direction Skills Through Emotional Control

The first skills to master in an Executive Effectiveness Program are what we call RET skills, which lead to self-direction through emotional control. To help teach the ideas and terminology of basic RET, we use reading assignments: for example, *Executive Leadership: A Rational Approach* (Ellis, 1972b) and *A New Guide to Rational Living* (Ellis and Harper, 1975).

Identifying feelings and emotions obviously is important to emotional control. We find that some business people are unaware of emotions or are unable to specify feelings they experience. And we have met a number of "charging" business people who try to push their feelings aside — thinking they are ignoring them and not realizing how much these troublesome emotions are affecting their work. We use various techniques to help people specify their feelings. One method is to get direct feedback within the group. We have given subjects homework assignments to get feedback from people in their environments about when they perceive the subject is upset or angry. We have successfully used individual and group exercises from a book called *Awareness* by John Stevens. Certain gestalt-type exercises help some people become more aware of their feelings, but we believe these methods must be used with caution among business people who, long after the seminar is over, must interact on a routine basis.

Being good RET therapists, we do not stop with an awareness of emotions. We spend a good deal of time teaching business people the A-B-C's of emotions. Like most people, individuals in business and management still have a number of irrational beliefs, especially the notion that things outside themselves directly upset them. They are not really aware of the *beliefs* that upset them. We spend considerable time working with the A-B-C's and giving examples. We use some of Maxie Maultsby's techniques in terms of getting people to write down the A-B-C's with the goal of making them aware of their belief systems. One thing we have been developing is a list of common irrational ideas found in business. In Table 1 you can see such beliefs as "I need the approval of my superiors, my subordinates, and my peers for everything I do." While it is a slight modification of Albert Ellis's original, it hits home with business people when it is tailored to their specific area. How often do many of us say, "I am justifiably and healthily upset when things are going poorly in my firm or in my department . . . it's terrible and awful when

TABLE 1

Common irrational ideas in business

1. I need the approval of my superiors, my subordinates, and my peers for everything I do.
2. Certain behaviors on the part of my fellow businessmen are terrible and awful and they should not do them.
3. People in business who do bad acts should be severely punished and blamed.
4. It is terrible when things go wrong, such as when we suffer a loss, lose a contract to a competitor, or one of our men makes a serious error.
5. Losses, management problems, errors, etc. cause me emotional pain and upset.
6. I am justifiably and healthfully upset when things are going poorly in our firm or my department.
7. It is often easier to avoid my business difficulties and self-responsibilities.
8. I need something stronger than myself on which to rely when making major decisions and taking business risks.
9. In my position I should be thoroughly competent, intelligent, and achieving in all possible respects on my job.
10. Many difficulties I have on the job today are due to past experiences and thus these problems will be with me indefinitely.
11. I will probably be most happy if I don't get too involved in anything at work but rather do as little as possible.
12. When things go wrong on the job, I can't help but get very angry or depressed or upset in some way.
13. If I do a better job than other people, I should be rewarded accordingly.
14. I should be able to outperform my colleagues.

things go wrong — when we lose a contract to a competitor or when one of our men makes a mistake . . . I should be able to outperform my colleagues"?

We have identified some irrational beliefs that block the goal specification we talked about in a previous section. We try to make people aware of irrational ideas like, "I will not come up with anything specific if I do these exercises" or "I'll never attain them anyway, so why do them?" or "I would have to do something drastic if I specified my goals and I can't stand major problems" or "If I knew my goals I would have to attain them and could never relax until I did so."

After teaching business people the A-B-C's of RET, we show them how to challenge irrational beliefs, using Criddle's pamphlet "Guidelines for Challenging Irrational Beliefs." We have also developed what we call a reaction sequence. Table 2 outlines

TABLE 2

Reaction Sequence

A Situation	The president of the company called John into his office and firmly, almost angrily, told him that he was very disappointed in his recent performance and expected him to increase his and his department's output immediately or expect to be terminated.		
B Possible Cognitive Reactions (Internal Ideas)	1. That goddamn no-good SOB! He has no right to accuse me of not doing my best. He should look at his own lousy performance! He shouldn't talk to me that way!	2. I guess I'd better get the details of his complaint and see if he has a valid point and discuss it with both him and my department. It sure is disappointing to have this happen but it is not the end of the world. I'll survive.	3. What a shit I am! I can't do anything right! I'd better seriously consider going back to my old job; this is too much for a failure like me. This just shouldn't happen to me — poor me!
C Feelings from B	Anger and blame	Concern and disappointment	Guilt, self-pity, and worthlessness
Probable Behavioral Reactions	Angrily yell at boss, subordinates, wife, kids; get drunk; plan revenge and carry it out.	Calmly talk to boss to get details, talk to department, plan ways to change and do them.	Complain to others to receive pity, cry, get drunk, resign, apologize to department.
Usefulness of Reactions	Destructive	Constructive	Destructive
Corrective Measures to Be Taken to Change Reactions	1. Identify ideas 2. Challenge ideas that are irrational 3. Replace with rational ideas 4. Plan constructive behavior	None needed	Same as under Column 1

a specific reaction sequence. We start with the A and give a business situation (the president of the company calls John into his office and chews him out.) Next we note possible cognitive reactions. First — the different internal ideas that produce anger: "That so-and-so has no right to accuse me of this," etc. Then we note alternative rational beliefs, such as, "I guess I had better get the details of his complaint and work on it. It's not the end of the world. It doesn't mean I'm a failure." Then we include possible behavioral reactions that might accompany the different emotional reactions, and note whether these emotional reactions are destructive or constructive. Lastly, we show corrective measures — both cognitive and behavioral — as a means of challenging irrational beliefs.

Self-Direction Skills Through Behavior Control

It is important to see how behavior modification has been incorporated into the RET approach. Certainly Maxie Maultsby has done it one way, Arnold Lazarus in another, and Albert Ellis in his own unique way. Figure 1 outlines how the A-B-C's can be

Fig. 1.   Elaborated A-B-C model.

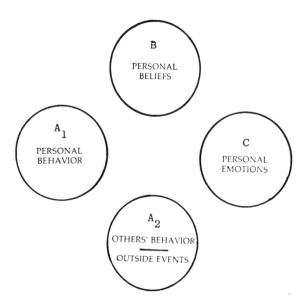

broken down a little differently. Notice that the typical A is broken into two pieces: personal behavior on the one hand, and other people's behavior and outside events on the other. Personal beliefs and emotional consequences remain the same as in the standard RET approach. We believe the subdivision of A has some implication in terms of presentation and allows us to present traditional concepts from behavior modification within this more refined RET model. For example, a typical problem is one in which another's behavior (criticism of me) filters through my irrational belief that "they should not do that and it's awful and they should really love me." Following this belief, one can become either angry or depressed. We believe that this leads to behavioral consequences and that the behaviors become more irrational as they flow from destructive emotions. This example would fit a typical A-B-C sequence of the RET model.

Many of us who do clinical work encounter clients who get depressed about having depression. In this case the activating event is some personal behavior which is filtered through one's personal belief system like, "I shouldn't be depressed and I should be perfect at RET." As you can see from Figure 1, the activating event for this example would take a little different form. Now it seems to us that one way of introducing behavior modication and putting it into perspective is to view it as the relationship between personal behavior and others' behavior. In looking at this relationship between personal behavior and others' behavior one can rather neatly introduce the behavior sequences discussed by more traditional behaviorists. For example, a person's calling me a name is an antecedent or "setup" for my responding in an equally aggressive way. This sequence does not deny the fact that the person's remark — others' behavior — is filtered through my belief system and results in an emotion. What it does highlight is the interaction between my personal behavior and the other person's behavior.

In showing business executives how to analyze problems, we teach them to view not only their internal beliefs and emotions but also to carefully notice the sequence of behaviors. Hence we talk not only of "setups" (situations that increase the probability of problems) but also of "payoffs" (consequences) which follow particular behaviors. The fact that I shout and an executive responds by throwing a tantrum because the secretary did not mail an order not only has emotional consequences for me but may have the behavioral consequence of a drop in staff production and morale.

Within the Executive Effectiveness Program we teach people to specify particular problem behavior sequences. In addition to analyzing problem sequences, we focus on particular desirable goal behaviors. Let's take an example. If the goal is report-writing, then it is important for business persons to gain the self-control involved in guiding their own behavior by becoming aware of certain learning principles which will increase the probability of that particular behavior. If report-writing is a major part of my job, then it is important for me to "set up" myself and also to "pay off" myself. If my optimum report-writing time is two or three hours free from distraction and interruption, then it is in my best interest to get that period of time. It is amazing how many people go into their offices to write reports and become upset when notified by a secretary that there is a telephone call on line three. From a behavioral approach it would be much more straightforward to tell the secretary ahead of time that you don't want to be interrupted for two or three hours. In short, it is your responsibility to set up the conditions which maximize report-writing.

Now at the payoff or consequences end of things we also conduct a behavior analysis. We want individuals to become very familiar with their own reinforcers or pleasant events. In having an executive list his reinforcers you may encounter initial resistance, but once the payoffs are experienced this usually dissolves. For small short-term tasks we ask people to identify short-term immediate rewards for themselves. For larger target behaviors we have them reward themselves with larger long-term rewards.

To demonstrate how RET and the behavioral approach combine both in terms of problem analysis and in terms of accelerating positive behavior, one must constantly teach business people how to challenge irrational ideas which block carrying out the behavioral approach. Frequently business people are extremely stingy with themselves. They have the puritan ethic to the nth degree. No wonder they are less efficient than their potential in view of the fact that they irrationally believe that a person should work without any reward.

Other sessions within the Executive Effectiveness Program highlight the need to attain self-direction through a series of specific executive skills. Frequently these skills cannot be taught in a two-and-a-half-day session, but the groundwork can be laid. Specifically, executives can combine the behavioral and RET approach in learning how to become assertive with their staffs. We believe it is a common myth that business has a corner on the market for assertive people. In business as in all of life there are many "doormats" as well as aggressive individuals.

The area of assertiveness training can use focused time and energy.

Another area of skill training is in rational decision-making. Again our approach in this session is to combine both RET and the skills from behavior modification.

Measurement

In speaking with business people who have attended seminars using psychological principles, we find there is frequently a positive feeling with little behavioral outcome. Although positive feelings may be a positive outcome, they do not necessarily match the corporate reasons for hiring consultants. While we have thought of a number of different outcome measures, we are intrigued by the work of Kiresuk. Kiresuk has developed an outcome measure being used in mental health called Goal Attainment Scaling. Briefly, the way the scale works is for an individual to specify various outcomes at specific follow-up dates. (We prefer ninety days.) Next the executive specifies on a five-point scale possible outcomes for significant target goals. In our use of Goal Attainment Scaling we ask that individuals block out both personal and business goals. One personal goal might be to spend more time with one's family. Another personal goal might be to decrease weight. Looking at business goals one might specify report-writing as an important concern. With a limited number of concerns or goals — say four or five — the individual works out a goal-attainment scale. At the end of ninety days the person reviews his goal-attainment scale to see what level of outcome he has attained on the particular goal. (The executive whose goal was to increase the amount of time spent with family members would report in ninety days how many hours each week had been spent with his or her family.) Because goal-attainment scaling forces people to specify in behavioral terms what the projected outcomes are, the level of achievement is easy to determine.

We are clearly committed to some form of measurement and find Goal Attainment Scaling an intriguing and fascinating approach. It offers the advantage of combining a person's unique goals with the possibility of assessing an entire group's goal achievements.

In summary, we believe the Executive Effectiveness Program combines goals, skills, and measurement in a way that blends nicely the advantages of rational-emotive therapy with behavior modification.

RET Applications in Rehabilitation Counseling

LARRY K. HILL, Ed.D.

Oklahoma Department of Institutions, Social and Rehabilitative Services, Oklahoma City

The first nationwide public program for work with the handicapped came in 1920 with the passage in Congress of the Civilian Vocational Rehabilitation Act. The year 1975 marked the fiftieth anniversary of the National Rehabilitation Association. During this span of a half century, tremendous progress has been made toward equalizing the opportunities of the handicapped person for a full and rewarding life based on personal and economic independence. Physical rehabilitation procedures have become exceedingly sophisticated. No small advance has been made in educative rehabilitation. The blind can be taught to read using the Braille system. They also can be trained to an astounding level of mobility. The deaf have highly functional methods of lip reading and sign language. Vocational evaluation and training have reached an advanced stage for the handicapped. There now remains one last frontier in working with disabled individuals to achieve total rehabilitation.

Psychological or attitudinal rehabilitation always has been and continues to be the weakest area within the field of rehabilitation. As physical restoration and educative rehabilitation techniques have advanced to the point where many of the more tangible barriers to successful rehabilitation have been eliminated, it has been increasingly recognized that the most crucial element in overcoming a handicap lies in the attitudinal area. Given proper attitudes, severely handicapped persons have been known to overcome formidable obstacles. Where poor attitudes have existed, even minor handicaps have proved overwhelming. This, of course, is an area where RET concepts are particularly applicable, and the field of rehabilitation, I believe, is now ready to receive such concepts.

This has not always been the case, however, because much of the appeal of the rehabilitation movement has been based on sentiment. Consequently — and not at all surprisingly, given this context — such concepts as empathy, genuineness, and warmth have been grasped with no little fervor. Nonetheless, as a trainer of field counselors, I have witnessed a growing disenchantment with "relationship" approaches to counseling. More and more I hear these vocational rehabilitation (VR) counselors saying, "Well, a relationship is all fine and good, but when do we get down to *doing* something about the client's problems?" And this is understandable upon the realization that it is the VR counselor who bears the brunt of the current emphasis on accountability in state-federal programs. No longer can the counselor savor the self-rewards of an extended "caring" relationship. Thus, it is the practitioner in the field who is demanding more efficient and effective techniques of moving clients through the rehabilitation process. And here we see an emergence of another side of the rehabilitation coin — one that is built less upon sentiment than upon tangible realities of service outcome.

How can RET concepts fill this void in the rehabilitation service delivery system? There are some popular but erroneous notions in the field that tend to limit the effectiveness of rehabilitation counseling — notions that can be corrected by the application of RET principles. For example, much of the current thinking regarding the emotional impact of disability continues to focus on a supposedly causative relationship between A, the event, and C, the emotion, with the implication being that the attitude, the B statement, is inherent within A. Thus, it is not uncommon to hear statements to the effect that an actress will respond in a more intensely negative manner to facial scarring than will a day laborer, while the latter will respond more intensely to a physically disabling condition than to a cosmetic one. This assumes that the attitude is somehow automatically associated with the event, thus providing the superficial appearance of A causing C. In turning to RET theory, however, we encounter the principle of the separateness of A and C, which tells us that neither the severity of the disability nor the special import it has for the future of the person afflicted dictates the intensity of the response: A does not cause C. The response of the actress or the day laborer to *any* type of disabling condition will be an individual one based on the individual's self-sentences. Neither of them has to experience intensely negative emotion under any condition.

Once this first erroneous assumption is made, it is not difficult to accept an even more detrimental one, this being that the individual as a whole is changed by the event of disablement. This overgeneralization is reflected in such statements as, "The client must die as a sighted person and be reborn as a blind person." The basic idea is that an individual who acquires a handicap essentially becomes a person different from the former self. This may be true in one sense — that is, the same sense that a man becomes a different person when he acquires a mother-in-law (or has any other experience for that matter). In either case, he subsequently will have different experiences in life than he would have had without either the handicap or the mother-in-law. But, fundamentally, the handicapped person simply is a person who has experienced a different kind of A, and this A, like all A's, will have pervasive emotional effects depending only upon the B statements applied to it.

In order to clarify this point, let us take the example of a recently blinded individual. It is not uncommon for such a person to feel that his or her entire life is shattered when, in fact, he or she simply has been denied one avenue (albeit a major one) of deriving satisfaction from life. True, blind persons no longer are able to achieve those satisfactions in life that are tangibly associated with sight. This means not that they must settle for half a loaf, so to speak, but only that they must seek satisfaction in different ways. They still can lead a full and satisfying existence. To say otherwise would be the equivalent of making the obviously fallacious claim that being deprived of the companionship of a specific member of the opposite sex would reduce the absolute satisfaction one is capable of achieving in life. Again, it is the attitude, the B statement, that determines the rapidity with which the individual accepts the limitation imposed, whether such limitation be physical, economic, social, or psychological, and moves on to seek out other areas of life satisfaction.

Now this is a most important point in working with the handicapped in that it generally is believed that the rehabilitation client *must* go through a period of mourning regarding the loss of certain physical capabilities. Although a common precursor to getting better, this is less a "must" than it is the result of clients' being left to their own devices in working through the loss. The application of RET principles enables them to move quickly through such catastrophizing and into more rewarding endeavors. This point is quite vividly illustrated in a single counseling session I had with a severely disabled quadriplegic individual suffering a reactive depression. After approximately thirty minutes of rational-emotive counseling, he made a very short statement, beginning with a tone of frustration and actually ending with a laugh. The statement was, "But you don't want me to feel awful about anything." Being a very bright and perceptive individual, he realized even before finishing the statement that *that*, indeed, was the objective. He also realized that he need not feel awful about anything, including his permanent physical limitations. The A in this case was extremely significant to this client — but B, the real source of the problem of depression, was a relatively simple case of catastrophizing and self-pity which, when eliminated, enabled him to resume his efforts to learn to drive and to enroll in college.

And so it is with all reactions to disability or to the handicaps deriving therefrom. The nature and severity of the handicap present the client with somewhat different A's — the B's encountered in counseling the handicapped are no different from the B's encountered in counseling the nonhandicapped (if, indeed, there is such a person).

I would like to conclude this discussion by mentioning several of the more common B statements found in standard RET practice and showing how they tend to become manifest in the practice of rehabilitation counseling. Let us look first at some fear-producing statements, each reflecting the basic self-sentence of, "What's going to happen to me?"

1. What if people won't help me if I get lost?
2. I can't ever make a living for myself. What am I going to do?
3. Now that I'm disabled and can't support my family, what if they desert me?
4. What will people think of my condition? How could they accept me this way?

Second, there are the depression-producing statements that reflect the basic self-sentence of, "What a worthless person I am!"

1. This happened as punishment for my sins. I must be a terrible person!
2. I'm so different, so repulsive, no one will ever let me be close to them.
3. I've lost my wholeness. I'll never be any good as a person.
4. I can't stand being dependent on others. Only a slob lives that way.
5. No one really understands what it's like. It's just awful being this way!

And finally, anger-producing statements reflecting the basic self-sentence of, "It shouldn't be this way!"

1. Why did this have to happen? I shouldn't have to go through life this way.
2. I don't deserve this. It's just not fair.
3. Why do those slobs have to look at me that way? They should mind their own business.
4. People are so insensitive. I'm blind. He knows I can't tell a one-dollar bill from a five.

When looked at within the framework of the irrational B statement, it becomes evident that the psychological adjustment of a handicapped person is a counseling task for which RET is eminently suited.

Dealing with the Irrationality of Alcoholic Drinking

ALBERT F. GRAU, S.J., Ph.D.

Clinical Director, Mt. Manor Treatment Center, Emmitsburg, Maryland; Professor Emeritus of Psychology and Consultant to the Counseling Center, Loyola College, Baltimore, Maryland

Alcoholism may be viewed as a dysfunctioning in the use of alcohol with four dimensions: physical, psychological, social, and ethical (in that it involves value systems).

Physical

I will not elaborate in this area, except to say that the actual biological factors involved in alcoholism are gradually being identified. I refer you to William Madsen's work, *The American Alcoholic* (1974), and the monumental work of Wallgren and Barry in two volumes, *Actions of Alcohol* (1971), dismissing over three thousand publications relevant to the many primary biological effects of alcohol.

Most alcohologists agree that in true alcoholism there is a physiological compulsion which becomes operative upon the ingestion of alcohol. Most agree that this compulsive character remains with the alcoholic even after sobriety, in that it can be reactivated upon the ingestion of any appreciable amount of alcohol.

Psychological

The alcoholic in his particular life situation, early in his drinking, has experienced a relatively emphatic payoff as the result of his drinking — perhaps he lost his feelings of inadequacy, or was "accepted," or could sleep, or was cheered up. Think of this as a formula where

$$S(ituation) + A(lcohol) = P(ayoff)$$

It may be useful to think of S also as S(tress). Although S is often a situation involving stress, it may be a situation involving a desire or "need" to celebrate. The principle is the same: He did experience a celebratory euphoria, hence a payoff. Whenever S repeats itself, it tends to be linked with A. The S's tend to be elaborated and proliferated, as well as generalized according to the laws of stimulus generalization. Later on, even when S is not present, the drinker will tend, through rationalization and alibi, to create S's. The drinker becomes psychologically addicted. In other words the drinker establishes "linkages" between his various life situations, as he perceives these, and a relief from these, or reward in these, through drinking. He now tends to drink "on cue," but denial and rationalization abort any insight into his "cue drinking."

As long as the P is relatively uncontaminated at the time of drinking, the drinker will continue to drink, since obviously his drinking is reenforced. However, in the context — true alcoholism — we assume that eventually the payoffs get combined with problems or penalties. These might be "blackouts," conflict with law or with significant figures, physical symptomatology such as morning tremors, or various kinds of accidents.

Social

We live in a society which has been called "drug dependent." Cultural chemicals are legion. Alcohol is one drug which is not only legally and socially permitted, it is sanctioned, approved, and encouraged by various types of motivational imagery: "You've got one life to live — live it with gusto," "Drink _____, the SOFT whiskey" (for the gals), relaxing with a beer after a hard chore, being elegant with wine, etc., etc. Alcohol is the focal point of social festivity. To be able to enjoy drinking is socially important.

Value Systems

It is obvious that drinking has become a social value, i.e., it is rated as *important*. It is associated with masculinity, femininity, elegance, sophistication, culture, relaxation, etc. As such, for many nonalcoholic drinkers, it is reasonably important and adjunctive. For the alcoholic, it is a *necessary* value. Drinking for the alcoholic, as time goes on in his progression, changes its ranking in his priority of values, and gradually moves toward the top ranking.

The progression of drinking as a value can be illustrated in these changes given *as examples* in the drinker's scale of values.

	STAGE I (Beginning)	STAGE II (Some Time Later)	STAGE III (Critical Period)
Most Important	job	job	DRINKING
	family	family	job
	health	health	family
	reputation	DRINKING	health
Least Important	finances	reputation	reputation
	DRINKING	finances	finances

All of the above dimensions, but especially the psychological, social, and value systems dimensions, are interactive and complementary. For example:

Drinking is a folkway in one's neighborhood (social).
The drinker wants to be one of the boys (value system), and wouldn't it be awful if he weren't (psychological)?
He drinks.

As can be seen, alcoholism is not merely a vicious circle, it is an enmeshment.

What gets the alcoholic started, after he knows or suspects that he is alcoholic? There are alternative answers. (1) If the alky is in the drinking mode, it is most likely a physical compulsion, as in any addiction. (2) If he is "dry," it is probably a psychological compulsion. How get the alcoholic stopped? Or: (a) How is this circle or enmeshment broken up? (b) How is the freedom from alcohol abuse maintained?

In answer to (a): Usually by some sort of crisis, which can be contrived. (This can be "benign coercion" by spouse, employer, etc.) Not infrequently, the crisis will develop directly from the excessive drinking; for example, a traffic accident or the threat of loss of job.

In answer to (b): By dealing directly and head on with the psychological compulsion through the rational-emotive approach. It is my belief that some kind of ongoing program of educational (therapeutic) confrontation is usually necessary and always useful. A specific segment of this confrontational process must deal with, and teach the alcoholic to deal with, his or her emotional hang-ups. The effectiveness of RET in dealing with the psychological component of alcoholism is receiving strategic recognition among professional workers in the field. Margaret Hindman in the respected experimental publication *Alcohol Health and Research World* (produced by the National Institute on Alcohol Abuse and Alcoholism through the National Clearinghouse for Alcohol Information) (Spring, 1976) discusses various uses of RET *in re* in "Rational Emotive Therapy in Alcoholism Treatment."

In a typical case, let me present a brief sketch of the process as used with an alcoholic female. She was divorced by her husband and her last drinking binge was precipitated in her mind by the refusal of her ten-year-old son to visit her.

(This exchange took place at Mt. Manor Treatment Center, a twenty-eight-day residential program at Emmitsburg, Maryland. The residents routinely receive two formal lecture classes a week on rational-emotive principles and are familiar with the A-B-C-D model made famous by Dr. Albert Ellis.)

F_1: But, doctor, you'd be upset too, if your own child refused to see you!

D_1: I would? Not if I kept my thinking straight, which obviously at that time you did not. Let's look at what happened to you. What was your life situation, your S, as you saw it?

F_2: Uh, my son did not come to see me and that was crummy. After all I *am* his mother.

D_2: OK, that was your S. Now what kind of P were you actually looking for when you began drinking? I hardly think it was to get your son to change his mind, was it?

F_3: I guess not. . . . I guess I just wanted to get away from the hurt. . . .

D_3: "To get away from the hurt" was what you were looking for . . . your payoff. And did you get it? What happened?

F_4: Drinking sort of consoled me — for a while, but as a matter of fact, I felt worse. And I was still drunk the next day and missed work.

D_4: So the formula in your case was

S = son not visiting — how crummy!
P = narcotizing effect of the boose *plus*,
    in this case, trouble with your job.

Did you really get a payoff?

F_5: No, not really — not enough to balance out.

D_5: Let's go back to S again. There are really *two* things there that can be separated.

F_6: Oh yeah — what?

D_6: Think of what we discussed in the class concerning the ABC model. What's the A?

F_7: The crumminess of my son not coming to see me?

D_7: No! Your son's not coming to see you is clearly A. Where does the "crumminess" come from?

F_8: From him not visiting . . . er, uh?

D_8: He simply didn't visit! *You* added the "crumminess." Now, what is A and what is B in this case?

F_9: A is . . . of course . . . his not visiting and B is what I told myself: "Isn't it awful and crummy?" Yes, I guess I did add that.

D_9: Of course, and you had to feel upset if you concentrated on your own awfulizing and calamitizing. So do you see that the S in this case, and in many similar instances, is seen by you in the light of what you are thinking or saying to yourself at B? What can you do about your S?

F_{10}: Separate the B part from the A part, I guess.

D_{10}: Yes, and what else can you do about S?

F_{11}: Yes, I know — you emphasized this morning in class that it would be better to develop new links . . . "linkages," you called them.

D_{11}: Yes! Linkages for what?

F_{12}: For my situation, my S . . . ?

D_{12}: Precisely! You want a payoff or a relief in your life situation. All *you* get from drinking is a lot of pain and grief. Why not try a new linkage? S might still be tough in itself. But using your A-B-C model can clarify what S *really* is, rather than what you have made it — or perhaps even what you wanted to make it: an excuse or alibi to drink! So, let's look at the formula:

S — your life situation

P — the payoff or the relief you want *without any penalty*

And now we have a blank that needs to be filled in where you are trying to eliminate the alcohol. Your formula now is

$$S + ? = P$$

What do you put in place of the booze? What do we suggest here in the Program?

F_{13}: Well, . . . I guess when S is *really* tough . . . go to a meeting [of Alcoholics Anonymous, where members reenforce new thinking to replace B sentences — Author].

D_{13}: If you can't get to a meeting . . . ?

F_{14}: Well, call a friend or sponsor (a more experienced AA buddy), review my motivations for sobriety . . . ?

D$_{14}$: Fine! Whatever will help you to see that, for you, resorting to booze is irrational drinking, resulting from irrational thinking: a totally self-destructive linkage. . . . Could you *now* rehearse in your mind your son's not visiting you and your starting to get upset? Try it! What would you see yourself doing in that situation?

F$_{15}$: Well, let's see. . . .

In review, in this substantially authentic summary of a typical case, we have engaged in a confrontational exchange, wherein we try to accomplish two objectives: The first objective is to teach the alcoholic drinker to challenge and review his or her perceptions of S. Particularly, we show the alcoholic that when S(ituation) becomes S(tress), it is because of his or her irrational B sentences. The second objective is to teach the alcoholic new linkages. The desired payoffs can be achieved — without any penalty mixed in — in other ways where

$$S(ituation) + \text{RATIONALITY} = P(ayoff)!$$

RET in Dealing with Alcohol-Dependent Persons

JANE N. HIGBEE, M.D.

Veterans Administration Hospital, Columbia, South Carolina

First, I want to emphasize that alcoholics have all the eleven or twelve irrational ideas outlined by Dr. Albert Ellis plus a few extra of their own. Although most alcoholics roundly resent being treated on a psychiatric service, in my opinion they are probably far nuttier than the average psychiatric patient. They not only believe a lot of junk and indulge in self-defeating behavior but they have the added disadvantage of a drug effect, a mind-altering drug that is a cell poison. There is, according to Drs. Knott and Fink of the University of Tennessee Medical School Department of Psychiatry, no social drinking in this country. All drinking, even in moderation, is done because of the effect of the drug — alcohol — on the brain. Drinking is a learned behavior, and can be unlearned, but like smoking or overeating it requires a change of beliefs and attitudes plus a great deal of work. As Nietzsche said, human beings tend to be lazy and scared as a group, so alcohol allows us scared humans to fog up our brains and be less afraid of rejection, less afraid of what others will think, and less afraid of the consequences of our actions. It also chemically loosens inhibitions so that we can "let ourselves go" and behave foolishly.

Alcohol dependents (a term I prefer to "alcoholics" because there is no medical evidence that boozing is a disease and there is a great deal of evidence that it is a learned habit such as smoking or gambling) usually believe two irrational ideas quite strongly; and they are, oddly enough, contradictory:

1. I am so worthless that it doesn't matter what happens to me. I'm an alcoholic and can't help drinking. I'll always be an alcoholic.

2. I can stop drinking any time I want. It won't hurt me because I'll quit before I get d.t.'s or cirrhosis.

To change any habit requires making a decision and working at the problem — not just once but over and over — and that is where the difficulty comes in. When a habit pattern is printed on the brain, we tend to repeat it automatically — sort of like a fat person with a box of candy. The pudgy one will keep getting up for another piece long after the craving for candy is satisfied. Alcoholics have the same sort of foolish belief. "I must keep drinking until I can't hold any more or until it is all gone."

Alcoholics are also notoriously lazy; they want a quick "cure." Although Alcoholics Anonymous has helped a great many people to stay sober, there is no scientific evidence that AA is the best form of management. It probably helps some people for irrational reasons:

1. They can depend on a "higher power" rather than themselves.
2. They can have some place to go and be with people with whom they feel equally or less worthless.
3. They can believe they are victims of a "disease" and that one drink will cause a spree.

In teaching alcohol dependents, it is probably best to be absolutely truthful in regard to this last statement. Almost all drunks will tell you that they have had one, three, or seven drinks and quit without winding up in serious trouble; and there is some evidence that a few alcohol-dependent people have learned to drink socially.

I usually tell my patients that it is probably better to avoid the first drink because the habit tends to repeat itself and not because one drink will inevitably lead to the gutter.

Alcoholics also have the silly idea that a person who can control his drinking is somehow a better person than one who drinks and gets into trouble. They will, therefore, go through all sorts of manipulations to convince themselves that they can have a few drinks and quit. Most of them don't stop with a few drinks though.

Another dumb idea that the general public absorbs readily is that most alcoholics wind up in the gutter. Less than 5 percent of drunks are "skid row" types; and they actually drink very little. Most of them probably have severe character disorders or behave as simple schizophrenics who want a life free of responsibility. They titrate their intake of alcohol and show little evidence of the severe physical damage seen in the heavy drinker who is a successful business person or executive.

Probably most alcoholics fall into the class of passive-aggressive personality disorders, although, in the state of acute alcohol withdrawal, they may show manifestations of psychosis — either short-lasting or long-lasting. Some are misdiagnosed schizophrenic because they develop a state of chronic alcoholic hallucinosis. If you want to do psychological testing, wait until the patient is over his acute withdrawal stage; otherwise, the MMPI will have almost every scale elevated. Consider, too, that in this test the Pa or paranoia scale is usually elevated in blacks, possibly a cultural factor.

Sobering up a drunk is a medical problem, but changing the thinking which leads to drug dependence is a teaching challenge. I believe it takes anywhere from months to a year to really cause any change in the attitude of most of these people. My greatest success has been with teaching — didactically for the most part — the principles of RET or RBT. I use many illustrations from ward life, my personal life, and patient experiences, but I refuse to allow therapy to turn into long accounts of past failures. I quickly and cheerfully shut this sort of harangue off by remarking that we are here to learn to think rationally and not to relive our past mistakes or injustices. Repetition is the road to success, and I am careful to tell the patients that they will hear the same thing over and over from me, both individually and in group. Fortunately, our ward psychologist and social worker are both converts to RET and there is no problem of the patient's playing one therapist against another. If there were, we would hope to deal rationally with the situation by pointing out that everyone is entitled to differ, there are no absolutely right answers to most of life's problems, and being wrong or mistaken is not horrible and awful. Our therapists are not ashamed to admit that they goof at times, and this is helpful to the perfectionistic "all or nothing" attitudes of the alcoholics.

We try to teach our drug dependees not to harp on the bad qualities of their relatives, and we also try to discourage relatives from covering up and refusing to let the patient suffer the consequences of misbehaving. In this, we borrow heavily from Rudolf Dreikurs, M.D., an Adlerian, who did much work and wrote many books and articles about children and their management. The four mistaken goals of children apply equally well to alcoholics: attention-getting, power, revenge, playing helpless.

It takes time and work to change thinking and thus change feeling and behavior, and we emphasize work, work, work — on changing your nutty ideas without believing that your past errors and rotten behavior have made you a rotten person. You are only a rotten person when you are dead!

The Treatment of Guilt Through Rational Stage Directed Imagery

DONALD J. TOSI, Ph.D.

Associate Professor, The Ohio State University Faculty of Special Services

JAMES R. REARDON

Adjunct Assistant Professor, The Ohio State University

Numerous writers have discussed the topic of guilt. Freedman, Kaplan, and Sadoch (1972, p. 770) describe guilt as "an affect associated with self-reproach and need for punishment." Ellis (1962) says overemphasizing guilt is the propensity to blame oneself for one's failures or perceived shortcomings. Maultsby (1971a) contends that there are rarely any rational reasons to feel guilty. The behaviors about which one feels guilty are generally acts one really wanted to do in the first place; since one usually controls the contingencies and determines the excuses that are acceptable to oneself as rationalization for having done things, guilt as a form of self-punishment is rarely effective as an inhibitor or motivator of behavior. Freedman *et al.* (1972, pp. 257, 265) assert that for the treatment of several major disorders with which guilt is commonly associated (such as manic-depressive psychosis, psychotic-depressive reactions, and depressive neurosis) an active psychotherapeutic approach in which the ideas of guilt or worthlessness are challenged is one of the treatments of choice. Rational stage directed therapy (RSDT) is such an approach.

Rational stage directed therapy is a therapeutic approach developed by Tosi (1974) and Tosi and Marzella (1977). It is a modification and extension of approaches previously described by Lazarus (1971), Ellis (1974b), and Maultsby (1971a). RSDT is a didactic, experiential cognitive-behavior therapy designed to guide or direct the client's growth through progressive stages. RSDT starts with self- and situational *awareness*, proceeds through self- and situational *exploration*, *commitment* to rational thinking and acting, *implementation* of rational thinking and acting, *internalization*, on through *change* and *redirection*. The modality of RSDT consists of vivid cognitive-emotive imagery when the client is in a deeply relaxed state (RSDI) or hypnotic-trance state (rational stage directed hypnotherapy [RSDH]). RSDT, being stage directed, places priority on high-level covert cognitive control over emotional, behavioral, and situational processes. Thoresen and Mahoney (1974) and Meichenbaum and Cameron (1974) cite the critical cuing value of covert behavior (cognitions) in influencing overt behavior. Cognitive symbolic activity (conscious or unconscious) is generally a contributing factor to emotional arousal whether such arousal is positive or negative. RSDT employs the basic Ellisian A-B-C cognitive restructuring technique. Through the imagination, the client directly confronts those external or internal events that serve to activate the specific irrational ideas generating his affective/physiological/behavioral disorders. In the initial stages of RSDT, the client learns the rudiments of cognitive or rational restructuring and later becomes more proficient in its use. RSDT is then augmented with "in vivo" behavioral tasks corresponding closely to the imagery content.

Specifically RSDT is designed to dislodge, to outgain, and to minimize internalized beliefs, attitudes, and emotions that are self-defeating in nature. The following case report is a specific example of how treatment through rational stage directed imagery is conducted and its effect on the reduction of the frequency of self-reported guilt responses.

Case History

The client, a twenty-five-year-old white female, was raised in a rigid Roman Catholic family. She was initially referred to a community mental health center with presenting problems of vocational and interpersonal dissatisfaction and acute periodic states of depression and guilt. She experienced irrational feelings of worthlessness, dire needs for approval, protracted negative affective states such as depression, anxiety, guilt, menstrual irregularity (prolonged duration and excessive flow), migraine headaches, and rheumatoid arthritis. Behaviorally, she was very passive, socially reticent, dependent (on family), lethargic, and self-destructive (beat hands to a bloody pulp).

During eight individual sessions over two months the client learned to apply the Tosi (1974) A-B-C-D-E elaboration of Ellis's A-B-C paradigm until she became proficient. Additionally, written homework and bibliotherapy enabled her to expand her behavior repertoire in more self-enhancing ways. As her depression and inertia abated, she began to experience frequent guilt. The guilt was registered cognitively both as a consequence of behavior and in anticipation of future actions. Because of its aversive nature, the guilt served two maladaptive functions: One, it detracted from the reinforcing strength of the pleasure accrued by engaging in some of these behaviors; two, it was a potential inhibitor of future adaptive responses.

Treatment

Baseline responses of client self-reported guilt were gathered over a period of two weeks, during which time standard rational-emotive therapy techniques were employed. Also the client was exposed to systematic cognitive muscle relaxation for part of each one-hour weekly session.

During a five-week experimental period the client was seen twice weekly for thirty-minute sessions. In these sessions, cognitive muscle relaxation was paired with rational stage directed imagery. In RSDI the client examined activating events of a disturbing nature (A), her perceptions, appraisals, or evaluation of these events (B), the emotional or affective concomitants or resultants (C), physiological responses (D), and behavioral motoric options (E).

The therapist, using A-B-C-D-E cognitive restructuring, guided the client's imagining through the stages of awareness, exploration, commitment to rational action, implementation of rational action, internalization, and change/redirection. In brief, the stages were defined as follows:

Awareness. The client sees both irrational and rational possibilities. She is made aware of more reasonable modes of functioning (thinking, feeling, acting) and conditions that are contradictory to her self-defeating thoughts, the need to interact more effectively with her environment.

Exploration. The client tests out her new awareness about herself via imagery and in real life. She submits her old as well as new ideas to the empirical test. The therapist asks her to engage in vigorous cognitive restructuring in an experimental way — to experience situations she previously avoided, try out new behaviors, and evaluate the consequences of her acts. Resistance becomes increasingly apparent in this stage.

Commitment to Rational Action. The therapist encourages the client to use her newly acquired knowledge and awareness and self-exploration to fight and attack resistances that prevent her from implementing rational strategies for effective living. She is more aware of the innermost thoughts that produce affective/physiological reactions associated with tendencies to approach or to avoid significant life situations or to develop the skills necessary to overcome her cognitive/emotional/behavioral and situational difficulties. The client realizes she needs to take risks or make behavioral commitments. At this juncture the client thinks of terminating therapy — the *point* of *choice* or *decision to act.*

Implementation. The client, after privately and/or publicly commiting herself to constructive action, is encouraged to implement the self-management skills (via imagery and in vivo) she is in the process of acquiring. Her skills at this stage may involve cognitive control over emotional/physical and behavioral states. She proceeds to practice "in vivo" and refine these skills.

Internalization. The client shows signs of making her new learnings and experiences a part of herself. She shows obvious signs of incorporating more reasonable modes of thinking and acting into her behavioral repertoire and she implements them with greater ease and proficiency.

Change/Redirection. The client observes herself, notes significant changes in her thinking, and sees that she can control significantly negative emotions and self-defeating actions. She transacts more effectively with her environment — thus maximizing positive consequences. She realizes the need for further growth.

In this case study, the content of each session was based on the most disturbing situation arising between therapy sessions. The client was assisted in relaxation, and then rational stage directed imagery was introduced. The client was asked to imagine the situation (A), her irrational ideas (B), emotions (C), physiological state (D), and behavioral response (E). She was then helped to become more *aware* of the consequences of both irrational and rational ideas and subsequently was guided in exploring both self-defeating and self-enhancing possibilities. Through imagery the therapist guided her to focus on rational alternatives (determined by the Maultsby criteria for rational thinking). The therapist then guided her to focus on making a *commitment* to *implement* rational thinking and acting, and subsequently guided her to observe herself internalizing the more rational modes of functioning — feeling the more desirable emotions — and engaging in rational self-talk. As the client observed herself acting, thinking, and feeling more desirably, she was instructed to observe a more permanent change in her behavior (reduced feelings of guilt).

In the case of this client, merely thinking about moving out of her parents' home or discussing it with her mother (A) produced self-depreciating thinking (B) which led to guilt, anxiety, and resentment (C), a tension headache and/or hyperventilation (D), and avoidance, withdrawal, and inactivity (E). Through RSDI the same (A) situation (moving out) would become associated with (B) thoughts of appropriate self-assertion, independence, and acceptance (of both herself and her parents), (C) feelings of confidence and relaxation, (D) physiological homeostasis, (E) productive behavioral activity such as apartment-hunting and more positive social interaction with parents and others. The same sequence was as applicable to the above-described behavior as to dating men not approved by the family, changing vocations, or sexual experimentation. The client was asked to engage in RSDI at home for fifteen to twenty minutes each day.

Results

Beginning on January 3, 1975, and ending February 21, 1975, the client was asked to self-observe and record any time when she experienced thoughts or feelings of guilt, and to note the date, time, and activating event/self-talk. In order to control for experimenter bias and to minimize the influence of self-recording on the subject, the following protocol was observed:

1. The subject recorded each individual incident of guilt on a 3×5 card which she then placed in a large manila envelope so that she would be minimally aware of any pattern or frequency of guilt.
2. The therapist/experimenter did not collect or examine any data (including baseline) until after the entire baseline/experimental period (1-3-75 to 2-21-75) was over, so that experimenter bias could be minimized.

Results are graphically represented both on a day-to-day and weekly basis. The frequency of self-recorded guilt was significantly decreased by the intervention of rational stage directed imagery.

Fig. 1. Daily frequency of self-observed/self-recorded guilt as a function of time in treatment.

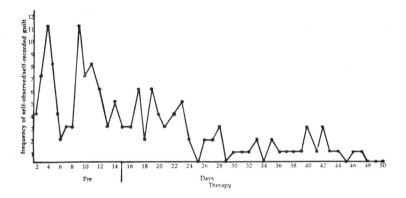

Fig. 2. Weekly frequency of self-observed/self-recorded guilt as a function of time in treatment.

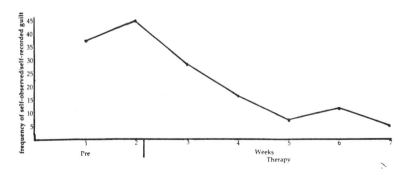

The client was further affected in the following ways:

A —Situations — a variety of situations, such as dating, sexual play, moving into her apartment, staying out late, became associated with

B —Cognitions — self-acceptance, tendency to face problems,

desire (but not dire need) for acceptance, objectivism and rationality rather than moralism

C — Affect — relatively guiltless, confident, happy, spontaneous, relaxed

D — Physiological — regular menstrual periods (normal duration, moderate flow), cramps and/or headaches (not migraine) very rarely, no recurrence of arthritic problems since early February

E — Behavioral — sleeping soundly, appropriately self-assertive, spontaneous, honest, responsible, socially adept, decisive, energetic, experiencing significant academic and vocational achievement

Follow-up

Three months following the cessation of RSDI the client continues to function very adequately. She has moved from her parents' home into her own apartment. She is working twenty to twenty-five hours a week in addition to doing straight "A" work through two quarters (twenty-three hours) of college — majoring in respiratory therapy. She is dating several individuals and is developing an intimate relationship with one of them. She experiences minimal psychological disturbance and has recently terminated therapy by our mutual agreement.

Rational-Emotive Therapy with Hospitalized Psychotics*

JOHN M. GULLO, Ed.D.

Private Practice, Springfield, Illinois

Psychotherapy with psychotics has traditionally been difficult primarily because of their basic thought disorder, which makes thinking rationally or logically quite hard. Probably most mental health professionals in inpatient facilities have not found it very rewarding to treat the psychotic, and have not cherished the tremendous effort and hard work required to affect behavioral change. I believe that many, if not most, psychotherapists (in an inpatient setting) have given up too easily in the treatment of these psychiatric casualties.

Many therapists also see group therapy with chronic regressed patients as largely valueless. They say, "They [the patients] don't talk or communicate," or "They are too far out." These reasons seem *specious*. Some success, though, has been obtained using Remotivation techniques. These are not of the psychotherapy variety as is usually conceived, though they are an important adjunct, if not in most instances a starting point. Even here, apparently, little beyond remotivation has been achieved. Moreover, a large part of the success obtained (increased patient responsiveness) frequently results from the remotivators' relating to the patient on the *patient's* terms. Thus there is no threat to his determined maintenance of his own chronicity. In actuality the patient would seem to be manipulating or "conditioning" the therapist, and not the reverse. The patient is saying, "I'll relate to you but only on *my* terms." One fallacy in the argument that verbal therapy is fruitless with chronic regressed patients is

* This paper was originally written in 1969 when the author was at the Jacksonville (Illinois) State Hospital. This is an edited version given at the First National Conference on Rational Psychotherapy.

the assumption that verbal response is a necessity for the therapist. Patients can learn and get therapy just listening. While this passivity may not be conducive to optimal benefit, it does have its place and can be helpful. In fact, a patient can be an active passive participant assessing his attitudes quietly.

And so it has been found empirically that these chronic regressed patients do, after a period of from three to six group sessions, begin to talk up in the group. Part of their responsiveness seems to be an outgrowth of the therapist's activeness and directness. In this connection, experience has shown that the more the therapist is talkative and active, the more the patient tends to become actively engaged in the process. As is well known, most schizophrenics, especially the chronic regressed cases, isolate themselves and are socially withdrawn. Therefore, it is necessary to badger and bedevil them into conversing with you. This, in the severe cases, is at the level of remotivation — getting them to speak simple things such as age, address, name, names of fellow patients. Usually the patient can be gotten to give more information by expanding questions about his address, such as inquiring about stores nearby, family members (names, occupation, etc.). Thus the patient is shown that he can talk to others and, more importantly, that it is not frightening — that he's not going to be "eaten alive" by others. Of course, he knows he can talk, but he refuses to do so because of fear of involvement with others, self-imprecation, and an inured pattern of isolation. Positive reinforcement of the social (verbal) interaction together with an excavation of the self-defeating underlying illogical beliefs can move these patients successfully in the direction of self-reliance.

Another avenue of entry into the patient's aberrant thinking is the exploitation of important side comments made by patients. These can be explored to ascertain underlying attitudes. For example, Alex, in giving the names of his sisters and brother, said, "Genevieve, Lily, Joseph — he'll never make it." This is not uncommon and at first thought would appear to reveal sibling rivalry. This may be queried and the insight expanded to include present relationships and its import into the patient's maintaining his hospitalization by this self-defeating belief. This is an idea that almost all, if not all, patients (and nonpatients for that matter) have — the idea that one should be thoroughly competent, adequate, and achieving in all possible respects if one is to consider oneself worthwhile. Many of these patients have had significant deprivations, and life truly has been "rough" for them, especially in view of their propensity to be so disturbed. And within the context of these deprivations, they observe their great difficulty in maintaining themselves and accepting the grim facts of reality. They fail — as *all* humans do — because of their humanity. Then they fail again . . . and again . . . and some more; and finally conclude falsely that these failures prove that they really are inadequate, nonachieving, and incompetent — that they *shouldn't* be doing perfectly well. It's not their failures that are doing them in, but their nonvalidated belief that they shouldn't be failing. Ergo, since they are failing, they are no-good, worthless slobs. They imprecate their whole beings because some of their acts are wrong, mistaken, or bad. They overgeneralize. This is the process that leads to their anxiety, guilt, and depression. It is this irrational thinking that has produced the self-defeating pattern of behavior. "After all, since I am so worthless, I am not now and never will be able to make it on the outside. I must remain in the hospital the rest of my life." Or, put into a second irrational idea, this would read, ". . . one's past history is an all-important determinant of one's present behavior and . . . because something once strongly affected one's life, it should indefinitely have a similar effect" (Ellis and Harper, 1962).

Equally important in the psychological self-immolation of chronic regressed patients is another unsubstantiated notion — the idea that it is an utter necessity for an adult human being to be loved or approved by virtually every significant person in his community. When this approbation is not accorded, again they conclude they are good-for-nothing . . . garbage. They execrate their whole selves merely because a part of them is not doing so well. With this illogical idea, they are forced to overpersonalize disapproval, thus maintaining their chronicity and hospitalization.

Of course, involved in any invalid belief there is a valid component. This is one's desires or preferences. Chronic hospitalized psychotics often *want* the goodies of life, which include love, money, material objects, and so on. But, especially in regard to love, they normally demand a *guarantee* that they'll always have love or be loved. Even if they are being approved of by all the people they value, they continually worry about how much they are being loved and whether or not others will continue to approve of them. This kind of guarantee one can't get. Thus, their self-defeating values maintain their hospitalization.

Corollary to their insistent need to be loved is their magnified dependency — the idea that one should be dependent on others and needs someone stronger than oneself on whom to rely. Hence, they believe that this dependent behavior will get them the demanded approbation — that gratuitously they should and

will be awarded the "goodies of life." Moreover, they erroneously think that "it is easier to avoid than to face certain life
difficulties and self-responsibilities." They resist doing the
work required to surmount the difficulties and build self-
reliance.

How could rational-emotive therapy effectively handle this?
Simply by *confronting* the patients with these and other negative
ideologies — the thinking that is absolutistic. The therapist
directly, forcefully confronts the patient with his "stupid ideas."
We give concrete homework assignments to get this process
going because, if we leave patients to their own devices, they
probably won't do anything about their "insight."

We make an all-out attempt to get the patient to see that *he or
she is responsible for his or her actions.* One may be "sick" or
"crazy" but he or she is still in the driver's seat, and being
"mentally ill" doesn't prove or mean one can't control oneself or
is immune to self-help. That the patient can be responsible is
more than an assumption. Empirically, I have seen this validated
for an increasing number of chronic long-term patients — many
of whom hallucinate, have troublesome delusions, and otherwise have serious psychological impairments. (Gullo, 1966).

Far too many psychotherapists and mental hospital employees
(not to mention most other people) have the same serious hang-
up as the patients' compelling need to be approved of. Accordingly, they are afraid and refuse to take the risk of confronting
patients with their (the patients') nonsense. Hence they maintain a deleterious status quo by "playing it safe." This is most
unfortunate because, in my estimation, almost anything short of
confronting the patient with reality is doing the patient a serious
disservice. Silence is all too easily interpreted as consent, and
patients go along their merry solipsistic way. Therapists have a
hard time accepting the fact that they *can* confront and "smash
patients' crazy thinking" over their heads. This produces positive results because ideas are attacked, *not* whole persons. From
a practical referent we know that, by and large, refusal to confront hospitalized psychotics' behavior does contribute significantly to their becoming chronic. Because of false premises,
therapists and staff have no guts, lack the courage of their convictions, and fear being considered mean and untherapeutic. Their
irrationality is believing that it is terrible if someone thinks
badly of them and that their censure proves they are worthless.
This even applies to the patients' attitudes toward the staff. The
patients generally in one way or another feel sorry for themselves, and in various ways let you know this. They begin collecting injustices both covertly and overtly. They exhibit themselves

as weaklings being abused by staff who are viewed un-euphemistically as "bastards" when they try to get patients to move out of their psychic slum. And, sad to say, therapists and staff alike fall for this game. They play it, nourish it, keep it alive by believing: "Yes, how awful it is that you are here, and are so disturbed, and are so weak." Instead of rationally believing, "It's just an unfortunate, unpleasant fact and no more," they declare, "It's tragic."

As a complementary tool, use *directness* therapeutically. Here the therapist outrightly *confronts* patients with their disturbances, shows in what way they are "off their rockers." Not confronting patients with reality allows them the luxury of continuing, in an uninterrupted fashion, to condition themselves to their unrealistic notions. It is most important to force the talking issue with the patient — to be *intrusive* upon his or her solipsistic existence — because any therapy is to a large degree an intrusion on the patient's "life space."

Assign minimal tasks with the foreknowledge that the patient will be able to do them successfully. Administer positive reinforcement to establish a more rational set of beliefs and debrainwash the negative values. You may employ penalties (not punishment, which involves both (1) penalization, deprivation, and (2) condemnation of the whole person and not just his acts) and utilize Premack's principle (Homme, 1965).

In order to get the patients to put into action what things they've learned about themselves or to just help them get *experience* in some particular facet of living, give concrete assignments. The withdrawn, autistic patient can have the assignment to talk to at least two or three persons between group meetings. Sometimes she or he may be asked to do this with specified members of the group or on the ward. And sometimes in the more serious cases, other members of the group are asked to volunteer to coerce the patient to talk to them. The required conversation is kept at minimal levels initially, such as the food or weather or clothes. Increasingly this is accelerated to include, for example, reading an article from a book. At an even higher level, the patient is encouraged, even forced, to join some social club. The homework assignments are checked on constantly — "What are you doing to get out of here?" — in order to keep the patient focusing on the advantages of getting discharged. In other words, continued prodding is necessary to get patients into motion and positively motivated. In this way, memory as well as reality confrontation can be facilitated.

The Theoretical and Empirical Integration of the Rational-Emotive and Classical Conditioning Theories

JEFFREY M. BRANDSMA, Ph.D.

University of Kentucky

I think you are all aware that Albert Ellis has presented a system of psychotherapy which has explicit in it a theory of the development of psychopathology. The key idea here is that thought inevitably precedes and accompanies emotion — then irrational self-talk maintains the negative emotions. These ideas have been summarized into his A-B-C theory, where A is the objective stimulus configuration, B the cortical evaluation of A, and C the emotional response. B gets loaded with culturally, parentally, or self-induced fallacious ideas, and their repeated usage directly causes emotional disturbance.

Rimm and Litvak (1969) did the only available study before ours looking at Ellis's assumption that relates implicit verbalizations (B) to emotional arousal. We (Russell and Brandsma, 1974) criticized their work extensively and came up with a clearer conception of the process in terms of the classical conditioning paradigm.

In their study they had male and female college students read triads of sentences to themselves. Each triad had a simple observation, an inferential-irrational statement, and an evaluative-emotional conclusion.

An Example of
Rimm and Litvak's Operationalization

A. Observational-Objective Statement

A. My grades may not be good much this semester.

B. Inferential-Irrational Statement

B. I might fail out of school.

C. Evaluative-Emotional Statement

C. That would be awful.

Dependent variables were galvanic skin response (GSR) and change in rate and depth of respiration. Each subject was presented with two triads of rated high concern (Relevance) and two of low concern. A control group read triads of syllogisms of an emotionally neutral variety.

Results: Nothing. Degree of relevance had no relationship to any of the dependent variables and no difference in response to the different sentences of the triad. The only difference was between the experimentals and controls on the respiration measure, and this merely indicates that loaded verbal stimuli are more arousing than neutral stimuli. This is trivial and does not add any new knowledge or support to Ellis's theory.

We criticized their procedures from two vantage points — methodological and (more important) theoretical. Two methodological problems: (1) *The manipulation of relevance.* Rimm and Litvak had thirty-five problem areas rated on an eight-point scale by a large number of students. The top ten of their items had a mean of 2.9, the lowest ten had a mean of 1.3. We contended that this difference was not meaningful — that the subjects were presented with content that was not of high concern to them. (2) *Rating of only twenty problem areas by their subjects in their experiment.* We contended that for any individual student this restricted range of problems would not allow relevance to be successfully manipulated.

Theoretically faulty inferences were drawn which can be shown by our model of the developmental process of emotional disturbance.

Three-Phase Model

Phase 1 —(In previous development the child learns to talk.)
— B = verbal symbols that function as conditioned emotional stimuli
— C = *actual* physiological reaction subjectively experienced as an emotion (not a stimulus to which arousal has been conditioned as Rimm and Litvak operationalized)

Phase 2 —A becomes associated with B. The child uses negative symbols to describe a neutral event by cultural conditioning, modeling, operant conditioning.

Phase 3 —A has become a second-order CS (conditioned stimulus) → CER (conditioned emotional response). B has dropped out.

The job of rational behavior therapy is to extinguish or change the B after making a person aware of it. In Phase 3, the discrete parts of A-B-C in effect occur simultaneously and are thus only *representative* of the previous conditioning process. Thus in Rimm and Litvak's study they allowed ten seconds for the Interstimulus Interval (ISI) in presenting the triad — *plenty* of time for a conditioned response to occur if the content of the triad is of concern. This would fall under Phase 3 of the model and would predict equivalent levels of responding for A, B, and C. Differential responsiveness would be predicted only when there was no prior aversive conditioning to the content of the triad (i.e., Phase 1).

This model leads to the predictions of (1) greater responsiveness to high-relevance triads than low, (2) equal responsiveness to A-B-C in high-relevance triads, and (3) greater responsiveness to parts B and C than to A within low-relevance triads.

To evaluate these predictions you would need 2 × 3 analysis of variance such as:

		A	B	C
Relevance	H			
	L			

but Rimm and Litvak analyzed them separately and couldn't tell. Predictions based on our model were:

1. Mean responsiveness of affectively loaded dyads will be greater than neutral, impersonal content.

2. High relevance will produce greater responsiveness than low relevance.

3. Sentence-type effects will *not* be significant but interaction effects will be.

4. Neurotics will respond more than normals (as measured by the Eysenck neuroticism scale [Eysenck and Eysenck, 1968a]).

The subjects (Ss) were females — ten control, thirty experimental — assigned at random. The galvanic skin conductance (GSC) was measured from the onset of stimulus to maximum deflection within twenty seconds. Respiration rate and respiration depth were measured by the change in twenty seconds after compared to a base-line rate. We developed a Co-ed Problem Rating List: One hundred items (personal, family, academic) were selected from a sample of thirty-five college females asked to list their and their friends' most important problems. New dyads were developed: A was an objective observation, B was a negative inferential-evaluative comment. The length of sentences was made relatively equal.

Example:

If student indicated problems with being overweight:

A. Compared to other girls who are my age and height, I am several pounds overweight.

B. I'm too fat . . . no one likes obese, ugly people like me . . . I just hate myself.

The control dyads were syllogisms.

Example:

A. Either history is wrong or Eli Whitney invented the cotton gin.

B. Patent records give unmistakable evidence to the fact that Whitney invented the cotton gin.

Procedure

Ss would fill out the EPI, rate the Co-ed Problem Check List, and then pick their two most and least important items. (On a seven-point scale the mean rating for high relevance was 6.8 and for low was 1.1.) Then the GSC electrodes and pneumograph were attached and after a ten-minute wait the dyads would be presented. All Ss were read instructions to "concentrate on the sentences and imagine that they are your own thoughts."

For half of the Ss the order of presentation was low- (relevance) -high-low-high. This was reversed for the other half to control for habituation effects. Control subjects were treated the same way except for being given the neutral, impersonal dyads. Results: No habituation effects, so groups combined for other analysis.

Hypothesis 1: Experimentals different from controls <.001 on GSC, not on respiration measures even when only the high-relevance items were analyzed alone (because low relevance would be functionally the same as controls). Thus respiration data were excluded from further analysis.

Hypothesis 2: Relevance was a significant main effect in the analysis of variance (<.01).

Hypothesis 3: As predicted, sentence type was not significant as a main effect, but the interaction effects were at the .05 levels as predicted (i.e., greater reponsiveness to low-relevance Type B sentences than to low-relevance Type A sentences).

Hypothesis 4: High vs. low neuroticism did not differentiate on GSC.

Discussion and Summary

Our study much more successfully manipulated relevance and sentence type. Lack of congruence between the three physiological measures is no surprise because there is documentation of tremendous variability in psychophysiological response channels in an individual. Lacey (1959) pointed out that no single psychophysiological measure correlates well with any other.

1. Our asking Ss to read the sentences aloud may have interfered with the respiration measures.

2. Respiration is easily capable of voluntary control and is thus not a very pure measure of autonomic arousal.

The model we derived made better predictions — in Hypotheses 2 and 3, i.e., that A would be the same as B in Phase 3, different only in Phase 1.

The personality data were of no use — a growing body of data that points to the conclusion that self-report personality variables (neuroticism, locus of control, etc.) are complexly related *(if at all)* to physiological arousal and are not good predictors of autonomic responding.

Three of four hypotheses received support from the GSC — the best measure of autonomic arousal in this study. This suggests support for the A-B-C Theory.

In future studies, a lot could be done methodologically:

Operationalize "cognitive mediation" better.

Check to see if group statistics are truly summaries representative of what individuals are doing.

Demonstrate that the stimulus itself is not arousing.

Determine whether mediation leads to the changes without the pairing of specific A's and B's.

Investigate whether it is negative descriptions or a process of deduction that produces negative emotions.

A Review of Rational-Emotive Psychotherapy Outcome Studies

LARRY D. TREXLER, Ph.D.

Camden County Psychiatric Hospital Community Mental Health Program, New Jersey

It could hardly be more appropriate on this first day of this First National Conference on Rational Psychotherapy, to examine the scientific validity, based on empirical referents in methodologically sound experimental studies, of RET. The purpose of a review of such studies is not deliberately to shake the equilibrium of any true believers among us, although it may inadvertently do so. The "true believer" attitude is, of course, inimical to the basic tenets of RET, which, as Albert Ellis so frequently expounds, is at heart a scientific method of thinking, based on the sometimes hard truths of reality.

Since Dr. Ellis's original paper twenty years ago, a "school" of sorts has slowly evolved, helped by his forthright and energetic proselytizing, until today RET is one of the more important and popular systems of therapy being practiced in the mental health professions. This is gratifying, but it suggests caution. The all-too-frequent evolution of "schools" of therapy has been well described by Blocher:

> "Much of the history of change in counseling and psychotherapeutic theory and practice contains elements which closely parallel those which tend to dominate the evolution of religious movements and political ideologies. In both cases a movement tends to be originated by a messianic figure, characterized by a kind of *élan vital*, who translates a deeply moving personal experience into universalistic terms. This leader quickly attracts a group of worshipful disciples who immediately begin to generalize the precepts promulgated by the master into the most widely applicable terms" (1967, p. 4).

Albert Ellis, while possessing impressive *élan vital,* is hardly regarded universally as "messianic," and I believe that Blocher's description does not apply to RET in other respects. Nevertheless, the implications of his statement hold true for us all. We must be careful that deeply held personal convictions are not defensively maintained by suppression of cognitive dissonance when faced with therapeutic failures (which can always be attributed to client shortcomings — clients can be "resistant" to RET as well as to psychoanalysis). Turning to learning theory, let us keep in mind that conditioning based on intermittent reinforcement is strongly resistant to extinction.

Lest I sound too pessimistic, let me say that this paper will, on the whole, lend room for optimism as to the scientific evidence supporting RET theory and practice. Not that such evidence is overwhelming and conclusive — it is not. In my doctoral dissertation (Trexler, 1971), I noted that relatively little research has been forthcoming from the semantic or cognitive schools of psychotherapy. I wish I could say that the situation has substantially changed, but it has not — although it is indeed better. My purpose here is to review the extent and status of psychotherapy outcome research that bears a fairly close relationship to rational-emotive therapy. I will try to be comprehensive and to present some evaluation of the methodological quality of studies discussed. Any omissions are inadvertent or due to limitations of time and energy rather than "editorial" in nature. The evaluative intent will not be to make a definitive statement on each study, but rather to bring to the reader's attention methodological strengths and weaknesses that can bear directly on the veracity of conclusions based on the data. In short, the purpose will be to educate and stimulate, first by way of illustrative RET-related outcome studies that will also, cumulatively, bear witness to the current scientific status of RET and later by general discussion of important experimental issues. One further qualification is that this paper will not deal with the much more extensive literature related to the cognitive theory (i.e., "we feel as we think") central to RET.

In any review of RET outcome studies, it is necessary to define what is meant by rational-emotive therapy. This is not as easy as it may seem. In some cases authors refer directly to Ellis and RET and say, in effect, this is what we are doing (which, incidentally, is no guarantee that that is what they do). Others are not so explicit. For the purposes of this paper I have adopted the thesis that studies that appear to be cognitive-behavioral are roughly equivalent to RET. While RET is unquestionably a cognitive-behavioral therapy (and Maxie Maultsby prefers to call it RBT, for rational behavior therapy), Ellis (1973a) notes that the two are not synonymous. RET, among other differences, is a more emphatically cognitive-didactic-philosophic approach to therapy. (The "hyphen emotive" must not be, and is not, lost sight of, but again is secondary to cognitive change. Note that the word "cognitive" or its equivalent is the invariable element in these varying titles.)

It is interesting in passing to note that what was once almost entirely behavior therapy has become so increasingly cognitive-behavior therapy. There seems to be much truth in Dember's statement that "psychology has gone cognitive" (1974, p. 161). In addition to Ellis, who all along has espoused a thinking-plus-action attack on neurotic problems, other prominent clinicians (including Aaron T. Beck (1970) and Arnold A. Lazarus (1971), who was originally a rather strict behaviorist but has recently emphasized a "broad-spectrum" behaviorism or multimodal approach to therapy) have contributed to this development. Bergin, among many others, has noted that "there may be highly specific interventions which have a behavioral or cognitive focus, but these are always embedded in a multidimensional context or have multiple consequences" (1970, p. 208). Behavior therapy can no longer detour around the role of cognitive processes in the production and alleviation of symptomatology (Beck, 1970).

These developments make the present undertaking both more challenging and more exciting. Surely the influence of RET has played an important role in their evolution, and it would be nice to receive full credit for it. More important, people who present themselves for help with psychological problems are receiving more effective and efficient treatment.

Or are they?

Survey of RET and Related Outcome Research

I hope the following discussion will have value not only as an informal annotated bibliography, but also as a survey that will give both the interested researcher and clinician an idea of where RET-related outcome research has gone and is going, how good or bad it is and why, and how it has fared along the way. Some of the studies may seem as much process- as outcome-oriented, but the emphasis will be on outcome alone, since, as Malan has stated: "Outcome is surely the crucial variable in psychotherapy . . . there is little point in studying other variables unless their relation to outcome can be established" (1973, p. 719).

First there will be relatively detailed discussion of some RET and RET-related studies deemed important historically, methodologically, or otherwise, followed by less-detailed discussion of other RET and related studies. In a number of cases (particularly unpublished doctoral dissertations in which there was time only to obtain the abstract), information on the study is unfortunately limited — and so will be any comments made thereon. Strictly laboratory analogues are for the most part omitted, as are case reports. There is an abundance of the latter, and the interested reader need only turn to issues of *Rational Living*, the journal of the Institute for Rational Living, or the book *Growth Through Reason: Verbatim Cases in Rational-Emotive Therapy* (Ellis, 1971b), in which Ellis presents and discusses cases handled by himself or by five other therapists. The reasons for this are that analogues do not closely enough approximate actual therapeutic practice, and case reports are generally lacking in experimental controls.

The Ellis 1957 Three Outcomes Study. It may surprise the reader, then, that this section begins with a study that is not much more than a collection of case reports, lacking adequate controls and that Meltzoff and Kornreich, in their review of psychotherapy outcome literature, summarize it as one in which "many things other than the method could account for the results and the case for rational therapy and against orthodox analysis is not advanced by this study" (1970, p. 187). Nevertheless, it is deemed the "granddaddy" of RET research, with both historical and motivational importance in the evolution of this method — which probably never would have gotten off the ground had the results been otherwise.

Ellis, as you may know, developed RET following training and experience first as an orthodox analyst and then as an analytically oriented therapist. He kept records of his effectiveness during these three periods, and then compared treatment results with 16 cases seen in psychoanalysis, 78 in analytically oriented therapy, and 78 in what was then called rational therapy. These were all closed cases, with a minimum of 10 sessions (averages: analysis, 93 sessions; analytic, 35; RET, 26). The percentages of those whom Ellis rated as having considerable improvement, distinct improvement, or little or no improvement were as follows: analysis, 13, 37, 50; analytically oriented, 18, 45, 47; and RET, 30, 44, 26. Ellis also saw considerable benefit in 22 RET patients with from one to five sessions, as compared to seven analytically oriented cases and no analysis cases with a similar number of sessions.

Ellis himself noted that these results should be taken with due caution, since he could have been prejudiced in his evaluations, and differed in the degree of enthusiasm and energy he employed in the varying methods. He noted further that the patients may have improved *with* therapy rather than *because* of it (since there were no controls for nonspecific or extratherapeutic effects), and that since the three techniques overlapped in some respects, the extent to which any of them worked could be attributable to some factor common to all. Added to the latter consideration is the possibility of therapist or client variables common in the three methods — the groups of patients were fairly comparable, and it is difficult to imagine the irrepressible Ellis in the traditional, stereotyped view of the classical analyst asleep behind his couch (but now it is I who am drifting into subjectivity — nay, amused speculation). An additional therapist variable with possibly confounding effects is that, during the roughly seven-year period of this study, Ellis's theoretical model and technical skills were both maturing (Mahoney, 1974). Further, to point up other disadvantages of this type of investigation, Meltzoff and Kornreich comment on the problem of maintaining implicit criteria of improvement over time, and that of generalizability: "The data from a single therapist is not representative and lacks generality, especially when he is the sole judge of his own case records and the founder of the approach that shows up best" (1970, p. 187).

For all its limitations, it is worthwhile to keep the study in historical perspective not only in relation to RET but to the rather sorry condition of the psychotherapy outcome literature in general at that time. It is noteworthy that Eysenck (1961) was able to include it as one of only three studies comparing psychoanalytic and other types of therapy. It was his hope that properly controlled studies would soon be initiated to test specific therapeutic hypotheses and compare methods.

The Maes and Heimann Study. The first major effort to fulfill Eysenck's wish in regard to RET was a study by Wayne Maes and Robert Heimann (1970) of Arizona State University sponsored by the U.S. Office of Education's Bureau of Research. It is still, at this writing, one of the few studies comparing RET with other methods of therapy and with a control group, and thus is deserving of attention. It does show some superiority for RET, but it has methodological weaknesses — which the authors candidly acknowledge — and the data supporting RET are by no means conclusive.

This study compared the relative effectiveness of client centered, rational-emotive, systematic desensitization, and ι no-treatment control group in reducing test anxiety among high school students. Of an original 48 students, attrition lowered the final sample to 33, predominantly female, with from 7 to 9 in each group. They had been selected by obtaining high state anxiety but average or low trait anxiety on the Spielberger State-Trait Anxiety Inventory (STAI). Each student was counseled individually by advanced graduate students (24 in all) for from seven to eleven sessions during a five-week period. Training manuals were drawn up for each treatment, and two weeks of training were provided. The pre- and post-test conditions were a "simulated" intelligence test along with being asked to imagine a classroom test-taking situation. Criterion measures were the STAI, psychogalvanic skin responses (GSR), and heart rate. There were no significant differences between the four groups on the STAI, but significant differences were found in the predicted direction between treatment groups and controls on the GSR and heart rate. Post hoc analyses disclosed significance for the desensitization group on GSR, the RET group on heart rate. A "more conservative test" (the Mann-Whitney U, as compared to the Multiple Comparison Rank Sum Test, both nonparametric) showed only RET "significantly" different from controls on heart rate, at less than the .10 level. While RET had the lowest post-treatment scores on the STAI and the heart rate, and it tied with desensitization on GSR, differences from other treatment groups were not significant.

Maes and Heimann have made a substantial step in the right direction of utilizing experimental controls, but, as they themselves substantiate, there are a number of qualifications. Some of these bear notice not just for the sake of criticizing this study, but because they are seen so frequently elsewhere, including other studies to be mentioned in this review. First, concerning the subjects: Selection of "test-anxious" students on the basis of the STAI has some rationale, but those scores do not pertain directly to test-taking anxiety, which is fairly specific. Apparently there was no attempt to match the groups on the basis of level of initial test-taking anxiety (randomization is no guarantee of initial equivalence, especially with small numbers of subjects [Ns]). The small Ns create further statistical problems (for one thing, preventing the use of more powerful parametric analyses), and the preponderantly female sample limits generalizability of results. There is no indication of how the seven to eleven sessions balanced out in the different groups.

Training of counselors was limited in time and scope, and there was little supervision of how they actually conducted the sessions. This would be particularly important when there are so many counselors involved. There are no data on counselor treatment effects, or on how the subjects perceived their counselors. In terms of experimental design, there was no attention-placebo condition to control for nonspecific therapy effects (e.g., expectation, suggestion), or any check on subject expectancies concerning the treatments offered. A more direct measure of subjective test-taking anxiety in the test situation would have been preferable. A behavioral measure would have been advisable in addition to the two physiological measures, which well may not have been independent of each other and also present problems of stability. There is also some question as to how well the "simulated" and imagined testing conditions aroused test anxiety. This problem would, of course, hold true across conditions; yet stress would be necessary to help differentiate the experimental from the control groups. One of the critical client variables in this case would be the ability to imagine vividly!

In regard to statistics (on which matters I shall attempt only elementary remarks), a probability level of less than .10 is not ordinarily accepted as significant. Other-than-ordinary significance levels require some rationale, and none was offered. Finally, no follow-up data were obtained.

It is easy, from an armchair position, to take to task a study laboring under what the authors refer to as "budgetary and personnel limitations." They deserve credit not only for their pioneering effort, but the candor with which they acknowledge limitations and suggest recommendations to help obviate such limitations in future research. This has a truly heuristic value in the cumulative progress of science that may well surpass that of the data obtained in any given study.

The DiLoreto Study.   The following year Adolph DiLoreto's book (1971) based on his doctoral dissertation at Michigan State University was published. A study of the relative effectiveness of systematic desensitization (SD), RET, and client-centered (CC) therapy in the treatment of introverts and extroverts who desired help with interpersonal anxiety, in scope and controls it is comparable with — and in some respects superior to — the Gordon Paul study (1966) that made such an impact on the field of psychotherapy outcome research.

The study involved 100 college student volunteers, high in interpersonal anxiety, randomly assigned to one of 10 introvert and 10 extrovert groups (with a modal composition of two males and three females), which were in turn randomly assigned to one of five conditions, the three treatments, a placebo no-treatment group and no-contact (other than pre- and post-assessment) no-treatment group, and finally to one of two counselors within treatments. The counselors were advanced graduate students who had had some experience in and commitment to DiLoreto's approach. The experimental subjects received roughly eleven hours of counseling, the placebo subjects an equivalent amount of attention. Measures included a behavioral checklist of inter-personal anxiety (completed by independent raters), self-report scales of interpersonal anxiety and activity, therapist ratings of client anxiety, and varied other subject personality scales and therapist self-ratings.

Besides the usual treatment-vs.-controls hypotheses, DiLoreto's hypotheses concerning the introversion-extroversion dimension are interesting. These were that, with regard to ex-troverts, the order of effectiveness in reducing interpersonal and "general" anxiety would be (from most to least effective): CC, RET, and SD. For introverts, the order would be: SD, RET, and CC. These hypotheses were partially supported, in that SD was equally effective with both personality types, CC was better with extroverts, and RET with introverts.

The main pre-post effects were that all treatments significantly differed from both control conditions on all scales (except that CC did not achieve significance on the interpersonal activity scale). There were no significant differences between CC and RET on any of the self-report or behavioral ratings of anxiety. Systematic desensitization, when subject personality type and individual counselor effects were not considered, achieved the greatest amount of anxiety reduction. RET produced a signifi-cantly higher increase in interpersonal *activity* than either SD or CC. Within its own subjects, it was three times more effective in reducing anxiety in introverts than in extroverts. While on this dimension, it is interesting to note that placebo benefits (which generally surpassed no-contact) were limited almost exclusively to introverts, and that group SD appeared to have a detrimental effect with introverts.

Commenting on this study at some length in the 1975 *Annual Review of Psychology*, Bergin and Suinn note its "elaborate ex-perimental controls and 72 pages of statistical analyses" (p. 511), and that "the phenomena and processes involved were some-what closer to the 'real thing' than in the Paul study" (p. 511). They conclude, nonetheless, that the results are limited some-what by the nature of the subjects and counselors. Michael Mahoney (1974), in his review of the cognitive therapy outcome literature, agrees that the clinical significance of the study is limited due to some of the outcome variance's being apparently related to counselor effects, and the absence of direct perfor-mance measures. Other problems include, if my impression is correct, that the placebo subjects were in effect told that what they were about to receive was *not* treatment, which because of financial limitations would begin at the end of the term, and they would be given informal help in the interim! Surely this would have aroused an expectancy effect inferior to those students receiving therapy (which effect, apparently, was not ascertained). The placebo group met for group discussions of university life, academic problems, and study skills in three sessions totaling eight hours, which is not, it seems to me, sufficiently commensurate with the total and distribution of counseling time.

One of the most commendable aspects of DiLoreto's monograph is that he invited prominent and knowledgeable practitioners from each of the three therapy areas to write critiques. In the case of RET, this was, most appropriately, Albert Ellis. His remarks were well balanced in terms of praise and constructive criticism, some of which is worth repeating for its applicability both to this paper and generally. Dr. Ellis found the RET procedures employed to be a watered-down method, the counselors not intensively trained and one of them lacking in experience, and the approach faulty on a number of points, including being too generally didactic and lecturing, not demonstrating to the client why his basic assumptions were irrational, making little use of the Socratic dialogue method, and not giving sufficient stress to the necessity of work and practice. He objected further that this "highly pale and wan approach" (1971a, p. 215), based on a narrow definition of RET, contrasted with a liberal definition of CC and SD that employed RET-flavored procedures, such as being didactic in teaching more rational attitudes toward themselves and others.

Commenting on RET's success with introverts and lack of it with extroverts, Ellis said he is not surprised by the former, since introverts need active-directive prodding and homework activity. Such success is important because, in his opinion, most actual psychotherapy clients are introverts. Nor is he surprised by the relative ineffectiveness with extroverts, because these people are more generally disturbed, defensive, unwilling to work at changing themselves, and resentful of those who try to make them listen to reason and actively work at changing. In order to attain success with such patients, Ellis states, it is necessary to have stronger, more effective RET counselors than were employed here. The other critics (Alan Goldstein and Joseph Wolpe for behavior therapy, Angelo Boy for client-centered) make similar reservations about how their respective techniques were employed. All of these objections point to the importance in a therapy outcome study of approximating as closely as possible the system that one purports to be testing.

Ellis finally warns against an "essentially false conclusion" that could be drawn from this study: "that individual clients tend to be so different that one type of therapy may well work best for a given client but not work at all well for another" (1971a, p. 219). The logical deduction would be for a therapist to become eclectic, or at least employ a large variety of techniques within his theoretical framework so he can work effectively with different types of clients. Ellis acknowledges that there is some validity to this position, and he himself has incorporated a wide range of cognitive-emotive-behavioral-experiential techniques into his practice of RET. But he emphasizes that this is not the same as eclecticism, since the techniques employed are consistent with his theoretical stance rather than being adopted on purely pragmatic grounds. Ellis goes on to say that, while a specific technique or method may seem to work better with one personality-type client than another:

> "It is still probable that (1) one technique will be more effective *most of the time* with *more* clients than will another, that (2) this same technique will bring about more elegant or 'deeper' solutions than will an alternative method, and that (3) this same technique, if practiced by competent therapists for a sufficiently long period of time, will achieve better results than an alternative method which over a shorter period *seems* to work better" (1971a, p. 220).

The Trexler and Karst Study. My dissertation chairman, Thomas O. Karst (currently at the Medical College of Ohio), and I reported (Trexler and Karst, 1972) a study evaluating the relative effectiveness of RET, attention-placebo (AP), and no treatment (NT) in reducing public-speaking anxiety in college students at Temple University who had been required to take a public-speaking course. It was inspired by the Gordon Paul (1966) study and the then dearth of cognitive therapy outcome research.

This paper was a partial replication and refinement of an earlier study by the authors (Karst and Trexler, 1970) comparing George Kelly's fixed-role therapy and Ellis's approach with a no-treatment group, also in reducing public-speaking anxiety. Of five self-report and two behavioral measures, predicted treatment differences over no treatment were obtained on three self-report measures, with a fourth approaching significance. At a six-month follow-up involving 15 of the 22 original participants, 12 reported anxiety to be "much" or "somewhat" less than before treatment. Neither treatment was found to be more successful than the other. The significance of this study was seen in its attempt to subject two of the more cognitively oriented therapies to objective analysis, much as had been done with behavior therapy, by defining the independent therapy variables by means of a manual and limiting the number of sessions, and by limiting primary concern to a target symptom.

In the 1972 study, RET was compared with placebo and no treatment, but not with another form of therapy. The 17 female and 16 male student volunteers, screened for a relatively high level of public-speaking anxiety (PSA), with groups matched on this dimension, were randomly assigned to treatments in groups of three. The AP procedure was relaxation training. The subjects gave an initial evaluation speech, followed by treatment (four sessions) for RET and AP, another speech by all subjects, RET treatment for the formerly AP and NT subjects, and a final speech by all subjects. The audience was two trained raters. This design permitted combining groups to increase N, and the use of immediate and delayed post-treatment data for the RET subjects. There were, thus, both "primary" (initial pre-post group differences) and "secondary" (combined group differences) analyses of data. There were three observational and five self-report measures, a post-therapy questionnaire (e.g., therapist and method acceptance, generalization effect), and a six-month follow-up. Only the finger-sweat print, a physiological measure, proved unreliable. Manuals for RET and AP were prepared, and RET involved structured sessions and homework activity and reading assignments. The senior author conducted all sessions, and was rated equally by both RET and AP subjects.

Analyses of variance gave significant Fs for the three self-report measures lending themselves to such analysis, with post hoc analyses showing RET significantly better on two, AP on the third. Two observational measures achieved marginal significance, using delayed post-treatment RET scores. Collapsed-groups analyses for RET combined with NT after treatment showed significantly greater improvement than AP on observational and self-report measures. This was also true of RET plus AP after treatment compared with NT. Comparison of all subjects initially and post-RET showed significant differences favoring treatment of all measures. We concluded that, while aspects of the study limited generalizations, it indicated that RET could be used effectively in short-term efforts to relieve specific emotional problems and also (by attempting to change the underlying ideas) bring about general improvement in the patient's life style.

Commenting on this paper in the *Annual Review of Psychology*,

Bergin and Suinn state: "Like most studies of outcome with a single technique, there was at least modest support for the effects of the therapy on some criteria compared with the control groups, but there was no comparison with any other form of therapy. The problems were mild and changes were more evident on an irrational beliefs test and self-rating of confidence as a public speaker than on a behavioral check list or an anxiety scale" (1975, p. 516). Mahoney further notes that the interpretation of the secondary, or collapsed-groups data, favoring RET "must take into account the resulting differences in time and intervening practice" (1974, p. 180), and that the repeated-measures analysis of all subjects pre- and post-RET, again favoring treatment, warrants only limited conclusions due to the absence of an untreated comparison group.

The most embarrassing finding, in the view of the authors, in relation to the hypothesis favoring RET, was that the situation-specific subjective rating of anxiety significantly favored AP in the primary analyses, nonsignificantly in the secondary. We discuss technical and empirical limitations to this one-item self-report scale, but also note that this scale may be particularly sensitive to social desirability influences (the "hello-goodbye" effect), which were mitigated against in the RET condition by subjects' being told that they did not *have* to give a better, less-anxious speech in order to please the therapist, the raters, or themselves. If the post-therapy speech was no better in that regard than the initial one, the world would not come to an end and they would still be worthwhile human beings, fully capable of self-acceptance.

Additional comment is also warranted concerning the Irrational Beliefs Test (IBT) (Jones, 1969; see also Trexler and Karst, 1973). This is a 100-item self-report test measuring, on a five-point scale, degree of agreement or disagreement with the then ten irrational beliefs listed by Ellis. It could be argued that this test measures only the acquisition of an RETish vocabulary rather than changes in anxiety level, and thus was not directly appropriate in a study of PSA reduction. Two counterarguments are that (1) empirically, among these subjects, the IBT was associated with other measures of PSA and thus possesses some generality and construct validity, and (2) theoretically "acquisition of such a grammar and language system could be a most important aspect of any type of counseling or psychotherapy. It is, of course, a specific tenet of rational-emotive therapy that the sentences one tells himself determine, at least in part, his emotional reactions to situations" (Trexler and Karst, 1972, p. 65).

The Straatmeyer and Watkins Study. Alvin Straatmeyer and John Watkins, two South Dakota psychologists, in a 1974 study also investigated the effects of RET on public-speaking anxiety. Their study was patterned somewhat after that of Trexler and Karst, and uses some of the same measurements and materials, but has the additional feature of comparing a "complete RET procedure" with "a procedure in which the disputing element of RET was omitted" (1974, p. 33). They further helped in the standardization of treatment by utilizing videotape presentations appropriate to two RET groups and the attention-placebo groups as portions of those treatments. The modified RET included insight into irrational beliefs, with counterpart rational beliefs, related to PSA, but no aid or encouragement in disputing the former. The placebo subjects were given a discussion of the problems of anxiety in general.

Subjects were 29 female and 28 male college students experiencing anxiety in a required speech course, randomly assigned to one of two doctoral-candidate therapists, both of whom were experienced in RET and both of whom conducted sessions with all groups. The PSA measures and procedure (both for treatment and testing) were essentially those of Trexler and Karst, although there was an additional (fifth) therapy session. To measure generalization effect, DiLoreto's (1971) Interpersonal Anxiety Scale was used.

Analysis of covariance showed no statistically significant difference among the four groups on any of the four measures (two behavioral, two self-report) related to speech anxiety. The "complete" RET group did better in terms of mean change scores than the other three groups, but not significantly so. On the generalization measure, both RET groups improved significantly more than the no-treatment group. Thus only the hypothesis concerning generalization to interpersonal anxiety was confirmed, with a trend in favor of RET over the other three groups for the hypothesis concerning reduction of PSA, but no statistical confirmation. There were no significant differences in the results obtained by the two therapists, due no doubt in part to the deliberate efforts to standardize procedures and content for the sessions.

Straatmeyer and Watkins attribute the lack of statistical significance regarding the main treatment effect to the "gross within-cell variances" (1974, p. 37). They recommend that in further studies subjects could be placed in equivalent groups, say in relation to initial level of PSA (as was done by Trexler and Karst), and then these groups could be randomly assigned to the various treatment conditions. This would reduce the within-cell variance and improve the chance of obtaining significant Fs from an analysis of covariance. The authors also suggest increasing the number of treatment sessions so as to enhance the treatment effect.

It is worth noting the increasingly widespread use of public-speaking anxiety as a dependent variable in outcome studies. It is a type of behavior that lends itself to behavioral, physiological, and self-report measures, and has the further advantage of being "relevant," common, and an aspect of more general interpersonal anxiety. We (Trexler and Karst) were impressed by the motivation of our required-speech-course students, none of whom once they had begun treatment, dropped out, despite heavy schedules and work loads. This was true even of the no-treatment subjects, while waiting the two weeks for treatment to begin. Missed sessions, however, appear almost inevitable. Both in our case, and that of Straatmeyer and Watkins, make-up sessions were scheduled. Some limits must be placed in order to insure equivalency of groups; the latter authors excluded from data analysis students who missed more than two sessions without make-up.

The Meichenbaum Studies on "Modifying What Clients Say to Themselves." While the work of Donald Meichenbaum and his colleagues at the University of Waterloo, Canada, is not strictly speaking an investigation of the effects of rational-emotive therapy, the "self-instructional training" — or what Meichenbaum has more recently termed "cognitive-behavior modification" (1975, p. 1) — is in theory and the procedures involved so relevant to RET as to merit serious consideration. Certainly at the heart of the matter is cognitive restructuring, so that what clients do say to themselves (Ellis's "internal sentences") is reasonably rational, in order to effect desired emotive and behavioral changes.

This subsection will be a sort of review within a review. No exhaustive or even thorough evaluation of the numerous studies completed in the space of only six years will be attempted. That would entail a paper in its own right, and the interested reader is referred to some excellent reviews by Meichenbaum (1972b, 1973, 1975) and Meichenbaum and Cameron (1974). Individual studies are not beyond criticism, but on the whole this body of research is extensive, and clinically and methodologically impressive.

The general research strategy has been to bring together the concerns of semantic or cognitive therapists and the technology of behavior therapy. This has led to studies assessing the efficacy of standard behavior therapy procedures relative to procedures including a self-instructional component. (More recently this has been broadened to include imagery- and fantasy-based factors, leading to the change in name.) Meichenbaum comments that his research program "evolved from an 'incestual' relationship between being trained in behavior therapy while having a theoretical commitment to the importance of cognitive processes. The offspring of this union . . . has been the production of a variety of new therapy procedures" (1972b, p. 23). He also notes, in an aside that could serve as an impetus to many of the rest of us, that his "concern with cognitive factors in behavior modification began where most clinical research ends, namely, with my doctoral dissertation" (1972b, p. 23).

This survey will also begin there, and proceed in quasi-chronological order. Meichenbaum's (1969) dissertation study involved a laboratory operant training program in which hospitalized schizophrenic patients were taught to emit "healthy talk" in an interview. A serendipitous finding was that these effects generalized to follow-up interviews and other verbal tasks. A number of the patients repeated aloud and spontaneously the previous instruction "give healthy talk, be coherent and relevant." This self-instruction appeared to mediate generalization by helping the patient in attending to the task at hand. The question arose: Could schizophrenics, and perhaps other clinical populations, be trained *explicitly* to talk to themselves in such a self-guiding manner?

A paradigm for the self-instructional model emerged from a series of studies with impulsive children (Meichenbaum and Goodman, 1969, 1971). The technique proceeded as follows: The experimenter performed a task while the child observed; the child performed the same task while being instructed aloud; then while instructing himself aloud; while whispering; and, finally, covertly. Meichenbaum credits inspiration for this paradigm to the developmental literature from the Soviet psychologists Vygotsky and Luria. Relative to placebo and control groups, this procedure resulted in significantly improved performance on a variety of tasks, including the Porteus Maze and WISC Performance IQ. This same modeling and overt-to-covert cognitive rehearsal procedure was then tested (Meichenbaum and Cameron, 1973) with schizophrenics trained to emit such self-instructions as "pay attention, listen and repeat instructions, disregard distractions." The investigators found significantly improved performance, relative to a yoked practice control group, on a variety of measures, including a digit symbol task.

The second phase of the research was directed at training

neurotics, who emit wide-ranging maladaptive, emotionally disruptive self-statements, to substitute more adaptive, rational counterparts. This first experiment (Meichenbaum, Gilmore, and Fedoravicius, 1971) was designed to assess the merits of such a basically RET group "insight-oriented" psychotherapy relative to systematic desensitization, a combination of the two, an attention-placebo "discussion group," and a waiting-list control group. Subjects were 35 male and 18 female high-speech-anxious volunteers, mainly students, who gave pre- and post-experiment speeches involving behavioral and self-report anxiety measures. Treatments consisted of eight group sessions conducted by two therapists who carefully followed the respective manuals. Results showed that the RET insight group was as effective as the SD group in significantly reducing speech anxiety over controls both at immediate post-treatment and three-month follow-up. The combined cognitive insight-SD group resulted in less consistent anxiety reduction; the authors conjectured that the treatment sequence did not leave sufficient time for adequate cognitive exploration of anxiety-creating self-verbalizations. What the authors considered a most interesting *post hoc* finding was that, despite the small Ns, subjects "for whom speech anxiety was a generalized response style significantly benefited from the group insight treatment . . . whereas Ss for whom speech anxiety was a circumscribed problem confined mainly to the public speaking situation significantly benefited from the group desensitization treatment" (Meichenbaum, Gilmore, and Fedoravicius, 1971, pp. 418-19). This is consistent with RET theory concerning "basic irrational ideas" underlying emotional disturbance in general, and research findings that SD tends to work best with subjects having fairly specific anxieties.

The above study was described in some detail to give a partial picture of the careful construction and reporting typical of Meichenbaum's work. More briefly, a second study with neurotics, this time with test-anxious subjects (Meichenbaum, 1972a), found significantly superior results for cognitive modification over desensitization and no treatment (despite small Ns of 8, 8, and 5). This was true in an analogue test situation, self-report at post-treatment and one-month follow-up, and grade point average. The cognitive-modification procedure included coping imagery on how to handle anxiety (as opposed to mastery imagery in which one is completely fearless), plus self-instructions to attend to the task and not ruminate about oneself. (This appears to be quite similar to what Maxie Maultsby calls "rational-emotive imagery.") Meichenbaum considers it most significant that "only the Ss in the cognitive modification treatment group reported a posttreatment increase in facilitative anxiety . . . (1972a, p. 377). Following treatment the . . . Ss labeled arousal as facilitative, as a cue to be task relevant, as a signal to improve their performance" (1972a, p. 376). In light of the inherent falli- bility of human beings, including a propensity to become and remain anxious, it would appear essential to teach people how to cope with the fact of being anxious.

Meichenbaum and Cameron (1974) report the application of like procedures in increasing the functioning of college students who perform poorly on creativity tests by training them to pro- duce more task-relevant and creativity-enhancing statements. Working with snake-phobic subjects, Meichenbaum (1971) found that models who explicitly model self-verbalizations, and who demonstrate coping behaviors (i.e., first showing fearful behavior, then coping behavior, and finally mastery behavior) vs. mastery behavior (fearless throughout) produced clearly superior results. In a later discussion of this paper, Meichen- baum and Cameron (1974) reinforce Ellis's stress on active- directive cognitive reeducation with their observation that while Bandura has emphasized that

> "the information which observers gain from models is con- verted to covert perceptual-cognitive images and covert mediating rehearsal responses which are retained by the client and later used by him as symbolic cues to overt behavior . . . results of the modeling study suggest that the explicit model- ing of self-verbalizations facilitates the learning process . . ." (1974, p. 112)

The research efforts of Meichenbaum and his colleagues con- tinue to date, with attention having been given to geriatrics, worrying, aversive conditioning of cigarette smoking, and the cognitive-behavioral management of anxiety, anger, and pain. A final noteworthy development is what Meichenbaum and Cameron (1972) term "stress inoculation training." This includes three goals: educating the client about the nature of his stressful or fearful reactions, having him rehearse various coping be- haviors, and finally giving him an opportunity to practice the rehearsed skills in a stressful situation. Particularly encouraging was the finding that, in working with multiphobic (rat and snake) subjects, training them in relation to one of these animals produced marked reduction in avoidance behavior to *both* phobic objects. The comparison desensitization group showed, instead, a specific treatment effect.

The differences and similarities of Meichenbaum's cog- nitive-behavior modification approach and RET mentioned earlier have been given thoughtful analysis by Mahoney, who states:

"An important performance focus in both RET and self-instructional training involves modification of dysfunctional thought patterns. Their respective *means* for effecting this goal, however, vary in emphasis. Ellis relies predominantly on Socratic dialogue and logical self-examination. Meichenbaum, on the other hand, places greater procedural emphasis on graduated tasks, cognitive modeling, and directed mediational training. He likewise encourages self-reinforcement of improvement" (1974, p. 191).

Mahoney goes on to note that the existing evidence on RET is insufficient and inadequate to allow a comparative evaluation between the two approaches. He encourages future research not only into the relative effects of these training strategies but also into their potential combination.

Meichenbaum and Cameron summarize their research results as indicating that when the standard behavior therapy procedures are augmented with a self-instructional package, greater treatment efficacy, generalization, and persistence of treatment effects are obtained. The common theme running through their studies is that:

"Behavior therapies in their present form have overemphasized the importance of environmental consequences, thus underemphasizing (and often overlooking) how S perceives and evaluates those consequences. Our research on cognitive factors in behavior modification has highlighted the fact that it is not the environmental consequences *per se* which are of primary importance, but what S says to himself about those consequences. However, what S says to himself, that is, how he evaluates and interprets these events, is explicitly modifiable by many of the behavior therapy techniques which have been used to modify maladaptive behaviors" (1974, p. 103).

In reading about "self-instructional training," it might be easy to gain the impression that what the subject does is mainly to parrot certain modeled or otherwise taught phrases that, however facilitative, lack the true cognitive restructuring pursued in RET. Meichenbaum and Cameron do not overlook this danger, cautioning against mechanical or rote repetition "without the accompanying meaning and inflection. . . . What is needed instead is modeling and practice in synthesizing and internalizing the meaning of one's self-statements" (1974, p. 106).

The Taylor and Shaw Studies. Two other neighbors to our north have us in their debt for recent doctoral dissertation studies comparing cognitive and behavioral approaches to depression — Frederick Taylor (1974) and Brian Shaw (1975). Taylor's contribution is especially noteworthy in that he found a *combination* of the two methods (following procedures outlined by Aaron T. Beck) results in greater improvement than either the cognitive or behavior elements alone. The superiority of the combined method was retained at one-month follow-up and on measures of self-esteem and self-acceptance as well as of depression. Another interesting feature of this study, derived from the cognitively oriented personal construct theory of George Kelly, was "the use of an individualized measure of self-esteem and self-acceptance which seeks to ensure that the self-measures are psychologically valid for each subject" (Taylor, 1974, p. ii).

Taylor worked with students showing mild to moderate depression as measured by the Beck Depression Inventory. The over-all methodology was acceptably good, considering the state of the art, but had some weaknesses, such as the lack of a placebo group to control for expectancy effects; the lack of behavioral or other external, more "objective" criteria to support the self-report measures; the relatively small N of seven in each group; lack of a treatment manual; and short follow-up. Since there was no check on expectancy effects, the question remains open whether the combined treatment might have been the most powerful in this respect. Limitations such as these call for qualification of conclusions. Nevertheless, the Taylor study is an important advance in the RET-cognitive-behavior literature.

The Shaw (1975) study is not as close to RET in that it separates the cognitive and behavioral components, yet is pertinent in that it found the cognitive approach (which is, if any one element must be singled out, the heart of RET) the most effective in alleviating depression as measured by both self-report and an objective clinical rating. The cognitive modification procedures resulted in significantly less depression following treatment than did the behavior modification, nondirective (placebo), and no-treatment groups. The behavioral and nondirective groups did fare better than no treatment.

As defined by Shaw in his abstract, the cognitive modification treatment was "designed to identify and modify subjects' idiosyncratic, maladaptive thoughts and ideation." The behavior modification treatment was "designed to restore an adequate schedule of positive reinforcement by training subjects to emit behaviors which are likely to be positively reinforced by others and to engage in activities which are intrinsically rewarding."

These definitions are fairly typical of those used in studies employing either or both of these procedures. Treatment was somewhat more extensive than is frequently seen in studies of this type (perhaps because students tend to be busy, and sometimes put the study of subjects other than themselves first — this was not intended as a pun, but will make do). The two two-hour sessions per week for four weeks provided sixteen hours of treatment. Follow-up was, as with Taylor, only one month, and apparently only the cognitive and behavior modification groups were assessed.

Additional RET and RET-Related Studies. The following will be a somewhat briefer discussion of other outcome studies related to rational-emotive psychotherapy. Not singling them out for special attention is by no means to diminish their importance, for it is no one study in and of itself, but all studies cumulatively, that will eventually provide the empirical basis for scientific validation of RET and analogous cognitive-behavioral approaches to therapy. The selection for inclusion — both in this paper as a whole and, further, in this subsection — is, of course, a matter of individual judgment, subject to whatever fallibility a dyed-in-the-wool RET therapist (among others) would insist I have. Some of the studies have poor, if any, methodological controls, and one was at this writing incompletely reported, yet they are brought to the reader's attention so that he or she may have a better idea of the directions that RET-related research is taking.

Critical comments will be more limited here, both because in some cases it would be repeating points made earlier (and the intent of the methodological criticism is as much for general education as it is to present evaluations of individual studies), and because in some cases full information about the study was not available. At times I had recourse only to abstracts; the interested reader will have more time to obtain the complete papers. The sequence in which the studies will be presented is, roughly, chronological (date of publication) and alphabetical.

The initial paper, by E. Lakin Phillips (1957), is similar in several respects to that of Albert Ellis with which this section began: It was published the same year, is of more historical than methodological importance, and was the other study cited by Eysenck (1961) as comparing a cognitive approach with psychoanalysis, to the latter's detriment. Phillips' "assertion-structured" or "interference" therapy is, like RET, an active-directive attempt to educate the patient to adopt more realistic assertions or hypotheses about life, and test them experimentally rather than accept them unthinkingly. Thus, there is considerable overlap with RET.

Phillips compared the effectiveness and efficiency of his approach with psychoanalytic depth-oriented therapy in outpatient, parent-child cases. Practically all his patients, on the basis of self-report, benefited from three or more sessions, while less than half the analytic patients did so. (The "or more" here would make a big difference, however, as one would not expect patients in classical analysis to derive much benefit from only three sessions.) A more telling comparison took into account that only 45 of 190 applicants were accepted for psychoanalysis, whereas Phillips accepted 53 of 59 applicants. Thus, the percentage of original applicants who benefited was 86.4 for assertion-structured therapy, 17.3 for psychoanalytic therapy. An improvement over the Ellis study was that other patients were treated by other therapists, and self-report as well as therapist ratings of improvement were obtained.

In a study comparing "reason versus reinforcement in behavior modification," Juanita Baker (1966) found that cognitive restructuring accelerated emission of positive self-reference statements in an interview significantly more than did behavior modification of a control group (given random reinforcement). Pre- and post-test of generalization effects showed that a combination of cognitive restructuring and reinforcement for positive self-references led to a significant increase on three measures of self-esteem, while cognitive restructuring alone led to an increase on anxiety and "unhappy" scales. It was hypothesized that merely being instructed to speak well of oneself was incongruent with the subject's experiential background ("don't blow your own horn"); with appropriate reinforcement, anxiety was decreased and generalization enhanced. This is essentially a laboratory analogue study, and methodologically limited in some respects (e.g., no follow-up), but has implications for psychotherapy in suggesting that direct methods of verbal communication can be used quickly and effectively to change clinically meaningful behavior, and that combined cognitive-behavioral techniques may, at least in terms of generalization effects, be superior to either component taken separately, as was supported later by Taylor.

John Gullo unpretentiously describes his study as "an anecdotal description of how patients responded to rational-emotive psychotherapy" (1966, p. 11). His paper is refreshing in other respects as well, such as in his discussion of "so-called vulgar language," an objection to which was a principal focus in the one patient's responding negatively. Gullo used a fairly open-ended follow-up questionnaire, sent by mail, with 12 of 22 returns. There were potential sources of bias in the voluntary returns, self-report, and rating of the replies by the therapist himself. The patients were a varied group of state mental hospital inpatients, all psychotic or borderline, seen in both individual and group therapy. The author concluded that while "the theory of RET may be practiced in a nondirective manner . . . being quite active and direct will produce better and quicker results . . . particularly . . . with psychotic patients whose problems are severe" (1966, p. 11). This is an aspect of RET that deserves more systematic, experimentally controlled observation.

Two rather similar studies, appearing in the same issue of *Rational Living*, are those of Alice Gustav (1968) and B. J. Hartman (1968). Both authors devised scales for measuring changes brought about by largely didactic exposure to principles of RET — Gustav through a sentence-completion format and Hartman with a sixty-item personal-beliefs inventory. The subjects in the former case were 12 people who attended at least 8 of 10 sessions of a lecture series at the Institute for Rational Living; in the latter case there were two samples, 8 therapy clients and 23 students in a college psychopathology course. The results were beneficial in both studies, but must be qualified by the lack of controls, the limitations in terms of supporting validity and reliability data for the two measures, and a question posed well by Gustav: "At this point we do not know whether those who showed positive change in the post-test had merely learned the correct words by listening to the lectures; or did their post-test responses reveal the initiation of *genuine* change in their emotions and behavior? Will they be able to continue to put such learning into *practice*?" (1968, p. 2).

Richard McFall and Albert Marston (1970) employed cognitive procedures not explicitly RET, but seen as being very similar thereto, as a "placebo" check on behavior rehearsal procedures. Behavioral, self-report, and physiological measures showed behavioral rehearsal significantly superior to the control conditions. On measures of situational anxiety and satisfaction with response, however, "placebo therapy" subjects reported significantly increased improvement and satisfaction over no-treatment controls, with no differences between treatment groups. On the whole, the placebo procedure, as described by the authors, appears to have been more akin to "positive thinking" than rational-emotive therapy in that it attempted to lay a superficial, positive veneer over the irrational ideas underlying fear of self-assertion rather than directly analyzing and challenging those ideas. An interesting feature of this study was the "unobtrusive *in vivo* assertive test" at follow-up (only two weeks later) in which a student with experience as a telephone salesman called each subject, ostensibly attempting to sell magazine subscriptions; the calls were tape-recorded and responses rated for sales "resistance," verbal activity, and social skill and poise. (This deception was later explained.)

In a doctoral dissertation at Washington University, Ann Montgomery (1971) compared three "behaviorally oriented" techniques — systematic desensitization, implosive therapy, and RET — with each other and a no-treatment control in treating a problem common with college students — test anxiety. All therapy was pre-recorded "in order to reduce therapist involvement as a factor affecting the outcome of therapy" (see abstract). Results were somewhat mixed, but in general favored SD. This is *one* way of controlling for therapist effects, and may be reasonably adequate for comparatively mechanical procedures such as SD and implosive therapy (although even here such a procedure would be far from ideal). Applied to RET, however, it would surely miss the critical philosophic dialogue in which the patient is taught to ferret out and actively challenge and refute irrational beliefs. A lecture-type, pre-recorded presentation can give information along these lines, but not the training that eventually helps the patient to become his own therapist.

Maxie C. Maultsby, Jr., the irrepressible rational behavior therapy (RBT) psychiatrist formerly with the University of Wisconsin, now at the University of Kentucky, fortunately does not stand on rhetoric alone. He has strongly encouraged a research orientation, as represented today by the report of two of his colleagues at the University of Kentucky on an extensive RBT program with alcoholics. Mention will be made here of three other studies (Maultsby, 1971e, 1971f; Maultsby, Stiefel, and Brodsky, 1972; Maultsby and Gram, 1974) dealing with written homework, group therapy, and dream changes following therapy, respectively.

Dr. Maultsby has been an ardent champion of systematic written homework ("rational self-analysis"). The present study, which in some respects examines process as well as outcome, divided sixty-seven male and female college students into three groups on the basis of degree of improvement from outpatient psychiatric treatment, as measured by self-evaluation forms that were then rated by Dr. Maultsby and three independent raters. Improvement was compared with self-report estimates of homework performance, with results that 85% of the improved patients reported that the homework definitely contributed to therapeutic progress, and that "diligence in homework performance was associated with psychotherapy progress" in a statistically significant manner. The Taylor Manifest Anxiety Scale

(TMA) was also employed as a self-report measure, but not correlated with improvement or homework.

The 1972 study concerned a similar sample in which patients rated the pleasantness and benefits of group therapy (they had also received individual therapy). Forty-one of 69 saw group as being of definite value, 11 of none; 28 as definitely pleasant, 10 as not (including 5 who found it valuable). The authors conclude that "RBT group therapy experience need not be enjoyable in order to be beneficial" (p. 30). In the 1974 study, 22 of 68 patients completing "successful" RBT reported changes in dreams, all but one of them favorable. The therapeutically desirable dream changes tended to be associated with moderate to excellent therapy response over-all. The TMA measure showed improvement generally, but these scores were not correlated with dream changes. All three of these studies show similar methodological weaknesses, including lack of placebo or no-treatment controls, and sole reliance upon patient self-report (the clinical ratings are simply categorizations of the self-report data). Nonetheless, investigations such as these are useful in directing our attention to how RET (or RBT) can be made more effective and efficient, and to innovative assessments of therapeutic results that, because they are not directly related to theory, might in some quarters be the more impressive.

James Bard reported on the effects of "rational proselytizing," in that six students in a university abnormal psychology class, in which there was emphasis on RET, attempted to teach the principles of RET to a friend, relative, or other willing listener. Compared with students from the same class, but in a different, non-RET project, they showed a significantly greater increase in scores on a "rationality scale." This scale was "validated by having Albert Ellis respond to the many items" (1973a, p. 24). This might be an excellent check on face validity, but would surely be weak on concurrent and construct validity, not to mention stability, unless Dr. Ellis and others were to make additional responses that could be related to the scale. Other methodological considerations are the lack of control over what the experimental subjects actually did, the comparative effects of RET exposure in the classroom for the two groups, the appropriateness of "other projects" as a placebo control, the lack of a behavioral check on self-reports of benefits, and, again, what Alice Gustav earlier raised as the question of true belief and ability to practice versus regurgitation of what one has learned is the proper thing to say. What role, too, might cognitive dissonance have had in influencing the experimental subjects to agree with what they were teaching? This study does not adequately answer those questions, but it does support the theoretical notion in RET that actively counter-propagandizing irrational beliefs (whether in oneself or others) enhances cognitive change. This, of course, is assumed to be one of the important ingredients of group therapy.

A study that involved RET along with three other methods of therapy without directly comparing them, but focused instead on client preferences concerning the treatment provided, is that of Donald Devine and Peter Fernald (1973) at the University of New Hampshire. Thirty-two snake-fearing subjects viewed a videotape of four therapists who described and illustrated their techniques for treating such a fear. The therapies were RET, systematic desensitization, encounter, and combined modeling and behavior rehearsal. Half the subjects were assigned to a therapy for which they expressed preference, half were not. Sixteen control subjects who had not gone through the aforementioned procedure were randomly assigned to the different therapies. Post-therapy measures showed that, in combination, the preferred treatments produced significantly more fear reduction than either the nonpreferred or randomly assigned treatments. Taken singly, the modeling-behavior rehearsal group improved the most, followed by RET. The authors conclude that the results "argue for the practice of having patients learn about available therapies and then choose one of them" (see abstract). This does not mean that clients cannot be educated to prefer, or at least accept, a given mode of treatment (and those who expect purely "supportive" therapy are often initially resistant to RET), but the matter of client attitude toward treatment deserves further research attention.

Thomas D'Zurilla, G. Terrence Wilson, and Rosemary Nelson of the State University of New York at Stony Brook, where the strongly behavioral orientation has of late been increasingly blended with attention to mediational factors, employed a cognitive restructuring procedure similar to, but not identical with, RET to control for "nonspecific factors" in a study comparing systematic desensitization and "graduated prolonged exposure" in imagination in treating female undergraduates who showed a high degree of fear of dead and bloody rats (1973). On a behavioral approach measure, only the latter group showed significant reductions in avoidance, with the cognitive procedure approaching significance. On a measure of subjective fear, there was a surprising (to the authors) finding that only the cognitive restructuring procedure (which had essentially been conceptualized as placebo in nature) led to significant improvement. Subjects were treated in groups, with the cognitive treatment emphasizing perceptual relearning and relabeling of the fear-provoking stimuli. On the basis of their results, obtained with good experimental controls, the authors suggest that behavioral therapists pay more attention to the patient's cognitions, and that the prolonged imagery and cognitive procedures be combined for still more effective alleviation of this type of irrational fear.

Note that in this study RET as a "placebo" fared somewhat better than in that by McFall and Marston (1970). In both cases the cognitive restructuring led to changes in self-reports of subjective feelings, but not much behavioral change. Rational-emotive therapy, as has been repeatedly stated, is more than cognitive restructuring; even within this narrow definition, the procedures described in these two papers would be viewed as weak.

The use of reading materials as an adjunct to therapy sessions in RET has been one of the hallmarks of this therapeutic "school." It is not surprising, therefore, to find at least one study attending to the effectiveness of bibliotherapy. David Jarmon, in his doctoral dissertation (1973), criticized previous work along these lines as making little effort to "structure the reading along the lines of a particular school of therapeutic thought" (see abstract). He presumably employed RET-related materials geared to the reduction of public-speaking anxiety, and compared this with group RET, a placebo, and a no-treatment control. Behavioral, self-report, and physiological measures with the fifty-four student volunteers showed bibliotherapy to be the most effective treatment; however, these gains were not maintained on follow-up. Jarmon discusses the ineffectiveness of live RET in terms of "the low level of initial anxiety among treated Ss, the brief nature of treatment, and the motivation of the student volunteers receiving treatment." He views his results as supporting the value of therapeutically oriented written materials in the treatment of anxiety, and recommends further research with both bibliotherapy and RET.

In a paper based on David Burkhead's 1970 dissertation at Western Michigan University, Burkhead, Travers, and Carlson describe a therapy analogue study in which live, taped, and taped "maladaptive" RET (in which subjects were told why they should be fearful), and no treatment were compared in reducing the stressful effects of threat of electric shock. The sixteen male and female subjects in each condition set an "annoying but not painful" level of shock in a pre-test procedure involving subjective and physiological measures, then received approximately three minutes of treatment, a three-tone series in which they were told they "might" receive shock (but did not), another one minute of treatment, and another tone series. The authors sum up the results and their implications as follows: "If the application of different kinds of cognitive messages from one to less than three minutes in a laboratory setting can significantly manipulate the Ss' emotional responses as measured by the GSR and a paper and pencil check list, it would appear that a therapist might be able to effect even greater change if he were to choose carefully the cognitive messages he provides his client during the usual fifty-minute hour" (1974, p. 101). It should be noted that "reverse treatment" (which resulted in increases in anxiety) is not a placebo, and would serve to enhance positive treatment effects, and it is not clear whether the groups were initially matched for level of anxiety. No differences were found between introverts and extroverts.

Preliminary findings from the application of "systematic rational restructuring as a self-control technique" in reducing speech anxiety were reported by Marvin Goldfried, Edwin Decenteceo, and Leslie Weinberg (State University of New York at Stony Brook). They describe a structured five-step procedure employing an imagery hierarchy of anxiety-eliciting scenes in which the patient is instructed to ferret out "any self-defeating anxiety-provoking attitudes or expectations he has about the situation," followed by rational reevaluation of those self-statements, and comparing anxiety levels before and after. This is a feedback loop model in which the individual develops the ability to use anxiety as a signal to seek out and rationally restructure the pertinent cognitions, and thus regulate his behavior and emotions. With only four subjects, significant and near-significant decreases in anxiety were found on two self-report measures "despite the brief duration of treatment . . . and minimal therapist contact" (1974, p. 252). Further experimental investigation is called for.

Howard Kassinove, in what is essentially a group case report, noted informal indications that doctoral students at Hofstra University (where a major emphasis has been placed on behavior therapy, with more recent additional emphasis on RET), were surprisingly benefiting in their personal lives from didactic exposure to and use of RET with clients. To further study this effect, a short questionnaire was answered anonymously by students completing the RET sequence. They generally perceived RET "to be of significant value in solving personal problems" (1974, p. 8) in a wide range of areas.

Eldon Morley and John Watkins analyzed partial data from an earlier outcome study by Straatmeyer and Watkins (1974) in terms of internal and external locus of control. Externally oriented subjects treated with conventional RET and internally controlled subjects treated with RET modified by removing the disputing element showed the greatest gains in reduction of public-speaking anxiety. These results held only for the behavioral, and not the self-report, measures. The authors conjecture that "internals" may view the directive disputing of orthodox RET as threatening, and react defensively. They suggest that "those therapeutic approaches which are client-centered may offer greater promise for internally-ordered subjects, while the more directive approach may be the therapy of choice for behavioral change with clients who are externally-controlled" (1974, p. 24). Such a suggestion has clear heuristic implications.

Two recent studies by Geoffrey Thorpe involve "self-instructional training" (SIT) procedures designed to replace unproductive cognitions with more positive attitudes that would facilitate more assertive responses and reduce public-speaking anxiety, respectively. The first, based on his 1973 doctoral dissertation at Rutgers University, compared the effectiveness of this method, systematic desensitization, modeling and behavior rehearsal, and a placebo control in increasing assertive-refusal behavior in thirty-two college students. There were self-report, behavioral, and physiological measures for a situational test in which subjects responded to a pre-recorded narrator who made "imposing requests." There were six sessions of group therapy in which twelve assertive-refusal situations (i.e., unreasonable requests) formed the basis for treatment. SIT was, over-all, the most effective technique. It and the modeling-behavior rehearsal procedure were superior to the control group on the behavioral test and an assertive questionnaire, and SIT subjects improved significantly more than SD subjects on some measures. The experimental design included initial within-sample matching on a self-report measure, and checks on subjects' expectancy of benefit and therapist likability and competence. Such variables may seem incidental to the independent and dependent variables, but can confound treatment effects if not controlled.

The other study (Thorpe, Amatu, Blakey, and Burns, 1975) utilized four variants of SIT aimed at reducing public-speaking fears in thirty-two British students (the equivalent of U.S. high school students). The roles of instructional rehearsal and of insight into unproductive cognitions were examined through the following conditions: general insight (RET), specific insight, instructional rehearsal, and specific insight plus instructional rehearsal. Behavioral measures showed general improvement, but self-report measures revealed superiority of the groups not receiving instructional rehearsal. This improvement was maintained at three-month follow-up. The authors concluded that " 'insight' into unproductive thinking is a more important ingredient of SIT than the overt rehearsal of statements evidencing productive thinking, at least in brief, analogue treatment" (see abstract). There was no comparison of RET "general insight" combined with instructional rehearsal, and it is puzzling that the specific insight plus such rehearsal did not do as well as insight alone. This would seem to contradict the finding (e.g., Taylor, 1974) that combining cognitive and behavioral techniques enhances improvement. Any number of methodological differences (including sample differences) can account for divergent findings.

Last, but by no means least, is a report from John Rush, a psychiatric resident at the University of Pennsylvania, of a study (Rush, *et al.*, 1975) presented at the Society for Psychotherapy Research Annual Meeting in Boston. This study was conducted (in some respects it is still ongoing) by Dr. Rush in collaboration with (among others) Aaron T. Beck, a research psychiatrist at the University of Pennsylvania well known for his cognitive-behavioral approach to psychotherapy in general and the treatment of depression in particular. It is the first to examine the effects of cognitive-behavior therapy (CBT) with depressed psychiatric outpatients. (The Taylor and Shaw studies involved depressed student volunteers.) This approach was compared with pharmacotherapy (Tofranil).

Patients with a primary diagnosis of depressive neurosis were divided into once-a-week CBT ($N=14$; 20 weeks), twice-a-week CBT ($N=10$; 10 weeks), and drug therapy ($N=10$; 10 weeks). There were a number of "dropouts" early in the study (in the case of chemotherapy, due principally to side effects), which points up a problem especially troublesome in outpatient research. Interestingly, all the dropouts in CBT were in the once-a-week condition, so that more intensive therapy was more effective in keeping people in treatment. From partial analysis of data it appears that it also gave better results, in terms of symptom reduction, than the less intense CBT. Utilizing the Beck Depression Inventory, a Hopelessness Scale (both self-report), the Hamilton Depression Rating (a clinical rating scale), and MMPI, Rush and Beck obtained results that over-all appear to be roughly equal in improvement for CBT and pharmacotherapy.

One of the strong points of this study methodologically was its use of a detailed treatment manual for training the psychiatric residents at the University of Pennsylvania Mood Clinic who served as therapists. It also compared CBT (which, as conceptualized by Dr. Beck, is very similar to RET) with another form of treatment; however, it lacked a check on placebo effects. Dr. Rush comments further, concerning limitations, that there were no external ratings by "significant others" or behavioral measures to support the self-report and clinician-rating data, the clinicians who made the Hamilton scale ratings were frequently not blind to the patient's experimental condition, and there is as yet only limited follow-up. It will be interesting to see if the results, which at this point are fairly equivalent, will hold up as well for chemotherapy as for CBT.

General Impressions and Conclusions

After a look in more or less detail at a variety of RET and RET-related outcome studies, ranging widely in methodological sophistication, what over-all impressions can be gained from them as to scientific validation of this therapeutic approach? Of the nearly thirty studies examined, some were too poorly controlled or are not adequately similar to conventional RET to be considered in answering such a question. Looking first at those that could, within reason, be termed RET, five comparing this method with other therapeutic approaches and employing adequate experimental controls gave mixed favorable-unfavorable results. Of three studies comparing RET with attention-placebo and no-treatment control groups, two showed favorable, and one mixed, results for RET. Secondly, there were a number of studies employing procedures, such as self-instructional training, "cognitive restructuring," and cognitive-behavior modification, that are closely related to RET but are not deemed sufficiently similar to include under that rubric. These generally compared such a procedure with others, and employed adequate controls. Eight such studies discussed in this paper gave favorable results; one was mixed. In the case of the more restricted analogue studies, two gave mixed, and one favorable, results for the cognitive or RET method.

These results would appear to call for cautious optimism. More specifically, there seems little question that RET is superior to placebo or no treatment, but there remain basically unanswered questions as to how it compares with other types of psychotherapy. The related procedures, which in these studies have tended to be more structured and narrow in scope, have fared better.

There are various points of view from which differing conclusions regarding RET outcome research can be drawn. Ellis, in a general article on RET that included a look at supporting research, stated: "Since most of these studies have been done with partial versions of full RET procedures, and still tend to find significant improvement in groups having RET, its record of clinical effectiveness is quite good" (1973d, p. 170). He has a valid point concerning the "partial versions," but again this leaves the research questions concerning the full version unanswered. As clinical-scientists we must be careful to avoid what Goldstein, Heller, and Sechrest (1966) refer to as a "double standard" in research. This is the common tendency to reject unfavorable results by pointing to methodological and control problems, and then to cite at the same time favorable studies with the same types of flaws to support the position one advocates.

Michael Mahoney, in a chapter reviewing cognitive therapies, concludes that:

> "In short, the extent, quality, and findings of the existing experimental work on cognitive restructuring do not warrant an evaluative conclusion. This, of course, means that the clinical efficacy of RET has yet to be adequately demonstrated. Depending on one's own conceptual biases, empirical criteria, and perhaps clinical experience with RET, the foregoing evidence may be viewed as tentatively promising or pessimistic. In either case, we are obliged to suspend a more confident judgment until further data are available" (1974, p. 182).

Donald Meichenbaum, who has also extensively reviewed the RET outcome literature, comments that "although therapeutic procedures such as Ellis' rational-emotive therapy (RET) have been available and professionally visible for well over a decade, there is a sparsity of controlled experimental data bearing on their efficacy" (1975, p. 14). He goes on to state that while a few encouraging studies of RET efficacy have been forthcoming, he is in full accord with the above assessment by Mahoney. It is one with which I, regretfully but within my own limits of objectivity, also agree.

Emphasis in such an evaluation is appropriately placed on investigations employing good experimental controls. Only by this means can we be sure that our results have what Campbell and Stanley (1966) refer to as "internal" and "external" validity (i.e., are they the effects of treatment, or some other confounding variable; and are they generalizable beyond the immediate sample?). This does not mean that relatively uncontrolled, or even case, studies have no value. I am also inclined to agree with Mahoney's statement that "their converging optimism should be borne in mind . . . although a poorly controlled case study may offer more modest 'empirical returns' than its more rigorous siblings, its possible contribution to our incremental confidence should not be overlooked" (1974, p. 178).

Lest we, irrationally, develop an inferiority complex in regard to the quantity and quality of RET-related research, I believe it is fair to say that we are no worse off than psychotherapy research in general, and well ahead of some other "schools" of therapy. The assessment made five years ago in an excellent article on design problems in such research by Fiske, Hunt, Luborsky, Orne, Parloff, Reiser, and Tuma, while deserving some qualification, still holds all too true today:

> "There have been few convincing research studies on the effectiveness of the various psychotherapies. The studies of large scope have typically had insufficient or inadequate controls. Other studies, often more adequate in methodology, have been so limited in scope that any generalization of their findings must be very tenuous. Until recently, few studies have built cumulatively on earlier ones to provide comparable rather than conglomerate data. As a consequence, we have little systematic experimental knowledge of psychotherapy, of its effectiveness, and of the factors facilitating its effects. Certainly the practice of psychotherapy has been influenced very little by the research literature" (1970, p. 22).

Much more than being an annotated-bibliography type of survey of the literature, this paper seeks to serve as a stimulus and (to some extent) guide in correcting some of the deficiencies found there, so as to provide RET and like procedures a more solid empirical base. Will this be easy? Assuredly not, as human behavior is "multidetermined," to use Freud's term; the variables affecting therapeutic change are many and complex. As Howard and Orlinsky admonish: "No area of psychotherapy has suffered so much from simplistic thinking in the guise of tough-minded pragmatism as has research on therapy outcome. The insistent demand to know if therapy 'works' has obscured the extreme subtlety of the question . . ." (1972, p. 645). It is no wonder, as Joseph Zubin observed a decade ago, that clinical investigators had made a "flight into process" (1964, p. 127). It appears that this trend is being reversed, especially in the behavioral and cognitive-behavioral literature, but there is still a long way to go.

Earlier here I made numerous remarks on a variety of

methodological considerations and problems in the course of reviewing outcome studies. My original intent to include a brief but comprehensive review of such factors will be largely aborted — in part because of the unexpected length of this paper. Many of you need no such general reminders, being able to hark back to that experimental design seminar with its attention to such variables as subjects, therapists, procedures, time, measures, and statistical analyses. Fortunately for those interested in inquiring further, there are some very good review articles and chapters on methodological problems in outcome research (e.g., Bergin and Strupp, 1970; Fiske, et al., 1970; Meltzoff and Kornreich, 1970; Paul, 1969; Strupp and Bergin, 1969).

Nevertheless, a few matters deserve brief discussion. One of these is the limited value of comparing a given treatment procedure with only a no-treatment control group. This is, as Blocher (1967) has pointed out, to stack the cards in one's own favor, since all kinds of intervention, from voodoo to Mesmerism to sugar pills, will produce some desirable effects. As DiLoreto sees it, this experimental design perpetuates "school" distinctions by maximizing the occurrence of "positive" results, so as to provide a "pseudo scientific base that makes these schools currently so implacable and unyielding" (1971, p. 27). As a remedy, he suggests:

> "In order to overcome this predicament, research in counseling and psychotherapy must move in two directions. First, we must move from research that emphasizes process to research that emphasizes outcome, but includes relevant process measures of client-therapist interactions as well as measures of sequential change in the target behaviors under study, so as to aid our understanding of why we got the results we did. Second, movement must occur from outcome studies that emphasize the treatment-no-treatment model to studies that emphasize research on a multivariate-comparative model" (1971, p. 27).

Grummon, in agreement, asserts that "if we are going to rest our case about the effectiveness of counseling on whether or not it promotes this or that desirable behavior, we must also consider whether some other procedure might not produce the result more economically and to an even greater degree" (1965, pp. 63-64). The inclusion of an attention-placebo control is, of course, an improvement over the treatment-no-treatment model, but it is only by attempting to fulfill DiLoreto's admonition that we can begin to answer what Paul terms the "ultimate questions": "What treatment, by whom, is most effective for this individual with that specific problem, under which set of circumstances, and how does it come about?" (1969, p. 44). This is a tall order, and Paul is quick to add that no single study will ever be able to provide all these answers. What is required, instead, is "for meaningful knowledge to accumulate across studies" (1969, p. 44). In order to achieve this, it is necessary for each study to specify those questions it does attempt to answer, and adequately describe, measure and control the pertinent independent, dependent, and at least major potentially confounding variables.

A number of the studies reviewed in this paper used a variety of outcome measures, including self-report, clinical ratings, behavioral observations, and physiological measures. But there were more that did not, and it is important that diverse measures be used, since they tend to have low inter-correlations (Fiske, et al., 1970; Garfield, Prager, and Bergin, 1971). It is evident that cognitive approaches tend to do better on self-report than on external measures, and whenever possible it is worthwhile to obtain the support of behavioral and physiological changes as well. When clinical or behavioral ratings are involved, it is essential that the raters be trained adequately. To obtain interrater reliability is important, but not enough, as A. V. Boy points out: "Although the raters agree with each other, they could both be 'wrong' in their ability to 'read' anxious behavior" (1971, p. 242). Speaking of measurements, it is interesting to note how often investigators in the methods section justify the use of a particular instrument, only to criticize it for inherent weaknesses when it does not provide data supporting the hypotheses — like trying to have one's cake and eat it too! What we are measuring, of course, is one or more dependent variables. In most of the studies reviewed, these were clinical problems relevant to clients and lending themselves to experimental investigation. Nevertheless, it is worth keeping in mind the principles in DiLoreto's (1971) explanation of his choice of interpersonal anxiety as a treatment focus because (a) the dependent variable is delineated enough to allow for fairly rigorous experimental methodology, (b) it is a sufficiently significant emotional problem to allow generalization from the findings and to suggest implications for further study in the broader field of counseling and psychotherapy.

When Ellis referred to "partial versions of RET," he was pointing up the two-pronged problem of approximating as fully as possible the procedure one purports to be using, and as carefully as possible defining it. This is necessary not only for replicability, but so that people know what is being studied. It is particularly inadequate to rely on the term "cognitive" therapy, as Meichenbaum emphasizes:

"The uniformity myth with respect to treatment procedures that Kiesler (1966) described can no longer be applied to semantic or cognitive therapies. Instead, we must encourage comparisons between different cognitive approaches in order to identify the parameters that underlie cognitive restructuring. What are the relative therapeutic merits of viewing our clients' cognitions from such perspectives as Ellis, Beck, Meichenbaum, D'Zurilla and Goldfried?" (Meichenbaum, 1975, p. 32).

His list of names is only a beginning. One means to such delineation is a good treatment manual. It is also preferable to use several therapists, competent in and committed to the approach they employ, and to verify, by means of audio or videotape, that they follow established procedures. In this way, results can more appropriately be attributed to the method rather than the therapist. The importance of controlling for therapist variables is played up by a study (Bobey and Davidson, 1970) in which there were three taped procedures for increasing pain tolerance in female student nurses. The tapes by a male "therapist" gave positive results in all three treatments, but only one of the tapes by a female gave positive results (calling women's lib!). One must also be cautious in generalizing from results obtained on volunteer student samples to a clinical population (Goldstein and Wolpe, 1971; Lazarus, 1971). With such safeguards we may avoid lending support to Perry London's wry observation of psychotherapy as "an undefined technique applied to unspecified cases with unpredictable results. For this technique rigorous training is required" (1964, p. 155).

After all these caveats, a few closing words may be in order to help offset growing feelings of what David Malan (1973) referred to as a general disillusionment with psychotherapy research. It would be nice to have that million-dollar large-scale study comparing the effectiveness of RET with other major forms of therapy that Ellis speaks of. Such an undertaking would help correct the research deficiencies that led him to say "as for the clinic, conclusive results are by no means in yet" (1971b, p. 11). That million dollars is by no means in yet either; in the meantime we must make do with more meager resources. A number of critics of psychotherapy research are encouraging in this respect, asserting that sample size is less important than controls (which, indeed, may be more difficult to maintain in large-scale studies), that confidence in findings increases with replication over a series of studies by different investigators, and that individual studies may be weak (but not too weak!), and still add to cumulative evidence (e.g., Fiske, et al., 1970; Malan, 1973).

Merely comparing the quantity and quality of studies reviewed in this paper with those reviewed in the introductory section of my dissertation four years ago persuades me that we are headed in the right direction. If one can metaphorically think of psychotherapy research as culminating at the end of a tunnel, no doubt the studies reported in this conference will add further to the light eventually to be found there — as well as that helping to guide the way.

S.H.A.R.P. (Self Help Alcoholism Research Project): A Descriptive Presentation

RICHARD WELSH, ACSW

Associate Professor of Clinical Social Work in Psychiatry

JEFFREY M. BRANDSMA, Ph.D.

University of Kentucky

S.H.A.R.P. (Self Help Alcoholism Research Project) is a four-year $347,746 research-demonstration project on alcoholism funded in 1972 by the National Institute of Alcohol Abuse and Alcoholism, and sponsored by the Outpatient Psychiatry Clinic, University of Kentucky Medical Center.

S.H.A.R.P. presently is examining efficacy of four treatment modalities with the treatment of alcoholism. In Group I, the subjects received rational behavior therapy (RET), including individual therapy sessions with a professionally trained therapist, utilizing tape recordings, written rational self-analysis techniques, and referral to a professionally led RBT group. Group II is designed to test self-help RBT, utilizing the basic theoretical principles of RBT. Patients received self-instructional tapes, and written rational self-analysis assignments; they then participated in a rational self-help group led by a nonprofessional counselor. These two approaches are being compared to Group III (traditional insight-oriented therapy) and Group IV (Alcoholics Anonymous). All four treatment groups will be compared to Group V, a "no treatment" control group. Individuals assigned to the control group were not offered any type of treatment — were left to seek what was available in the community.

The major goal of S.H.A.R.P. is to examine the efficacy of four treatment modalities in the treatment of alcoholism. Psychiatric literature has produced very little scientific evidence (Hill and Blane, 1967) that traditional approaches in the treatment of alcoholics have any significance and/or long-lasting effects. In an overview book summarizing research and psychotherapy (Meltzoff and Kornreich, 1970) the point is repeatedly demonstrated that the results of studies comparing the efficacy of treatments of alcoholism (in both controlled and uncontrolled designs) are variable. Apparently no conclusive evidence exists that any specific treatment approach consistently produces optimum results. In the context of a society whose major behavioral problems are chronic alcoholism and chronic drug abuse, we believe that new approaches must be tried and evaluated.

In addition to comparing systematically four treatment modalities to discover which treatment, if any, is generally more effective, S.H.A.R.P. is investigating the possibility that there are certain predictor variables that may tell what type of person responds better to one mode of treatment than to another. If so, it would be possible to assign selectively certain treatment modalities with some assurance of success. Further research objectives include: (1) the investigation of possible physiological predictors of response to treatment, and (2) the evaluation of the effectiveness of court probation on retention and treatment.

Those alcoholics selected for this study are males between the ages of twenty-four and fifty-eight (mean age 39.7 years) living within a thirty-mile radius of Lexington, Kentucky. Seventy percent of our sample were referred by the local municipal court system and probated to S.H.A.R.P. for treatment.

Five hundred and thirty-two alcoholics (532) were referred to the project for screening. From that number, 260 or 49% of those screened were acceptable. The above number includes 184 individuals who were court-referred and 76 individuals who were self-referrals or referrals from hospitals or other social agencies. However, only 197 initiated treatment. Three factors account for most of the 65 individuals lost between screening and treatment initiation. They are: (1) individuals who lived out of town and were unable to commute regularly for treatment; (2) potential clients who were involved at that time in other alcoholic treatment programs which prevented their participation in this study; (3) respondents who were unwilling to accept the random nature of treatment assignment and the possibility of assignment to a nontreatment control condition. Treatment, as defined by S.H.A.R.P., consisted of ten or more therapy sessions within a forty-six-week period. A subject who did not attend at least ten therapy sessions was classified as a dropout.

In order to be accepted as part of the treatment sample, each alcoholic was first screened to eliminate those individuals with a nonsignificant drinking problem, or possessing low intelligence, gross organic impairments, or severe psychiatric disturbance. When evidence of gross disturbance existed, the individual was not accepted as part of the sample.

Following the screening procedure, each alcoholic was given various psychological and physiological tests, and then was randomly assigned to one of the four treatment groups or the control group to begin one year of treatment or no treatment (if assigned to the control group).

Measurement of treatment effectiveness will include evaluation of pre- and post-test results of various physiological and psychological measures, cross-validation of behavioral rating scales, arrest records, and subjective evaluations made by the therapists. A one-year follow-up with evaluations every three months is in process to evaluate several measures of social and psychological functioning as well as the criteria of relative abstinence.

Uniquely then, this study aims to find new predictors, as well as to specify what types of outcome are obtained from what types of therapy. Further, it aims to assess whether the changes caused by therapy are stable over a one-year period of follow-up.

At this early stage in the research, we have little data available except therapy attendance rates, since most alcoholics are still involved in the one-year follow-up program. To date, however, 197 out of 217 (91%) of the alcoholics did initiate the first therapy session. Sixty percent of those alcoholics who initiated therapy completed at least ten or more sessions. Table I shows a comparison of alcoholic attendance rates according to treatment modalities.

In Group I (Professional RBT) 66% of those alcoholics completed ten sessions or more. The dropout rate was 4%. In Group II (Self-Help RBT) 59% completed ten sessions or more with a dropout rate of 9%. In Group III (Insight Therapy) 60% of those who initiated therapy completed ten sessions or more with a dropout rate of 12%. In Group IV (Alcoholics Anonymous) 28% of those individuals who initiated AA treatment completed ten sessions or more. The dropout rate for Group IV was 19%.

We are reluctant at this point to speculate or offer conclusions regarding patient-retention rates and treatment effectiveness because complete analysis of the data has not yet been made and a one-year follow-up is still in process. Yet, a significant over-all view of S.H.A.R.P. patients indicates a very favorable retention

Table I

Treatment Modality	Number Taking Initial Battery	Initiated Therapy		Percent Dropout Rate	Attendance of Ten Therapy Sessions or More	
		No.	%		No.	%
Group I Professional RBT	50	48	96	4	33	66
Group II Lay Leader — RBT	46	42	91	9	27	59
Group III Insight Therapy	43	38	88	12	26	60
Group IV AA	47	38	81	19	13	28
Group V Control	31	N/A	N/A	N/A	N/A	N/A

rate in comparison to many outpatient alcoholism programs (Gerard and Saenger, 1966; Kissin, Platz, and Su, 1970; Ditman and Cohen, 1959; and Mendelson and Chafetz, 1959). The high retention rate of S.H.A.R.P. patients may have significant implications for treatment effectiveness and new innovative treatment programs.

Within the next year, S.H.A.R.P. will begin systematically to evaluate its data. We hope it will have important implications for the treatment of alcoholism.

In summary, we believe this type of research has several significant aspects. First, there is a great need for controlled investigations and new approaches to alcoholism. Second, there are many viewpoints regarding self-help techniques, the efficiency of AA, the role of physiological addictions, and the attempt to predict treatment success. We hope S.H.A.R.P.'s research results will prove crucial and valuable in terms of evaluating treatment effectiveness. Specifically, RBT and its systematic utilization of self-help may prove to be the superior treatment choice for alcoholics. If validated this will have important economic, social, and philosophical implications for self-administered self-help treatment programs which will be capable of reaching large numbers of patients at a minimal cost.

Assessment of Irrational Beliefs and Irrational Thinking

HERDIE E. BAISDEN

University of Minnesota and St. Joseph's Home for Children

Since the concept of irrational beliefs is central to rational-emotive theory, it is not surprising that there are several reports of attempts to develop instruments to assess the degree to which individuals hold these beliefs. Ellis (1957) determined the basic irrational beliefs held by a group of 59 patients he studied but he does not report the procedures used to make this determination.

Most of the assessment attempts reported in this presentation involve the development and application of some kind of rating scale. For the most part these scales are inadequately developed; they are typically not constructed on the basis of conventional procedures of sound test theory. For example, in some instances there is little in the way of reliability and validity investigations on sufficiently large samples. Since the usefulness of any assessment device is a function of its reliability and validity, the value of most of these instruments in assessing irrationality (however this is demonstrated testwise) is dubious.

Hartman (1968) constructed a 60-item, self-administered, objectively scored, 6-point rating scale for assessing specific levels of irrational thinking. Item-selection (from a pool of 135 items) was based on item-total mean-score correlations in a sample of 500 college students. The instrument, the *Personal Beliefs Inventory* (PBI), was then given to one group of thirty college students and readministered five days later. Analysis of scores yielded a test-retest reliability coefficient of .89 and split-half reliability of .95. Analysis of scores, after one week, of another group of 85 college students yielded a test-retest reliability coefficient of .91 and a split-half reliability of .90.

While .89 and .90 represent "good" reliability estimates, the fact that they were obtained after so brief a time span (five and seven days, respectively) provides limited evidence of the effectiveness of the instrument in assessing irrational thinking. On theoretical grounds alone, it seems reasonable to expect an instrument designed to assess irrational thinking to demonstrate fairly good stability over a longer period of time. The high split-half reliabilities for the two groups of scores (.95 and .90, respectively) suggest that the instrument has good internal consistency — for the specific population, and in the specific conditions, with which it was used. Furthermore, due to the small number of subjects ($N=30$, $N=85$) upon which the reliability estimates are based, generalization to other populations is inadvisable. No formal validation or cross-validation procedures are reported, although Jones (1969), based on the following study, believes that such procedures would be successful.

Hartman (1968) obtained the mean scores on the PBI of a sample of eight patients before and after undergoing ten sessions of RET and of a sample of 23 students in a psychopathology class which emphasized rational-emotive principles and which, incidentally, was taught by the investigator. Although the differences in pre-post treatment mean scores of the two groups appear impressive, no significance tests of these differences are reported. In short, it appears to me that sample size, sample description, descriptive statistics, and reliability and validation/cross-validation procedures are inadequate. In view of such deficiencies, I wholly disagree with the investigator's statement that his findings " . . . have empirically shown the *Personal Beliefs Inventory* to possess a high level of validity and reliability to be extremely sensitive to irrational thinking" (p. 7). For such a claim to be tenable, it is recommended that the test development procedures be repeated with a large validation sample and that the PBI be subjected to more rigorous analysis.

In an attempt to determine the cognitive changes of patients in a human relations training program, O'Connell and Hanson (1970) administered the PBI to 143 male veterans. Their use of the PBI seems inappropriate in light of my earlier comments regarding the deficiencies of the instrument. But, even if the PBI were a most elegant instrument, it seems inappropriate for use with this population: The PBI derivation samples included most nonhospitalized college students, whereas this sample included mostly hospitalized veterans. ranging in age from 19 to 61 years, with three to twenty years of education! Nevertheless, the PBI was administered to these veterans at the beginning and end of the four-week training program. The training program emphasized "action therapy" involving "psychodramatic techniques" and based upon Adlerian theory. One aspect of this therapy involves distinguishing between active patients " . . . who volunteer to present their problems and practice new social solutions, and are the principals or 'stars' of the sessions" and inactive patients " . . . who remain on the periphery" (O'Connell and Hanson, 1970, p. 59). Although the specific procedures employed in making this distinction are not stated, 39 patients were determined to be active and 104 to be inactive. It appears that this distinction was made during the course of the program after the first administration of the PBI. At the end of the program, pre-post treatment scores were subjected to analyses of variance.

Pre-post treatment total scores were significantly different for the entire group. To say, however, that this difference represents "a decrease in irrational beliefs" or "negative nonsense" is unwarranted, since we do not know the meaning attached to various scores on this instrument (O'Connell and Hanson, 1970, p. 59).

Of the 60 items on the test, 29 yielded significant pre-post differences; however, one of these 29 items changed in the unexpected direction. Several of the items were found to be endorsed significantly more by active than inactive patients, and vice versa. However, the design and methodology of this study do not permit determination of the meaning or significance of these results; for example, there is no control group. Also, since we do not know the reliability of the PBI for this population, apparent score "improvement" might be nothing more than chance fluctuation.

O'Connell and Hanson (1971) report another study using the PBI which is very similar to the study reported above. However, this report provides too few details to allow for extensive critical review. In this study, the investigators derived a total of six items from the PBI which significantly ($p \leq .30$) favored inactive patients and 13 items which significantly ($p \leq .30$) favored active patients. In justifying their use of a 70-percent, as opposed to the conventional 95-percent, confidence level in determining significance, the investigators state: " . . . neither population nor instrument lent themselves to the detection of subtle differences" (O'Connell and Hanson, 1971, p. 30). This statement may be construed as supporting evidence of the inappropriate use of the PBI in this and the earlier study. Most of my comments on the earlier study apply here as well.

In another study, Argabrite and Nidorf (1968) devised a 15-item, 5-point rating scale to investigate the possibility of the irrational beliefs' being used as a measure of neurosis. Scale items were anchored at one end by a description of a rational belief and at the other end by its corresponding irrational belief. The scale was administered to a sample of 204 college students; the mean, range, and standard deviation for their scores was determined. No other orthodox test-development information is reported. Nevertheless, the investigators state: "Although this test tends to correlate positively with other, more traditional tests of psychopathology in the main, the correlations are not particularly high" (O'Connell and Hanson, 1971, p. 11). Just what these correlations are, and in what manner they were derived, is unclear — rather, unstated by the investigators.

Jones (1969) developed a 100-item, 5-point, factor-analyzed instrument to quantify the relative presence or absence of irrational beliefs in individuals. In constructing the instrument, he wrote 40 items for each of 10 major irrational beliefs. This pool of 40 items per scale was reduced to 20 items per scale, for each of 10 scales, based upon the consensus of three judges, including the investigator. The 200 items were administered to an initial validation sample of 131 college students; based upon item-item and item-total-score correlations *for each scale*, and subsequent factor analysis, a 100-item, 10-scale instrument was obtained. The factor-scales were labeled:

1. Demand for approval
2. High self-expectations
3. Blame proneness
4. Frustration reactive
5. Emotional responsibility
6. Anxious overconcern
7. Problem avoidance
8. Dependency
9. Helplessness
10. Perfectionism

Mean loadings of scale items for each of the 10 factor-scales ranged from .358 to .628; factorial validity coefficients ranged from .850 to .991 for the scales.

The instrument was then cross-validated on a heterogeneous sample of 178 college students, 72 state mental hospital patients, and 177 volunteers selected from a general adult population. To provide external criterion measures, the cross-validation sample was also administered the *Sixteen Personality Factor Questionnaire* (16PF) and a 25-item symptom rating scale which had been rationally (as opposed to empirically) derived by the investigator. The IBT scores of the cross-validation sample were factor analyzed and the resulting factor structure compared with the factor structure obtained in the initial validation sample. For the cross-validation sample, mean loadings of scale items for each of the 10 factor-scales ranged from .248 to .362; factorial validity coefficients ranged from .561 to .824.

The IBT undoubtedly demonstrates high factorial validity, but its relationship to external criteria is not well established. Although 8 of the 10 IBT factor-scales correlated significantly with the 16PF *clinical* scales, IBT scores correlated significantly with the 16PF *nonclinical* scales as well; discriminant validity is not demonstrated. The two IBT factor-scales which did not correlate significantly with any 16PF scales are factor-scale 8 (Dependency) and factor-scale 10 (Perfectionism). As with the 16PF, the same eight factor-scales correlated significantly with the symptom rating scale; however, the meaning of these correlations is questionable since the scale was not formally validated prior to use. Comparison of IBT scores of the state mental hospital patients with those of the general population adults yielded significant differences, in the expected direction, for all factor-scales except factor-scale 1 (Demand for approval), factor-scale 8 (Dependency), and factor-scale 10 (Perfectionism). The instrument did not reliably discriminate with regard to age, sex, or intelligence, but a strong negative relationship is suggested between IBT scores and educational level.

Although this research is by far the most successful attempt to develop an instrument to assess irrational beliefs, as Jones (1969) points out, there is a possibility that the initial validation sample was too small ($N=131$) for the number of variables (items) investigated ($N=200$) and might have resulted in an inordinate increase in chance communality unique to his sample. In view of this fact as well as the questionable relationship of the instrument to external criterion measures, it is suggested that the IBT be subjected to further validation.

Another irrational beliefs scale, a version of the *PIRL Rating Scale*, is reported by Oda (1969). This scale (referred to by Oda as the *VA Rating Scale*) is a self-administered rating scale devised by Ells and Stieper of the VA Mental Health Clinic, Fort Snelling, Minnesota. The scale includes statements such as: "How long do you usually hold a grudge?" and "How important is your reputation to you?" The extremes of each statement are clearly labeled, and an individual rates himself along an 8-point scale for each statement.

At the time Oda (1969) reported using the instrument, she noted that no reliability and validity information was available. However, examination of her data suggests that the instrument might be of value in assessing irrational thinking. The instrument was administered to 62 University of Minnesota undergraduate students before exposure to two different programmed instructional treatments: a rational-emotive treatment and a client-centered treatment. Analysis of pretreatment scores reveals no significant differences; however, analysis of posttreatment scores shows that subjects in the rational-emotive treatment obtained significantly lower (.05) scores than those in the client-centered treatment on the *PIRL Rating Scale*, indicating a decrease in self-rated emotionality.

McClellan and Stieper (1971) administered the *PIRL Rating Scale* along with several other measures to four couples undergoing group marriage counseling (the version of the *PIRL Rating Scale* used in this study was referred to as the *Irrational Beliefs Scale*). Pretreatment scores on the scale correlated significantly ($p. \leqslant .10$) with Welsh's "A" scale on the *Minnesota Multiphasic Personality Inventory* (MMPI). Pre-post treatment scores were significantly different at the .05 level, suggesting improvement in self-ratings and less "psychic distress." Both the study by Oda (1969) and the study by McClellan and Stieper (1971) suggest that further development of the *PIRL Rating Scale* might prove valuable.

Using a sample of 60 undergraduate students, MacDonald and Games (1972) developed the *Ellis Scale* — a 9-point, 9-item irrational beliefs rating scale. Items for the scale include 9 of the 11 major irrational beliefs. Scores on the scale can range from 9 to 81; mean score for this sample was 35.07, with a standard deviation of 10.99. Item-total correlations for the 9 items ranged from .42 to .74. Analysis of scores yielded an internal consistency estimate (Cronbach Alpha) of .74.

To further investigate the reliability of the *Ellis Scale,* the investigators administered it along with the *California Psychological Inventory* (CPI) to 37 graduate students. Analysis of scores yielded an internal consistency estimate (Cronbach Alpha) of .79. Mean score for the group was 27.73 with a standard deviation of 11.90. Item-total correlations ranged from .27 to .75. For the total sample, all of the correlations between the *Ellis* and the CPI subscales (such as "Dominance" and "Capacity for status") were negative; 10 of these correlations were significant at the .05 level. These results were interpreted as "evidence in support of Ellis's proposal that endorsement of the irrational values or ideas is an indication of poor psychological adjustment" (MacDonald and Games, 1972, p. 27). The data also supports the reliability and validity of the *Ellis Scale.*

To determine the relationship between the *Ellis Scale* and more direct measures of maladjustment, MacDonald and Games (1972) administered the scale — along with the *Eysenck Personality Inventory*, the Taylor *Manifest Anxiety Scale*, and the Marlowe-Crowne *Social Desirability Scale* — to a sample of 84 undergraduate students. The MacDonald-Tseng *Internal-External Locus of Control Scale* was also administered to 37 of the 84 students. Several students were dropped from the study due to high lie-scale scores and other reasons. For the remaining 75 students, analysis revealed significant correlations ($p \le .01$) between *Ellis Scale* scores and the *Eysenck* neuroticism scale, *Manifest Anxiety Scale* scores, and *Internal-External Locus of Control Scale* scores. Correlations between the *Ellis Scale* and the *Social Desirability Scale* were nonsignificant, suggesting absence of social desirability response bias on the *Ellis*. For this sample, the mean score was 29.81 with a standard deviation of 12.27; the internal consistency coefficient was .79. No significant relationships were found between *Ellis Scale* scores and age, father's level of education, academic level, the lie and introversion-extroversion scales on the *Eysenck*, the lie scale on the *Manifest Anxiety Scale*, family size, or frequency of church attendance.

The results of this series of studies are interpreted by Mac-Donald and Games (1972) as providing construct validational data for Ellis's notions as well as for the *Ellis Scale*. The investigators point out: "The present set of results give strong justification for the instigation of additional validation" (MacDonald and Games, 1972, p. 28). It is recommended that further reliability studies include investigation of the stability of the instrument.

Laughridge (1972) mentions an inventory which he developed, the *Test of Irrational Ideas*, which is based on the 11 major irrational beliefs; however, he presents no other information on the instrument.

The only other irrational beliefs rating scale of which I am aware is the scale presently under development by Bard (1973b). This investigator devised a self-administered, 20-item, 5-point rating scale similar to one used to measure attitude change. Item-selection procedures are not explicated, but it is stated that all of the items were derived from the writings of Ellis. In the only two publications of the scale found in the literature, item 11 is missing. A "perfect score" on the instrument is reported to be 100, but no scoring procedures are reported. The "face" validity of the scale is supported by a statement that Ellis "ruled" on each item, but no reliability and validation procedures are reported, except for the following study.

Bard (1973a) administered the scale to students enrolled in a course in Abnormal Psychology during the first week of the course. The course, which emphasized rational-emotive principles, was taught by the investigator. A treatment group of 10 students was randomly selected from among the students who indicated a willingness to participate in class projects. A matched group of 10 students was selected to function as a control group. The treatment group was assigned to teach rational-emotive principles to anyone who would listen; three students dropped out of the group. The rating scale was read-ministered to the class at the end of the course. Pre-post treatment mean scores were significantly different (.05), in the expected direction, for the treatment group. Bard (1973a) indicates, however, that we do not know what a high rationality score means; he suggests that the observed increase in rationality scores might be due to "a greater familiarity with the text of the *Guide to Rational Living*" which students were required to read (p. 25). Plans have been made by the investigator to further develop the scale.

It was difficult for me to decide just where to include the following study. Gustav (1968) developed a ten-item sentence completion test to evaluate the effectiveness of a series of ten lectures on the rationale of rational-emotive therapy; the lectures were conducted for the general public by the Institute for Rational Living. The instrument, designed to measure concomitants of various irrational beliefs, includes items such as "High standards of performance . . . " (thought to measure a need for perfection) and "When someone criticizes me. . . . " (thought to measure a need for approval). Three of the ten items included " . . . were intended to be relatively pleasant for many people, and therefore [intended] to function as buffers at the beginning, middle, and end of the testing" (p. 1).

The instrument was administered to 89 male and female subjects at the beginning of the lecture-series. Unfortunately, lecture attendance was sporadic and only 12 subjects, each of whom had attended a minimum of eight lectures, were available for post-test. However, the investigator combined the pre-post treatment protocols and had three judges conduct a Q-sort of all of the responses into five categories: good adjustment, poor adjustment, neutral response, cannot say, and no response. Although Q-sort results are incompletely presented, the investigator states that the inter-judge agreement ranged from about 50 to 100 percent, depending on the item. A tabulation of the pre-post treatment responses, on which all three judges agreed, of the 12 subjects attending at least eight lectures was examined. Positive changes were suggested in several categories; however, as the investigator points out, it is impossible to determine the meaning of these changes. One might also note that the investigator, in conducting her analyses, included the three items she had placed in the test as "buffers," and evidently some subjects even show "improvement" on these items.

For further development of this instrument, it is recommended that additional studies be conducted on large validation and cross-validation samples. Future samples should also include comparison of the instrument against some external criteria, statistical analysis of data, and other conventional test development procedures which were not included in this study.

Summing Up

Based upon the studies reviewed, it appears that further research is indicated in developing an instrument to assess the degree to which an individual holds the irrational beliefs or engages in the irrational thinking postulated by rational-emotive theory. Several of the attempts reported seem most promising in this regard (e.g., Jones, 1969; MacDonald and Games, 1972).

Irrational Beliefs Assessment: Perspectives

SAM H. LANE, Ph.D., JUDITH L. BESSAI, M.A.,
and JAMES A. BARD, Ph.D.

Cleveland State University

Research related to rational-emotive therapy falls into three broad categories. First, it has been demonstrated that inaccurate beliefs can affect behavior (Nisbett and Schachter, 1966; Valins, 1966; and Valins and Ray, 1967), and that behavior and emotions can be modified by self-verbalizations (Coleman, 1971; Meichenbaum and Goodman, 1971; Palkes, Stewart, and Kahana, 1968; Rimm and Litvak, 1969; Rimm and Masters, 1974; and Velten, 1968).

A second area of concern has been the effectiveness of RET as an educational tool (Keller and Crooke, 1975) and its relative effectiveness when compared with psychoanalysis (Ellis, 1957), systematic desensitization (DiLoreto, 1969; Meichenbaum, Gilmore, and Fedoravicius, 1971), and client-centered therapy (DiLoreto, 1969).

A third group of efforts has involved the development of scales to assess "irrational beliefs." An overview of these scales reveals that approaches have been diverse, have differed in their objectives, have not given much attention to the specification of terms (Bard, 1966), and have differed in their concern with traditional steps in scale construction. The focus of this review is to determine the areas of convergence and divergence among the scales and the degree of their individual usefulness for further development. Several of these scales (Argabrite and Nidorf, 1968; Bard, 1973b; and Maultsby, 1974a, b, c) were generated primarily to elicit information from patients or potential patients, or as a workshop evaluation (Gustav, 1968), with little effort being allocated to the various steps associated with rigorous scale construction. Fox and Davies (1971) were more systematic in their development of the Adult Irrational Ideas Inventory (adapted from Zingle's [1965] Irrational Ideas Inventory, which had been constructed for use with secondary school students), but the usefulness of the instrument is limited. Many of the items solicit information regarding feelings or symptoms rather than beliefs, and the factorial complexity of the scale was not examined. These same limitations apply to the Personal Beliefs Inventory developed by Hartman (1968).

MacDonald and Games (1972) did not develop a scale as such. Instead they had subjects indicate their endorsement of each of Ellis's (1962) list of eleven irrational beliefs on a nine-point scale. Their premise was that " . . . the endorsement of the eleven values collectively would be a more reliable indicator of psychopathology than each value separately" (p. 25). The authors found a sufficient number of substantial relationships in the predicted directions between the "Ellis Scale" and various personality measures such as the California Psychological Inventory, Eysenck's Neuroticism Scale, the Taylor Manifest Anxiety Scale, and a measure of locus of control to conclude that the data provided construct validation for Ellis's system. While the results reported with this "scale" are striking, it does not provide a way to examine the factorial structure of "irrationality," and the procedure for generating a total score by summing responses across all eleven irrational beliefs raises some questions regarding the assumed unidimensionality of the construct.

In many ways the most systematic·scale development work was done by Jones (1969) and is represented in the "Irrational Beliefs Test." He generated a large pool of items, and then systematically developed scales based on factor analytic procedures. This instrument would be the most promising candidate for further development except that: (1) the subject sample for his final factor analysis was heterogeneous in a problematical way (it included 105 junior college students, 73 college seniors, 72 mental hospital patients, and 177 adults from the general population); (2) the ratio of his sample size to the number of items entered into the factor analysis was small, thus reducing the probability that the structure could be replicated; (3) 15 factors were extracted and only 10 were used (factors 1-8, 12, and 14), which raises questions as to the extent to which his structure is the best fit to the data; and (4) 41 out of the 100 items were not placed on the scale on which they had their highest loading (in fact, 9 of the 41 were placed on the scale on which they had one of their five lowest loadings). Of the 41 items, 14 had loadings less than .100 and 13 had loadings less than .200 on the factors on which they were placed. In some respects, it is a commentary on the robustness of the phenomenon that an instrument with all of the problems of the "Irrational Beliefs Test" can still be useful in evaluating the effects of differential treatments as in the study reported by Trexler and Karst (1972).

In summary, a review of the existing scales indicated that no one scale seems to be sufficiently comprehensive and well-developed psychometrically and theoretically to warrant using it as a starting point. A more promising initial strategy appeared to be to try empirically to determine common domains of content that were judged to be related to Ellis's system.

Research Project I described below details some of the problems that led us not to consider such instruments as viable candidates for further development. Project II describes our efforts to develop a rationality scale using items primarily from existing measures. Project III is still in the conceptualization stage and grew out of attempts to understand the structure of Ellis's list of irrational beliefs.

Project I: Self-Rating Scale for Rationality

The twenty-item Self-Rating Scale for Rationality (SRSR) developed by Bard (1973b) was concerned primarily with eliciting useful information from patients in a clinical setting. Upon closer examination some of the problems discovered with the scale brought into sharp question exactly what the scale was measuring. In our judgment, these problems would probably be found to exist in other somewhat similar scales such as those of Argabrite and Nidorf (1968), Gustav (1968), and Maultsby (1974a,b,c). Following are specific examples of why these scales do not serve as a good starting point for further development.

With regard to reliability, Waugh (1975) found test-retest reliability of .80 after one week, but in a different study reliability dropped to .50 after thirty days (Crabtree and Ward, 1975). Split-half reliability was found to be .56 for university undergraduates and .67 for mental health clinic outpatients (Waugh, 1975).

Data from research correlating the scale with other personality measures provide a confusing composite. Crabtree and Ward (1975) found correlations of only .41 between the SRSR and two other measures of rationality: the Common Belief Scale (Maultsby, 1974a) and Ellis's list of eleven irrational values set in Likert scale format. They found no significant correlation between the SRSR and anxiety, as measured by the A-Trait scale of the State-Trait Anxiety Inventory (Speilberger, Gorsuch, and Lushene, 1970); however, Waugh (1975) reported a significant correlation between anxiety, measured by the Taylor Manifest Anxiety Scale, and a modified version of the SRSR in which the five least discriminating items were dropped. Waugh found no significant correlation between the modified version of the SRSR and neuroticism, as measured by the neuroticism scale of the Eysenck Personality Inventory (Eysenck and Eysenck, 1968b).

Bard (1973a) found that scores on the SRSR were more "rational" for a group of undergraduate students after they were required to teach the principles of rational living to others than for a control group over the same time period. However, when Waugh (1975) administered the SRSR to several different groups, his findings were inconsistent. A significant difference in rationality in the expected direction was found between university undergraduates and the most maladjusted mental health clinic outpatients, and between patients who were moderately maladjusted and those who were the most maladjusted, but no significant difference in rationality was found between university undergraduates and moderately maladjusted mental health clinic outpatients. In fact, the scores of the patients were slightly more "rational" than those of the university students.

The results from two studies that factor-analyzed the scale provide further support for the notion that the use of the scale is limited. Waugh (1975) administered the SRSR to 231 subjects (155 university undergraduates and 76 mental health clinic outpatients). His three-factor solution, which used only items with factor loadings of at least .400, resulted in only ten usable items. These items loaded on the factors as follows:

Factor I — Control of others

    Item   8 — It is justifiable to be angry when people don't keep their word.

    Item 17 — If we do everything we can to be friendly to others, they should be friendly in return.

    Item 19 — Unhappiness is usually the result of being treated badly by others.

    Item 20 — Everyone needs to feel worthwhile.

Factor II — Self-worth

    Item   1 — Unless people get very anxious about how well they perform, they won't achieve much.

    Item   2 — Sympathy is the best remedy when a person's feelings have been hurt.

Item 9 — A person's values can be judged fairly well by the number of people who like him.

Item 11 — People really can't help thinking less of themselves when they fail.

Factor III — Control of self

Item 10 — We should be upset when other people are unhappy.

Item 18 — Everyone has the right to be ill tempered and malicious.

In an effort to replicate this structure the SRSR was administered to 151 university undergraduates and the resulting three-factor solution, also using only items with factor loadings of at least .400, generated fourteen usable items.* Only 6 items (1, 2, 10, 11, 19, 20) had loadings of over .400 in both Waugh's analysis and the authors' analysis, and of these only two items (2 and 19) loaded on the same factor in both analyses. Of the five items which Waugh found to be the least discriminating (5, 6, 7, 14, 16) three (5, 7, 14) had loadings of over .400 in the authors' analysis. The fourteen usable items in the authors' analysis loaded on the factors as follows:

Factor I

Item 1 — Unless people get very anxious about how well they perform, they won't achieve much.

Item 4 — Self-confidence comes from working hard enough to insure success.

Item 7 — The reason that people "break down" is that other people expect too much of them.

Item 11 — People really can't help thinking less of themselves when they fail.

Item 13 — To think well of oneself it is necessary to be liked by at least a few people.

Item 19 — Unhappiness is usually the result of being treated badly by others.

Factor II

Item 2 — Sympathy is the best remedy when a person's feelings have been hurt.

Item 5 — People who do wrong should feel guilty about it.

Item 10 — We should be upset when other people are unhappy.

* We wish to express our appreciation of the efforts of C. K. Simpson in collecting this data and making it available.

Item 12 — Whether other people like us or not is entirely up to us.

Item 14 — The person who gets disgusted with himself for failing is not so likely to improve.

Factor III

Item 3 — We can live comfortably whether other people like us or not.

Item 15 — The best way to achieve happiness is simply to pay no attention to the opinions of other people.

Item 20 — Everyone needs to feel worthwhile.

At this point, our conclusion is that the SRSR may be useful as a training device and as a clinical tool to provide the therapist with information about a patient's irrational thought patterns. However, from a psychometric standpoint, results concerning its reliability, its relationship to other measures, and the results from the two factor analyses have been inconsistent and generally unsatisfactory, and the measure does not warrant further developmental effort.

Project II: Development of Rationality Measure from Existing Scales

As noted earlier, a review of the existing scales indicated a need to determine empirically the areas of overlapping content among the existing scales, and the extent to which that content was related to Ellis's system. The optimal procedure for accomplishing this objective was judged to be the examination of the factor structure of a pool of items composed of nonoverlapping items drawn from existing scales, and items that were generated by slightly rewording each of Ellis's list of twelve irrational beliefs (see list at the beginning of this book). The first step in this procedure involved the selection of items.

The initial pool consisted of 419 items. A screening of the content and form of the items revealed some large differences both within scales and across scales. In particular some items seemed to have been derived from different versions (1958b, 1962, 1973b) of Ellis's Irrational Beliefs, some items were not related to any specific beliefs, but seemed to be related to other aspects of Ellis's system, and some items were not related to any of Ellis's ideas, but did seem intuitively to be getting at "irrationality." Some items were worded in the first person, and some were worded in the third person. Some items were not stated as beliefs, but rather referred to the presence or absence of a symptom. Given the nature of the ambiguity it was decided to adopt a rather liberal selection criterion by excluding outright only those items that were judged not to be relevant to some aspect of Ellis's system.

Five judges (two RET practitioners and three individuals who were knowledgeable of the system and scale construction procedures) reviewed each item. One of the following options was exercised based upon a consensus of at least three of the five judges: (1) The item was accepted as it was stated. (2) If the item was stated in the first person, it was reworded to change it to the third person. If this was not possible without a major change in the meaning or if the third person wording became nonsensical, the item was discarded. (3) If the item was not stated as a belief, it was reworded to make it a belief. If this could not be done, the item was discarded. (4) If the item contained more than one idea (usually in the form of multiple sentences or clauses), it was discarded. (5) If the item was ambiguous and the ambiguity could not be clarified through rewording, it was discarded. (6) If the item solicited information regarding the presence or absence of a symptom, it was discarded. The items were then grouped on the basis of content similarity, and redundant items were discarded based upon consensual agreement among three of the five judges. These procedures resulted in a pool of 172 items from the following sources:

- 16 — Adult Irrational Ideas Inventory (Fox and Davies, 1971)
- 5 — Common Perception Scale (Maultsby, 1974b)
- 19 — Common Belief Scale (Maultsby, 1974a)
- 4 — Common Trait Scale (Maultsby, 1974c)
- 19 — Questions for Rating Reason (Argabrite and Nidorf, 1968)
- 64 — Irrational Beliefs Test (Jones, 1969)
- 30 — Personal Beliefs Inventory (Hartman, 1968)
- 1 — Ellis Scale (MacDonald and Games, 1972)
- 14 — A Self-Rating Scale for Rationality (Bard, 1973b).

The items were then screened to insure that there was a pair of items, one worded such that a positive response would be scored as rational and one worded such that a positive response would be scored as irrational, which were direct statements of each of Ellis's list of twelve irrational Beliefs (Ellis and Harper, 1975). It was intended that these pairs would serve as "markers" in the factor structure. The directionality of each of the other 172 items was examined, and it was determined that there were approximately twice as many items to which a positive response would be scored as irrational as there were items to which a positive response would be scored as rational. Rewording some of the irrationally scored items resulted in an overall balance of 91 items on which a positive response would be scored as rational and 98 items on which a positive response would be scored as irrational. Item responses were placed in a five-point Likert scale format ranging from "strongly disagree" to "strongly agree." At the time of the present paper, data are being collected on the instrument. The plan is to factor analyze the correlation matrix of items, and to determine the extent to which the items from the existing scales are related to each other and to the "marker" items. Additionally, it will be possible to determine whether the twelve irrational beliefs will emerge as separate factors or will combine in various ways. It is intriguing to speculate on the possibility of being able to generate interpretable second-order factors following an oblique rotation, and then begin to explore whether or not the beliefs can be conceptualized in a hierarchical arrangement.

Project III: Irrational Belief Structure

A third area of consideration emerged from our efforts to understand the intent and content of the existing scales within the perspective of Ellis's system. A guiding notion was that Ellis's ideas represented a theoretical starting point upon which other formulations should be based. To some extent that had been the case with the development of the existing scales, but the fact that Ellis altered to greater and lesser degrees the list of irrational beliefs confused the issue. Additionally, some rather perplexing issues emerged from the process of determining whether or not items were minimally related to Ellis's system. In particular, upon close examination it appeared that what was being tapped in Ellis's statement of twelve irrational ideas differed greatly across the list.

The basic premise of RET is that functional emotional disturbance is fundamentally cognitive, i.e., human beings emote and behave inappropriately and disfunctionally because the beliefs they hold (content) are false and/or their reasoning (process) is faulty. It is useful to this analysis to realize that the term "irrational idea" can refer to either a false belief/content or a faulty reasoning process, if not a combination of both. The twelve irrational ideas enumerated by Ellis (as listed at the beginning of this book) are proposed to be most commonly held by persons described as maladjusted or emotionally disturbed. His statement of these irrational ideas is presently nothing more than a guideline to cognitive therapists who are seeking to determine which of the patient's ideas are causing trouble, so that appropriate corrective homework assignments may be formulated. The issue became one of how to refine the guidelines in ways that would help to develop diagnostic instruments, enable them to serve as therapeutic devices, and in the long run possibly help elaborate and validate a theory of psychopathology.

This *"refining"* is primarily a sorting task. If people are disturbed because they hold inappropriate content in their heads and/or process whatever the content disfunctionally, then the mass of words that comprise the twelve statements should indicate some leads to understanding these verbalizations. For example, Irrational Idea 1, "The idea that you must have sincere love and approval almost all the time from all the people you find significant," clearly is based on irrational content. However false that belief might be, however firmly it might be held, it cannot produce emotional disturbance unless (1) there is an implicit irrational reasoning process (i.e., "or else you're awful, or you will die" and (2) some significant person says "go to hell." (In this connection it is useful to consider the distinction between *active* and *latent* pathology. If a person believes Irrational Idea 1 and gets what he believes he needs most of the time, whether from persons or Jesus, the person won't be actively disturbed.) In this case, faulty reasoning is added to the original false belief. The "stinger" is implied by the "must." According to RET, the words "must" or "should" can make practically any statement irrational. The "should" clearly implies an "or else" which amounts to reasoning from a premise. If the person says "I must . . . or else I will be very disappointed and inconvenienced by having to look for someone else to love me," there is little for the rational therapist to debate, since the person's reasoning process is rational.

Viewing the remaining eleven statements in the same way, it appears they fall into one of three categories. The first category of irrational ideas contains simple "content" statements (Irrational Ideas 5, 7, 8, 10, 12). These statements seem to contain false beliefs (thus the term content) which without any additional processing probably will operate to misdirect the believer's efforts to achieve better results and longer-term satisfactions. If it were really true that "emotional misery comes from external pressure," then the hurt feelings of the berated wife would remain hurt until her husband admitted he made a terrible mistake and was indeed no good, and promised never to behave that way again. Students who believe "you can achieve happiness by inertia and inaction" may have fun for a time, but face grave consequences later on.

The second category is labeled "content and process" and is composed of statements that contain a false or at least a highly improbable belief, plus implicit or explicit irrational processing of that belief (Irrational Ideas 1, 2, 3, 9). In the case of Irrational Idea 2, "you must prove yourself thoroughly competent, adequate and achieving . . . ," it is implicit that this is necessary "in order to feel worthwhile," an example of faulty reasoning. In the case of Irrational Idea 3 the process is made explicit, i.e., because people who commit misdeeds are bad, it follows that they should be punished for their sins. Even if it were true that they were bad, it does not follow that they necessarily should be punished. So both content and explicit process are faulty.

The third category is comprised of statements that seem to represent only faulty processing (Irrational Ideas 4, 6, 11). The idea that if things do not go the way you would like them to go then life is awful or terrible is simply faulty reasoning. Things frequently do not go the way we would like, so there is no doubt about the premise in this case. Similarly, Irrational Idea 6 — because something seems dangerous (which things frequently do) one must become terribly occupied with and upset about it — seems to be essentially a case of faulty processing.

If the parameters of "irrationality" are these twelve irrational ideas, then one is behooved when developing an assessment instrument to be aware of the heterogeneity discussed above. At the present time we are attempting to expand upon the conceptual distinctions among "content," "process," and "content and process" aspects of irrationality. The next step will be to generate a measure for each aspect, or a measure that allows for separation, to explore further the dimensionality of the construct.

General Issues in the Assessment of Irrational Beliefs

The following set of issues and observations emerged over the course of our efforts, and suggested guidelines for future efforts to clarify and expand Ellis's system as well as the development of assessment techniques.

The first point is the observation that "scale-developers" have not been very creative in their consideration of alternatives to the self-report questionnaire. With the exception of Gustav

(1968) every scale has utilized this format. Several other possibilities would seem to merit exploration. For example, it might be possible to construct stories similar to Kohlberg's moral dilemmas and ask questions that tapped differential interpretations. A second possibility would be to expand upon the work of Gustav (1968) and Rimm and Litvak (1969) and use incomplete sentences with alternative tags provided. A third possibility would be to explore whether it would be possible to score Thematic Apperception Test protocols for irrationality. Some initial attempts at this have not proved fruitful, but perhaps cards depicting other scenes might be more powerful in eliciting this type of content.

A second point is that, in our judgment, Ellis's system does not seem at this time to provide the basis for formulating a "complete theory of personality" similar in form and intent to "classic" theories of personality. In a similar vein, it is not imagined that assessment efforts would have as an objective the development of some omnibus instrument like Cattell's "16-PF" or the "Guilford-Zimmerman Temperament Survey." Rather it would seem that the more appropriate theoretical analog would be Rokeach's conceptualization of "dogmatism." As in that system, it might be possible in the future to demonstrate the pervasiveness throughout an individual's behavioral repertoire of a belief system which functions irrationally.

A third point is that any derived system should make explicit its differences from other conceptualizations in its theory and its supporting data base. To some degree this can be accomplished by examining the relationship between rational-irrational cognizing and other cognitive approaches to personality, as well as the established literature on values and beliefs. The study by MacDonald and Games (1972) is a step in this direction, but research questions should be posed in regard to points other than maladjustment. For example, a wide gamut of research questions and possibilities is associated with attempts (as discussed earlier here) to conceptualize the *process* of irrationality. In another context, the question can be posed as: What is the nature of the functioning of the cognitive processes of someone who scores high or scores low on any particular assessment technique? This kind of question leads to a more fundamental and general question: What is the appropriate referent population for norming considerations? What assumptions are to be made regarding the distribution of rationality-irrationality in the general population? It would seem important to address and resolve these questions before significant steps could be taken to achieve anything resembling a useful validation study.

Irrational Beliefs of Psychotherapeutic Professionals

STEVEN J. STEIN

University of Ottawa and Royal Ottawa Hospital

The present investigation includes an attempt to examine one of the many testable hypotheses set forth in Dr. Albert Ellis's rational-emotive theory. My first live exposure to Dr. Ellis occurred over a year ago when he gave a workshop in Ottawa, Ontario. One of the first assumptions made by Dr. Ellis at this workshop postulated that "all psychotherapists are out of their fucking minds." This existed as a corollary of the larger assumption that "all people are out of their fucking minds." Ellis did admit, however, that these statements somewhat overgeneralized. The overgeneralization did not occur through the use of the word "all" but rather the verb "are." Ellis pointed out how all forms of the verb "to be" overgeneralize and introduced the first books written in E-prime (Ellis, 1975; Ellis and Harper, 1975) eliminating the use of all forms of the verb *to be*. This present paper also uses the linguistic device known as E-prime.

Upon entering my internship at the Royal Ottawa Hospital, I initially became surprised to find myself noticing "irrational beliefs" not in the patients only — but fully integrated in the belief systems of staff. At first I doubted my impression; but as my internship progressed, the impression remained constant — in fact, it grew as empirical evidence seemed irrefutable. A study which would deal with the "irrational beliefs" of mental health professionals seemed in order.

The present investigation attempted to examine the irrational beliefs of the professional staff at the Royal Ottawa Hospital. The sample obtained could thus serve as a small local norm group. It would prove interesting to see how the norms obtained would compare to other institutions. The results of the present study could also prove useful educatively in that they would point out to psychotherapists and trainers of psychotherapists some of the irrational beliefs that prevail among those in the professions. This could prove of great use in facilitating development of more effective therapists. The sixty-item Adult Irrational Ideas (AII) Inventory served as the measuring instrument as it was circulated to 198 members of the professional staff of the hospital — a group that included psychologists, psychiatrists, psychology interns, psychiatric residents, nurses, social workers, and occupational therapists. Before discussing the psychometric data, I believe it interesting to point out that some of the staff manifested resistance to filling out the inventory. Although the questionnaires allowed for anonymity, some of the staff reported fears of "opening up" and felt that studies of this kind usually "are a waste of time and of no value except to some so-called higher values of science." Some of the more threatening items of the scale include "Jeers humiliate even when I know I am right," "I worry about situations where I am being tested," and "I have sometimes had a nickname which upset me." Some professionals — mostly psychiatrists in the hospital — boycotted the study on the advice of the psychiatrist-in-chief, due to some of the ongoing politics in the hospital. Only 73 of the questionnaires were returned, representing 36.87 percent of those sent out. Although a relatively small sample made up the present study, I believe the results prove interesting enough to warrant discussion. Many studies of this nature report returns as low as 33 percent. Also, speaking *very* subjectively, those members of staff known to have submitted their inventories (by including their names) appeared generally the better-adjusted members of staff known to me.

This investigation utilized the sixty-item Adult Irrational Ideas Inventory (Davies, 1970) which consists of an adaptation for adults of an original inventory designed by Zingle (1965). The scale measured the degree to which individuals exhibit the eleven (there presently exist twelve) irrational beliefs postulated by Ellis (1959, 1962). The eleven beliefs, as hypothesized then, included:

1. The idea that it is a dire necessity for an adult human being to be loved or approved by virtually every significant other person in his community.
2. The idea that one should be thoroughly competent, adequate, and achieving in all possible respects if one is to consider oneself worthwhile.
3. The idea that certain people are bad, wicked, or villainous

and that they should be severely blamed and punished for their villainy.

4. The idea that it is awful and catastrophic when things are not the way one would very much like them to be.

5. The idea that human unhappiness is externally caused and that people have little or no ability to control their sorrows and disturbances.

6. The idea that, if something is or may be dangerous or fearsome, one should be terribly concerned about it and should keep dwelling on the possibility of its occurring.

7. The idea that it is easier to avoid than to face certain life difficulties and self-responsibilities.

8. The idea that one should be dependent on others and needs someone stronger than oneself on whom to rely.

9. The idea that one's past history is an all-important determiner of one's present behavior and that because something strongly affected one's life, it should indefinitely have a similar effect.

10. The idea that one should become quite upset over other people's problems and disturbances.

11. The idea that there is invariably a right, precise, and perfect solution to human problems and that it is catastrophic if this perfect solution is not found.

The items of the scale consist of single statements scored on five-point Likert scales ranging from "strongly agree" to "strongly disagree." The scores range from 60 (highly rational) to 300 (highly irrational). A test-retest reliability of the inventory (administered to 110 senior education students, with a three-week interval) yielded a Pearson r of .77. A Kuder-Richardson formula 20 yielded coefficients of .74 and .78. There exist studies of construct validity carried out by Zingle (1965), Taft (1968), and Conklin (1965). Other studies with this scale reported positive relationships between the possession of irrational thoughts and depression (Beck, 1966), marital adjustment (Eisenberg, 1971), alcoholic tendencies (Davies, 1970), delinquents (Hoxter, 1967), prison inmates (Morris, 1974), and underachievement (Zingle, 1965).

The present study attempted to examine patterns of irrational beliefs as they relate to sex, profession, years of experience, and psychotherapeutic orientation of psychotherapeutic professionals. One of my first thoughts upon contemplating the present study included the possibility of a group as well-versed and educated in psychological assessment as psychotherapeutic professionals to score quite homogeneously, creating a very limited range of scores. However, to my surprise, the scores ranged from 105 to 193 with a mean score of 147.12 and a standard deviation of 15.94. The number (and percentage) of respondents examined in each of the professions follows (residents were included with psychiatry, and psychology interns with psychology): psychology, 20 (50%); social work, 16 (41.03%); occupational therapy, 7 (36.84%); nursing, 15 (30%); and psychiatry, 14 (28%).

The over-all pattern of the percentage of scores in the irrational-rational directions can be seen in Figure 1. Psycho-

Fig. 1. Percentage of Rational and Irrational Responses to the Eleven Irrational Beliefs for a Sample of 69 Psychotherapeutic Professionals

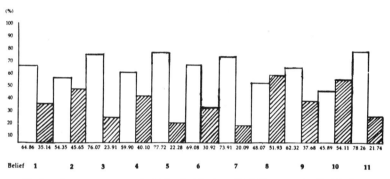

Note: Empty bars represent percentage of beliefs in rational direction and hatched bars represent irrational direction.

therapeutic professionals tend to possess a greater percentage of irrational than rational beliefs on the irrational ideas number 8 and number 10. These consist of (8) the idea that one should be dependent on others and needs someone stronger than oneself on whom to rely and (10) the idea that one should become quite upset over other people's problems and disturbances. The differences for number 8 appear to be quite small.

The first analysis consisted of male-female differences in over-all scores (these combine number of irrational beliefs with degree of acceptance) and number of beliefs in the irrational direction. No significant differences occurred between males and females on either mean scores on AII Inventory or number of irrational beliefs. However, interesting differences in the percentage of each of the irrational beliefs held occur upon examination of the patterns of responses. One can see in Figure 2 that both groups show a greater percentage of irrational than rational

Fig. 2. Percentage of Rational and Irrational Responses to AIII for a Sample of 46 Females (A) and 23 Males (B)

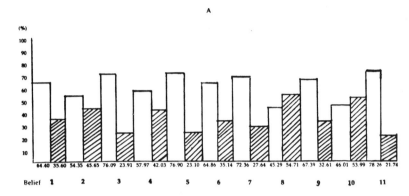

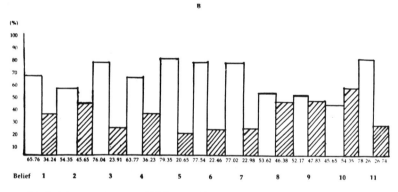

Note: Empty bars represent percentage of beliefs in rational direction and hatched bars represent irrational direction.

beliefs for idea number 10. However, only the female group shows greater irrationality on idea number 8 — the idea that one should be dependent on others and needs someone stronger than oneself on whom to rely.

The next analysis consisted of differences among the various professions — psychology, social work, nursing, psychiatry, and occupational therapy. A one-way analysis of variance yielded no differences in terms of both mean AIII scores and number of responses in the irrational direction. However, interesting differences occur when examining the patterns of responses of each of the professions. (A two- or three-level

ANOVA did not get performed due to the small numbers of some of the cells, i.e., male nurses and occupational therapists.) Figure 3 shows that psychologists and social workers possess a greater

Fig. 3. Percentage of Rational and Irrational Beliefs for Each of the Professions

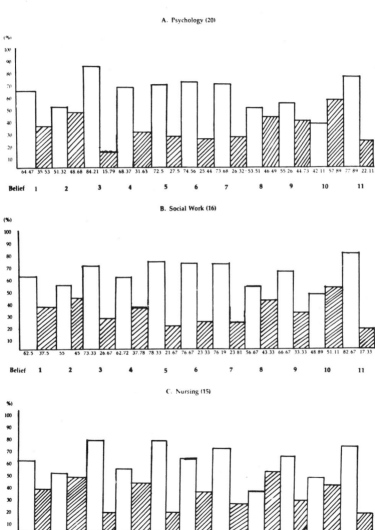

A. Psychology (20)

B. Social Work (16)

C. Nursing (15)

Note: Empty bars represent percentage of beliefs in rational direction and hatched bars represent irrational direction.

Fig. 3. (cont.)

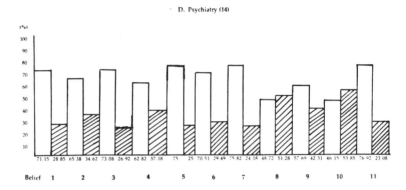

D. Psychiatry (14)

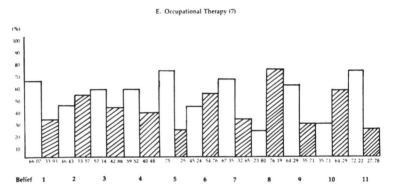

E. Occupational Therapy (7)

Note: Empty bars represent percentage of beliefs in rational direction and hatched bars represent irrational direction.

percentage of responses in the irrational direction for idea number 10, while nurses showed a greater percentage of irrational responses on idea number 8. Psychiatrists presented a greater percentage of irrational beliefs on both ideas number 8 and number 10. The occupational therapists showed greater irrationality on ideas number 2 (the idea that one should be thoroughly competent, adequate, and achieving in all possible respects if one is to consider oneself worthwhile), number 6 (the idea that, if something is or may be dangerous or fearsome, one should be terribly concerned about it and should keep dwelling on the possibility of its occurring), and ideas number 8 and number 10. Previous research with this inventory (Morris, 1974) has found differences in scores due to amount of education.

However, that study consisted of a lower-educated group (prison inmates) than the present one. In the present study, amount of education does not appear of importance, as evidenced by the fact that the nurses, who displayed greater irrationality on only one of the ideas, generally have less education than the psychiatrists and occupational therapists who showed greater irrationality on more than one of the beliefs.

The psychotherapeutic orientation did not get analyzed in the present study due to the large number of professionals who did not show any willingness to ally themselves with a particular orientation. Of the 63 people who indicated any orientation, 17 chose more than one. The majority (28) considered themselves eclectic, although I find it difficult to believe that any more than a handful of them display any form of eclecticism in terms of Dr. Arnold Lazarus's meaning of the term.

Finally, the number of years of experience received attention. This referred to the number of years of experience obtained after completion of the most recent degree (Ph.D., M.D., R.N., M.S.W., etc.). No significant differences relating to number of years of experience occurred.

Thus the present study attempted to examine some of the beliefs by which certain helping professionals operate. I believe this information can prove quite useful if it becomes available to professionals along with constructive educative material such as *A New Guide to Rational Living* by Ellis and Harper (1975) and other such material put out by the Institute for Rational Living in New York. In reality, I don't believe that a great many of the people where I intern will take advantage of the opportunity to reexamine their attitudes. However, if more of you could conduct similar studies where you work, I believe the results could prove quite interesting. I think it especially useful if one could compare rationality scores of professionals in (1) institutions where RET exists as the primary mode of treatment to (2) institutions such as the one in the present study, where it practically does not exist. Comparisons would also prove interesting in terms of length of inpatient stay, numbers of readmissions, patients' self-reports regarding treatment, reports of significant other people in the patient's life on behavioral, affective, and attitudinal changes of the patient, and many, many other possibilities. In any case, I hope I have provided one way in which we can better understand the people who work at trying to improve the lives of others.

Rational Skills Training Material

VIRGINIA ANNE CHURCH, J.D., Ph.D.

Former Dean of Lewis University College of Law, now Executive Director, Institute for Rational Living, San Francisco Branch

Rational Skills is a basic course for students electing the Area I, Human Rights and Relationships concentration, as well as for all students planning to engage in office practice or trial advocacy. Others may be exempted from taking the course. It is required of all students entering on provisional status and those placed on academic probation who have not taken rational skills previously through exemption. The logic and reasoning skills and the cognitive-learning-theory orientation of the Rational Skills course material will be taught pervasively in the other courses by the faculty who have had in-service training in these techniques and theory.

This course uses a skill-training, workshop approach to develop the critical thinking necessary for success in law school and the practice of law. Among the reasoning skills emphasized are: the critical stance . . . a certain necessary skepticism, an objective approach to facts and events; the ability to draw distinctions, for example, between factual statements and evaluative statements; the analysis of situation descriptions into basic elements; the application of evaluative opinions (and statements of law) to fact situations; the development of appropriate conclusions or decisions based on the facts and the evaluation.

These are the major skills necessary to the successful understanding of the basic premises and forms of logic required in law school. They are usually assumed to be in the behavioral repertoire of the law students, but they often have not been explicitly laid out or taught. That such an approach to reasoning and conceptualizing can be taught to people of average and higher intelligence is known, but methods of teaching it have not often been considered outside of logic and philosophy courses, where students may struggle with entirely abstract concepts.

Rational skills training is an attempt to teach these skills at once on two levels — both of immediate relevance and value to the law student: (1) in terms of learning to manage his or her emotional overreactions to ambiguous or stressful stimulae, and (2) in terms of applying the same reasoning skills to the writing of examinations, thinking through legal-counseling problems, and eliciting more nearly accurate and rational information and collaborative preparation with a client. To the extent that the course is taught as legal-counseling techniques, using selected written materials from Maultsby, Ellis, and Church, it is used as a personal self-help course in gaining the emotional objectivity necessary to proper analytic handling of emotionally charged cases and unpopular causes. The course understood as an introduction to legal reasoning and analysis relates to materials assigned from the areas of jurisprudence, logic, and philosophy. These parallels are illustrated through the use of audio-visual tapes and other media, tying legal and psychological rational methods together in mixed settings, and demonstrating them with legal and psychological problems.

This course uses the cognitive learning model for the understanding of the creation of emotions and dysfunctional behavior. Students are taught to analyze the facts of a presenting situation, breaking the described event into its component parts: (1) the objectively determinable perception, the ultimate facts; (2) the evaluative overlays, which are examined and related to emotional consequences on the assumption that these evaluative beliefs, attitudes, and learned responses produce the feelings and behaviors. It is taught that, as Epictetus observed in the 1st century A.D., "Men are not disturbed by events, but by the views they take of them."

Students are then taught how to understand change in emotional responses in reaction to the same presenting situation. This is studied in relation to the observed ambivalence of clients, and humans generally who "feel" one day one way and another day quite differently in response to the same general life situation. It is also studied in connection with determining what elements underlie this observable phenomenon, and how it can be understood by the lawyer and manipulated to produce this change by choice and in a rational direction to help lawyer and client see long-range satisfying legal and holistic goals. This model can be demonstrated in relation to a variety of live examples with the students themselves during the first year of law school. Typical anxiety reactions, stress, responsive escalation of oversensitivity, resentment, blame, guilt, or depression are usually all available as genuine feeling responses in members of any class. Volunteers present their uncomfortable feelings and the situation they generally believe is "causing it." The professor uses this to demonstrate the basic model, while assisting the student in management of anxiety, relief of depression, and generally retraining both the volunteer and the watching classmates in a useful self-help method called rational-emotive or rational behavior training (or therapy).

The teaching methods provide the students with an opportunity to develop or retrain these highly specialized conceptualizing, analytical, and analogical reasoning skills within the meaningful context of anxiety reduction in the high-stress first year so that they can learn to handle frustration, ambiguous stimuli, and their own cognitive dissonance as the new habits take hold, but do not immediately feel natural due to well-learned prior-feeling responses to the same types of situations. This permits the students to experience and test out the results of rational thinking in personal life situations and to reenforce the use and refinement of these skills as their results improve the quality of their work and lives.

Students are encouraged to discuss current situations which are popularly considered as "anxiety producing." The professor selects appropriate materials from both the rational-therapy literature (including Behavior Law and Remedies, introducing juro-psychologist expressly written for the law student and practitioner) and from semantics, logic, legal philosophy, and jurisprudence. Personally meaningful practice opportunities are provided in classes for the students, leading to the rapid development and reenforcement (for long-range retention) of the new skills through live group demonstrations, role playing, game simulations of law office counseling problems, and audio-visual tapes and taping, as well as the use of graphic aids. Assignments vary from class participation to analytical homework assignments using rational self-analysis methods, to written critiques of films, tapes, and class presentations requiring an analysis of facts, separation of elements, evaluative beliefs and opinions, emotional and practical consequences of application of these evaluative opinions and rules, the development of choices and alternatives personal, for the client, and in developing a theory of a case or application of law to resolving problems in practice.

The Course Outline

I. Introduction to Assumed Legal Basic Cognitive Skills
    Skepticism and the objective stance; drawing distinc-

tions, deriving elements, delineating and choosing evaluative rules, and predicting their consequences in application or distinguishment. In A-B-C terms these would be:

A. conceptualizing and breaking out objective or ultimate facts from presenting story and evaluative opinion overlays

B. considering alternative evaluative opinions and applicability with long-range consequences

C. prediction of determinations, holdings, or setting long-term legal goals, or advice-giving

II. Introduction to Rational Behavior Theory (and Rational-Emotive Psychotherapy)

Study of Albert Ellis and Maxie Maultsby, psychiatrists' conceptualizations of the brain's function to produce emotional and behavioral and automatic responses to the evaluative processing of perceptions and events. This includes the Anatomy of Emotions:

A. the activating event, broken into its elements: perceptions, labels, and the objective reality of the event

B. the evaluative beliefs, attitudes, conditioned responses, patterns of thought and behavior, and the self-talk language that supports and maintains them

C. the feeling, conditioned behaviors (automatic-responses to stimuli) the emotionally based decision or goal

D. disputation, challenges, and methods of substituting rational for irrational beliefs and the parsing of the nonempirical and misleading self-talk

E. the new cognitive effect, new alternatives, and their relationship to the new conceptualizations and understandings

III. Techniques for Resolving Dissonance and Conflict Between Evidence, Goals, and Legal Achievable Results

A. Legal Methods: legal research and analysis, trial preparation and relating facts to theory, cross-examination, preparing witnesses against emotional stress, defensive lying, and anxiety

B. Psychological Methods: rational self-analysis (by client or lawyer) (emotional reeducation techniques); rational-emotive imagery and desensitization; disputing, challenging, and restructuring evaluations and belief systems or responses to obnoxious or socially threatening events or future possibilities

IV. Components of Good Legal Counseling

    A. Interviewing Techniques

        1. fact-gathering
        2. fact-sorting
        3. fact-verifying or disputing and reinterpretation

    B. Problem Evaluation

        1. statement of problem; clarification of values, underlying goals, and probabilities of achievement
        2. evaluation of the emotional or irrational-belief-based goals, and the likelihood and value in the client's best interest of attempting value clarification and attitude change through referral or counseling
        3. setting flexible goals, and working toward them cooperatively and holistically with the client

    C. Examples of Strategy for Developing Alternatives

        1. consideration of alternatives, critiquing choices, building or developing wider alternatives (emotional or legal)
        2. techniques for guiding a client to choose rationally strength-appropriate goal, selected despite ambivalence or dissonance or stress
        3. strategy for achieving goals through legal process
            a. assertion of rights and motivation towards strong preferences
            b. negotiation or settlement methods
            c. trial strategies and goal achievements

V. Group-Counseling Techniques

    A. Ellis and Maultsby's zeroing in on techniques, empirical challenging, and semantic-reasoning techniques

    B. Assertive and/or sensitivity training

    C. Desensitization and promotion of attitude change in legal counseling groups through peer change and reenforcement

A Model Course in Rational-Emotive Psychology

RICHARD WESSLER

Associate Professor and Chairman, Department of Psychology, Pace University, Pleasantville, New York

In 1974 I began the development of a "model" course in rational-emotive psychology, suitable for presentation to general adult populations as well as to typical college populations. The purposes of the course were to teach basic concepts and principles of rational-emotive theory and to help people learn to think rationally. The result is a course that is intended for adult-education classes, weekend workshops, college courses in the psychology of adjustment, self-help study groups, and seminars in counseling and psychotherapy.

From the beginning I tried to avoid a lecture method of presenting information. This decision stems from a bias acquired over a decade of college teaching — that people learn least when they are passive listeners and learn most when they are active participants. So I held lectures to a minimum — both in numbers and in length — and sought other means to convey RET ideas and to involve people in the learning process.

Lessons were devised and field-tested several times at the Institute for Rational Living in New York City, with an unselected or self-selected adult education population. They were also tested with undergraduate students at Pace University in Pleasantville, New York, where the students ranged from a high school senior taking a personal adjustment course by special arrangement, to mothers taking the course as part of their return to college after their children reached high school age.

Each lesson was revised, or in some cases discarded altogether. The final set of lessons seems to communicate the basic points about RET and to hold the interest of most participants.

The format is flexible, to permit use with various audiences having various objectives. The materials work especially well with small classes, discussion groups, and seminars.

The lessons are constructed around issues in which the participants themselves expressed interest. In general, the adult population at the Institute for Rational Living seemed more concerned about self-help and problem-solving issues. Undergraduate students wanted more information which they thought they could apply to other people. With such different orientations, the discussion of issues follows different lines of thought and the instructor will do well to prepare for many possibilities.

The outline includes three parts — any one of which can be used by itself. However, I would not ordinarily omit Part I unless participants were already familiar with the basic concepts of RET. The lesson plan allows basic issues to be discussed and fundamental concepts presented in as many or as few sessions as the instructor, school, or organization may deem practical.

Part I is an introduction to rational-emotive psychology. It includes a basic lecture on the A-B-C theory of emotions, and experience in applying the A-B-C theory to the detection of expressions of anger, guilt, depression, and anxiety. These emotions are ones that are most frequently described in RET literature as negative, dysfunctional emotions that interfere with human happiness.

Part II deals with specialized topics and application of RET principles to concerns of widespread interest. Examples are assertiveness, risk-taking, and habit-modification. This part extends coverage of basic principles through application, is largely experiential, and can be especially useful in courses and workshops with a self-help purpose, as well as in some college courses in psychological adjustment.

Part III deals with theoretical and technical issues, and features analysis of therapy and counseling approaches, either through films and tapes, or typescripts (e.g., Albert Ellis's *Growth Through Reason*). Here the instructor can consider the relations between RET and general psychology, social psychology, personality theories, logic and ethics. This part does not find much favor with the general public (nor with many college students), but is intended to provide a close look at the theoretical, philosophical, and empirical underpinnings of RET.

Summarizing the course objectives, they are:

—to show understanding of RET principles, especially through their application

—to show understanding of oneself and of other people, using RET concepts

—to be able to conceptualize personal problems and those of other people in RET terms

—to show competence to plan ways to resolve personal problems by applying RET principles

Each instructor may wish to extend this list of behavioral objectives.

The lessons are designed to inform people about the principles of RET and to help them apply these principles to their own lives, if they wish. The lessons are not intended to prepare people to help other people, although they could be used in this manner. Some students have tried applying RET principles to others through peer counseling, but I found that they were not doing it very well. Close supervision is the better answer to inept applications of RET to other people. These students could have tried applying the principles after reading a book (rather than after taking the course), but the instructor would do well to caution underprepared students about overestimating their own levels of skill.

Because the lessons are not aimed at producing new practitioners of RET, I have deliberately chosen to give them a broader label: rational-emotive psychology. I hope this label also conveys the idea that RET, though developed in a non-academic setting, fits nicely into current general psychology.

Instructor Qualifications

It is tempting to list a long set of qualifications for teaching this course, but I suspect that such a listing would merely parallel my own qualifications. I can safely say, however, that the instructor had better have a thorough grounding in RET. He or she would be well prepared by having read such basic references in RET as Albert Ellis's *Reason and Emotion in Psychotherapy* (1962), *Growth Through Reason* (1971b), *Humanistic Psychotherapy* (1973b), and Ellis and Harper's *A New Guide to Rational Living* (1975).

The instructor does not necessarily have to be a practitioner of RET, but would be much better prepared if he or she were. The instructor would be advised to have some experience in leading group discussions, especially to prevent a single talker from dominating the class meetings.

The instructor would also do well to know about other approaches to rational-emotive therapy and counseling, and to have read such standard references as Maultsby's *Handbook of Rational Self-Counseling* (1971a), Knaus's *Rational-Emotive Education* (1974), and Tosi's *Youth: Toward Personal Growth* (1974).

The instructor had better be well grounded in basic psychology and abnormal psychology, and may wish to prepare or review by reading basic texts which take a cognitive-behavioral approach to psychology. I can recommend Kagan and Havemann's *Psychology: An Introduction* (1972), Davison and Neale's *Abnormal Psychology* (1974), Mischel's *Introduction to Personality* (1971), Hayakawa's *Language in Thought and Action* (1949), and Zimbardo and Ebbesen's *Influencing Attitudes and Changing Behavior* (1969). Undoubtedly others would add to or replace some of the above, but these are my preferences.

Finally, the instructor had better be prepared for discussing therapy and counseling systems closely related to RET. Read books by A. T. Beck, Harold Greenwald, Arnold Lazarus, Michael Mahoney, Donald Meichenbaum, and Victor Raimy. Since students and adult participants seem to like to discuss approaches unrelated to RET, the prospective instructor may want to review these in Robert Harper's *Psychoanalysis and Psychotherapy: 36 Systems* (1974) and *The New Psychotherapies* (1975).

Students can appropriately read many of the books listed above. I have recommended *A New Guide to Rational Living, Humanistic Psychotherapy, Growth Through Reason,* and *Youth: Toward Personal Growth.* Most students report that these are enjoyable and informative, and they especially like the case presentations of therapist-client dialogues.

Since RET is a comprehensive system that spills into many areas, instructors will find that they have ample opportunity to bring in their favorite topics, and their individual observations. Though RET can be as simple as ABC, its foundations and implications touch on many areas that well-prepared students will wish to discuss: theory of emotions, self-theory, cognitive control of behavior, existential philosophy, situational ethics, semantic analysis, epistemology, and the newly emerging field of sociobiology.

Since RET is very much unlike some popular approaches to therapy or self-help, the instructor may find participants want to show how transactional analysis or gestalt or primal scream or whatever is "clearly superior" to RET. Be prepared (rationally as well as intellectually) for students who wish to dispute what you have to say rather than learn what you have to teach.

A Sample Lesson

One of the first lessons I like to give groups, I call Building an Emotional Dictionary. It works well in small groups up to about twenty persons.

I begin by telling the group that communication is easier if we understand each other's meanings. To help us mutually understand, we will construct a dictionary of common English-language words we use to describe human emotions. Each person is to call out at least one word that labels an emotional experience. I record these on a chalkboard. (Sometimes to get people started, I furnish the first word — such as *anxiety*.)

After the chalkboard is full of words, I ask the group to classify each word as representing either a positive or negative emotional state. I mark a plus (+) or minus (−) by each word after the group votes. Sometimes there is disagreement: The word *anger*, for instance, often gets rated positive. If discussion does not produce consensus, I simply point out how some words can mean one thing to the speaker and another thing to the listener, and that *anger* is a label used to express a wide range of feelings, from mild indignation to enraged hostility.

After all words have been classified as negative or positive (only one word, *apathy*, has defied classification, and properly so — it means absence of emotion), I ask participants to say whether a word is mildly or strongly negative (or positive). I acknowledge that there can be many gradations in between, but most people will agree to use a two-point scale rather than a continuous one. Again I record their ratings.

The results might look like this:

anxiety −2   depression −2
love +1   guilt −2
sadness −1   ecstasy +2

Participants by this time have communicated with each other and with the instructor, and have begun to loosen up. We also know about how each other uses words. I, at some point, probably have mentioned that words mean different things in different contexts. If not, some participant is almost certain to raise that valid point.

But now, the lesson shifts to teaching a basic assumption of RET. RET theory states that negative, dysfunctional emotions are caused by irrational beliefs, while mild to moderate negative emotions are caused by rational beliefs. In other words, −1 emotional words are due to rational thinking, but −2 emotional words are due to irrational thinking. (I mention that the same principle holds for positive emotions.)

This lesson aims to teach one of the most difficult concepts for people to learn about RET — rational thinking *can lead* to negative feelings, but extreme, sustained unhappiness is due to irrational thinking.

Another Example

Another difficult RET principle for many people, including many professionals, is that one challenges irrational beliefs without being overly concerned whether an activating event has occurred in the way a person has described.

Cognitive therapies in general focus upon the likelihood that an "A" has happened or will happen in the way a person reports. These therapeutic approaches may help the person reinterpret what happens and this may prove beneficial. A person might report, for example, that he is fearful because his boss might fire him. Many cognitive therapists would help him assess more accurately the probability that he was correct. RET, of course, would focus upon what the man was saying to himself about the boss's possibly firing him, and help by challenging irrational ideas.

Through a lecturette, using examples like the one given above — or, better, ones brought up by the group's members — I show the difference between empirically challenging the truth or falsity, the probability or improbability of any "A's" occurring, and the challenging of an irrational belief or evaluation of the "A."

In RET, I later add, we do promote more accurate perception of reality, but most elegantly this is done *after*, not before, disputing the irrational beliefs. This key issue in RET that distinguishes it from other cognitive-behavioral approaches might create great interest among college students, and get easily accepted by adult-education groups.

Summary

A well-prepared instructor will know both RET in detail and those relevant aspects of abnormal, personality, and social psychology to which RET relates. Not every group of participants or students will want to cover every possible aspect, but classes can be unpredictable, as every experienced instructor already knows. I recommend overpreparation rather than underpreparation, in order to do an effective job of using prepared lessons from the "model" course in rational-emotive psychology.

A Programmed Course in Rational Living

DONALD R. STIEPER, Ph.D., and EDWARD ELLS, Ph.D.

Veterans Administration, Minneapolis/St. Paul, Minnesota

Historical Perspectives (Ells)

Programmed Instruction in Rational Living (PIRL for short) was adapted from the writings of Albert Ellis to teach concepts of RET to a group of psychiatric patients who were not psychologically minded. We (Stieper and Ells) started this book in 1966 and later included Albert Ellis as editor and co-author. Actually, PIRL has many more than three authors. The patients with whom we developed PIRL really were co-authors too, since their responses to the program significantly shaped our writing. Other professional colleagues helped as well, and some of them will be mentioned in this presentation.

We became interested in RET in 1961 through reading and listening to tapes of Ellis's therapy interviews and through Ellis's appearance at the VA Mental Health Clinic in St. Paul, where we developed PIRL. We found the RET approach rewarding in our personal lives and useful with patients. RET fit with our predilection toward viewing psychotherapy as a teaching situation. The content of RET seemed clear and sensible. We assigned RET literature to our patients for bibliotherapy, but it seemed that only some of the more intellectually able and motivated patients completed their reading assignments. We thought we could more effectively present RET if we simplified the vocabulary and programmed the RET material. Also we felt that PIRL might be used in psychotherapy research as a treatment method which has less variance when applied to different patients and which could be used to compare the variable of what is taught with the variable of the patient-therapist relationship.

In 1963 our Day Treatment Center opened and among the materials purchased for the center was a teaching machine. However, there was no bibliotherapy-type material available for use with our teaching machine. This lack provided impetus for developing PIRL. We didn't begin writing PIRL though until 1966, when about sixty patients were assigned to us who were considered untreatable by psychotherapy. These patients had a history of psychotherapeutic treatment in excess of three years, two or more therapists, no improvement in psychotherapy, little or no likelihood of termination, and a generally nonpsychological, somatic orientation. In working with this group, it became apparent very soon that, in order to teach them about the psychology of emotion, we had to begin in a very simple, repetitive manner, starting with defining concepts of happening, belief, and emotion. We avoided the usual A-B-C format as being too abstract. These groups (roughly six groups of ten) met monthly because they resisted coming more frequently and also because we needed time to do the writing of PIRL. Originally there was quite a bit of repetition from one session to the other in order to compensate for the infrequency of meeting times. Even with a slow pace and repetition, there were four patients who were unable to master the material, although they went through the seven basic lessons three times. This first version of PIRL was revised several times so that the groups averaged approximately 80 percent or more correct answers to each of the questions in the program. This resulted in a high probability that participants would have the rewarding experience of frequently reciting correct responses before the group. Some of our patients told us that this experience helped them to speak before other groups where they had previously been silent. We did not collect data on the effectiveness of the program on their emotional condition because both PIRL and the built-in questionnaire were in a state of developmental change.

PIRL has also been used in our Day Treatment Center (mostly chronic psychotics), with college students (Bednar, Oda), with married couples groups (McClellan and Stieper), in The Living School and in a televised version developed by Herdie Baisden, and with VA patients in Palo Alto, California.

The need for a short form of PIRL to be used with groups who met more frequently and needed less repetition led to MINI-PIRL, which shortened the original seventeen lessons to ten. More about this later.

At Albert Ellis's suggestion, we revised PIRL to make it suitable for individuals as well as groups. Presumably that could have made it more marketable by a commercial publisher but, because of the difficulty getting it published, MVAH helped us publish one hundred copies in 1970. In 1972 Albert Ellis made suggestions for extensive revision of PIRL. In August, 1973, we decided not to revise PIRL because of our pessimism about publishing it and our lack of time to work on it. Then, with strong encouragement from Albert Ellis and Herdie Baisden and with more time available, we started thoroughly revising PIRL in December, 1973. Albert Ellis became a co-author of the 1975 revision. It incorporated his suggestions about deleting language which might be construed as absolutistic, made the terminology consistent with RET's A-B-C-D format, redefined "emotional problem," and presented the "elegant" solution to the self-worth problem — not rating the self. A new chapter encouraged risk-taking and served to dispute the irrational belief that uncertainty in life is "awful" and can best be coped with by erecting a fictitious world of absolutes. The last chapter discusses habit-breaking and sensitizes the reader to five elements of irrational thinking: *OVERGENERALIZATION, DEMANDING, SELF/FULFILLING PROPHECY, RATING PERSONS*, and *ABSOLUTISM*.

Structure of the Program (Stieper)

Philosophy of a Programmed Text.   A programmed text is simply another way of presenting materials. The student learns the materials by "interacting" with them, rather than by passively reading or listening. The student responds to a short paragraph of information by answering a question at the end of the paragraph. The correct answer is imbedded very clearly in the short paragraph of information. "Cues" may appear in the space given for the answer, such as the first or last letter of a term, the number of letters or words in the answer, several words if the answer involves a sentence, etc. The paragraphs or "frames" of information are usually standardized so that 90 to 95 percent of the "base group" have been able to obtain the correct response.

In a linear program, the student then goes on to the next frame. The linear program's stepwise progression encourages the student to move in a straight-line fashion through the lesson. In another programming variation, the student may proceed along several alternative lines, called "branches," depending upon his answer. An incorrect answer may lead him back through a review lesson. A correct answer may lead him, via branching, to shortcuts or new areas of material. The advantage of the branching program over the linear program is that it moves the more facile student along more rapidly, thereby reducing the boredom factor which is an inherent disadvantage in most programmed materials. B. F. Skinner developed linear programs and N. Crowder developed branching programs.

In contrast to most other instructional methods, programming gives the student continual feedback about how well he is doing. In our program, the student also receives a "score" at the end of each section or lesson. It is quite possible to "flunk" a section of material, whereupon the student preferably repeats the flunked materials.

Crowder states that the paradigm for programmed instruction is the tutor-student relationship, wherein the tutor leads the student to discovery, employing the Socratic method with immediate feedback to the student's proposed answers to problems. In one variation of the use of our program, in which we use one leader (who reads the material aloud) and several students, dialogue among students and leader often expands beyond the one-to-one interchange to a series of interchanges among members concerning a particular concept or idea. Consequently, the virtues of immediate positive reinforcement are enhanced by the social value of the group interchanges. Since there is a high likelihood of being correct on publicly made responses, there is a high likelihood of being publicly rewarded. This group-programming method (PIRL can also be administered individually, of course) is unique to PIRL and carries some of the advantages of programmed instruction one step further, capitalizing upon the virtues of small-group functioning.

Structure of PIRL. PIRL consists of three sections referred to as "phases."

Phase One, made up of eight programs (each requiring about forty-five minutes to take), instructs the student in basic RET concepts. It provides numerous examples to which the student responds, giving opportunities to manipulate each part of the basic A-B-C formula. It instructs the student in identifying emotions and gives guidelines for separating thinking from feeling, consequences from beliefs, and beliefs from activating events.

Phase Two contains seven programs, each self-contained, which are directed toward instructing the student in the following three areas: (1) Four common irrational beliefs (since they are *irrational*, and since they are *beliefs*, they are called "superstitions" in the program) — the need to be loved, the need to be perfect, the need to have everything one's own way, the need to blame. Imbedded in the test and examined are several other irrational attitudes — one's inability to control one's feelings, the need to rate oneself, and the need to tie consequences directly to activating events (ignoring beliefs). (2) Instructions on how to change one's feelings and behavior by focusing on Step D (disputing). (3) Discussion of several "cultural" expectations with which we all have to deal — coping with the absolutes (villains and heroes), battling the "shoulds" and "musts" (dogmatism), assuming the worst in "risk-taking" (it's going to turn out badly), and so forth.

Phase Three contains a potpourri of RET materials. There are several workbook-type sections which students may use to broaden their use and knowledge of RET principles. There is also a two-program Marital Interaction series, directed toward some of the more common problems of marital (or any kind of interpersonal) discord and focusing on two major concepts — *respecting* and *expecting*. The marital interaction series may be used by one individual in the usual programmed fashion, by both members of a pair, or by a group of students with a leader in the manner described earlier.

In our original textbook, we selected several "key" programs from Phases One and Two and combined them into a speeded-up series for more facile students (MINI-PIRL). The current format has forsaken MINI-PIRL, but there are instructions in the preface indicating the ways in which the student can construct his own MINI-PIRL, depending upon his current requirements. For example, in addition to learning about RET concepts (Phase One), he may be interested in how these apply to risk-taking behavior (Phase Two) or to marital interaction (Phase Three), skipping the rest of the text (at least, for the moment).

One of the virtues of PIRL is that it provides built-in scales by which the student can assess the degree of his own hang-ups on certain of the irrational beliefs. These "scales" are programmed into the materials and are used as takeoff points for discussion in the text.

A final word needs to be said about our text's versatility. It can be adapted for either individual or group use. A special section in the Appendix describes our experiences with and recommendations for use with small groups of students.

New Developments

One of the momentary drawbacks of RET is its strong emphasis on intrapsychic phenomena (self-blaming, etc.) and its relative de-emphasis of interpersonal influences. The next development in RET may very well be to broaden working concepts to involve more interpersonal relationships and "systems theory" data. Although PIRL does not contain materials directly relating to this approach, the current materials can — in the hands of an experienced group leader — readily apply in this fashion.

The Evaluation Aspects of PIRL

PIRL has several built-in evaluation features which make it one of the few instructional-therapeutic programs where students can continuously monitor their progress. In addition to learning immediately whether his or her responses to individual frames are correct or incorrect, the student can obtain a score at the end of each program to compare with scores of normative groups contained in tables in the Appendix. Also, Program Eight, Phase One, has a special scale designed to test the basic RET concepts discussed in Phase One. The score on this test will indicate whether the student would best proceed with Phase Two, "refresh himself or herself" by reviewing Programs Three and Six, or repeat all of Phase One.

The four principal irrational beliefs (or superstitions) contained in Phase Two are accompanied by ten- or eleven-item "scales" which permit the student to assess the degree of his or her involvement with the particular superstitions.

Assessment of PIRL

In Ethel Oda's dissertation (1969), she reported combining the four scales assessing the superstitions into a single "test" which she administered to subjects before and after exposing them to MINI-PIRL. She found that they showed significant improvement in the post-testing. This is one of the few available experimental studies designed to test the "therapeutic" power of PIRL. McClellan and Stieper reported (1971) on the use of PIRL with a structured marital group. And Richard Bednar compared nondirective and RET programs in a fairly extensive study using university students (1968). (All of the above studies had positive findings.) However, other than these, there is relatively little experimental data on the therapeutic effectiveness of PIRL. On the other hand, there is a great deal of clinical data (particularly in the heads of the authors of PIRL) which attest to its usefulness, novelty value, and therapeutic value to students and patients alike.

Limitations (Ells)

Of PIRL's several limitations, the foremost appears to be its limited availability. Until it is more widely published, distributed, used, and researched, its utility will remain meager. Research is needed to determine which people can benefit from it — both in mastering the content as well as applying it. For better retention and application of the material, some follow-up appears necessary, such as periodic review or (better) individual or group therapy. We don't recommend using it with either high- or low-IQ people. The high-IQ people tend to be bored with the pace, although using PIRL with groups dispels some of the boredom. Some below-average-IQ people lack the ability to attain the basic concepts covered in Phase One.

Advantages (Stieper)

PIRL is adaptable to both group and individual approaches. It has built-in controls over many group phenomena, exerting pressure on "monopolizers" and moving the group along over a carefully laid-out series of ideas. In this sense it at least provides the illusion of therapeutic movement. It also encourages inhibited and withdrawn patients and provides reinforcement to their public responses. It provides a good orientation to therapy (particularly RET) which may be followed up by RET, role-playing, assertiveness training, etc. Because PIRL is pre-written (rather than depending upon what happens to come up in the interaction between therapist and patient), it guarantees coverage of all important concepts. It has several built-in evaluation systems which check out how well the student is learning the materials. It has a number of devices for slowing down or speeding up the learning process, by directing the student back to poorly learned sections or by providing him or her the opportunity of selecting specialized programs. Because of its highly structured format, it may be used as an Independent Variable in research projects designed to assess therapeutic outcome, etc. Because of the nature of the material, PIRL focuses on concepts — not on patient weaknesses; on problem-solving — not on diagnosis. Because of its novelty value as an instructional/therapeutic device and because PIRL is filled with stories, examples, and bon mots, the text can be entertaining.

The Revolution, Phase II: Training Lay People to Teach RBT

BETTY MATTINGLY BARRY

© ART, 1975

I debated long and hard about calling this "The Revolution, Phase II." I hesitated because the word "revolution" is a rather strong emotion-eliciting word and might convey more than I really intend. But ultimately I realized that I do see the process that Albert Ellis began and that all of us in RET and RBT are continuing as a revolutionary process. Hardly an overnight sort of thing. Certainly nothing violent. It is more a very quiet process of change that is going on throughout this country and in some other parts of the world.

When Albert Ellis developed rational-emotive psychotherapy twenty years ago, he broke with the Freudians and with traditional psychotherapeutic theory and methods. In doing so, he posited two ideas: (1) that each of us creates and maintains his or her emotional states and thus is fully responsible for his or her own behavior; and (2) that we are all fallible human beings, neither worthwhile nor worthless. Period.

That second idea isn't exactly new. We've heard "All men are created equal" from the time we were children. And our parents heard it before that and their parents before that. The catch is that nobody really believed it. Before Ellis built a usable, workable therapeutic system on that idea, it wasn't seen as particularly useful. For those who considered themselves worthless or inferior because of low social status and income, it didn't appear true. Given the cultural standards, there was no evidence to support it. And for those who (at least at times) considered themselves worthwhile and superior — again, because of social status and income — it was an idea that they could give lip service to but would rather not see the society act on.

But then Ellis came along and used the concept of the fallible human being as a basis for RET. Suddenly, it became a very useful idea. It was useful as a means to emotional health. And it's useful toward that end for all people whether they have money or status, or not. It became the key to productive and creative living — for everyone.

As Martin Grossack aptly pointed out in the fall (1974) issue of *Rational Living*, "By explicitly challenging cultural values, Ellis lays the groundwork for individuals to assume more responsibility for their lives and to become free of conformity pressures from society. RET appears to say that most people's best interests are served by learning how not to conform without dreading failure, rejection, and censure. RET encourages free expression and self-directed growth. To this extent, rational-emotive therapy is a revolutionary social attitude therapy." I agree with him.

Phase II began five years ago. It began when Dr. Maxie C. Maultsby made a very interesting discovery in his RET group at the University of Wisconsin in Madison. He discovered that the people in the group who had been around for a while were teaching newcomers the concepts, were helping them identify their irrational self-talk, and were rationally challenging their self-defeating ideas. Members of the group reported to him with delight that they were teaching family members and friends the ideas they had learned from him. And gradually, Dr. Maultsby's role as group leader decreased as he turned the group over to the members.

On the basis of this discovery and his reading about a lay self-help group called Recovery, Inc., he formed the first chapter of the Association for Rational Thinking (ART). That was the first chapter of a lay organization founded for the purpose of teaching RET and providing ongoing groups for people involved in the process of learning to think more rationally.

The resultant working-together of professionals, paraprofessionals, and lay people in rational self-help and mutual-help seems to me to be a tremendous breakthrough in the field of emotional health. There are many other self-help/mutual-help groups around besides ART. But most, if not all, of these avoid professionals like the proverbial plague. ART, on the other hand, provides a common ground. In an ART group, the group leader may or may not be a mental health professional.

And whether or not the leader is a professional, he or she is not expected to "have it all together." When the members of the group learn RBT, they learn the mechanism of emotional upset and the resulting self-defeating behaviors. They also soon come to realize that *no one* has it all together, all the time, but that learning to think and live more rationally is a lifelong process. They also soon realize that all people have problems to deal with. And in spite of this, a person can be of great help to others through the process of RBT. Those health and mental health professionals who do avail themselves of membership in ART usually find it an exhilarating experience to no longer be expected to have all the answers and solutions, but to be a part of a supportive group of people who are working each for themselves and to help each other.

So, basically, I see the development of ART as revolutionary for two reasons. First, there is a sort of leveling effect in that, whether a person is a psychologist or a housewife or a student or a government employee, in ART he or she is primarily seen and treated and reacted to as a person, a fallible human being. And secondly, I see all this as revolutionary because — let's face it — there are more people with problems than there are mental-health professionals to help them out. And private sessions are expensive. So mental and emotional health through the professional network has been regrettably out of range for many people. ART, on the other hand, is expanding the network by training lay volunteers so that effective help can come within the means of anyone who is interested in pursuing rational growth.

Some Helpful Distinctions

At this point, I would like to distinguish among professional, paraprofessional, and lay persons. You are, of course, welcome to disagree with my definitions. But for clarity, I'll tell you what I'm talking about when I use these terms.

I define a professional as a person who has developed expertise through extensive training in a particular field and makes his or her living working in that field. I think that I would add that recently the word "professional" has acquired the added connotation of one who has received a graduate degree or degrees in his or her field. Also, when I use the word here, I am referring to people involved in the health and mental health professions.

The word paraprofessional is so new that it doesn't appear in the dictionary. By this term, I mean a person who has more than average knowledge and skill in a specific field and does not have graduate degrees, but does make his or her living assisting professionals in that field.

By lay person, I mean someone who is interested in and pursuing a field, has no degrees in that field, and does not make his or her living in that particular pursuit. All of us are lay people with regard to many, many fields of knowledge. A lawyer is usually a lay person in the field of psychology and a psychologist is usually a lay person in the field of business.

I also like to make a distinction among therapy, counseling, treatment, and training. Professionals and some paraprofessionals do therapy, counseling, and treatment. As a lay person or paraprofessional, I do training.

This distinction is important for me to make for two reasons. First, I cannot (at least in the state of Wisconsin) call what I do "therapy, counseling, or treatment" without advanced degrees. I call it "training" to avoid a lot of environmental conflict. And secondly, the words "therapy, counseling, and treatment" carry connotations of illness that I prefer to avoid. My reasons for this are twofold: First, I think that "illness" is inaccurate in most cases. With the exception of people with organic disorders or psychosis, people who are emotionally distressed are suffering because of their mistaken ideas and beliefs — not because they are ill and need to be "cured." And secondly, because of people's hesitancy to seek help of any kind, more individuals are attracted to rational behavior *training* than are likely to seek help through rational behavior *therapy*.

So what we do in ART is to *teach* people the concepts and theory of RBT and *train* them in such techniques as rational self-analysis (RSA) and rational-emotive imagery (REI). I see it as a meaningful and useful philosophy that has built-in mechanisms for learning it.

Training Lay Leaders to Teach RET

We have, in Madison, the only program I know of in the country for training lay people to teach RBT in groups and individual sessions. From the results we have seen so far, the program is very effective. It is based, to some extent, on the training programs at the University of Kentucky Medical Center and, to some extent, we have made our own adaptations. The program has been run once, this past winter. We will run it again in the fall.

Background. To gain some perspective on the development of this program, I will briefly describe the history of ART in Madison. The development of the chapter has had much to do with our initiating our own training program.

When Dr. Maultsby left Madison in 1971, the ART group practically disbanded. One member of the group, however, was determined to keep it going and built it. With these objectives in mind, Connie Walling (who, by the way, does not have advanced degrees and was at that time a lay person) worked diligently, talking to people at almost any time, teaching RBT concepts, training a small core of leaders, and promoting ART. In January, 1972, Connie started a series of introductory classes in RBT. At the end of six weeks of classes, students were invited to join the ART group.

Working closely with Connie Walling were three other people — Robin Alexander, Fran Kaplan, and me. At that time, we had no formal training program at all, but we were getting a lot of experience leading weekly groups and talking to people on an individual basis. We held two or three marathons a year and learned a great deal at them from participating in groups with Dr. Maultsby. We also started holding workshops. The first was sponsored by Dane County Social Services. Later ones have been sponsored by ART and open to the public. Again, as we invited speakers in for these, we learned from them.

As we led the various groups, we discovered other people — just as Dr. Maultsby did — who were responding and teaching in group. These people were then asked to help lead groups, as the organization grew. Still there was no formal program.

During this growth process, various members of the professional community became interested in RBT. To make a long story somewhat shorter, there are now some twenty or thirty physicians, psychiatrists, psychologists, nurses, and social workers who refer clients to ART. Connie taught a course in RBT for the staff of the psychiatric ward of Madison General Hospital. I teach courses periodically for Dane County Social Services, and we are called on frequently to explain RBT to various professional and lay groups involved in mental health and related fields. Another indication of our success is the fact that two social workers whose training in rational thinking was through the ART chapter have recently been hired into new jobs and reported that their knowledge of RBT and their experience in ART were instrumental in their being hired. One is working in the Alcoholism Treatment Program at the state mental hospital and the other is a behavioral specialist in the pediatrics section of a local medical clinic.

I guess I've outlined the above to back up my statement that our program is effective. Another indicator is the growth of the local organization. We have grown in this past year from two groups of ten or fifteen people to five groups with a total active membership of seventy-one people. With regularly scheduled introductory classes and several workshops and marathons each year, along with referrals from the professional community, we are continually adding new people.

It became apparent this year in light of greatly increased numbers that we could no longer rely on haphazard training for group leaders and rational associates (these are people who primarily see people on an individual basis). In order to keep up with the rapid growth of ART, we established a leadership training program. I went to the University of Kentucky last October to go through the paraprofessional training program there and set up a training program for rational associates in Madison in January of this year.

Who are the people involved? The people who went through our first training series represent a rather varied background. The group included an editor for the University of Wisconsin Extension, a veterans' service officer, a woman who is currently a car rental agent and operates a small business making and selling health food snacks, three social workers, a boiler room operator, an aide at the state home for the retarded, two students, an insurance agency legal assistant, a lawyer, and an interior decorator.

This may seem an unlikely crew to be training to help people learn RBT. But all have two main things in common: They are all using RBT effectively in their own lives and they are all willing to spend time working with others to help them learn RBT.

How did they get into the training program? Basically, they were invited. In the absence of degrees or work-related experience that give some idea of what a person's background and abilities are, we rely on other criteria for choosing people to go through the training program. We look and listen a great deal.

We look for the successful use of RBT in people's own lives and a demonstrated ability to do RSA and REI. We think that people are better able to teach something they are doing themselves.

We listen for the ability to clearly verbalize the concepts and challenges in group. But we also recognize that the verbal skills are only a part of the learning process — what Maultsby would call the first step of intellectual insight. So the verbal skills are helpful and useful, but only part of the picture. We look to see if people are doing what they say they want to be doing in their lives.

We also listen for the ability to identify other people's self-talk, to fill in the missing self-talk that a person may not recognize.

We look to see if people are attracting newcomers to the group. If a person is talking to friends and relatives and getting the ideas across clearly enough to influence those people to take a course, or go to a workshop or marathon, we have a pretty good idea that this person is ready to train to teach others.

And finally, we look for a willingness to spend time as a volunteer group leader and rational associate over the next six months to a year. There are some people who might do very well as group leaders who either scare themselves too much or simply don't want to spend their time this way.

Stated Requirements. The stated requirements stem from the criteria above. They are: six months' experience in group and/or individual sessions, completion of a basic course in RBT, reading that includes *A Guide to Rational Living* (Ellis and Harper, 1962) and *Handbook of Rational Self-Counseling* (Maultsby, 1971a) or *Nine Client Handouts* (Maultsby, 1971c), and a demonstrated ability to do personal Rational Self-Analysis and Rational-Emotive Imagery.

The Course Itself. I like to consider the course both flexible and open-ended. In other words, it will continue to change as new materials are available through the RET/RBT network. And it will continue to change as I get feedback from participants. As it stands now, the course this fall will include:

1. Review of Basic Concepts and Hints on How to Teach Them. 4-6 hours. This includes tapes by Dr. Maultsby; Jeff Brandsma's paper on "Self-Concept, Science, and the Concept of a Fallible Human Being"; emphasis on the use of analogy and personal experience as teaching tools.

2. How to Begin Someone in RBT. 1 hour. In this section, we cover (1) asking simple and direct questions to help the person tell his or her story (this is often called taking a case history), (2) helping the person to define his or her own problems accurately, and (3) beginning the training with the RBT concept of an emotion.

3. Teaching RBT Informally. 1 hour. Here we cover such things as: (1) working with people whose verbal skills are not well developed, (2) getting beyond the RBT jargon to present the concepts in easily understood terms, and (3) using questions to help individuals discover the concepts in their own terms.

4. Teaching RSA and REI. 2 hours. In this section we deal with common problems that people encounter when they start doing RSA and REI. (Examples: How do you help someone identify self-talk they are unaware of? What do you do when RSA's have become a "magical ritual" but no action results? What do you do when someone doesn't feel better after doing an RSA?)

5. Styles of Teaching and Training. 2 hours. In this section we use tapes and live demonstrations of various styles, discuss adapting one's own style, and stress both flexibility and creativity.

6. How to Recognize and Refer People Who Are in Need of Professional Help. 2 hours. While we don't go very heavily into diagnosis, we do invite a doctor from the University Medical Center to cover this particular section so that we will be able to recognize psychosis and medical problems.

7. Common Problems in Teaching RBT and Leading Groups. 2-4 hours. Here we take up such questions as how to recognize defensiveness and deal with it; techniques for dealing with group sidetrackers and monopolizers; what to do about advice-seekers and advice-givers; dealing with one's own fear of leading a group or doing an individual session; what to do about dependency, hostility, and upsetting one's self about other people's problems.

8. Summary and Feedback. 2 hours.

During the course, people observe both group and individual sessions. We suggest that they evaluate what they see both in terms of what they are learning and in terms of what they would do in the situation. Toward the end of the course, they begin responding to RSA's under supervision — both in group and individual sessions. The course meets for two hours a week for eight or ten weeks.

Maintaining Quality. This is a rather slippery area, I think. It is so partly because I haven't defined for myself just what I mean by "quality." Here, as in deciding who is ready to train as a leader, we look and listen a great deal. I sit in with the various groups from time to time. I listen to people's comments about what goes on at group. I talk with people in the chapter a lot — both the group leaders and the other members of the group.

We also ask for written evaluations at workshops and marathons. Some of the things I look for: Are people getting help? Over a period of time are they working through their problems and behaving as if they were using rational concepts in their lives? Is it RBT that's being taught? Or is it RBT in combination with something else? (I personally don't have any objections to people's branching out and using other theories and techniques. But within the ART framework, I don't think this is appropriate.) Are the group leaders trying to influence people to adopt their personal values? Are they giving advice, rather than teaching concepts and techniques? Are the groups staying on the topic?

Continuing Education. This part is probably the most fun. For one thing, we hold a monthly meeting of all group leaders and rational associates. At this time we discuss problems, and various techniques that people have found especially helpful in teaching or problem-solving. New materials from the Institute for Rational Living and from the RBT section of the University of Kentucky Medical Center are brought to everyone's attention. We also review audio and video tapes, critique tapes made by people in the groups, and the like.

We encourage people to attend RBT workshops in other cities. We hold about three major workshops a year and bring in such speakers as Albert Ellis, Maxie Maultsby, Janet Wolfe, Linda Carpenter, and Sol Gordon.

And by having our group leaders run small groups for these programs, they usually attend the workshop free. This helps us keep up with new developments in the field.

ART and the Professional Community

There are a few physicians, psychiatrists, and psychologists in Madison who primarily use RBT with their clients. We rely on these people for help and expertise from time to time. When we think it's advisable, we refer people to them. They, in turn, refer clients to us.

RBT is being used in the Alcoholism Treatment Unit at the State Hospital and on the psychiatric ward of Madison General Hospital. These programs, of course, then feed into our ART groups.

The people on our growing list of referral sources are alerted to our classes, workshops, marathons, and other activities. Some of these people are in our groups and we see many others at various ART functions, so that we are maintaining a lively and mutually beneficial liaison. It is a network we are continually working to expand.

The Results So Far

As I said earlier, we had two groups of ten or fifteen people each a year ago. Each group had two leaders and we had a few people who were trained informally who could take over when necessary.

Right now we have five groups meeting regularly, with a total active membership of seventy-one people. Our mailing list of three hundred includes people who are former ART members and people who have heard about us and would like to be involved in the future. There are many reasons for this dramatic increase in membership in the past months. But obviously we would never have been able to provide leaders for these groups if we hadn't begun a formal training program. And as a result of the training, we held our first marathon without professional leadership (Dr. Maultsby used to come for all our marathons) in March of this year and ran four groups of ten or twelve people. The evaluations we asked for at the end — without exception — praised the skill of the group leaders. By next fall, I don't doubt that we will have one or two more groups meeting regularly. By this time next year — well, I hesitate to predict a number at this point. Fortunately, there are already people who have expressed an interest in taking our training program — the course I've outlined here — in the fall.

The results — in terms of numbers — are gratifying. But numbers hardly tell the whole story. Doctors who have referred clients to us have reported back their pleasure at the progress made. We see people changing — in healthy self-defined directions — constantly. Some changes, of course, are more dramatic than others. This, too, is gratifying. And what we're doing, basically, is building a helping network that is beginning to extend farther and farther.

A woman from one of our groups came to see me at my house the Saturday evening before Easter. She was upsetting herself about a family situation that had just occurred. She said she had gone to see her doctor — who does RBT in his practice — but he wasn't home. She came to my house, but knew that if I wasn't in or didn't have time to talk, she could go to Mary Sue's or Mary Anne's or Larry's. "I know I would get the same kind of help from any of you," she said. "That's what I really like about ART."

The helping network we have formed extends beyond dealing with people's emotional upsets. We have a network of people who help in other ways and with each other's real life difficulties. When someone moves or needs babysitters or has an emergency of some sort, there are people to call on. Not just friends, but friends who will help deal with the situation in a relatively rational way. And we're friends during the "good times," too. We party together and get together socially to share the benefits we've gained from RBT in having fun together. I suppose this group of people who are working for themselves, who are concerned about each other, who are willing to help each other, and who then enjoy being together to celebrate our personal and mutual successes is the most gratifying aspect of my involvement in ART.

Implications for the Future

As I said earlier, I think we're involved in a revolutionary process. By this I mean a dramatic change in the whole social order of things. Again, we're certainly not doing it overnight. And it may be that those of us who are involved in the rational process won't actually be the ones to make the ultimate changes. But I do think the potential is here.

I recently had lunch with a social worker from a nearby town who was in our ART group two years ago and with whom I worked on an individual basis for about three months. He told me of an experience he'd had at work where one of his clients, a child, was being denied necessary medical and dental care because of something in the political structure of the community. This man went far beyond what was called for in his job description to obtain the needed care for the child. He knew that his job was most likely not at stake, but he did risk the disapproval and censure of people in his agency and his community to do this. "Before I knew RBT," he said, "I would never have done anything like this. But I knew I had the tools to deal with the conflict, and it made sense to me to pursue it."

This, of course, is an isolated example of how a person can use the rational concepts and techniques to work for change. But is it so isolated? Actually, I've heard a number of similar stories. And you probably have, too.

But perhaps more important than this example, in considering the implications of the network of professionals and lay people involved in the rational process, is the idea that the personal changes made by one person rarely stop with that person. More often we see that the changes made by one person in a family eventually bring about dramatic changes in the family itself. I know, for example, of a good many parents who are teaching their children RBT. Not to mention the number of people who join ART because they work with or know someone else who is involved.

Now when one person frees himself or herself from emotional upset, stops blaming the society and other people, stops feeling sorry for himself or herself, and believes and acts as if we really are all fallible human beings, that person has more time and energy and greater motivation to become more creatively involved in his or her family, work, and community. And that person is able to effect some changes toward alleviating the nonsensical and irrational things going on around him or her. And when two people are doing this, they are able to effect even more changes. Just think about what happens when — if I may dream a little — hundreds or even thousands of people in the same community are doing similar things. What happens, as people learn to think and behave more rationally, is that they cease to be societal problems and begin to create solutions. These solutions are based on what is really happening, are life-preserving and life-enhancing, are likely to get most people most of what they want now and in the future, and are likely to minimize each individual's emotional conflict and people's conflicts with each other.

If masses of people did what I'm describing, I think it's an understatement to say that major changes would take place in our society. On a small scale, this is happening right now. But perhaps we'd best not call it a revolution. Perhaps we'd best just quietly go on doing what we're doing and enjoying the results.

Founding a New Institute

VIRGINIA ANNE CHURCH, J.D., Ph.D.

Former Dean of Lewis University College of Law, now Executive Director, Institute for Rational Living, San Francisco Branch

I suppose my main contribution to this area is in the organizational sense, legally and conceptually. I was instrumental in founding the Florida Branch in Clearwater and we faced a number of problems that will be faced by others. It seems likely that sharing some of my learning experiences and problem solutions with those of you considering founding Institutes will prove worthwhile.

The basic problems could be arranged into (1) financial, (2) collegial and staffing, and (3) community public relations. Most people who want to start an Institute don't usually cite the expense of getting it off the ground.

Actually, founding an Institute is no different from founding any other kind of group practice. Financially, you would need to find a building or suite of offices, get a telephone, buy supplies, etc. The problem often arises because people wanting to start an Institute are or tend to be "100% security seekers" or are presently employed by someone else so that they have jobs with guaranteed incomes — which are indeed spooky to risk.

If you are already in private practice you know what is involved and you are simply expanding the risk a bit, while giving yourself a large number of new possibilities for increasing your practice more than enough to offset the increased overhead. A full-time secretary is a must, in my view. It lends both permanence and respectability and is the difference between one image and the other.

The main space requirement an Institute needs that a group practice does not is a convertible large room which can be used for open houses, lectures, etc. This does require more space than the usual group room for six people. However, it can be a multipurpose room housing the bookstore (in locked cabinets or enclosed shelves), providing space for volunteer public-relations people and ART meetings and the like. Since this room is what allows you the educational center title, it can be conceived of as the largest potential for "big-money" production not possible without it.

That leads into my concept of an Institute. I disagree that the most useful format is for training other therapists in RET methods! While I enjoy doing that, it is largely a self-defeating activity for most of us. If all trained people go out pyramid-club-wise training everybody else they can talk into it, what happens? We have lots and lots of semi-trained competition claiming to be rational therapists. If they are good, competent people, fine! But even then you lose the edge of your own uniqueness. If they are poorly trained or have personal problems which affect their functioning (rather out of the judgment of the weekend trainer), we as a network get blamed for their poor use of RET and of themselves as therapeutic tools.

My concept of a productive Institute is a three-pronged one that covers community counseling and psychotherapy, community education and public services, and research. The construct subsumes organization as a nonprofit corporation, which is eligible to receive grants and donations — the education and research warrant that.

How do you make a living on this basis? As an employee of the corporation. You set up the charter to allow you to pay incorporators and/or directors, provided that they are working as therapists, teachers, or in paid administrative positions. You set their salaries at whatever you need to make and believe you can reasonably bring in within the new setting — minus thirty or forty percent for overhead — and assign that as a salary. You provide in the minutes of the first board meeting that all salary contracts will be pinned to actual earnings by the Institute's paid services and grants to cover those salaries, and that each employee must agree to receive a lesser amount than that contracted for if he or she does not gross at least another third more than the figure set as his or her salary.

That overcomes the major reservation most people have about the nonprofit format, while remaining honest and (so far as I have experienced) acceptable to IRS, since donated funds and surpluses over what you estimate do in fact go into the Institute accounts for use for nonprofit purposes. These would include financing low- or no-profit educational programs (such as the open house), publications, public service spots for radio, and the like.

Most states have some sort of licensing requirements for mental health or psychology group practices or for Institutes. It is well to be sure your corporation meets those standards or is excluded from them by specifying itself to be something else which is also acceptable in that area.

In using the nonprofit nature to drum up business, I lean toward a free open house once a week with a printed schedule of topics, free coffee, and conversation. The open house serves as a meeting place both for potential clients and for rationally thinking people who want a home away from home and will serve as a strong referral network. Its ability to be freely plugged by newspapers and radio, and invitationally used in talks and speeches, far exceeds the fact that the incorporators are required to donate some free speakers' time in order to establish a practice for the Institute! That, of course, is a matter of personal priorities; but little is gained without investing time, energy, and money . . . and lots can be reaped for the effort it takes to sow and tend before the reaping.

References

Adler, Alfred. *Understanding Human Nature*. New York: Greenberg, 1929.

Alberti, Robert E., and Emmons, Michael L. *Your Perfect Right: A Guide to Assertive Behavior*. San Luis Obispo, Calif.: Impact, 1974.

Alexander, Franz, and French, Thomas. *Psychoanalytic Therapy*. New York: Ronald Press, 1946.

Ard, Ben N., Jr. "The A-B-C of Marriage Counseling," *Rational Living*, 1967, 2 (2): 10-12.

Ard, Ben N., Jr. "Communication in Marriage," *Rational Living*, 1971, 5 (2): 20-22.

Ard, Ben N., Jr. *Counseling and Psychotherapy*. Palo Alto, Calif.: Science & Behavior Books, 1966.

Ard, Ben N., Jr. "A Rational Approach to Marriage Counseling," in Ben N. Ard, Jr., and Constance Ard (eds.), *Handbook of Marriage Counseling*. Palo Alto, Calif.: Science & Behavior Books, 1969.

Ard, Ben N., Jr. *Treating Psychosexual Dysfunction*. New York: Jason Aronson, 1974.

Argabrite, Alan H., and Nidorf, Louis J. "Fifteen Questions for Rating Reason," *Rational Living*, 1968, 3 (1): 9-11.

Baker, Juanita N. "Reason Versus Reinforcement in Behavior Modification." Doctoral Dissertation, University of Illinois, 1966.

Bandura, Albert. *Principles of Behavior Modification*. New York: Holt, Rinehart and Winston, 1969.

Bard, James A. "Cognition and Motivation," *Rational Living*, 1966, 1 (1): 34-38.

Bard, James A. "Rational Proselytizing," *Rational Living*, 1973a, 8 (2): 24-26.

Bard, James A. "A Self-Rating Scale for Rationality," *Rational Living*, 1973b, 8 (1): 19.

Beck, Aaron T. "Cognitive Therapy: Nature and Relation to Behavior Therapy," *Behavior Therapy*, 1970, 1: 184-200.

Beck, Aaron T. *Depression*. New York: Harper & Row, 1967.

Beck, Aaron T. "Thinking and Depression," *Rational Living,* 1966, 1: 4-13.

Bednar, Richard L. "The Role of Persuasibility, Expectation for Improvement, and Treatment Methods in the Process of Behavior Change." Doctoral Dissertation, University of Minnesota, 1968.

Bender, Lauretta. "Mental Illness in Childhood and Heredity," *Eugenics Quarterly*, 1963, 10: 1-11.

Bergin, A. E. "Cognitive Therapy and Behavior Therapy: Foci for a Multidimensional Approach to Treatment," *Behavior Therapy*, 1970, 1: 205-12.

Bergin, A. E., and Strupp, H. H. "New Directions in Psychotherapy Research," *Journal of Abnormal Psychology*, 1970, 76: 13-26.

Bergin, A. E., and Suinn, R. M. "Individual Psychotherapy and Behavior Therapy," *Annual Review of Psychology*, 1975, 26: 509-56.

Beritoff, J. S. *Neural Mechanisms of Higher Vertebrate Behavior.* Boston: Little, Brown, 1965.

Blocher, D. "What Counseling Can Offer Clients: Implications for Research on Client Selection," in J. M. Whiteley (chair), *Invitational Conference on Counseling: Reevaluation and Refocus.* Symposium Presented at the Central Midwestern Regional Educational Laboratory, Conference Proceedings Series No. 2, Washington University, September, 1967.

Bloom, Lynn Z., Coburn, Karen, and Pearlman, J. *The New Assertive Woman.* New York: Delacorte Press, 1975.

Bobey, M. J., and Davidson, P.O. "Psychological Factors Affecting Pain Tolerance," *Journal of Psychosomatic Research*, 1970, 14: 371-76.

Bourland, D. David, Jr. "A Linguistic Note: Writing in E-Prime," *General Semantics Bulletin*, 1965-66, 32-33: 111-14.

Boy, Angelo V. "A Critique," in Adolph O. DiLoreto, *Comparative Psychotherapy*. Chicago: Aldine-Atherton, 1971.

Breuer, Josef, and Freud, Sigmund. *Studies in Hysteria.* New York: Basic Books, 1957.

Browne, Harry. *How I Found Freedom in an Unfree World.* New York: Avon Books, 1974.

Browning, Robert M., and Stover, Donald O. *Behavior Modification in Child Treatment: An Experimental and Clinical Approach.* Chicago: Aldine-Atherton, 1971.

Burkhead, David E., Travers, R. M. W., and Carlson, W. A. "An Experimental Reduction of Emotional Responses Through Rational-Emotive Therapy," in David S. Goodman and Maxie C. Maultsby, Jr., *Emotional Well-Being Through Rational Behavior Training.* Springfield, Ill.: Charles C Thomas, 1974.

Campbell, Donald T., and Stanley, Julian C. *Experimental and Quasi-Experimental Designs for Research.* Chicago: Rand McNally, 1966.

Chess, Stella, Thomas A., and Birch, H. G. *Your Child Is a Person.* New York: Viking, 1965.

Church, Virginia Anne. "Public Forum: Rational Therapy in Divorce Practice," *Rational Living*, 1974, 9 (2): 34-38.

Coleman, R. E. "The Manipulation of Self-Esteem — a Determinant of Elation-Depression." Doctoral Dissertation, Temple University, 1971.

Conklin, R. C. "A Psychometric Instrument for the Early Identification of Underachievers." Doctoral Dissertation, University of Alberta, 1965.

Crabtree, R. G., and Ward, G., II. "A Note on Three RET-Related Scales." Paper presented to the West Virginia Academy of Science, April, 1975.

Criddle, William D. "Guidelines for Challenging Irrational Beliefs," *Rational Living*, 1974, 9 (1): 8-13.

Davies, R. L. "Relationship of Irrational Ideas to Emotional Disturbance." Doctoral Dissertation, University of Alberta, 1970.

Davison, Gerald C., and Neale, John M. *Abnormal Psychology: An Experimental-Clinical Approach.* New York: Wiley, 1974.

Dember, W. "Motivation and the Cognitive Revolution," *American Psychologist*, 1974, 29: 161-68.

Devine, Donald A., and Fernald, Peter S. "Outcome Effects of Receiving a Preferred, Randomly Assigned, or Nonpreferred Therapy," *Journal of Consulting and Clinical Psychology*, 1973, 41: 104-7.

Diamond, Leonard, and Songor, Eleanor. "Eight Rational Principles of Effective Communication in Relationships," *Rational Living*, 1972, 7 (1): 36-38.

DiLoreto, Adolph O. *Comparative Psychotherapy.* Chicago: Aldine-Atherton, 1971.

DiLoreto, Adolph O. "A Comparison of the Relative Effectiveness of Systematic Desensitization, Rational-Emotive and Client-Centered Group Psychotherapy in the Reduction of Interpersonal Anxiety in Introverts and Extroverts." Doctoral Dissertation, Michigan State University, 1969.

Ditman, K., and Cohen, S. "Evaluation of Drugs in the Treatment of Alcoholism," *Quarterly Journal of Studies on Alcohol,* 1959, 20: 573-76.

Dubois, P. *The Psychic Treatment of Nervous Disorders.* New York: Funk & Wagnalls, 1907.

D'Zurilla, Thomas J., Wilson, G. Terrence, and Nelson, Rosemary. "A Preliminary Study of the Effectiveness of Gradated Prolonged Exposure in the Treatment of Irrational Fear," *Behavior Therapy,* 1973, 4: 672-85.

Eisenberg, J. M. "Marital Adjustment and Irrational Ideas." Doctoral Dissertation, University of Alberta, 1971.

Ellis, Albert. "Are Cognitive Behavior Therapy and Rational Therapy Synonymous?" *Rational Living,* 1973a, 8 (2): 8-11.

Ellis, Albert. *The Art and Science of Love.* New York: Lyle Stuart, 1960.

Ellis, Albert. *The Civilized Couple's Guide to Extramarital Adventure.* New York: Peter Wyden, 1972a.

Ellis, Albert. "A Critical Evaluation of Marriage Counseling," *Marriage and Family Living,* 1956, 18: 65-71.

Ellis, Albert. "A Critique," in Adolph O. DiLoreto, *Comparative Psychotherapy.* Chicago: Aldine-Atherton, 1971a.

Ellis, Albert. *Executive Leadership: A Rational Approach.* Secaucus, N. J.: Citadel Press, 1972b.

Ellis, Albert. "Experience and Rationality: The Making of a Rational-Emotive Therapist," *Psychotherapy: Theory, Research and Practice,* 1974a, 11: 194-98.

Ellis, Albert (ed.). *Growth Through Reason: Verbatim Cases in Rational-Emotive Therapy.* Palo Alto, Calif.: Science & Behavior Books, 1971b; North Hollywood: Wilshire, 1974b.

Ellis, Albert. *How to Live with a "Neurotic": At Home and at Work.* New York: Crown, 1975.

Ellis, Albert. *Humanistic Psychotherapy: The Rational-Emotive Approach.* New York: Julian Press, 1973b; New York: McGraw-Hill Paperbacks, 1974c.

Ellis, Albert. *The Intelligent Woman's Guide to Man-Hunting.* New York: Lyle Stuart, 1963a.

Ellis, Albert. "My Philosophy of Psychotherapy," *Journal of Contemporary Psychotherapy,* 1973c, 6: 13-18; reprinted New York: Institute for Rational Living.

Ellis, Albert. "Neurotic Interaction Between Marital Partners," *Journal of Counseling Psychology,* 1958a, 5: 24-28.

Ellis, Albert. "Outcome of Employing Three Techniques of Psychotherapy," *Journal of Clinical Psychology*, 1957, 13: 344-50.

Ellis, Albert. "Psychotherapy and the Value of a Human Being," in J. W. Davis (ed.), *Value and Valuation: Essays in Honor of Robert S. Hartman*. Knoxville: University of Tennessee Press, 1972c; reprinted New York: Institute for Rational Living.

Ellis, Albert. "Psychotherapy Without Tears," in Arthur Burton (ed.), *Twelve Therapists*. San Francisco: Jossey-Bass, 1972d.

Ellis, Albert. "Rational Emotive Theory," in Arthur Burton (ed.), *Operational Theories of Personality*. New York: Brunner/Mazel, 1974d.

Ellis, Albert. "Rational-Emotive Therapy," in R. Corsini (ed.), *Current Psychotherapies*. Itasca, Ill.: F. E. Peacock, 1973d.

Ellis, Albert. "Rational Psychotherapy," *Journal of General Psychology*, 1958b, 59: 35-49.

Ellis, Albert. *Reason and Emotion in Psychotherapy*. New York: Lyle Stuart, 1962.

Ellis, Albert. "Requisite Conditions for Basic Personality Change," *Journal of Consulting Psychology*, 1959, 23: 538-40.

Ellis, Albert. *Sex and the Liberated Man*. Secaucus, N.J.: Lyle Stuart, 1976.

Ellis, Albert. *Sex and the Single Man*. New York: Lyle Stuart, 1963b.

Ellis, Albert. "Sexual Problems of the Young Adult," *Rational Living*, 1971c, 5 (2): 2-11.

Ellis, Albert. *Sex Without Guilt*. New York: Lyle Stuart, 1958c; revised ed., North Hollywood: Wilshire, 1970.

Ellis, Albert, and Harper, Robert A. *A Guide to Rational Living*. Englewood Cliffs, N.J.: Prentice-Hall, 1962.

Ellis, Albert, and Harper, Robert A. *A Guide to Successful Marriage*. North Hollywood: Wilshire, 1973.

Ellis, Albert, and Harper, Robert A. *A New Guide to Rational Living*. Englewood Cliffs, N.J.: Prentice-Hall, 1975; North Hollywood: Wilshire, 1975.

Ellis, Albert, Krassner, Paul, and Wilson, Robert Anton. "An Impolite Interview with Albert Ellis," *The Realist*, 1960, 16: 9-14; 1960, 17: 7-12.

Ellis, Albert, Wolfe, Janet L., and Moseley, Sandra. *How to Raise an Emotionally Healthy, Happy Child*. North Hollywood: Wilshire, 1972.

Erickson, M. H. *Advanced Techniques of Hypnosis and Therapy: Selected Papers of M. H. Erickson.* Edited by Jay Haley. New York: Grune & Stratton, 1967.

Eysenck, H. J. "The Effects of Psychotherapy," in H. J. Eysenck (ed.), *Handbook of Abnormal Psychology.* New York: Basic Books, 1961.

Eysenck, H. J., and Eysenck, S. B. G. *The Eysenck Personality Inventory.* San Diego, Calif.: Educational and Industrial Testing Service, 1968a.

Eysenck, H. J., and Eysenck, S. B. G. *Manual for the Eysenck Personality Inventory.* San Diego, Calif.: Educational and Industrial Testing Service, 1968b.

Fenichel, Otto. *The Psychoanalytic Theory of Neurosis.* New York: Norton, 1945.

Fiske, D. W., Hunt, H. F., Luborsky, L., Orne, M. T., Parloff, M. B., Reiser, M. F., and Tuma, A. H. "Planning of Research on Effectiveness of Psychotherapy," *Archives of General Psychiatry,* 1970, 22: 22-32.

Fox, E. E., and Davies, R. L. "Test Your Rationality," *Rational Living,* 1971, 5 (2): 23-25.

Frank, Jerome D. *Persuasion and Healing: A Comparative Study of Psychotherapy.* Rev. ed. Baltimore: Johns Hopkins University Press, 1973.

Freedman, Alfred M., Kaplan, H. I., and Sadoch, B. J. *Modern Synopsis of Comprehensive Textbook of Psychiatry.* Baltimore: Williams & Wilkins, 1972.

Freud, Sigmund. "Mourning and Melancholia," in *Collected Papers,* Vol. 4. London: Hogarth Press, 1950.

Garfield, S. L., Prager, R. A., and Bergin, A. E. "Evaluation of Outcome in Psychotherapy," *Journal of Consulting and Clinical Psychology,* 1971, 37: 307-13.

Gerard, Donald L., and Saenger, Gerhart. *Outpatient Treatment of Alcoholism: A Study of Outcome and Its Determinants.* Toronto: University of Toronto Press, 1966.

Glasser, William. *Reality Therapy.* New York: Harper & Row, 1965.

Goldfried, Marvin R., Decenteceo, Edwin T., and Weinberg, Leslie. "Systematic Rational Restructuring as a Self-control Technique," *Behavior Therapy,* 1974, 5: 247-54.

Goldstein, A. P., Heller, K., and Sechrest, L. B. *Psychotherapy and the Psychology of Behavior Change.* New York: Wiley, 1966.

Goldstein, Alan, and Wolpe, Joseph. "A Critique," in Adolph O. DiLoreto, *Comparative Psychotherapy*. Chicago: Aldine-Atherton, 1971.

Goodman, David S., and Maultsby, Maxie C., Jr. *Emotional Well-Being Through Rational Behavior Training*. Springfield, Ill.: Charles C Thomas, 1974.

Gordon, Thomas. *Parent Effectiveness Training: The "No-Lose" Program for Raising Responsible Children*. New York: Peter Wyden, 1970.

Grace, W. J., and Graham, D. T. "Relationship of Specific Attitudes and Emotions to Certain Bodily Diseases," *Psychosomatic Medicine*, 1952, 14: 243-51.

Graham, D. T. "Some Research on Psychophysiologic Specificity and Its Relation to Psychosomatic Disease," in Robert Roessler and Norman S. Greenfield (eds.), *Physiological Correlates of Psychological Disorders*. Madison: University of Wisconsin Press, 1962.

Graham, D. T., Kabler, M. D., and Graham, F. K. "Physiological Response to the Suggestion of Attitudes Specific for Hives and Hypertension," *Psychosomatic Medicine*, 1962, 20: 257-66.

Graham, D. T., Lundy, R. M., Benjamin, L. S., Kabler, J. D., Lewis, W. C., Kunish, N. O., and Graham, F. K. "Specific Attitudes in Initial Interviews with Patients Having Different 'Psychosomatic Diseases,' " *Psychosomatic Medicine*, 1962, 24: 257-66.

Graham, D.T., Stern, J. A., and Winokur, G. "The Concept of a Different Specific Set of Physiological Changes in Each Emotion," *Psychiatric Research Reports*, 1960, 12: 8-15.

Graham, D. T., Stern, J. A., and Winokur, G. "Experimental Investigation of the Specificity of Attitude Hypothesis in Psychosomatic Disease," *Psychosomatic Medicine*, 1958, 20: 446-57.

Greenwald, Harold. *Direct Decision Therapy*. New York: Jason Aronson, 1975.

Gregory, J., and Diamond, M. J. "Increasing Hypnotic Susceptibility by Means of Positive Expectancies and Written Instructions," *Journal of Abnormal and Social Psychology*, 1972, 82: 363-68.

Grossack, Martin. "The Revolutionary Social Philosophy of Albert Ellis," *Rational Living*, 1974, 9 (2): 17-21.

Grummon, D. L. "Client-Centered Theory," in B. Stefflre (ed.), *Theories of Counseling*. New York: McGraw-Hill, 1965.

Gullo, John M. "Counseling Hospitalized Patients," *Rational Living,* 1966, 1 (2): 11-15.

Gustav, Alice. " 'Success Is —': Locating Composite Sanity," *Rational Living,* 1968, 3 (1): 1-6.

Harper, Robert A. "Marriage Counseling as Rational Process-Oriented Psychotherapy," *Journal of Individual Psychology,* 1960, 16: 192-207.

Harper, Robert A. *The New Psychotherapies.* Englewood Cliffs, N.J.: Prentice-Hall, 1975.

Harper, Robert A. *Psychoanalysis and Psychotherapy: 36 Systems.* New York: Jason Aronson, 1974.

Harrison, B. "In Defense of Jealousy," *McCalls,* May, 1974.

Hartman, B. J. "Sixty Revealing Questions for 20 Minutes," *Rational Living,* 1968, 3: (1) 7-8.

Hartman, Robert S. *The Measurement of Value.* Carbondale, Ill.: Southern Illinois University Press, 1967.

Hauck, Paul A. *Overcoming Depression.* Philadelphia: Westminster Press, 1973.

Hauck, Paul A. *Overcoming Frustration and Anger.* Philadelphia: Westminster Press, 1974.

Hauck, Paul A. *Overcoming Worry and Fear.* Philadelphia: Westminster Press, 1975.

Hauck, Paul A. *The Rational Management of Children.* New York: Libra Publishers, 1967.

Hauck, Paul A., and Grau, Albert. "Comparisons: Christianity and Rationality," *Rational Living,* 1968, 3 (2): 36-37.

Hayakawa, Samuel I. *Language in Thought and Action.* New York: Harcourt, Brace, 1949.

Hebb, Donald O. *The Organization of Behavior.* New York: Wiley, 1960.

Herzberg, Alexander. *Active Psychotherapy.* New York: Grune & Stratton, 1945.

Hilgard, Ernest R. *Introduction to Psychology.* New York: Harcourt, Brace, 1967.

Hill, M. J., and Blane, H. T. "Evaluation of Psychotherapy with Alcoholics: A Critical Review," *Quarterly Journal of Studies on Alcohol,* 1967, 28: 76-104.

Hindman, Margaret. "Rational Emotive Therapy in Alcoholism Treatment," *Alcohol Health and Research World,* Spring, 1976.

Homme, L. E. "Perspectives in Psychology, XXIV: Control of Coverants, the Operants of the Mind," *Psychological Record,* 1965, 15: 501-11.

Howard, K. I., and Orlinsky, D. E. "Psychotherapeutic Processes," *Annual Review of Psychology*, 1972, 23: 615-68.

Hoxter, A. Lee. "Irrational Beliefs and Self-concept in Two Kinds of Behavior." Doctoral Dissertation, University of Alberta, 1967.

Hudgins, C. V. "Conditioning and Voluntary Control Reflex," *Journal of General Psychology*, 1933, 8: 1-49.

Jakubowski-Spector, P. *An Introduction to Assertive Training Procedures for Women.* Washington, D.C.: American Personnel and Guidance Association, 1973.

Jarmon, David G. "Differential Effectiveness of Rational-Emotive Therapy, Bibliotherapy, and Attention-Placebo in the Treatment of Speech Anxiety." Doctoral Dissertation, Southern Illinois University, 1973.

Jellinek, R. "Mythology as a Science," *New York Times*, May 12, 1973, p. 31.

Jones, Mary Colver. "Elimination of Children's Fears," *Journal of Experimental Psychology*, 1924, 7: 382-90.

Jones, Richard G. "A Factored Measure of Ellis' Irrational Belief System, with Personality and Maladjustment Correlates." Doctoral Dissertation, Texas Technological College, 1969.

Kagan, Jerome, and Havemann, Ernest. *Psychology: An Introduction.* New York: Harcourt Brace, 1972.

Karst, Thomas O., and Trexler, Larry D. "Initial Study Using Fixed-Role and Rational-Emotive Therapy in Treating Public-Speaking Anxiety," *Journal of Consulting and Clinical Psychology*, 1970, 34: 360-66.

Kassinove, Howard. "Some Effects of Learning RET on Graduate Student Adjustments," *Rational Living*, 1974, 9 (2): 7-8.

Keller, J., and Crooke, J. "Effects of a Program in Rational Thinking on Anxieties in Older Persons," *Journal of Counseling Psychology*, 1975, 22: 54-57.

Kelly, George A. *The Psychology of Personal Constructs.* New York: Norton, 1955.

Kiesler, D. J. "Some Myths of Psychotherapy Research and the Search for a Paradigm," *Psychological Bulletin*, 1966, 65: 110-36.

Kiresuk, T. S., and Sherman, R. E. "Goal Attainment Scaling: A General Method for Evaluating Community Mental Health Programs," *Community Mental Health Journal*, 1968, 4: 443-53.

Kissin, B., Platz, A., and Su, W. H. "Social and Psychological Factors in the Treatment of Chronic Alcoholism," *Journal of Psychiatric Research*, 1970, 8: 13-27.

Knaus, William J. *Rational-Emotive Education.* New York: Institute for Rational Living, 1974.

Korzybski, Alfred. *Science and Sanity.* Lancaster, Pa.: Lancaster Press, 1933.

Kroger, William S. *Clinical and Experimental Hypnosis.* Philadelphia: Lippincott, 1963.

Lacey, J. I. "Psychophysiological Approaches to the Evaluation of Psychotherapeutic Process and Outcome," in E. A. Rubinstein and M. B. Parloff (eds.), *Research in Psychotherapy,* Vol. 1. Washington, D.C.: American Psychological Association, 1959.

Lakein, Alan. *How to Get Control of Your Time and Your Life.* New York: Signet, 1974.

Lange, A. J., and Jakubowski, P. *Responsible Assertive Behavior: Cognitive/Behavioral Procedures for Trainers.* Champaign, Ill.: Research Press, 1976.

Laughridge, S. "An Approach to Handling Resistance to Interpretation," *Rational Living,* 1972, 7: 29-31.

Lazarus, Arnold A. *Behavior Therapy and Beyond.* New York: McGraw-Hill, 1971.

Lazarus, Arnold A. "The Use of 'Emotive Imagery' in the Treatment of Children's Phobias," *Journal of Mental Science,* 1962, 108: 191-95.

Lazarus, Arnold A., and Fay, Allen. *I Can If I Want To.* New York: Morrow, 1975.

Lechnyr, R. "Evaluation of Student Effectiveness," *Social Work,* 1975, 20, 148-50.

Lehman-Olson, Dana. "Assertiveness Training: Theoretical and Clinical Implications," in D. Olson (ed.), *Treating Relationships.* Lake Mills, Iowa: Graphic, 1976.

Lehman-Olson, Dana. "Cognitive-Behavioral Approaches to the Reduction of Anger and Aggression." Doctoral Dissertation, Oklahoma State University, 1974.

Lembo, John M. *Help Yourself.* Niles, Ill.: Argus Communications, 1974.

London, Perry. *The Modes and Morals of Psychotherapy.* New York: Holt, Rinehart and Winston, 1964.

MacDonald, A. P., Jr., and Games, Richard G. "Ellis' Irrational Values," *Rational Living,* 1972, 7 (2): 25-28.

McClellan, Thomas A., and Stieper, Donald R. "A Structured Approach to Group Marriage Counseling," *Mental Hygiene,* 1971, 55: 77-84.

McFall, Richard M., and Marston, Albert R. "An Experimental Investigation of Behavioral Rehearsal in Assertive Training," *Journal of Abnormal Psychology*, 1970, 76: 295-303.

Madsen, William. *The American Alcoholic: The Nature-Nurture Controversy in Alcoholic Research and Therapy*. Springfield, Ill.: Charles C Thomas, 1974.

Maes, Wayne R., and Heimann, Robert A. *The Comparison of Three Approaches to the Reduction of Text Anxiety in High School Students*. Final Report, Project 9-1-049. Washington, D.C.: Office of Education, Bureau of Research, U.S. Department of Health, Education and Welfare, 1970.

Mahoney, Michael J. *Cognition and Behavior Modification*. Cambridge, Mass.: Ballinger, 1974.

Malan, David H. "The Outcome Problem in Psychotherapy Research," *Archives of General Psychiatry*, 1973, 29: 719-29.

Maslow, Abraham H. *Motivation and Personality*. New York: Harper, 1954.

Maultsby, Maxie C., Jr. "Common Belief Scale," in David S. Goodman and Maxie C. Maultsby, Jr., *Emotional Well-Being Through Rational Behavior Training*. Springfield, Ill.: Charles C Thomas, 1974a.

Maultsby, Maxie C., Jr. "Common Perception Scale," in David S. Goodman and Maxie C. Maultsby, Jr., *Emotional Well-Being Through Rational Behavior Training*. Springfield, Ill.: Charles C Thomas, 1974b.

Maultsby, Maxie C., Jr. "Common Trait Scale," in David S. Goodman and Maxie C. Maultsby, Jr., *Emotional Well-Being Through Rational Behavior Training*. Springfield, Ill.: Charles C Thomas, 1974c.

Maultsby, Maxie C., Jr. "Controlled Study of Effect Psychotherapy on Self-Reported Maladaptive Traits, Anxiety Scores and Psychosomatic Disease Attitudes," *Journal of Psychiatric Research*, 1974d (10): 121-32.

Maultsby, Maxie C., Jr. *Handbook of Rational Self-Counseling*. Madison: Association for Rational Thinking, 1971a.

Maultsby, Maxie C., Jr. *Help Yourself to Happiness: Through Rational Self-Counseling*. Boston: Esplanade Books, 1975a; New York: Institute for Rational Living, 1976.

Maultsby, Maxie C., Jr. "How and Why You Can Naturally Control Your Emotions," in *Nine Client Handouts*. Lexington: University of Kentucky Medical Center, RBT Section of Psychiatric OPD, 1971b.

Maultsby, Maxie C., Jr. "The Neurotic Fear of Being a Phony," *Corrective Psychiatry and Journal of Social Therapy*, 1972, 18 (4).

Maultsby, Maxie C., Jr. *Nine Client Handouts*. Lexington: University of Kentucky Medical Center, RBT Section of Psychiatric OPD, 1971c.

Maultsby, Maxie C., Jr. *Overcoming Irrational Fears*. (Auto Tape Series Covering Common Irrational Fears) Chicago: Instructional Dynamics, 1975b.

Maultsby, Maxie C., Jr. "Rational Behavior Therapy for Acting-Out Adolescents," *Journal of Social Casework*, 1975c, 56: 35-43.

Maultsby, Maxie C., Jr. "Rational Emotive Imagery," *Rational Living*, 1971d, 6 (1): 24-26.

Maultsby, Maxie C., Jr. "Systematic, Written Homework in Psychotherapy," *Psychotherapy: Theory, Research and Practice*, 1971e, 8 (3): 195-98; *Rational Living*, 1971f, 6 (1): 16-23, 26-27.

Maultsby, Maxie C., Jr. "Theoretical Basis and General Information on RBT Concepts of Homework," in *Nine Client Handouts*. Lexington: University of Kentucky Medical Center, RBT Section of Psychiatric OPD, 1971g.

Maultsby, Maxie C., Jr., and Gram, Joyce M. "Dream Changes Following Successful Rational Behavior Therapy," *Rational Living*, 1974, 9 (2): 30-33.

Maultsby, Maxie C., Jr., and Hendricks, Allie. *RBT Cartoon Booklet*. Lexington: University of Kentucky Medical Center, RBT Section of Psychiatric OPD, 1974a.

Maultsby, Maxie C., Jr., and Hendricks, Allie. *You and Your Emotions*. Lexington: University of Kentucky Medical Center, 1974b.

Maultsby, Maxie C., Jr., Stiefel, Leanna, and Brodsky, Lynda. "A Theory of Rational Behavioral Group Processes," *Rational Living*, 1972, 7 (1): 28-34.

Meichenbaum, Donald H. *Cognitive Behavior Modification*. Morristown, N.J.: General Learning Press, 1974.

Meichenbaum, Donald H. "Cognitive Factors in Behavior Modification: Modifying What Clients Say to Themselves," in C. M. Franks and G. T. Wilson (eds.), *Annual Review of Behavior Therapy Theory and Practice*. New York: Brunner/Mazel, 1973.

Meichenbaum, Donald H. "Cognitive Modification of Test Anxious College Students," *Journal of Consulting and Clinical Psychology*, 1972a, 39: 370-80.

Meichenbaum, Donald H. "The Effects of Instructions and Reinforcement on Thinking and Language Behaviors of Schizophrenics," *Behavior Research and Therapy*, 1969, 7: 101-14.

Meichenbaum, Donald H. "Examination of Model Characteristics in Reducing Avoidance Behavior," *Journal of Personality and Social Psychology*, 1971, 17: 298-307.

Meichenbaum, Donald H. "Toward a Cognitive Theory of Self-Control," in G. Schwartz and D. Shapiro (eds.), *Consciousness and Self-Regulation: Advances in Research*. New York: Plenum Press, 1975.

Meichenbaum, Donald H. "Ways of Modifying What Clients Say to Themselves," *Rational Living*, 1972b, 7 (1): 23-27.

Meichenbaum, Donald H., and Cameron, Roy. "The Clinical Potential of Modifying What Clients Say to Themselves," *Psychotherapy: Theory, Research and Practice*, 1974, 11: 103-17.

Meichenbaum, Donald H., and Cameron, Roy. *Reducing Fears by Modifying What Clients Say to Themselves: A Means of Developing Stress Inoculation*. Unpublished manuscript, University of Waterloo, 1972.

Meichenbaum, Donald H., and Cameron, Roy. "Training Schizophrenics to Talk to Themselves: A Means of Developing Attentional Controls," *Behavior Therapy*, 1973, 4: 515-34.

Meichenbaum, Donald H., Gilmore, J. B., and Fedoravicius, A. "Group Insight vs. Group Desensitization in Treating Speech Anxiety," *Journal of Consulting and Clinical Psychology*, 1971, 36: 410-21.

Meichenbaum, Donald H., and Goodman, J. "Reflection Impulsivity and Verbal Control of Motor Behavior," *Child Development*, 1969, 40: 785-97.

Meichenbaum, Donald H., and Goodman, J. "Training Impulsive Children to Talk to Themselves: A Means of Developing Self-Control," *Journal of Abnormal Psychology*, 1971, 77:115-26.

Meltzoff, Julian, and Kornreich, Melvin. *Research in Psychotherapy*. Chicago: Aldine-Atherton, 1970.

Mendelson, J., and Chafetz, M. "Alcoholism as an Emergency Ward Problem," *Quarterly Journal of Studies on Alcohol*, 1959, 20: 270-75.

Mischel, W. *Introduction to Personality*. New York: Holt, Rinehart and Winston, 1971.

Montgomery, Ann G. "Comparison of the Effectiveness of Systematic Desensitization, Rational-Emotive Therapy, Implosive Therapy, and No Therapy, in Reducing Test Anxiety in

College Students." Doctoral Dissertation, Washington University, 1971.

Morley, Eldon L., and Watkins, John T. "Locus of Control and Effectiveness of Two Rational-Emotive Therapy Styles," *Rational Living*, 1974, 9 (2): 22-24.

Morris, G. B. "Irrational Beliefs of Prison Inmates," *Canadian Journal of Criminology and Corrections*, 1974, 16: 1-7.

Morris, Kenneth T., and Kanitz, H. Mike. *Rational-Emotive Therapy*. Boston: Houghton Mifflin, 1975.

Mowrer, O. H. "Integrity Groups: Basic Principles and Objectives," *Counseling Psychologist*, 1973, 3 (2): 1-24.

Mowrer, O. H. *Learning Theory and Behavior*. New York: Wiley, 1960a.

Mowrer, O. H. *Learning Theory and the Symbolic Processes*. New York: Wiley, 1960b.

Neuman, D. "Using Assertive Training," in J. D. Krumboltz and C. E. Thoresen (eds.), *Behavioral Counseling Cases and Techniques*. New York: Holt, Rinehart and Winston, 1969.

Nisbett, R. E., and Schachter, S. "Cognitive Manipulation of Pain," *Journal of Experimental and Social Psychology*, 1966, 2: 227-36.

Oates, W. J. (ed.). *The Stoic and Epicurean Philosophers*. New York: Random House, 1940.

O'Connell, W. E., and Hanson, P. G. "The Negative Nonsense of the Passive Patient," *Rational Living*, 1971, 6: 28-31.

O'Connell, W. E., and Hanson, P. G. "Patients' Cognitive Changes in Human Relations Training," *Journal of Individual Psychology*, 1970, 26: 57-63.

Oda, Ethel A. "Value Commitments and Attitudinal Changes in Simulated Therapeutic Encounters." Doctoral Dissertation, University of Minnesota, 1969.

Osborn, Susan M., and Harris, Gloria G. *Assertive Training Procedures for Women*. Springfield, Ill.: Charles C Thomas, 1975.

Palkes, H., Stewart, W., and Kahana, B. "Porteus Maze Performance of Hyperactive Boys After Training in Self-Directed Verbal Commands," *Child Development*, 1968, 39: 817-26.

Palmer, R. D., and Field, P. B. "Visual Images and Susceptibility to Hypnosis," *Journal of Consulting Clinical Psychology*, 1968, 32: 456-61.

Paul, Gordon L. "Behavior Modification Research: Design and Tactics," in C. M. Franks (ed.), *Behavior Therapy: Appraisal and Status*, New York: McGraw-Hill, 1969.

Paul, Gordon L. *Insight Versus Desensitization in Psychotherapy: An Experiment in Anxiety Reduction.* Stanford, Calif.: Stanford University Press, 1966.

Pearlman, J., Coburn, K., and Jakubowski-Spector, P. *A Leader's Guide to Assertive Training Procedures for Women.* Washington, D.C.: American Personnel and Guidance Association, 1973.

Phelps, Stanlee, and Austin, Nancy. *The Assertive Woman.* San Luis Obispo, Calif.: Impact, 1975.

Phillips, E. Lakin, *Psychotherapy.* Englewood Cliffs, N.J.: Prentice-Hall, 1957.

Piaget, Jean, and Inhelder, Barbel. *The Psychology of the Child.* New York: Basic Books, 1969.

Raimy, Victor. *Beliefs in Psychotherapy.* San Francisco: Jossey-Bass, 1975.

Razran, G. "The Observable Unconscious and the Inferable Conscious in Current Soviet Psychophysiology: Interoceptive Conditioning, Semantic Conditioning, and the Orienting Reflex," *Psychology Review,* 1961, 68: 81-147.

Rimland, Bernard. *Infantile Autism: The Syndrome and Its Implications for a Neural Theory of Behavior.* New York: Appleton-Century-Crofts, 1964.

Rimm, David C., and Litvak, Stuart B. "Self-Verbalization and Emotional Arousal," *Journal of Abnormal Psychology,* 1969, 74: 181-87.

Rimm, David, and Masters, John C. *Behavior Therapy: Techniques and Empirical Findings.* New York: Academic Press, 1974.

Rokeach, Milton. *Beliefs, Attitudes and Values: A Theory of Organization and Change.* San Francisco: Jossey-Bass, 1968.

Rosenthal, D. *Genetic Theory and Abnormal Behavior.* New York: McGraw-Hill, 1970.

Rush, A. J., Beck, A. T., Kovacs, M., Khatami, M., Fitzgibbons, R., and Wolman, T. "A Comparison of Cognitive and Pharmacotherapy in Depressed Outpatients: A Preliminary Report." Paper Presented at the Meeting of the Society for Psychotherapy Research, Boston, Massachusetts, June, 1975.

Russell, P. L., and Brandsma, J. M. "A Theoretical and Empirical Integration of the Rational-Emotive and Classical Conditioning Theories," *Journal of Consulting and Clinical Psychology,* 1974, 42 (3): 389-97.

Salter, Andrew. *Conditioned Reflex Therapy.* New York: Farrar, Straus, 1949.

Satir, Virginia M. *Conjoint Family Therapy: A Guide to Theory and Technique.* Palo Alto, Calif.: Science & Behavior Books, 1964.

Schacter, S. "The Interaction of Cognitive and Physiologic Determinants of Emotional States," *Advances in Experimental Social Psychology*, 1964, 1: 49-80.

Schwartz, Dan. "The Spatial Distribution of the Diffuse Component of Cosmic X-Rays." Doctoral Dissertation, University of California.

Shaw, Brian F. "A Systematic Investigation of Two Psychological Treatments of Depression." Doctoral Dissertation, University of Western Ontario, 1975.

Skinner, B. F. *The Behavior of Organisms.* New York: Appleton-Century, 1938.

Skinner, B. F. *Science and Human Behavior.* New York: Free Press, 1960.

Skinner, B. F. *Verbal Behavior.* New York: Appleton-Century-Crofts, 1957.

Slater, Eliot, and Cowie, Valerie. *Psychiatry and Genetics.* London: Oxford University Press, 1971.

Smith, Manuel J. *When I Say No, I Feel Guilty.* New York: Dial Press, 1975.

Speilberger, C. D., Gorsuch, R. L., and Lushene, R. E. *STAI Manual.* Palo Alto, Calif.: Consulting Psychologist Press, 1970.

Sperry, R. W. "Science and the Problem of Values," *Zygon: Journal of Religion and Science*, 1974, 9 (11): 7-21.

Stevens, John O. *Awareness: Exploring, Experimenting, Experiencing.* New York: Bantam, 1973.

Straatmeyer, Alvin J., and Watkins, John T. "Rational-Emotive Therapy and the Reduction of Speech Anxiety," *Rational Living*, 1974, 9 (1): 33-37.

Strupp, H. H., and Bergin, A. E. "Some Empirical and Conceptual Bases for Coordinated Research in Psychotherapy," *International Journal of Psychiatry*, 1969, 7: 18-90.

Taft, L. M. "A Study to Determine the Relationships of Anxiety to Irrational Ideas." Doctoral Dissertation, University of Alberta, 1968.

Taylor, Frederick G. "Cognitive and Behavioral Approaches to the Modification of Depression." Doctoral Dissertation, Queen's University, Kingston, Canada, 1974.

Thoresen, Carl E., and Mahoney, M. J. *Behavioral Self-Control* New York: Holt, Rinehart and Winston, 1974.

Thorpe, Geoffrey L. "Short-Term Effectiveness of Systematic Desensitization, Modeling and Behavior Rehearsal, and Self-Instructional Training in Facilitating Assertive-Refusal Behavior." Doctoral Dissertation, Rutgers University, 1973; *European Journal of Behavior Therapy,* in press.

Thorpe, Geoffrey L., Amatu, H. I., Blakey, R. S., and Burns, L. E. *Contributions of Overt Instructional Rehearsal and "Specific Insight" to the Effectiveness of Self-Instructional Training: A Preliminary Study.* Unpublished manuscript, 1975.

Tillich, Paul. *The Courage to Be.* New York: Oxford University Press, 1953.

Tosi, Donald J. *Youth: Toward Personal Growth.* Columbus, Ohio: Merrill, 1974.

Tosi, Donald J., and Marzella, J. Nick. "Rational Stage Directed Therapy," in Janet L. Wolfe and Eileen Brand (Eds.), *Twenty Years of Rational Therapy: Proceedings of the First National Conference on Rational Psychotherapy.* New York: Institute for Rational Living, 1977.

Trexler, Larry D. "Rational-Emotive Therapy, Placebo, and No-Treatment Effects on Public-Speaking Anxiety." Doctoral Dissertation, Temple University, 1971.

Trexler, Larry D., and Karst, Thomas O. "Further Validation for a New Measure of Irrational Cognitions," *Journal of Personality Assessment,* 1973, 37: 150-55.

Trexler, Larry D., and Karst, Thomas O. "Rational-Emotive Therapy, Placebo, and No-Treatment Effects on Public Speaking Anxiety," *Journal of Abnormal Psychology,* 1972, 79: 60-67.

Valins, Stuart. "Cognitive Effects of False Heart-rate Feedback," *Journal of Personality and Social Psychology,* 1966, 4: 400-8.

Valins, Stuart, and Ray, Alice A. "Effects of Cognitive Desensitization on Avoidance Behavior," *Journal of Personality and Social Psychology,* 1967, 7: 345-50.

Velten, E., Jr. "A Laboratory Task for Induction of Mood States," *Behavior Research and Therapy,* 1968, 6: 473-82.

Wallgren, H., and Barry, Herbert. *Actions of Alcohol,* 2 vols. New York: American Elsevier, 1971.

Watts, Alan W. *The Way of Zen.* New York: New American Library, 1959.

Waugh, N. M. "Rationality and Emotional Adjustment: A Test of Ellis' Theory of Rational-Emotive Psychotherapy." Doctoral Dissertation, Case Western Reserve University, 1975.

Wolfe, J. L., and Fodor, I. "A Cognitive-Behavioral Approach to Modifying Assertive Behavior in Women," *The Counseling Psychologist*, 1975, 5 (4): 45-52.

Wolpe, Joseph. *Psychotherapy by Reciprocal Inhibition.* Stanford, Calif.: Stanford University Press, 1958.

Wolpe, Joseph, and Lazarus, Arnold A. *Behavior Therapy Techniques.* New York: Pergamon Press, 1966.

Young, Howard. Rational Casework with Adolescents. *Journal of School Social Work*, 1975, 1: 15-20.

Zimbardo, Philip G., and Ebbesen, Ebbe B. *Influencing Attitudes and Changing Behavior.* Reading, Pa.: Addison-Wesley, 1969.

Zingle, Harvey W. "A Rational Therapy Approach to Counseling Underachievers." Doctoral Dissertation, University of Alberta, 1965.

Zubin, Joseph. "Technical Issues: Discussion," in P. H. Hook and Joseph Zubin (eds.). *The Evaluation of Psychotherapy.* New York: Grune & Stratton, 1964.

Index of Contributing Authors